WEST-INDIA POLICY
UNDER THE RESTORATION

SIR THOMAS LYNCH

Lieutenant-Governor of Jamaica, September 1670–November 1674
Governor and Captain-General of Jamaica, August 1681–August 1684

Attributed to Kneller

WEST-INDIA POLICY UNDER THE RESTORATION

BY

A. P. THORNTON

Lecturer in British Imperial History
in the University of Aberdeen

OXFORD

AT THE CLARENDON PRESS

1956

Oxford University Press, Amen House, London E.C.4

GLASGOW NEW YORK TORONTO MELBOURNE WELLINGTON
BOMBAY CALCUTTA MADRAS KARACHI CAPE TOWN IBADAN

Geoffrey Cumberlege, Publisher to the University

PRINTED IN GREAT BRITAIN
AT THE UNIVERSITY PRESS, OXFORD
BY CHARLES BATEY, PRINTER TO THE UNIVERSITY

PREFACE

TWENTIETH-CENTURY Europe has seen a number of Restorations in recent times, but fewer Acts of Indemnity and Oblivion; and many administrations have found themselves stumbling because they carried passengers with 'black records' of one sort or another, exiles from another age. The manner in which the Restoration Government of King Charles II in England dealt with these problems in the seventeenth century therefore continues to deserve some attention and respect. It made many errors, indeed, but it did not go hunting heresies of its own volition. Titus Oates, like many of his spiritual descendants, had his friends in high places; but he still fills a particular niche in English history, as an exception that proves the tolerant rule.

But political sophistication does not grow so readily on the far frontier, and in the world of the West Indies memories of who was and who was not an 'Old Stander', a follower of the 'Old Cause', died hard, and underlay many a quarrel over freehold, privilege, illicit commerce, and the perquisites of a patent office. The temperature in the colonial Assembly of Barbados and Jamaica in the Restoration period was always much higher than that at Westminster: it was always easier to appeal to passion than to principle, but the contemporary protests of 'no taxation without representation'—a Barbadian assertion—and of 'no standing army and the laws of England'—one from Jamaica—were rooted deep in both. In an examination of the metropolitan colonial policy, and of one particular field in which it went to work, such as this book seeks to make, this difference in atmosphere, in temperature, and in outlook, needs always to be borne in mind. 'We are but a month from you by sea, if the wind be good,' wrote Peter Beckford, the secretary of Jamaica, to his sister in Bedford in 1672, 'but indeed those who talk much of a new world of the Indies say more than they ofttimes know.' It was a point that continued to tell, in the world that produced the American revolution in the following century: it is a point still arguable in the twentieth.

I owe much to the encouragement and advice of Professor Vincent Harlow, under whose generous guidance I first set to work on this study. Professor Richard Pares prevented me from making it twice as long, which is a service that everyone who reads what there now is will certainly appreciate; and Professor Bruce Wernham did for the book and its author another service which he will remember. The faults that remain are no fault of theirs. I am also grateful to the President and Fellows of Trinity College, Oxford, in whose company a young scholar could not fail to learn much. And to the Principal and Court of the University of Aberdeen, whose generosity removed the financial burden of prolonged research in the London depositories, my warm thanks are also due.

A. P. T.

King's College
Aberdeen
12 May 1955

CONTENTS

ABBREVIATIONS

The following abbreviations are used in the notes:

B.M.	British Museum.
Add. MS.	Additional Manuscripts, British Museum.
Bodl.	Bodleian Library, Oxford.
Rawl.	Rawlinson Manuscripts, Bodleian Library, Oxford.
SP	State Papers, Public Record Office.
Adm	Admiralty Papers, Public Record Office.
CO	Colonial Office Papers, Public Record Office.
GD	Gifts and Deposits, Public Record Office.
T	Treasury Papers, Public Record Office.
E	Exchequer Papers, Public Record Office.
PC	Privy Council Register, Public Record Office.
APCC i, ii	Acts of the Privy Council, Colonial (printed), vols. i (1613–80), and ii (1680–1720).
CSPC	Calendar of State Papers, Colonial (printed).
CSPD	Calendar of State Papers, Domestic (printed).
Cal. T.B.	Calendar of Treasury Books (printed).
Cal. S.P. Ven.	Calendar of State Papers, Venetian (printed).
HMC	Historical Manuscripts Commission (printed).

I

A SURVEY OF POLICY

1660–85

THE Restoration of the English monarchy in 1660 involved the shoring-up of an administrative structure whose weaknesses war and revolution had already made plain. England had to make her way in a jealous world, obtain political unity, increase her wealth, and maintain her population. How all these things were to be done was the subject of many pamphlets and broadsheets. Some publicists emphasized the dangers of underpopulation, and mourned those who had settled overseas as so many good Englishmen gone, who had better, for security's sake, stayed home. People were the wealth of the nation, and it was folly to squander them. The 'long continued diverting of the young and prolifick people to the plantations', this 'unpeopling' of the kingdom, would surely prove its ruin.[1] Others attacked this notion. The English who were scattered abroad could not now be recalled—but if the interdependence of the lands they lived in could be secured, if some unity of control could be set up there, then surely the whole realm, all the King's dominions, could not but be very greatly strengthened? English courage, English capital, had been heavily invested in the plantations overseas. The value of these 'colonies' was indeed such as to need a much firmer control than that which ruled the Englishman who had limited the area of his enterprise and unproductively stayed in his own parish. Every subject settled oversea earned £60 *per annum* 'for the Publick', and consumed more than ten times the amount of English manufactures than did his English cousin: so said one calculation.[2]

Colonies were primarily sources of supply for the home

---

[1] 'Essay concerning the Decay of Rents and their Remedies', *c.* 1670, B.M., Sloane MS. 3828, f. 205*b*; report of the Customs Commissioners, 14 Apr. 1679, CSPC 1677–80, 967.

[2] Josiah Child, *A New Discourse of Trade* (London, 1693), 212.

B

country, and on the volume of demand for that supply their reputations depended. The New England colonies in America raised similar produce to that of old England, were a poor market for English manufactures, and had anyway added insult to these injuries by entering into competition with the home country in the trade to the West Indies and to Europe. Their reputation was accordingly low. The 'Southern colonies' of Maryland and Virginia were regarded more favourably, although their over-reliance on the tobacco-staple worried economists of the day; while the Caribbean colonies were the most highly respected of all. For in the West Indies Englishmen could produce commodities that all Europe was eager to buy —sugar, ginger, pepper, indigo. The islands imported their necessities and provisions from England. Without this mutual commerce, one observer commented in 1668, 'this Nation must long since have totally sunck'.[1]

National self-sufficiency was the goal desired, and thus such valuable possessions required a strict commercial control. The Navigation Act of 1660 combined the regulations of two Commonwealth Acts of 1650 and 1651, and added a clause 'enumerating' all the subtropical produce of the West Indies, confining it solely to English ships, and consigning it solely to English ports. Enumeration was not necessary in the case of Newfoundland's fish, and not worth imposing on the produce of New England, but the same regulation of shipping was insisted on. The Act should be read in conjunction with three other contemporary measures: the issue of a new Book of Rates, laying down imperial protection as a policy (setting, for example, on foreign tobaccos imported three times as much duty as was paid by tobacco from English plantations, and nearly as much on foreign sugars); the renewal of the East India Company's Charter (1661), which 'enumerated' all the produce of the East as a matter of course; and the Act of 1663, usually called the Staple Act, which laid down that all trade between Europe and the English colonies must pass through England as a staple, and that foreign or manufactured goods must be unladen in an English port and there reladen on an English ship as if they were English goods.[2] In a broad view, it

[1] 14 Aug. 1668, Bodl. MS. Rawl. A. 478, f. 48.
[2] L. A. Harper, *The English Navigation Laws* (New York, 1939), 59-60.

was immaterial whether individual planters and merchants lost or gained an immediate profit under this system, so long as the future of their whole trade was secure. The enumeration of sugar led at first to a glut of it in the English market. Prices fell, and planters talked of ruin. Throughout this period Barbados pleaded to be granted the old free trade of Cromwell's day, 'before these chains were cast about her'; the planter disliked the whole system of regulation, both the enumeration of his produce and its restriction to English shipping, for it was a fact that there was just not enough authorized shipping in existence to carry all he could produce—and he disliked, too, to be told he was producing too much.[1] Henceforth his economic grievance tainted all his politics, and he early attained the intransigence peculiar to the frontiersman, ever resentful of the meddling of a bureaucracy whose problems are never his own.

It was always clear to the statesmen at Whitehall that the drive towards commercial self-sufficiency could not be established by the Crown alone. Parliament must act as its ally. It willingly did so. The resultant alliance of Crown with Parliament accomplished a work that endured, for although the old English monarchy fell for ever in 1689, the 'Old Colonial System' that was the product of its partnership with Parliament survived its fall for a century and a half; its principles continued to animate the governance of newer Empires, and are by no means dead now. Devotion to the pursuit of a surplus revenue involved the various officials and departments of State in a closer co-ordination than had hitherto existed, and a genuine attempt to reconstruct the methods of government was made from the year of the Restoration.

The expansion of England that had occurred under the early Stewarts and during the Interregnum had made necessary some similar development in the machinery of the administration of the realm. So much was plain. Thus, although the King's Privy Council was also restored, it did not regain the powers it had previously enjoyed. The vital work of government was

[1] Barbados's terms of capitulation to the forces of the Commonwealth, 11 Jan. 1652, have much to say on this point: Add. MS. 11411, f. 95; G. L. Beer, *The Origins of the British Colonial System* (New York, 1908), 209, 389, 392; Harper, op. cit. 243. A report of 1664 says that Barbados's shipping fell from 400 to 150 sail in five years, and that both imports and exports dropped by a third.

henceforward done in its Committees. While the Committee had
long been accepted as a convenience of administration, it had
heretofore been designed to meet only temporary needs. But in
the summer of 1660 pressure of business was naturally extreme.
Twenty-eight Privy Councillors could not cope simultaneously
with State affairs, with the ecclesiastical settlement, with the
prorogation of the old and the programme for the new Parliament; with Treasury problems, and military business; with
local government, and personal petitions and memorials; as
well as with the affairs of Ireland, Scotland, the Channel
Islands, and the American Plantations.[1] So formidable an
agenda would have strained the capacity of the closest-knit
administration. The Councillors (many of them uneasy com-
panions from the outset) had no smooth-running machine at
their disposal. They could only resort to Committee as to a
retreat, and pray that the flood would subside.

Fortunately, much of it did. Between 1660 and 1667 no fewer
than 50 Committees fell into abeyance as soon as their Reports
had been presented to the parent Privy Council.[2] Nevertheless,
there never came a day when there were no foreign affairs to
see to, when the business of the navy could be left to run itself,
and when the Treasury might be abandoned to the moth and
the rust. Nor could colonial and commercial matters (and the
two were one) be quietly forgotten. It was clear that a Committee which dissolved as soon as it had deliberated was not an
adequate instrument to deal with such issues, which were all
perpetual. Accordingly the Committees appointed to oversee
these, and in particular the business of 'Trade and Plantations',
were to attain a significance, and eventually a permanence,
which matched the affairs with which they had to deal.

The new aristocracy which set the pace at Court and dominated the Privy Council was composed of clear-headed men who
had survived adversities by the continuous use of their wits.
All of them, from King Charles II down, possessed the tenacity
peculiar to the *arriviste*. Opportunists, they followed no 'Grand

[1] E. R. Turner, *The Privy Council* (Baltimore, 1928), ii. 369. Of 54 Committees
established between 1660 and 1664 the two Secretaries of State were members of
43, Ashley of 41, and Anglesey of 36—to name only four of the major figures in the
Administration.

[2] E. I. Carlyle, 'Clarendon and the Privy Council', *English Historical Review*,
xxvii. 251–73.

Design', and no one of them could hope to graduate to such a ✓
position as Colbert was soon to hold in France. Their outlook on
politics was thus at least free from preconceived ideas. Simple
patriotism, for example, many of them never acquired; while
others, like Buckingham, discovered its value by chance and
wore it thereafter as a badge of their own virtue. Men of this
stamp, 'mutable and slippery',[1] did not turn their backs on the
past with that revulsion which marked the attitude of the orthodox Cavalier. They were temperamentally well fitted to assess
the sources of Cromwell's power; and even the one great
imponderable element in this, the personality of the Protector
himself, many of them were able to gauge from their own
knowledge and experience.]

The composition of the Privy Council Committee appointed ⟵
on 4 July to consider the accumulated business of Trade and
Foreign Plantations, well illustrates this.[2] All its members were
men of importance. It consisted of the Earl of Manchester,
appointed Lord Chamberlain on 30 May; the Earl of Southampton, appointed Lord High Treasurer on 8 September; an
unimportant exception in Robert Sydney, Earl of Leicester;
Viscount Saye and Sele; John Lord Robartes, appointed Lord
Deputy of Ireland, later to be Lord Privy Seal; Denzil Lord
Holles; Arthur Annesley, to be created Earl of Anglesey on
20 April 1661; Sir Anthony-Ashley Cooper, created Viscount
Ashley the same day, and appointed Chancellor of the Exchequer on 13 May; together with the two Secretaries of State,
members *ex-officio* of every Committee—Sir Edward Nicholas
and Sir William Morice. All but three of this group were also ⟵
Commissioners of the Treasury, all but two were Commissioners
for Irish affairs, and all but four sat as a Committee for the
affairs of the Navy.[3] Manchester, who had led the Parliamentary
Army against the King's father, was Governor of the Bermuda
Company. Morice was Monk's kinsman, agent, and nominee
for the office he now held. Saye and Sele, 'Old Subtlety',
had held considerable properties in New Hampshire and

---

[1] 'So ... as that they spend their whole time and thought in securing themselves,'
says Petty, no bad judge of the practice; Lord E. Fitzmaurice, *Life of Sir William
Petty* (London, 1895), 202.

[2] C. M. Andrews, *British Committees, Commissions, and Councils of Trade and
Plantations, 1622–1675* (Baltimore, 1908), 62; APCC, i. 484.

[3] Turner, *Privy Council*, ii. 264-6.

Connecticut, and had been, like Robartes, a member of the old Providence Company.[1] Like Annesley, Holles, and Robartes, he was a strong Presbyterian. Only two, Southampton and Nicholas, could show a purely Royalist record.

These men were among those who now stood by as Cromwell's Army—the force that had been the mainstay of his authority in England and the admiration of Europe—fell before the verbal onslaught of the Convention. But the Protectorate's other prop, a sound economic policy operated by an able central government, was still available to their hands. Accordingly the new Councillors of the new King turned with alacrity to those others who had stood at the usurper's ear to murmur magic measures of success.

The mercantile interest had been prominent in the inner counsels of State ever since the passing of the Navigation Act of 1650. Chief among these merchants were Martin Noell, Thomas Povey, Andrew Riccard, Maurice Thompson, and Thomas Kendall.[2] Noell, the Saltmaster, with interests in the trade of Scotland, Ireland, and the Levant, had been the 'very good friend' of the Cromwell family, Thurloe's brother-in-law, and the principal contractor for the expedition to the West Indies in 1655. Both he and his friend Povey, who had been in his day Lord Willoughby's agent in Surinam as well as secretary to the Protectorate's Committee of Plantations, had long been angling for the creation of a West-India Company on East-India lines. On their colonial and commercial expertise Cromwell had heavily relied, and their influence remained considerable while they were Members of Richard Cromwell's Parliament.[3] Riccard was a prominent capitalist, Master of the Drapers, Governor of the Levant Company, and a Director of the East-India Company. Thompson had interests in both the East and the West Indies, in Virginia and on the Guinea Coast, all of which he was anxious to expand.[4] Kendall was a leading West-India merchant, kin to the Kendalls of Barbados, both an

[1] Cf. A. P. Newton, *The Colonizing Activities of the English Puritans* (New Haven, 1912).

[2] Cf. Maurice Ashley, *Financial and Commercial Policy under the Cromwellian Protectorate* (Oxford, 1934).

[3] A. P. Watts, *Une Histoire des colonies anglaises aux Antilles de 1649 à 1660* (Paris, 1924), 391 et seq.

[4] V. T. Harlow, *Colonising Expeditions to the West Indies and Guiana, 1623–1667* Hakluyt Society, London, 1924), 26 n.

intimate and a cousin of Colonel Thomas Modyford of that Island—yet another of Cromwell's advisers on West-India policy,[1] who was even then trimming his sails to the fresh Royalist wind. Of this group Thomas Povey was the thinker and planner.[2]

These men were of much the same type as the Restoration statesmen themselves: quick to see the main chance, ready to do the State some service if the State would make it worth their while. Yet adept as they were in getting and pushing home an advantage, these merchants were to meet their match in the politicians, who had also been trained in a fiercely competitive school. Although they were now made welcome in the outer halls of the Administration, they were not admitted to its inner sanctum. Much was made of them while their brains were picked, but their presence was never allowed to become indispensable, nor their political importance to reach the level that had been attained under the Protectorate. Those who were now in control had no intention of delegating any part of their hard-won responsibility. The matter was handled with finesse; the Administration chose to adopt a commercial programme which the merchants could not but applaud. They could not fairly protest that their interests were being ignored, or that commerce was betrayed. They were left with no cause for grievance. They could only accept their knighthoods, rally to the aid of such State enterprises as the two African Companies, prosper under the protection of the Acts of Trade, and reconcile themselves to a position of comfortable subordination in the political scene. From that position, their class was not thereafter to move.

But this yet lay in the future. Now in 1660 the merchants confidently asserted themselves. They recalled the great part they had played in fomenting the 'Western Design'. It was true that the Design had suffered some distortion in translation from theory to practice, but in the blundering of soldiers and in the ravages of climate the merchants had seen no reason to change their minds as to the suitability of the West Indies as a field for

---

[1] Cf. 'A paper of Colonel Muddiford concerning the West Indies', Dec. 1654, printed in Watts, op. cit. 457–61.

[2] His letter-books, Add. MSS. 11410–11, and Egerton MS. 2395 provide a mass of proof. For further personalia on Povey, cf. G. A. Jacobsen, *William Blathwayt* (New Haven, 1933).

English commercial exploitation. Their unanimity on the point could not but impress those who were genuinely anxious to learn: and the decision to reorganize the method of dealing with commercial and colonial business was therefore taken in August 1660, only a month after the official plantations Committee had been set up.]

The King-in-Council sent a letter, to which Hyde, Monk (now Earl of Albemarle), Robartes, Annesley, and Morice put their hands, to the Lord Mayor and aldermen of London, directing them to circulate it to the Members of the Turkey, East India, Greenland and Eastland Companies, to the Merchant Adventurers, and to the Incorporated Traders for Spain, France, Portugal, Holland, and the West-India Plantations. Each of these bodies was asked to forward the names of four 'of their most knowing and active men' to the King, as His Majesty intended to select two such from each Company, dignify the resultant group with the presence of 'weighty Councillors', and thus constitute a standing Council of Trade under the Commission of his Great Seal.[1] While this was in train, the Chancellor, Hyde, kept Parliament informed. He said he was certain that the creation of this new Council of Trade would greatly benefit national commerce, a matter that the King considered as of the highest importance: His Majesty, confident that days of prosperity would soon return, was naturally also very 'solicitous' for the welfare of his overseas Plantations, 'where there is such large room for the industry and reception of such who shall desire to go thither'. Because he was so, still another new Council was planned, composed of 'well-qualified persons', who should take under their charge all the business of these Plantations.[2] So it fell out. On 4 December 1660 the affairs of Trade and those of Foreign Plantations were officially divided.[3] Each was transferred to the care of a loose, large organization, a Council swollen to great size by the merchants and stockholders of the principal trading Companies. In the midst of two such great clouds of witness—the Council of Trade had 62 members, the Council of Foreign Plantations

[1] Letter to Lord Mayor and Aldermen, 17 Aug. 1660, APCC, i. 488.
[2] 13 Sept. 1660; L. F. Stock, *Proceedings and Debates of British Parliaments respecting North America*, i, *1542–1688* (Washington, 1924), 282; *Lords Journals*, xi. 173, 175; *Commons Journals*, viii. 171, 173–4.
[3] Andrews, *Committees*, 67 et seq.

48—it seemed more than likely that even the weightiest Councillors might be hard to discern.

The Chancellor personally disliked this development. Cautious and charmless, the royalism of Hyde was always of a different order from that of his colleagues. With them it was a garment they had hastily flung on: with him it was an instinct. In the old days, to which this regretful exile always looked back, the privilege of advising the King on the conduct of State business had been that of Privy Councillors alone. The Governments of the Commonwealth and the Protectorate had doubtless farmed out the care of colonial and commercial affairs to ragged committees of merchants and the like, but Hyde saw no reason why Cromwell's principles should survive his régime. He did his duty by warmly approving this new system of Councils in public, but privately he termed them 'a crowd of commissioners'.[1] However, as the surest way to prevent merchants from obtaining an undue political influence was to supervise their proceedings himself, he became reconciled to the new conditions, and henceforward, as he tells us himself, 'took more pains than other men'[2] in these two departments of the public business.

The future before the Council of Trade was indeed as blank as Hyde foretold. It suffered always from the presence of too many experts, none of whom was interested in each other's knowledge. No Turkey merchant would bother to improve the market for West-India sugar: West-India merchants were correspondingly careless about the prospects of the spice trade. The Council had no real work to do. It was designed 'to consider English commerce primarily as affected by our relations with Forraine Powers',[3] but the control of foreign trade and commercial relations, as of all foreign affairs, remained the prerogative of the Crown. The Crown maintained that control by the grant or continuance of exclusive Charters and monopolies, such as were issued to the Levant, East-India, and Royal

[1] Clarendon, *Continuation of 'Life'* (Oxford, 1857), ii. 442. But this was not the opinion of the Venetian envoy in England, who wrote to his Senate that 'the Council of Trade will do harm to all the marts for trade and especially the Dutch'; 17 Dec. 1660, Cal. S.P. Ven., 1659–61, 250.

[2] Clarendon, op. cit. ii. § 1308; but cf. David Ogg, *England in the Reign of Charles II* (Oxford, 1934), 193: 'The Chancellor . . . was not interested in colonies.'

[3] Add. MS. 25115, f. 20.

Fishery Companies in 1661, to the Royal Company of Adventurers trading into Africa in 1663, to the Canary Island Company in 1665, to the Hudson Bay Company in 1670, and to the Royal African Company in 1672. The Council of Trade thus became a debating society of merchants whose interests lay elsewhere. It was not worth the Privy Councillors' while to attend it. Executive measures, like the successive Acts of Trade, were drafted not in any Council of Trade but in their proper place— the Privy Council. Thus the Council of Trade eventually died of inanition in 1667.[1]

And although the Council of Foreign Plantations had a different career, it came to much the same end as its fellow. It was at least able to avoid the danger of aimless deliberation, for the colonial business on its agenda was at once specific, urgent, and interrelated. Charged by its Commission to ensure a 'uniform Inspection & Conduct' of the colonies, and to do everything requisite for 'the rendering of those Dominions usefull to England', it instituted a regular correspondence with colonial Governors and officials, and amassed a great deal of statistical information, which was classified and registered.[2] Members of both the new Councils were instructed to keep close contact with one another—a simple condition enough, as 28 members were common to both Boards. Unlike the Council of Trade, the Council of Foreign Plantations was well attended by the Privy Councillors when there was urgent business before it; but, although planters and merchants were urged to contribute their particular specialized knowledge, the inordinate length of Thomas Povey's 'Overtures' hints that there were many occasions when he was not allowed his full say at the Board. The Privy Councillors wished to use the Plantations Council as a sounding-board of mercantile opinion, but not to devolve on it any executive power. It was still the exclusive duty of the politicians who were members of the Plantations Council to pass on its recommendations to the Privy Council—for no merchant had the *right* to tender his advice on a State matter directly to the King. Privy Councillors did not always, or indeed often, agree with the Chancellor, but this was one opinion that they shared.

[1] Andrews, *Committees*, 85.
[2] The Register is CO 1/14, No. 59, 1–27. It ends in Nov. 1664.

On the other hand, when the business before the Plantations Council was more factual than political, the merchants outnumbered the politicians. Sir Anthony-Ashley Cooper, who took a personal interest in colonies, was the only Privy Councillor present at the first meeting of the Plantations Council held on 7 January 1661.[1] He met there such old Barbados hands as Sir Peter Leare, Sir James Drax, and Sir John Colleton, all very conscious of their new knighthoods;[2] Thomas Jefferies and William Watts, who both had interests in St. Christopher and Nevis; Noell and Povey, as a matter of course; and, among others, Colonel Venables, son to the conqueror of Jamaica. The Plantations Council held 40 meetings in 1661 alone, convened suitably enough in Grocers' Hall.[3] It was from that address that they sent a message to Francis Lord Willoughby, asking him to take note of their creation and constitution; there they studied Richard Povey's first-hand accounts of Jamaica; there they began to collate all patents that concerned public offices in the Plantations. There they drafted letters for the King and Privy Council to approve, and in so doing early met the difficulties implicit in their own ignorance of the political situation, as distinct from the commercial conditions, in the colonies—for it was certainly hard 'to frame a Letter which required severall things to be done without some knowledge of who shall do them'. The letters they did frame were passed to a Privy Councillor for transmission above—'any of the Committee may speak to the sense thereof' they were told, 'but nothing contrary thereto'.[4]

Collation and investigation of facts could not go on for ever. As this sort of work diminished, and as issues of policy increased, the utility of the Plantations Council became questionable. From June 1662 it had to report all its doings to the Plantations Committee of the Privy Council,[5] and at any time a group of Privy Councillors might discuss colonial business in committee

---

[1] Minutes of the Council of Foreign Plantations, 7 Jan. 1661, CO 1/14, No. 59, 3, 8.

[2] Drax was originally one of Cromwell's knights (9 Jan. 1658); V. T. Harlow, *A History of Barbados, 1625–1685* (Oxford, 1926), 121.

[3] Andrews, *Committees*, 78.

[4] Plantations Council to the King, 25 Jan. 1661, CO 1/14, No. 59, 9–12.

[5] Normally the Council's secretary, Philip Frowde, acted as intermediary with the Secretary of State.

without necessarily informing or referring to either the Council
of Plantations or the Council of Trade. For example, the task
of framing a system of government for Jamaica was appointed,
on 3 July 1661, not to the Plantations Council but to a Privy
Council Committee.[1] The Scottish protest against the exclusion
of the Scots from the benefits of the Navigation Act was dealt
with by the politicians.[2] It was the responsibility of Lord High
Treasurer Southampton and his subordinates, the Commissioners of the Customs, to see that the colonies complied with
that Act.[3] In 1662 it was not the Plantations Council but the
Privy Council Committee that was further 'dignified' by the
presence of weighty Councillors: Clarendon, Portland, Hatton,
and Sandwich were added to it, and thereafter it convened
twice a week in the Privy Council Chamber.[4] Although the
Plantations Council called both Lord Willoughby and Lord
Windsor before it prior to their taking up their respective
appointments as Governors of Barbados and Jamaica, it was
only to brief them on the economic facts of the West-India
world. It was the Privy Council Committee which examined
Willoughby's subsequent opinions on the ill effects of the
Navigation Act on the trade and prospects of the Leeward
Islands; which dealt with the dispute concerning the Patent of
the Provost-Marshal's office in Barbados; and which considered
Sir Thomas Modyford's recommendations for the better settlement and organization of Jamaica in 1664.[5] The Plantations
Council had meanwhile to confine its attention to such minor
matters as the difficulty of collecting bad debts in Barbados.[6]

Moreover, how to serve the King and their own interests at
once presented merchants with a delicate problem. Noell, Leare,
Middleton, and Colleton were among those who petitioned the
King against allowing Willoughby to resume his proprietary in
the West Indies. This they did in their capacity of absentee
planters[7]—but it was odd conduct for men, themselves members

[1] 3 July 1661, APCC, i. 522.

[2] Cf. 6 Nov., 22 Nov. 1661, ibid. 536–7. The Council of Trade recommended that
Scots shipping should have the benefit of the Act of Navigation, although no inter-
course with the plantations.   [3] 15 Aug. 1662, ibid. 569.

[4] 29 Jan., 5 Sept. 1662, ibid. 544, 572.

[5] 24 Aug. 1664, ibid. 630.

[6] 10 June 1663, ibid. 595.

[7] 'Petition of planters of Barbados inhabiting in and about London to the
King', 1 Mar. 1661, CO 1/15, No. 25. They hoped that this intervention would

of a council constituted by royal Commission, thus publicly to object to the declared intentions of the King. The fact that serving the King was often a financial risk made the issue no simpler: Drax and Middleton both lost money handsomely supplying Jamaica with brandy and stores.[1] Perhaps it needs no comment, then, that it was Drax who gave his friend Humphrey Walrond, President of the Council in Barbados, the first hint of the plan to put a percentage duty on the exports of the colony—and so set the Assembly there in a roar.[2]

It was anyway not to be expected that mercantile and political views could for long coincide. The West-India interest inevitably disagreed with the politicians as to the beneficence of the Navigation Act as applied to the West-India trade. Their original chorus of propaganda—that the West-India trade was a veritable gold-mine—had, they found, done its work somewhat too well, for the politicians were now talking at large of placing even heavier duties on West-India produce. The politicians, particularly those who had worked for Cromwell, had not forgotten the Protector's conviction that a new Eldorado was to be won in the Caribbean. They therefore discounted a suggestion from Walrond that the wealth of the Island colonies was generally over-estimated, and did not heed his diagnosis that colonists themselves were 'generally poore & Vainglorious, makeing ostentation of Riches which they have not'. Walrond they distrusted as a time-server—and his gibe at those who had insinuated themselves at home into royal favour 'so as to creep back to that Power which they had in the Rebells time'[3] cut too deep for comfort. Thus, from an accumulation of reasons both personal and political, the Restoration statesmen preferred to shake themselves free of mercantile expertise as soon as they could effectively manage to do so.

In 1664 the Privy Council decided that the situation in Jamaica was stable enough to render the existence of a per-

---

lead the King to appoint 'commissioners' with Willoughby in Barbados, who might thereafter restrain that peer from any authoritarian excess; ibid. No. 52.

[1] Cf. CO 1/14, No. 59, 23–24.

[2] Cf. the Declaration of the President and Council of Barbados to the inhabitants of their reasons for dissolving the Assembly, 19 July 1661, CSPC 1661–8, 134.

[3] President and Council of Barbados to Nicholas, 10 July 1661, CO 1/15, Nos. 70–71. Walrond in fact was referring to the machinations in London of the Modyford faction, his sworn foes.

manent Committee for its supervision unnecessary.[1] The Island would perhaps require more money from time to time, but that was a matter which the interested parties, the Lord Treasurer and the Chancellor of the Exchequer, might arrange. Elsewhere it now appeared that order and method had been successfully imposed on the governance of the American estate. Since its trade, which was its only significance, was now closely regulated by Statute, its internal business might be left to the management of the royal Governors. Official care had still to be taken to protect that monopoly of supplying slaves to the West-India plantations which belonged to the Company of Royal Adventurers trading into Africa, in whose organization Court, Council, and mercantile interest enjoyed a closer communion than in politics; the sanctity of royal Patents to colonial offices was always to be guarded; and watch had continuously to be kept on the movements of those foreign nations to whom the Caribbean was at once a haven and a highway. Still, Empire of itself had no *mystique*: in the short run both Dunkirk and Tangier proved to be imperial embarrassments, and were summarily disposed of; and in 1668 the King would have accepted cash down from the French for the ruined island of St. Christopher had it been possible to do so. There is no reason so suppose that other English colonies might not have shared this fate, or that of Bombay (transferred as a bad bargain to the East India Company in 1669, at a rent of £10 a year), had they not measured better to the economic and strategic standards of the time.

Overmuch can be made of the work of Empire-building in the Restoration era. The Administration lacked cohesion and grip. The laws of Jamaica could be sent home for confirmation and there mislaid for ten years; a Privy Council decision that laws in Barbados and the Leeward Islands should be valid for one year only, before they must be confirmed by the King, could escape both notice and implementation.[2] In both foreign and home affairs, the Government had to wrestle with forces it could not gauge. At last it sank discredited beneath an accumulation of crisis, the vanquished in the war with the United Provinces on which it had staked its reputation. When

---

[1] 1 July 1664, APCC, i. 625.
[2] 19 Apr. 1665, ibid. 653.

Clarendon fell the administrative system that he had presided
over was demolished, on the principle (not so reckless, perhaps,
as his apologists assert), that any other must be better. While
amateur auditors examined baffling accounts, or hunted for
others that did not exist, colonial business was naturally left
even more at large. The degree of confusion may be judged
from the tone of a questionnaire sent by the Privy Council to
its Committee for Trade and Foreign Plantations in August
1667. What supplies were wanted by the American colonies?
What orders should the King send? And to whom?[1] There is
no firm colonial policy very evident there. Nor is there in the
instruction to William Willoughby, the new Captain-General
and Governor of Barbados and the Leeward Islands, to obey all
former orders sent to his late brother and predecessor, Francis
Lord Willoughby, 'except when these are contrary the one to
the other'.[2] The contrariness could be safely assumed.

But by 1669 some sort of order had been restored to the
Administration. Restoration, in the strict sense, was now over,
and its principal architects, both Royalist and Presbyterian,
were passing from the scene. Nicholas, Clarendon's Secretary
of State, had been superseded by Henry Bennet in 1662.
Southampton the Treasurer died in 1667, Clarendon's last year
in power. Ormond was dismissed from Ireland in 1669. Of the
Puritan members of the coalition that had restored the Crown,
the second Secretary of State, Morice, resigned in 1668. So did
his patron Albemarle in 1669, just a year before he died. The
way was thus clear for new men, the émigrés whose outlook was
not English at all, men whose model in this was the King
himself. Clarendon's successor as Lord Keeper, Sir Orlando
Bridgeman, was one of Buckingham's men. So was Morice's
successor as Secretary, Sir John Trevor. Diligent Sir Thomas
Osborne was another. Arlington's disciples included his secretary, Joseph Williamson (who was to succeed him in 1674 as
Secretary of State), Sir Thomas Clifford, and Sir William
Temple. Ashley, rising fast, brought the capable Coventrys,
William and Henry, up with him. It is, however, misleading to
speak of this as the period of the rule of a 'Cabal'; for the use
of this term implies at least some sort of co-operation, even if

[1] 30 Aug. 1667, ibid. 717.
[2] 23 Jan. 1667, ibid. 697.

only a partnership in crime. There is little of the kind here. Arlington and Buckingham were generally at odds—although both might conjoin to bring down a common foe, like William Coventry or Ormond. It was Arlington who felled the Catholic Clifford with the weapon of the Test Act. It was Buckingham who instigated Arlington's impeachment. Lauderdale lived his own life, and sensibly lived a lot of it in Scotland, out of sight if not out of mind; while Ashley, slow to decide where and on what to make his stand and his name, was to make it at last perilously close to the 'Good Old Cause'. Certainly all these men left their individual mark on the Administration, but the impression they made on its policies was less clear than that made by their master, the King.

That Charles found all public business tedious has perhaps been over-publicized.[1] A man who dislikes committees is not necessarily either an idler or a fool.[2] (It may well have been to defend himself from the ravages of tedium that he formed his resolve, on Clarendon's departure, to conduct affairs himself.) Certainly once he had bestirred himself to adopt a particular position, he was a hard man to move. His habit of 'sauntering' had already been remarked—but that it usually took him along a path of his own choosing was not always so plain to his contemporaries. At any rate his determination to cut leading-strings, to have his own way, to employ his own agents, to amass his own resources, backed policies that had previously been flaccid with a lining of steel. Although his interest in the welfare of plantations was based on their commercial value, as was that of everybody else, it did not depend on this alone. To the merchant, the Englishmen who lived in colonies overseas were just so many producers, or consumers, or preferably both; beyond these roles they had no further significance. The King

[1] Cf. the letter sent by Secretary Morice to Sir Richard Fanshawe, envoy at Lisbon, on 19 Nov. 1662: 'I have received both your packets, and abridged the first sixteen pages for His Majesty, who else would never have had the patience or given the time to have heard a quarter thereof . . .'; HMC Heathcote, 48. Fanshawe later thanked him ironically for 'reducing their tedious length to a compass supportable by His Majesty'; ibid. 69.

[2] Even while spinning his famous 'Dover' Plot, he did not lose sight of realities. He wrote his sister, 'You cannot choose but believe that it must be dangerous to me at home to make an entire league [with France], till first the great and principal interests of this nation be secured, which is trade'; Ady, *Madame* (London, 1900), 271.

of England could not look upon them quite in this way. He was no less King in America. The inhabitants of that continent were his subjects, who owed him their allegiance and trust, for which in return they deserved his good governance and protection. To the King, that independency of New England, which merchants bemoaned as a regrettable lapse from accepted economic standards, could only appear seditious. And the sedition might easily prove to be contagious. The thriving trade from Salem to the Indies (much of it illicit anyway) might very well carry the virus there.

The actions of the last two Stewart Kings in American affairs are thus perfectly consistent. They are not those of disgruntled economists, anxious to erase a discrepancy from their commercial tables; but of rulers determined to end a situation that allowed their commands to be flouted. They canvassed the views of their Councillors, but they made their own decisions. Charles no less than James believed that one was company;[1] he had plans in mind that would not bear outsiders' inspection. 'Od's fish!' was his cry in 1679, when encircled by a ring of new and suspicious Privy Councillors, 'they have put a set of men about me, but they shall know nothing!' Expert advice on the proper management of his affairs might be well-intentioned, but too much of it amounted to presumption. The authority of the Crown must be the supreme factor in every activity of Government: any weakening of that executive power not only unlawfully diminished the prerogatives of the monarchy, but injured the security and prospects of the realm.

The 1670's and 80's therefore saw the reins of colonial administration firmly drawn up. A close co-ordination between the departments of State was now not only asked for but ensured. Privy Council Committees were strengthened, and on new Councils of Trade and Plantations merchants were relegated to the background.[2] So, too, to their surprise, were the grandees—who had to be content to find in unusual corporate unity, such as that of 'the Lords of the Privy Council appointed a Committee of Trade',[3] the political influence which most of

---

[1] 'He did not think he was a King, as long as a company of fellows were looking into all his actions, and examining his ministers as well as his accounts.' Burnet, ed. O. Airy, *A History of My Own Time* (Oxford, 1900), ii. 3.

[2] Andrews, *Committees*, 96–114.

[3] Cf. R. P. Bieber, *The Lords of Trade and Plantations, 1675–1696* (Allentown,

them would have preferred to wield in person. The public officials of the time, not excluding the two Secretaries of State, were now men of importance only as servants of the Crown, no longer in their own right; a list of their names reveals them as loyal, industrious persons of correspondingly mediocre ambitions—Williamson, the Coventrys, Robert Southwell, William Blathwayt, Leoline Jenkins. These ancestors of the Permanent Civil Servant were neither sufficiently distinguished to be allowed the luxury of playing politics, nor foolish enough to expect to command obedience from Englishmen overseas if they were not themselves willing to obey their King. Under their aegis the effort was made to link every sphere of colonial governance more securely to the authority of the Crown. The previous emphasis on the commercial utility of colonies was now overlaid by the royal insistence, one which the royal agents took up with a will, that they were something more than markets: they were adjuncts of the royal power, jewels in His Majesty's Crown, preserved from harm by the magic of his grace and favour alone. And as a consequence, they were also places where no voice but that of Caesar might be heard.

This is the high tone that informs the official correspondence of the later years of the reign. This is the point of view that accounts for the institution of new, and the renovation of old, methods of administrative control. In the Parliament of England peers had to acquiesce in angry deadlock with the Commons over *Shirley* v. *Fagg*; but when their Lordships sat in Committee to deal with the affairs of Trade and Foreign Plantations, they would brook no correction and allow no dispute. When Barbadians had nothing else to complain of, they complained of the Acts of Trade, from whose mesh they ceaselessly sought to escape; but the previous official indifference to this habit was now changed to an attitude almost of horror. 'Of what evill Consequence it is', the Lords Committee of Trade reported to the King, 'that any of your Subjects should presume to petition Your Majesty against Acts of Parlament (which are the Laws they live under) and call them Grievances!'[1] Crown

Philadelphia, 1919); 'British Plantation Councils of 1670-4', *English Historical Review*, xl. 93-106; W. T. Root, 'The Lords of Trade and Plantations', *American Historical Review*, xxiii. 20-42.

[1] 8 Nov. 1676, CO 1/38, No. 31.

officials and royal patentees assumed new power in colonial life. The colonial Governor became a lesser figure. The old independence, the old discretion of action, were taken from him; these were attributes no longer considered essential to the commander of a frontier post, as Sir Jonathan Atkins in Barbados found to his cost. 'You are not to imagine', Secretary Henry Coventry warned his friend, 'His Majestie will endure to have so important a part of his Plantacons as Barbados to be governed so that neither he nor his Councill must know how.'[1] The best Governors were those who did exactly what they were told. The days when they tricked and deported their political opponents, filled local offices with their own kin, leagued with buccaneers to finance unlawful expeditions against a foreign neighbour, or maintained cordial relations with illegal traders, were now over. The impression is inescapable that the monarchy was testing its strength in a field far removed from the scrutiny of a factious, turbulent Parliament. 'Distance of place', runs an ominous royal message of the time, 'shall shelter none from our Justice and Power.'[2] Redoubtable Massachusetts herself was to fall before the sincerity of this resolve and the skill of its enforcement. Colonial history in the more confined quarter of the Caribbean provides a still more telling commentary on the stresses that were then weakening the domestic English structure.

The Stewart Monarchy is not reckoned a successful institution, but it won at least a sizeable victory in America. The Parliament of England, absorbed as always in the assertion of its own importance, never noticed these laurels of its adversary. In 1689 it made no charge against King James II that he had broken the 'contract' with his subjects in America. It was just as well it did not, for in fact monarchy had made no such contract, and this the King might easily have proved in a court of law, had he had the opportunity to do so. Each colony had its sanction for existence, and each sanction bore a royal Seal. In America the monarchy had been left free to define its terms. Colonial Assemblies, in particular those of Massachusetts and Jamaica, might choose to style themselves miniature Houses of Commons, and talk at large about representation and the rights

[1] Coventry to Atkins, 25 July 1679, Add. MS. 25120, f. 143.
[2] The King to Deputy Governor, Council and Assembly of Barbados, 22 Nov. 1671, APCC, i. 931.

of Englishmen; but this conduct had short shrift from both Whitehall and Westminster alike. The Stewart attitude was consistent throughout: all political assemblies, as in Tudor times, were 'of grace'. Charles II never dared take too strong a tone with his English Parliament of 1661–79, Cavalier and pensionary though its majority was: but 'unheard-of extravaganties' was the phrase he used in 1677 of the conduct of the Speaker of the Jamaican Assembly, who had usurped the royal prerogative of pardon by reprieving a condemned pirate—'a thing never presumed in England by any Speaker but Mr Lenthall, and that when the House of Commons pretended to sovereignty.'[1] In truth the House of Commons was busy making this pretension again when these words were written; but it was as yet decently veiled, and the Members would not support the more tactless claims of the colonial Assemblies, either then or later. No Parliamentarian made that language his own, nor any English jurist.[2]

Thus it came about that although Englishmen at home attained their political liberty in 1689, another century was to pass before Englishmen in America won the privilege they protested in vain before Charles II and James II: to be governed 'according to the known laws of England'. Not until the very name of Stewart had become a romantic tradition in England, were the bonds of rule first set upon 'Americans' by the princes of that house finally loosed—and, even then, not all Americans chose to break free. The continental American colonies—'the unfortunate results of misdirected effort'[3]—took a new path,

[1] Coventry to Vaughan (Governor of Jamaica), 21 Nov. 1677, Add. MS. 25120, f. 118.
[2] In the 18th century Chatham, Camden, and Mansfield all saw eye to eye on this point, a remarkable circumstance. Pratt (Camden) said in 1755: 'The constitutions of the two assemblies [i.e. the House of Commons and a colonial Assembly] differ, fundamentally in many respects; our house of commons stands upon its own laws, the *lex parliam.*, whereas assemblies in the colonies, are regulated by their respective charters, usages, and the common law of England, and will never be allowed to assume those privileges which the house of commons are entitled to justly here, upon principles that neither can, nor must, be applied to the assemblies of the colonies. . . . I am satisfied neither the crown nor the parliament will ever suffer those assemblies to erect themselves into the power, and authority, of the British house of commons'; George Chalmers, *Opinions of Eminent Lawyers on various points of English Jurisprudence chiefly concerning the Colonies, Fisheries, and Commerce of Great Britain* (London, 1814), ii. 31; and cf. i. 263–4, 265–6, 296.
[3] G. L. Beer, *The Old Colonial System* (New York, 1912), ii. 234.

but the West-India colonies, where the imperial effort had not been misdirected and where the results had been far from unfortunate, remained to animate new theories of imperial commerce. The best estimate of the 'Old Colonial System' is not arrived at by pondering the intangible causes of the American Revolution, but by calculating the profit of those economic institutions in the West Indies that were fostered under its care. As Osgood pointed out: 'The precedents which were favourable to active imperial administration were first established on a large scale in the government of the island colonies. The system was most thoroughly tested there.'[1] Those precedents, and that system, may now be more fully examined.

[1] H. L. Osgood, *The American Colonies in the Seventeenth Century* (New York, 1907), iii. 140.

II

RESTORATION IN BARBADOS AND INNOVATION IN JAMAICA
1660–4

I

IN 1660 affairs in the Caribbean were complicated in the extreme. Barbados and her satellite Leeward Islands were at once rent by internal faction and enmeshed in a net of claim and counter-claim for their possession.[1] Francis Lord Willoughby of Parham claimed the governance and ownership of the whole by virtue of the proprietorial grant awarded by Charles I in 1627 to the first Earl of Carlisle; a grant which the Earl's son had transferred to Willoughby in 1647, on a lease of 21 years. This second Earl, dying in 1660, entangled the matter further by leaving to a kinsman, the Earl of Kinnoull, his West-India rights and interests, as well as the heavy Carlisle load of debt. The rich and influential Earl of Marlborough had also a word to say on ownership, since his grandfather and the first Earl of Carlisle had trafficked together in Caribbean property; certainly there was a pension due to him from the proprietary revenues. Then there were the creditors of both Carlisles, who claimed this tangible asset in compensation for other disappointments they had suffered. Moreover, the heirs and creditors of Sir William Courteen, an authentic pioneer of settlement in the West Indies, had their own protestations to put forward. Lastly, Barbadian planters and merchants contested not only these claims, but the legality of the original proprietorial patent itself, whoever held it.

All this was difficult enough, but still other players crowded this narrow stage. The Caribbean was also an area where Europe's frontiers met. As yet, however, the Frenchmen, Dutchmen, and Englishmen there had more cause to agree than

---

[1] Cf. J. A. Williamson, *The Caribbee Islands under the Proprietary Patents* (Oxford, 1926), 198 et seq., an exhaustive survey of this whole matter.

to quarrel.[1] All three deeply resented that Spain should continue to monopolize the resources of the New World without
having the power to make that monopoly effective. This resentment had already brought into being one international agency
—one that had chosen the curious incorporation of *flibuste et
boucane*, with Tortuga as its fortress and Spain as its foe. But
the Spanish leviathan was not to be moved by these hornets
alone. Although Jamaica was now in English hands, Spain still
felt secure in America. Her grip was strong in the other islands
of the Greater Antilles, and as yet she ignored the raffish settlements *déracinés* Frenchmen were building in the western half of
Hispaniola. To the Lesser Antilles she had never paid much
attention since Cortez's time. They were a no-man's-land,
where swarmed the misfits of all nations, renegades and refugees. French planters were already prospering in Martinique
and St. Croix. They shared St. Christopher with the English,
and St. Martin with the Dutch. To windward they were colonizing Guadeloupe and coveting the Carib islands of St. Vincent,
Grenada, Dominica, and St. Lucia. But in 1660 their form of
proprietary government was failing, the islands' political future
uncertain, and Colbertism not yet come.

The ubiquitous Dutchman, too, had a nexus of warehouses
to do business in. In the Caribbean he held strategical points on
the trade-routes, using them as slave-factories, as bases for his
shipping, and as entrepôts for all the commerce of the American
seas. Saba and St. Eustatius (Statia) served| him thus to leeward. In the south Curaçao throve enormously, Tobago and
Aruba began to prosper, and in Surinam in Guiana he impinged
on the frontiers of Lord Willoughby's own settlement there. But
to the Dutchman peace was an essential if he was to prosper;
the born middleman, he had nothing to gain from the bloodshed of his customers. No harbour from Cape Cod to the Main
was unknown to him, no person who would do business with
him a foe. 'The Dutch have a proverb,' drily commented
England's Governor of Jamaica in 1673, ' "Jesus Christ is good,
but trade is better." '

Till now, what went on 'beyond the Line' was better guessed
at in Europe than known, and the shrug of French, Dutch, or

[1] For how they came there and what they did there, see A. P. Newton, *The
European Nations in the West Indies, 1492–1688* (London, 1933), 224 et seq.

English shoulders when the subject was brought up had been for long a rankling insult to Spanish pride. But soon both the *camaraderie* and the lawlessness of this frontier were to clash with the imperial policies of the expanding European nations. Their eyes turned on the Caribbean with new purpose, and their national rivalries were gradually superimposed on this older internationalism of the Indies.

The process was slow, because the problem was great. For England it was particularly difficult. Had the English Government in 1660 set out to pursue some comprehensive policy of action in America, it must assuredly have failed. English colonial America was not yet even 'a geographical expression'; it was not until after 1670, when England's absorption of New Netherland and her plantation of Carolina had knit together her Atlantic seaboard territories, that the fashioning of some common administrative system could be considered a practicable aim.

The assertion of its authority had thus to be the first care of the new Administration in 1660. It had to impress and ingrain the fact of its existence on men's minds. This must take precedence over any nice regard for proprietary rights, whether these lay in Caribbean islands or at home. A step to this end had already been taken prior to the King's return: on 7 May Parliament had ordered that all officers of the State should continue to carry out their duties in the King's name.[1] Colonial offices were not specifically mentioned, but those who held them hoped that silence on that point implied a similar consent to their own continuance. In June the Government began to draw up a detailed inventory of the structure it was taking over: scanning the roll of the sheriffs, inspecting the Charter of Bristol and the Constitution of Ireland. Examination of colonial business quickly followed,[2] and a special committee, as already noted, sat from 4 July. The immediate cause was the presentation to the Board of two petitions about the West Indies— clearly the forerunners of many. One group of merchants was praying that the Commission granted in April by the

[1] CSPD 1659–60, p. 433. Povey had heard 'discourses & drifts' that Governors were to be removed; 20 Sept. 1659, Add. MS. 11411, ff. 90–94.

[2] The Attorney-General was later sent all patents concerning land-grants in America, in order to certify their legality and utility, and draw up a 'reviate' of their powers; CSPD 1660–1, 16, p. 175.

Protectorate's Council of State to Colonel Russell as Governor of Nevis might be confirmed. A second group asked that Colonel Ward might continue as Governor of St. Christopher. To the Committee was assigned the task of assessing the merits of these pleas.[1] But it was, of course, pointless for the Crown to authorize particular rights in the Leeward Islands before its own in the parent island of Barbados had been secured. Accordingly, only five days after the Committee of the Council had been appointed,[2] the King issued a letter which had been in draft and ready since 2 June,[3] ordering Francis Lord Willoughby of Parham 'instantly to applye himself' to the Government of the Islands of the Province of 'Carliola'.[4] He might either go there himself, or appoint a deputy. In each case, the Instructions of Government were to follow those originally set out in the Patent of the first Earl of Carlisle.

This order, an interim measure, bid fair to raise a greater emergency than the one it hoped to avoid. The fact of Restoration was, as it happened, safely accepted in Barbados, despite reports which came to hand that the Island was 'disaffected to all but Parlament ways'.[5] There the 'Planter-Governor',[6] the nimble Colonel Thomas Modyford—confidant and cousin of General Monk himself—had proclaimed both his own Commission and the King, in despite of Governor Searle, the appointee of the Protectorate's Council of State.[7] The gentlemen of the Assembly, who desired two things above all, 'immediatt protection and free trade' (thereby involuntarily striking at the outset that note of paradox that was seldom to be absent from their deliberations), were hastening to take the Oath of Allegiance and Supremacy, and to draft a loyal address for presentation to the King. They expunged any terms or comments,

[1] Ward's Commission, 24 Apr. 1660, CSPC 1574–1660, p. 479. Both petitions are dated 25 June, ibid. 482.

[2] 4 July 1660, APCC, i. 484.

[3] B.M., Egerton MS. 2395, f. 267.

[4] The King to Francis Lord Willoughby, 9 July 1660, CO 1/14, No. 18.

[5] D'Oyley (Captain-General, Jamaica) to the Commissioners of the Admiralty, 1 June 1660, CSPC 1574–1660, 5, p. 480.

[6] His own expression in a speech to the Assembly; 1 Aug. 1660, CO 31/1, 13.

[7] Colonel Modyford, as were Colonels Ward and Russell, was appointed to his Governorship on 24 Apr. 1660: the form of Searle's Commission was copied, the words 'Council of State' being struck out and the phrase 'by the keepers of the liberties of England by authoritie of Parlament' substituted; Egerton MS. 2395, f. 245.

contained in previous Acts of the legislature, that might seem derogatory to the name and dignity of Majesty.[1] They had also hastily voided all Patents made in the Caribbean Islands under the Seal and authority of the two Cromwells—a gesture some of them were later to have cause to regret. But these Assemblymen, although genuinely welcoming the King's return, had no love for royalism. Abetted by their Governor Modyford, they were already considering ways and means to prevent any resumption of the proprietary claims that Carlisle's heirs, Carlisle's cronies, or Carlisle's creditors would certainly make to Barbados and the Leewards. Colonel Modyford—ever a shrewd judge of a predicament, whether his own or another's—believed that a gift of money to the King stood the best chance of effecting this, but the Assembly would not follow his lead. It preferred to play politics. The planters and merchants who had had a say in the making of high policy under the Commonwealth and Protectorate, were not prepared to retreat into obscurity merely because the Government of England had changed hands and form. They objected strongly to the imposition of a feudal Governor over them, whose powers would permit him to deal with them as so many subjects palatine. Above all things they feared a detailed investigation, which such a one would assuredly put in train, into the rights of their tenure in the Islands. It was this sense of tenurial insecurity—vieing in intensity with the fear of a negro insurrection—which was to underlie and envenom all the petty quarrels of West-India politics for more than a century to come.

Of course the planters' anxieties on this point reflected the similar fears that were then agitating the minds of many *nouveaux riches* at home in England; but the miniature scale of the island-world they lived in only intensified their problem. During the great sugar boom of the Interregnum, land in Barbados and the Leeward Islands had passed from the small-holding settler to the control of a group of wealthy planters who economically ran the estates accumulated by squeeze not with white labour but with black. 'The like Improvement was never made by any People under the Sunne', was said of this process by one enthusiast who assuredly did not speak for the displaced

[1] Minutes of the Council of Barbados, 26/27 June 1660, CO 31/1, 10–12; 31 July 1660, ibid. 17; 2 Aug. 1660, ibid. 25–27.

persons.[1] Ranking high in importance and wealth among the magnates were Modyford and his numerous kin, the Colletons and the Kendalls, together with their 'loveing Freinds'[2] in London, the very capable advocates of the rich man's point of view. The Restoration thus found a considerable number of absentee planters in the lobbies of Westminster, gearing themselves for a struggle to maintain the social and commercial *status quo* in the West Indies.

The political din that arose from Barbados was at first construed in London to signify more a local dislike of governmental authority *per se* than of any one form of it. But the Administration soon saw that although West-India voices might hector, they were by no means unanimous: one had only to go down to the Exchange to find that out. The politics of Barbados were understood to be so contradictory, the fortunes of local faction so uncertain, and Governor Modyford's control so precarious, that as late as December 1660 the King found it necessary, having optimistically addressed a dispatch to the Colonel as Governor of Barbados, to add a rider—'or to any other Governour of the Iland'.[3] This showed some prescience, for in fact Modyford was in the custody of his own Provost-Marshal ere the New Year of 1661 was a day old.[4] It was, accordingly, the Colonel's gaoler, Humphrey Walrond, who took it upon himself to reply to another royal letter that had graciously acknowledged Modyford's earlier assurance of the loyal devotion of every inhabitant of the Island to His Majesty. This swing of fortune was of no great moment to the Administration, however, so long as both sides in Barbados declared for the King; and all was well as far as that went, for indeed the two factions were angrily competing in a profusion of devotion to the royal name.

The Committee of the Privy Council appointed to investigate the business of Trade and Foreign Plantations spent a lot of its time in July 1660 gathering data on Barbados and on the proprietary question as a whole. Its members were no more anxious than the colonists themselves that some particular person, rather than the direct authority of the royal Government, should

[1] Egerton MS. 2543, f. 123.
[2] CO 31/1, 25–27. Thomas Kendall, as agent for the Courteen Interest, had a further reason for opposing Willoughby's claims.
[3] 10 Dec. 1660, CO 1/16, Nos. 7, 8.
[4] Minutes of the Council of Barbados, 2 Jan. 1661, CO 31/1, 38–40.

control these valuable West-India properties. For a Proprietor who was by Patent a law to himself was scarcely the best agent to carry out the injunctions of the Navigation Act, which was about to receive the royal assent.[1] Although the 'Laws of England', to which ringing appeals were being made at this time, were remarkably loose in so far as they concerned colonies at all, they certainly clearly held that the reversion of a Proprietary Colony lay in the Crown. The Committee therefore decided to advise the King to press for his full rights of dominion in the West Indies.

Francis Lord Willoughby indeed soon had much more cause for grievance against authority than had the anxious planters of Barbados. A warrant had been issued granting him full Proprietary rights over Surinam in Guiana, the colony he had founded and constructed, on the same day (9 July) as he received the royal instruction to reassume his Proprietary authority in 'Carliola'; but he was quickly aware of a design on foot to maim his rights in this sphere also. Hyde spoke out against the extent of the territory so granted.[2] A memorandum later drawn up by Nicholas[3] advised that Willoughby might go to Surinam as Governor, but not as Proprietor; for a Proprietor of Surinam who also owned Barbados could drain the surplus population of the latter colony off into the former, whereas a Royal Governor would have to obey an order to send it to Jamaica, the new and exclusively royal property, where it would plainly do the most good. Two other members of the Committee, Sir Anthony-Ashley Cooper and his father-in-law, the Earl of Southampton, concurred with this argument, and kept it alive throughout the wrangle about the ownership of the 'Caribbees'.[4] Hyde and Nicholas made the point, too, that the ruler of Spain, with a century and a half of colonial experience to guide him, knew better than to parcel out his American dominions to his nobles in this way; Spanish Viceroys enjoyed a term of three years in

[1] 30 July 1660. It was formally approved in Privy Council on 9 Sept. *Lords Journals*, xi. 330.

[2] The King to Willoughby, 9 July 1660, CSPC 1574–1660, 18, p. 483; cf. J. A. Williamson, *English Colonies in Guiana and on the Amazon, 1604–1668* (Oxford, 1923), 170.

[3] Minutes of a Committee of Foreign Plantations concerning Barbados, 7 May 1661, CSPC 1661–8, 83; CO 1/15, No. 52.

[4] L. F. Brown, *The First Earl of Shaftesbury* (New York, 1933), 132; and cf. Minutes of the Committee of Foreign Plantations, 5 June 1662, CO 1/16, No. 61.

their great office, but no longer. No doubt Willoughby had a fair enough claim to Surinam as he had been its first settler and explorer, but

if that Rule had always held he would have but an ill Pretence to the Caribee Ilands uppon the accompt of the Earl of Carlisle, for that those Ilands or the greater part of them were setled by Sir Thomas Warner before the Earl of Carlisle ever had anything to do with them.[1]

The Attorney-General was therefore set to drafting a new Patent for Willoughby as the King's Governor in Barbados and the Leeward Islands,[2] a document that should make no mention of the Earl of Carlisle, or of his rights, his pretensions, his heirs, or his successors. (But his debts could not be so simply ignored.)

The opposition thus met with in the very heart of the Administration to Willoughby's claims as Lord Proprietor in the West Indies could not, of course, be kept secret. Ashley for one, whose company these days was largely mercantile, had no intention that it should. The knowledge that there was this dissension in high places naturally encouraged the Barbadians, who now redoubled their efforts to rid themselves of the burden of the Proprietary. It was in vain that Willoughby sought to disabuse them of their fears, assuring them that on his part bygones were bygones, and that they would do well to support his claim, as a set of royal officials would be harder taskmasters to them by far than any appointed by a Proprietor.[3] They did not believe him. It was the Crown alone that had power to grant them that *de facto* recognition of their right of tenure; and therefore it was to the Crown that the planters turned for rescue. The London 'Interest' asked leave to proceed against the Carlisle Patent in the Exchequer Court—and they would not have done so had they not been confident of securing its repeal. That gained, the King should assume the Proprietary to himself, as was his right in law. They mentioned, moreover, an ace they held in their hand—though not at this juncture their reluctance to play it. In return for the grant of this royal favour,

---

[1] Cf. draft, 16 July 1660, in Hyde's hand; CO 1/14, No. 19.
[2] Minutes of the Council of Plantations, 7 May 1661, CO 1/15, No. 52.
[3] Cf. his letters of 4 Sept. 1660, Add. MS. 11411, f. 28; of 9 Feb. 1661, ibid., f. 30; Egerton MS. 2395, f. 329.

they would use all their influence with their loving friends in the
Assembly of Barbados, to procure for the Crown some percentage duty from the revenue of the Caribbees, which 'they
confidently averred would amount in the year to ten thousand
pounds at the least; out of which His Majesty's government
might be well supported, and His Majesty dispose of the over-
plus as he should think fit'.[1] This was matter to be thought on:
at any rate, until a new Parliament had met and the Crown
had satisfactorily arranged with it the great question of Supply,
the West-India Interest could not be rebuffed.[2] Everybody
knew this—and so the clamour both from Barbados and from
the counter-claimants against Willoughby continued *crescendo*.

Willoughby, knowing that time was on the side of his opponents, did not wait on events. Since the King's letter of 9 July
had not been recalled, he had a right to avail himself of the
powers it allowed him. In September, 'by vertue of the Powers
entrusted to him by James Earl of Carlisle dated 26 February
1647', he appointed Humphrey Walrond to act as President
of the Council in Barbados *ad interim*—a move skilfully con-
ceived to disarm the opposition in the Island. In October he cast
his net wider, by appointing a Governor to St. Christopher and
Anguilla: the merchant William Watts, to whom he delegated
authority to choose his own Councillors and to convene a
General Assembly.[3] The King cannot have known of this burst
of activity on Willoughby's part, else he would not have written
cordially to Colonel Modyford in November, confirming him in
his post as Governor of Barbados. But Willoughby did not allow
this to deter him; indeed, he was quick to see how he might
profit from the resultant uncertainties in the Island. In Humphrey Walrond he had chosen a man who was dedicated for

---

[1] Clarendon, op. cit. ii, § 1297. The planters had already stressed the argument,
privately agreed to by some Councillors, that the Patent had anyway usurped the
private enterprise of planter-pioneers in the Caribbean. Other Councillors fell back
on the conviction that a quick establishment of authority under some colour was
better than none at all; on 30 Aug. 1660, therefore, Hyde, Saye, Robartes, and
Nicholas had given their opinion that Willoughby ought to be restored to power on
the terms of the Carlisle Patent, from which he had been dispossessed 'by the
illegall power of Cromwell'; CO 1/14, No. 42. But although a Warrant to this
effect was drawn up by Nicholas for the royal signature, it never passed the Great
Seal; cf. draft, ibid., No. 45, date left blank.

[2] The Convention was dissolved on 24 Dec. 1660. The 'Cavalier' Parliament
opened its first session on 8 May 1661.

[3] Commission to Watts, 27 Oct. 1660, CO 29/1, 17–24.

reasons of his own to a rigid enmity to Modyford and all his faction. From December 1660 the self-styled planter-Governor and the new President of the Council, each with a different Commission of authority in his pocket, glared at each other across the Council board in Barbados. Willoughby himself was now content to remain in England. His regular correspondence with Walrond in Barbados, Osborne in Montserrat, and Russell in Nevis,[1] kept him in close touch with the political intricacies of the local situation. In England, too, he was able to add his weight to the new Councils designed for the care of Trade and of Foreign Plantations, and there gain first-hand information on the present state of West-India affairs from the merchants who were his colleagues.[2] There, too, he could ensure that no claimant gained the ear of the Administration or the Court to his own detriment, and that the machinations of the planters made little headway.

As the months passed the Administration strengthened its grip on affairs and walked less warily. The Crown Law Officers had already advised the King that the Carlisle Patent stood little chance of being upheld in law. This diagnosis, if correct, did not only weaken the case of the counter-claimants who were bidding for possession of the Patent; it threatened also to undermine the position that the Crown itself had taken up. The Patent issued to the Earl of Carlisle, like every other such, had been an instrument of the royal authority. Were subjects of the King, however wealthy and influential, to be allowed to bring their case against his prerogative in his own Courts? It was clear that any such suit could very easily resolve itself into nothing other than a *quo warranto* inquiry into the validity of Patents held under the Great Seal in America—and quite possibly elsewhere too. This was no time to allow either the legality of the grants of King Charles I to be called in question or to set limitations on the prerogative rights of King Charles II. While the restored Monarchy was still an innovation, it had to display a confidence it did not necessarily feel. Made bold, therefore, by its necessity, the Administration shook itself free of the bonds of legalism.

[1] Cf. Add. MS. 11411, ff. 31b–32; and Watts to Povey, 19 June 1661, Egerton MS. 2395, f. 303.

[2] He had previously been concerned in Noell's and Povey's schemes for a West-India Company and a trade to Florida; C. S. S. Higham, *The Development of the Leeward Islands under the Restoration* (Cambridge, 1921), 7.

This mass of evidence, this accumulated testimony, had to be sheared through by a political knife. On 28 March 1661 Morice was instructed to tell Barbados that the Proprietary was now vested in his Majesty.[1] Here can be seen the first clear assertion of the reign's 'colonial policy'—to uphold the supremacy of the royal power, and to discount the pretensions of all other interests. A mould was thus fashioned for later use.

The protracted investigation begun by the Privy Council in March 1661 and continued for over a year, made a great show of the Administration's determination to dispense impartial justice. This display served as a useful façade for its true purpose: it was now time, not merely to look or to hope for a compromise settlement, but to arrange one. The King should assume the Proprietary of the Caribbean Islands to himself: this would preserve the initiative in governance to the Crown. The other parties to the dispute would then be compensated by the Crown for their resignation of that initiative. Emphasis would be placed on the King's graciousness in so acting, for petitioners and subjects generally must learn to consider any royal acquiescence in their requests, not just as no more than they plainly deserved—which was too much their habit—but as a splendid boon from a warm-hearted Sovereign. And so it now fell out. Powerful allies of the Administration in this assertion of the Crown's authority were of course the planters and merchants of Barbados, who were so delighted to gain their main point—the extinction of the old Proprietary—that they were prepared to subordinate their personal dislike of Willoughby to a loyal obedience to him as the King's representative. Nor could the other claimants, who represented no other interest than their own, afford to take an independent stand: if the King was resolved to obliterate the Carlisle Patent and himself become Proprietor of the West Indies, then their best course was to seek to ingratiate themselves with him, so that the justice at least of their monetary claims on Carlisle's estate should not be entirely overlooked. They were indeed in no position to rebuff any gracious acts of royal generosity which might be going. Lord Willoughby also acquiesced. He was a royalist before he was a Proprietor, and he accepted as fitting the King's desire to 'drawe under his immediat authoritye & Councell all

[1] 28 Mar. 1661, APCC, i. 305-6.

the severall plantacons that they may have the same dependance
with the rest of His Maties Dominions'.[1] He accordingly declared
his willingness to submit his rights and title to the King, attach-
ing these unexceptionable conditions: that he should be Governor for the remaining period of his lease (seven years); that he
should be allotted half the profits of his Government, but no
salary; and that he might go to Barbados at once.

The Administration now pushed home its advantage. It took
up the offer previously made by Kendall and Colleton to pay
for just such a royal service as had now been rendered by
obtaining 'some Rate per cent on the Comodityes in ye Island'
as well as the customs duties on imports from the plantations.
At this suggestion of the merchants the planters retired in alarm
into recrimination among themselves, protesting that Barbados
could not afford any such thing, that the Modyford group had
had no authority to commit them to so rash a pledge. In this
attitude they were naturally able to count on the firm support
of Humphrey Walrond and the Council of the Island, who had
already given tongue to the dismay and indignation with which
they viewed the project.[2] The suggestion that a 4 per cent. duty
on exports from Barbados and the Leeward Islands would bring
in a revenue of £25,000 a year was, to them, 'a strang[e] wild
computation', since Barbados, as every planter there could
testify (or at any rate certainly did throughout this period), was
growing ever poorer both in soil and in its ability to command
a ready market for its commodities.

The planters, however, were in an awkward position. Their
lands had not yet been confirmed by their new royal Proprietor
in free and common socage. They had still to walk softly. Now
the Council of Barbados came to see the wisdom in an early
suggestion of Modyford's that had been passed over at the time.
To make a 'handsom Present' to His Majesty might not only
dispose him to the granting of this favour, but it might also
deflect him from these designs on the revenue.[3] The gentlemen
of the Assembly, however, would still have no truck with
subtlety. They demurred to the Council's idea of a 'free' gift—
unless it were made a plain *quid pro quo*. That the monarchy

---

[1] Willoughby to the King, 1 Oct. 1661, CO 1/15, Nos. 169-70.
[2] Cf. Walrond to Nicholas, 29 Mar. 1661, ibid. No. 36.
[3] Minutes of the Council of Barbados, 19 July 1661, CO 31/1, 53-57.

could not bargain in this way—that the Crown must be privately bribed, not publicly bought—they were too preoccupied with their own cares to comprehend. To them the most urgent domestic issue was the threat made to their trade and its future by the implementation of the Navigation Act. They were therefore already wondering whether they might not more advantageously bargain the promise that had been made of a fixed Caribbean revenue for the Crown against some royal relaxation of this odious Statute in Caribbean waters.

For to them it seemed that the boom years of sugar production were over; a planter who, in 1658, had been able to get a price of 28s. per 100 for his raw sugar was to think himself lucky to get 12s. by 1670.[1] In the 1650's the sudden expansion of the sugar-culture had made a few men very wealthy: now many men were to be merely rich. To have a competence in a world that promises plenty is hardship indeed. To see their produce 'forct into one Markett' by the Navigation Act dismayed planters who were accustomed to take their pick of several. On these subjects they petitioned the King, the Secretary of State, the Privy Council Committee, the Councils of Trade and Plantations—anyone who would listen, and many who would not. 'Ruin' became the most overworked word in their vocabulary.[2] (Yet they had friends at home who wrote their own terms in the new Book of Rates: sugar was rated at 30s. per 100.) The future of the sugar-economy was much debated at this time: it must not, like tobacco, become a 'Drugg', though few stressed that the real cause of the trouble was over-production. But in seeking to put commercial pressure on the public policy of the Government as embodied in the Navigation Act, Barbadians went too far. They over-estimated the significance of mercantile opinion and interests, and indeed the self-importance assumed by their own agents in London misled them for a considerable time to come; in fact the Barbadians were living in a world that had gone, and talking at large in terms that were no longer valid.

As yet, however, they were free to express themselves in

[1] Cf. Egerton MS. 2395, ff. 639–41; Higham, op. cit. 194. The Royal African Company rated Barbadian muscovados at 10s. per 100 in 1675, but this was sharp practice.

[2] And their text is Edward Lyttelton's *The Groans of the Plantations*, published in 1688.

extravagant language; no one troubled to call it treasonable. Moreover, it was well known that the island politicians were men who had never been able to agree on anything for very long. The fact that the President and his Council now fell out with the Assembly amid the customary hubbub of accusation and countercharge, naturally weakened what negotiating power remained to the London Interest, whose members were never certain which faction in the Island was in the ascendant, which would next gain the ascendancy, or what odd alliances would be made. How could one gauge a situation wherein Colonel Modyford was actually the Speaker in Walrond's newly summoned Assembly—which was the case from the autumn of 1662?

The Administration did not attempt the task. It was not disposed to wait for the problematical calming of the Barbadian waters. The people of that Island had always been, in Ashley's words, 'apt to create more difficulties than God and Nature had made them',[1] and were likely to remain so. Lord Willoughby was rewarded for his acquiescence in the designs of the Crown by being invited by the Privy Council in June 1662 to draft what he considered necessary for insertion into the official Instructions that were to be issued to him as Royal Governor of His Majesty's Proprietary of Barbados and the Leeward 'Caribbee' Islands. He had the satisfaction of seeing these Instructions drawn up to his own specifications by the end of September.[2] His jurisdiction was complete, save that he was not granted Vice-Admiralty powers in the Caribbean, as all colonial Admiralty jurisdiction was vested in James Duke of York as Lord High Admiral, and York was no believer in the virtues of delegation.[3] His Letters Patent as Governor 'of all Plantacons between 10° and 20° N. latitude & east of Porto Rico, with enjoyment therein', was ready by the end of November, with his own terms 'corrected and approved' therein. The principal

[1] Ashley's report, 19 Nov. 1661, CO 1/15, No. 89. This may be contrasted with Clarendon's earlier opinion, that Barbados was 'principally inhabited by men who had retired thither only to be quiet, and to be free from the noise and oppressions in England'; cf. *The History of the Rebellion and Civil Wars in England*, ed. W. D. Macray (Oxford, 1888), v. 262.

[2] 5 June 1662, CSPC 1661–8, 309; 25 Sept. 1662, APCC, i. 576; CO 5/903, 9–10.

[3] H. J. Crump, *Colonial Admiralty Jurisdiction in the 17th Century* (London, 1931), 102–3. Willoughby, however, was under the impression that he had Vice-Admiralty powers.

correction made had been the exclusion of Surinam (which lies between 5° and 8° N. latitude), and the determination of Willoughby to have this matter adjusted to his own satisfaction caused a further delay.

The back of the Caribbean Proprietary question was, however, broken, and the full Patent resolving all its intricacies finally passed the Seals in June 1663.[1] It laid down that Willoughby should retain the office of Governor in Barbados and the Leeward Islands for the remaining period of his lease of the Carlisle Patent. That instrument was officially declared void at law, and therefore in the King's power. The revenue of the Islands was divided into two parts, one half being allotted to Willoughby so long as he held the Governorship, the other to be shared in stipulated sums among the claimants for the Patent. Whenever all such claims had been fully met, the entire revenue was to revert to the Crown.

Lord Willoughby, content both in this and in his grant of Surinam (settled to his satisfaction and in significant partnership with the Chancellor's son, Lawrence Hyde),[2] was at last able to 'applye himself', as instructed three years previously, to the government of Barbados. He arrived there on 10 August 1663, administered the Oath of Allegiance and Supremacy to the members of the Council,[3] and turned to deal with the Assembly. This was already in session, being that which Walrond, as President, had summoned under the now-superseded Proprietary authority that Willoughby had been using for the past three years. Strictly speaking, therefore, the Assembly was illegally convened and constituted, and ought to have been dissolved at once.[4] This point was not made at the time, but the circumstance was not forgotten by the Islanders themselves. It was certainly not expedient for the Crown to insist on so narrow an interpretation of the matter. The fact that there was an Assembly in Barbados at all was not, of course, the result of any

[1] 13 June 1663, APCC, i. 599; Williamson, *Caribbees*, 212; CO 1/16, No. 41.

[2] Williamson, *Guiana*, 173, sees Hyde as a 'sleeping partner'. In the same month, however, Hyde shared with Willoughby 'the sole Use & Benefitts' of a new type of sugar-mill in Barbados, for a lease of 14 years; warrant of 22 June 1663, CO 1/17, No. 55.

[3] Minutes of the Council of Barbados, 18 Aug. 1663, CO 31/1, 79–80.

[4] Compare the care taken by Lord Vaughan on his arrival in Jamaica as Governor in Mar. 1675, to issue writs for a new Assembly, 'to avoid all scruples'; CSPC 1675–6, 471.

action of the Crown; Charles I, who dispensed with a Parliament in England as long as he could, was not the man to stud his overseas territories with Parliaments in miniature. Representation in Assembly was the fruit of an ingenious device of Governor Hawley in 1639 and of the subsequent constructive policy of Governor Bell.[1] The years of Interregnum had fashioned its existence into a custom of the country. The statesmen of the Restoration did well to recognize it as such, and Willoughby's Instructions assumed the existence of an Assembly in Barbados as part of the constitution of his Government.[2] Willoughby himself, although irked by the Assembly's presence and the attitude of a number of its members, could accordingly not question its right to be there, any more than could Charles II have questioned the existence of the Convention Parliament that had restored him.

Moreover, it suited the Governor to avoid the delay an election would entail. He knew that the Administration in Whitehall was anxiously awaiting some concrete result from the new colonial régime it had at last set up after so prolonged a deliberation. So was he himself. It was all very well for a royal Order-in-Council to satisfy the monetary claims of Carlisle's creditors, together with the Governor's own financial future, out of the Caribbean revenue; the plain fact was that no such thing existed. The figures that interested parties so often referred to, whether £8 or £10 or £25,000, were all figments of their various imaginations. The revenue had to be annually created by production and export. Barbados, as an economic institution, could therefore only operate with the consent of the representatives of the Islands. Thus Willoughby's Instructions insisted that he was to take especial care for

that Revenue that is and shal become due to us . . . that as our goode Subjects in these Remoat parts are neere us in affection, they may bee made sensible that some Returne of Proffit as wel as Dutie ought to bee made us for our continuall & unwearied Care of them[3]

and to emphasize both this point and the 'very great pains His Majestie had been att' in purchasing the Proprietary. He

---

[1] Cf. Harlow, *Barbados*, 25–55.

[2] e.g. he had power to order the Council and Assembly to sit either together or apart.

[3] Instructions to Willoughby, read at the Council Board, 13 June 1663, APCC, i. 598.

appointed a committee, four of the Council and eight of the Assembly, to settle the revenue. He assured the freeholders that the King had refused all sorts of financial blandishments that had been made him for the Caribbean revenue by gentlemen in England, out of his sheer goodness of heart and affection for his subjects; and the Assembly, after much wrangling, proved amenable to his pressure at last.[1] On 12 September 1663 was born the famous duty that was to remain in being for 175 years. The Assembly of Barbados passed an Act, decreeing

that an Impost or Custome . . . uppon all dead Comodityes of the Groweth or Produce of this Iland, that shall be shipp'd off the same, shall be paid to our Soveraign Lord the King, his heirs and successors for ever, Four and a half in Specie for every Five Score.

The preamble recited the terms on which this was given: the Proprietary settled in the King, the old dues and rents cancelled, lands to be held, at long last, in free and common socage.[2] The revenue raised from the duty was to be

in some measure proportioned to the publick charges and expences . . . in maintaining the Honour and dignity of His [Majesty's] Authoritye here; the publick meeting of the Sessions, the often Attendance of the Councell, the Reparation of the Forts, the building of a Session-house and a prison, and all other charges incumbent on the Government.[3]

In this phraseology there was ample ambiguity, as events were to prove; but for the moment the terms gave great satisfaction in London.[4] When once Willoughby had toured the Leeward Islands in the summer of 1664 and gained assent to a similar duty from each Assembly there—but minus the appropriation clause—a new fiscal link of empire had been forged, the old Proprietary was dead, and the 'Caribbees' had become solely dependent, politically and economically, on the

[1] Minutes of the Council of Barbados, 25 Aug. 1663, CO 31/1, 80–81; Sir R. Harley to Sir E. Harley, 11 Sept. 1663: 'The main point is that they would not confess the King to be proprietor, and so receive confirmation of their estates from him, but wd. have their possessing it during the troublesome times to be a good title'; HMC Portland, iii. 277.

[2] For one ear of Indian corn as rent. The King confirmed the Act on 21 Apr. 1665; CO 29/2, 14.

[3] CO 29/1, 47–50. The session-house and the prison were not completed until 1730; Bryan Edwards, A History, Civil and Commercial, of the British West Indies (London, 3 vols., edn. of 1801), i. 335, note (k).

[4] Harley reckoned that the duty would annually amount to 1m. lb. sugar; HMC Portland, iii. 277.

authority of the Crown. The significance of this precedent in
West-India and American affairs was later to be made plain.

II

Thus four years passed before the Restoration Government
was able to declare that its writ ran securely in the Lesser
Antilles. The work it did there does not, indeed, deserve the
name of 'restoration', in its strict sense. Rather was it reconstruction: a new authority was imposed on the foundations of
the old. A problem different in kind confronted the Administration as simultaneously it dealt with its other great legacy in the
West Indies, the Island of Jamaica.

Again this was no straightforward issue of restoration. There
were no precedents to follow, or even to adapt, for Jamaica had
never previously known any monarchy but that of Spain. It
lay in isolation, the last evidence in existence of the scope of
Cromwell's imperial Design. New foundations, as well as a
new structure of government, had there to be built.

In every respect the contrast with 'Carliola' was striking. In
1660 Jamaica, an involuntary possession, was not a settled,
opinionated colony like Barbados, a rich prize sought for by
many contenders. It had little security, less law. Its inhabitants
indeed had opinions, but these could be discounted, for the
men who held them had neither influence nor future.[1] Containing the stragglers of an army, about 2,000 masterless men,
the Island presented a formidable study in anarchy and confusion. In nominal command both of this ribbon of a force and
of the Island itself, was a disgruntled officer of General Venables's original army, Edward D'Oyley. He was a brave man
and a resourceful soldier, but like those under him he had no
hope of preferment from the new order in England and was not
even sure his life was safe. His acid comments on the condition
of Jamaica had dismayed the Plantations Committee of the
Protectorate's Council of State as early as March 1660, for the
evidence in his reports reinforced the representations that had
been submitted by traders and merchants, whose high hopes of
pursuing a profitable commerce at Jamaica had been dashed by

---

[1] Political refugees of various hues, but none of these Royalist, had flocked to
the Island in 1659; cf. Edwards, op. cit. i. 213; and many planters had come over
from Nevis and St. Christopher.

their discovery that there was no possibility of doing any business there at all while the chaotic conditions prevailed. A trader could neither buy nor sell there without loss. There were neither goods nor cash. Stores, provisions, arms, equipment, confidence, health, and sobriety—all were wanting. The negro population, which had seized their chance in 1655 to revolt from Spanish rule, had by now set their hand against every white man, and had retired to the mountain strongholds of the interior. The intention of Spain to regain the Island, although hourly magnified, could not be discounted; it was not two years since D'Oyley, with considerable skill and courage, had repulsed the last attempt.[1] The condition of Jamaica as it appeared to the English Government at that time confronted it with the two clear alternatives: either the Island must be effectively reinforced and its government reconstructed, or it must be entirely abandoned. Mere 'expediants and dilatorie Propositions'[2] were worse than useless.

Even a dying Protectorate had no wish to discard the trophy of its hey-day.[3] The mercantile chorus, to which it had always lent so willing an ear, yet insisted on a prosperous future for Jamaica.[4] Accordingly at the end of March the Council of State instructed Thomas Povey, at that time Secretary to its Committee for Foreign Plantations, to confer with all the officers and traders who knew conditions in the Island at first hand.[5] With their advice and help he was to work out some practicable scheme for its retention and preservation. By 9 April he presented his Report, listing the most pressing necessities of Jamaica. A fleet of ships should be sent to the Island forthwith,

[1] I. A. Wright, 'The Spanish Resistance and the English occupation of Jamaica, 1658–60', in *Transactions of the Royal Historical Society*, IV. xiii (1930), 117–47.

[2] Report of the Committee of the Councell, 'The State of affaires of the English in Jamaica', 27 Mar. 1660, Egerton MS. 2395, f. 241.

[3] Povey told Searle in 1659, however, that the 'Old Protector' did not think Jamaica worth keeping; Add. MS. 11411, f. 4.

[4] 'Being so large and fertile, is very capable of retaining those greate numbers of people that are forced to desert the Carribbee Islands, their plantacons being worn out . . . Jamaica hath an advantage of Ireland in its setting for that [Ireland] can only bee planted by persons that have estates or moneys, for a gentleman will not pay a poore man's transportation, cloth him and keep him well for his service there, neither can any person live there that may not subsist better in England: but 'tis not soe in the Indies'; 'Considerations relating to the English affaires in America', Egerton MS. 2395, f. 614. Martin Noell already owned 20,000 acres of Jamaican soil, and Richard Povey was his agent there.

[5] Order signed Edward Harley, 29 Mar. 1660, ibid., ff. 243, 245.

carrying three months' provisions sufficient for 2,000 men; together with clothing, ammunition, and arrears of pay for the Army. The Army itself should at once be reorganized, re-established, and disciplined for the proper defence of the Island. Since the shortage of money ruined all hopes of a successful trade, a temporary credit for the Islanders should be allowed in the New England colonies. The embittered D'Oyley should be replaced as Commander by someone who had confidence in the plantation's future, preferably by some person of consequence who was also equipped to deal with problems of navigation, planting, and commerce. This paragon—is it possible Povey was subconsciously describing himself?—should 'beate the Drumm' throughout all the Indies on Jamaica's behalf, recruiting not only soldiers but settlers too. By promoting the settlement of Jamaica, England might simultaneously relieve a pressing social problem of her own. She could send there her prisoners, felons, vagrants, and all 'noxious and Unprofittable persons', where they would find ample work for their idle hands to do. It may be assumed that both the Plantations Committee and its parent Council of State pondered this forthright Report with care, perhaps comparing its views with those of an optimistic petition presented by the West-India merchants at the end of April.[1] But that spring of 1660 the sands were running out. Not the Government of Jamaica, but that of three Kingdoms was the matter at stake. Now the tableau of Restoration, its excitements and its implications, riveted everyone's attention. All eyes were raised from all manner of Reports to watch the return of the King. All Administration paused as the Executive changed hands.

But General D'Oyley, not a witness to this drama, continued to pound away at whatever authorities there might be that this issue of Jamaica could not safely be shelved for long. The letters he sent that summer to the Commissioners of the Admiralty[2] —one bureau of administration that he knew must survive even the greatest of revolutions—reiterated his desperate theme. He

[1] 24 Apr. 1660, Egerton MS. 2395, f. 251.
[2] The patent to James Duke of York as Lord High Admiral of England was issued in May 1660: and as Lord High Admiral of Dunkirk, New England, Jamaica, Virginia, Barbados, St. Christopher, Bermuda, Antigua, Guinea, Binney, Angola, and Tangier in 1662. The passage of the Test Act in 1673 did not invade these latter rights; Crump, op. cit. 103.

had no money, no victuals, no pay, either for his troops or himself. No news came to him save wild and probably malicious rumours from Barbados of an impending Spanish descent upon him.[1] His own powers as Governor had been only on paper for long enough—but where was even that paper now? He warned that if he did not speedily receive explicit recognition of his authority from someone qualified to give it serious mutiny would result. There already existed a dangerous antagonism between the demoralized Army-men and the civilians on the Island, for 'Souldiers, in time of peace, are look'd uppon in the worst sense'. While they were drunk, which they were a great part of the time, they were politically harmless; but shortage of liquor would soon sober them, and then what they would do no one knew. D'Oyley's own control over them was one of personalitys rather than rank. He knew well enough that he himself, as a soldier, shared in the general odium with which the Army was regarded. William Beeston wrote sourly of him that he con-sidered only Army men and Army interests,[2] and certainly D'Oyley had some good words to say for his own officers: he assured Secretary Nicholas later that they were 'mostly Gentle-men of good Familys' whom the jealousy of Cromwell had banished.[3] This is questionable indeed, but on the whole his letters have a ring of truth in them. His tone throughout is that of a man anxious to break his chains. But he did not carry out his threat to return to England in the *Coventry* frigate. He let it go alone,[4] although with its departure one more tie with the authority of the English Government was broken. 'Without shipping', he sensibly remarked on this, 'this Place appears to mee of noe use to the Comonwealth.'[5] Nevertheless he re-mained at his post, urging always that Jamaica would sink into anarchy and be lost by default, unless action was at once taken to prevent it.

[1] But the frigate *Convertine*, which arrived in August, brought the news of the King's Restoration.

[2] Beeston's Journal, of great value for Jamaica's salad days, is printed in *Interesting Tracts relating to the Island of Jamaica* (St. Jago de la Vega, 1800), 271–300.

[3] D'Oyley to Nicholas, 11 Sept. 1660, CSPC 1574–1660, 43, p. 489.

[4] No provisions had been sent to Jamaica for over three years; 'The necessitys of Jamaica', Egerton MS. 2395, f. 617. The four frigates there in Mar. 1659, *Diamond, Hector, Coventry,* and *Chestnut,* were then 22–32 months in arrears of pay; A. W. Tedder, *The Navy of the Restoration* (Cambridge, 1912), 14.

[5] D'Oyley to Commissioners of Admiralty, 1 June 1660, CO 1/14, No. 7.

The West-India 'Interest' in London, as has been seen, had
lost no time in gaining first the attention and then the partial
confidence of the royal Administration. The asseverations they
had previously made to the Council of State—that Jamaica,
although admittedly in parlous condition at present, was capable of a grand redemption—were redoubled before the Committee of the royal Privy Council. What would be better able
to secure this redemption, they argued, than the august and
farseeing guidance of a great King?[1] So blessed, the Island
would become the market and entrepôt for the trade of the
entire Caribbean, now unfortunately a perquisite if not a
monopoly of rapacious and immoral Dutchmen. These were
attractive arguments.[2] In September the Privy Council called
for a report on Jamaica from its Committee of Plantations,
while the King assured merchants that he was indeed going to
retain the Island.[3] In October a sub-committee was formed,
composed of four members only, all men of the first importance
—Albemarle and Annesley in their own right, the two Secretaries of State in virtue of their office.[4] They sifted D'Oyley's
letters and Povey's overtures, and then recommended that
D'Oyley should be given a Commission as royal Governor in
Jamaica, 'untill further order'. By the end of November the
Commission was drafted, and the Privy Council ordered the
Jamaica Committee to expedite the dispatch of all essential
Instructions to the Island;[5] nothing would contribute more use-
fully to the Island's security than 'theyre knowledge of affayres
here and of His Maties gratious Purpose towards them'.[6] On

[1] 'Consideracons relating to the English affaires in America', c. 1660, Egerton
MS. 2395, f. 614.

[2] The Venetian envoy in England [hereafter VE] wrote to his Senate on 2 July
1660: 'The merchants here point to great advantages for the Crown', Cal. S.P.
Ven., 1659–61, 168; but added his own opinion (1 Oct.) that the Island was
'costly and useless', ibid. 218.

[3] Evelyn, Diary, 27 Sept. 1660.

[4] 17 Oct. 1660, APCC, i. 491.

[5] In November Captain Thomas Lynch presented the first of what was to be a
long series of recommendations for the better government of Jamaica, and he was
the first to suggest that it would be a great example to present and potential
settlers in Jamaica if the King himself were to set out a plantation in the Island;
CSPC 1574–1660, 54, p. 491. The Earl of Marlborough also put forward some
proposals, including a suggestion that Jamaica should be made a staple for the
trade in negroes from the Guinea Coast that was then in process of reorganization;
ibid. 56. Both of them agreed that the trade of Jamaica should be free of duty.

[6] 28 Nov. 1660. Provisions and shipping were to be sent, the ships to call at the

5 December four more members were added to the Jamaica Committee;[1] on the same day, a final courteous dismissal was given to the representations of the Spanish Ambassador that Jamaica should be restored to its rightful master, His Most Catholic Majesty of Spain. Until the Spanish reaction to this had been gauged, no direct step in regard to the Island could safely be taken. By February 1661 the assessment had been made: Spain would fulminate and threaten, but she would not move.[2] D'Oyley's Commission was therefore finally sealed.[3]

It did not, however, arrive in Jamaica until the end of May. So protracted a delay, of course, only served to increase D'Oyley's doubts that the royal Government in England had any serious intention of settling and ordering the Island's affairs, despite all his efforts to convince it that 'all the soberest sort of people' desired the royal protection above all things. He continued to write both to his cousin, Secretary Nicholas,[4] and to the Lords Commissioners of the Admiralty. The latter had at least taken some notice of him, for in August 1660 they had sent him two frigates, and on 12 December they had appointed him Commander-in-Chief of all His Majesty's ships in Jamaica.[5] True to a military conservatism, he never entered into direct communication with a new-fangled Council of Plantations of whose permanence he had no guarantee and of whose existence, indeed, he was never officially informed. In March 1661 he was still pressing Nicholas for the King's commands. As he had just shot two of his own colonels for a republican insurrection, there can be no doubt but that he was seriously in need of them.

Thus, despite his vow that he would hail the day when he might resign his irksome position to a successor (with whom he expressed sympathy),[6] D'Oyley was very glad to receive the official Commission and Instructions brought to him by the *Diamond* on 29 May. Both of these instruments stressed the

'Caribbees' for prospective settlers. Someone also considered that a thousand pairs of footmen's pumps were a great need in Jamaica at this time; CO 1/14, No. 55.

[1] York, Sandwich, Holles, and Sir George Cartaret; APCC, i. 501.
[2] See Chapter III, *infra*.
[3] Commission, 8 Feb. 1661, in CO 1/15, No. 10.
[4] He had to remind him of the kinship, 11 Sept. 1660.
[5] Adm 2/1732, 65a. York later ordered D'Oyley to keep up a correspondence with him, 19 Feb. 1661, ibid. 82.
[6] D'Oyley to Nicholas, Mar. 1661, CO 1/15, No. 37; D'Oyley to the commissioners of the Admiralty, 13 Apr. 1661, ibid., No. 40.

King's particular goodwill towards his distant subjects. Of these subjects the General was now pleased to count himself one; certainly D'Oyley the man with a royal Commission became a different fellow from D'Oyley the discarded Protectorate officer. His appointments of dubious Army men to office raised for him even more civilian enemies than he had had before. Perhaps in this he is not to be blamed, for his Commission is rather an oddment, its civil and military strands closely interwoven.[1]

It begins with the looked-for assurance of royal protection for the people of Jamaica. The General was empowered to do what he thought would conduce to the security of the Island and the welfare of its inhabitants. These powers were modelled on the 'just & reasonable Customes and Constitutions' that obtained in the government of other colonies—provided always that these same customs, together with any other enactment that the Governor might authorize, were not 'repugnant to our Laws of England'. (This was a necessary safeguard, for there had not yet been time to subject the constitutions of the other colonies to close scrutiny—and who knew what might not have crept into them?) With the advice of an elected Council of 12, of whom five were to make a quorum, D'Oyley was to set up civil courts and judicatures. He should administer the Oaths of Allegiance and Supremacy to the gentlemen of this Council, who must do for him the same service. He was to give every encouragement to trade, and smile upon merchants. At the same time, he should continue to act as Commander-in-Chief of the Island's forces, and 'fight kill slay represse & subdue' any who sought to disturb Jamaica's peace. In the case of any external invasion, or internal disorder, he was to proclaim martial law—'the Lawes Martiall according to the practice & Constitution of Court Martiall upon Souldiers only'.

In the event of his death or recall, seven of the Council should take over the administration of the Government, and within one week appoint a successor to him, who should act until the King's wishes were known.

D'Oyley's Instructions contained fifteen clauses, many of which repeated the style and sense of those in the Commission.[2]

---

[1] Commission, 8 Feb. 1661, Bodl., MS. Rawl. A. 347, ff. 3–6.
[2] Instructions to D'Oyley, 8 Feb. 1661, CO 138/1, 6–8; Bodl., MS. Rawl. A. 347, 7–10.

(The two Instruments were attached, and not drawn up on separate dates, as was later the practice.) The Governor was to publish his Commission and proclaim the King. Eleven of the Council were to be chosen by as many of the officers of the Army, planters, and inhabitants in general as could 'conveniently gather Togeather'—an Assembly, therefore, in embryo. The twelfth member of Council was always to be the Secretary and Recorder of the Island, an office that had already been granted by Patent to Thomas Povey's brother Richard. Exports should be free of duty for seven years, when a 5 per cent. impost would be charged. All judges, including those 'for the Admiralties'[1]—whom presumably D'Oyley was to appoint —should also take the Oath. Drunkenness must be extirpated, and respect both for the clergy and a decent mode of life inculcated in the inhabitants. Everyone must take his turn to help restore the Island's neglected fortifications; D'Oyley was given especial disciplinary powers to ensure that this was speedily pressed forward.

The Instructions, like the Commission, insisted that Jamaica was no longer an orphan of the storm. Land should be set aside for a royal demesne; and, to allay any doubt that might linger in the public mind concerning the good intentions of the Administration, D'Oyley was charged to

incourage our Subjects in our name and from Us that wee shal from time to time give them all Necessary Protection & Assistance to their industry & Traffique, it being our Royall Intention and wee requiring it from yourselfe and the Councill that all the Inhabitants of what quality soever be encouraged to Plant & Trade & Improve the said Island to ye best Advantage

—until conviction on the point had sunk home.

In Whitehall, Jamaica's affairs continued to command attention. The Admiralty, under York's control, efficiently carried out its task of supplying provisions and stores.[2] The Council of

---

[1] There had been an unofficial Admiralty Court set up in Jamaica in 1657 to try prize cases, but D'Oyley's actions in this connexion were presumably legalized by the Act of Indemnity and Oblivion. He took care, however, to apply for the benefits of that Act to cover all his actions in Jamaica, when he returned to England; CSPC 1661-8, 724; Crump, op. cit. 105.

[2] *Diamond*, besides taking D'Oyley's Commission to Jamaica, carried a clergyman to regulate morals, Colonel Ward going to St. Christopher, and orders to seize any foreign ships found trading to the colonies; 21 Feb. 1661, Adm 2/1732, 83.

Trade's advice on the Island's potentialities were referred to the fraternal Council of Foreign Plantations. Every member of the Privy Council Committee was asked to bring before it 'the best information he cann' on Jamaica. The Jamaica Committee conferred with the Plantations Council,[1] and both presented reports to the Privy Council Board in June 1661. In July the Board officially notified them of what had been freely rumoured since March, that the King had chosen Thomas, Lord Windsor, to succeed General D'Oyley as his Governor in Jamaica; and the Jamaica Committee was ordered to prepare the official Commission and Instructions for that nobleman.

The Committee had already asked the indefatigable Povey to draw up yet another collection of 'Overtures', this time 'for the better provideing of Jamaica before the Lord Windsors going away Governour of that place'.[2] The terms of their request showed signs of a lingering desire that this should be done as cheaply as possible; but Povey in the preamble to his Report, which he submitted on 10 June, made short work of this. He pointed out that if expense was to be the main consideration in the business, clearly the most inexpensive policy would be to disown Jamaica entirely, and leave the people there to their fate. Both honour and common sense demanded an end to parsimony in this matter. Generosity could best be shown by reviving the boon granted by Cromwell to settlers in Jamaica— freedom from any duty on imports for seven years, and on exports for ten.[3]

The merchant Thomas Middleton and others were granted permission to take over the *Charity*, man her, store her, pay all costs, and carry to Jamaica over 150 tons of goods and 250 prospective planters. The contractors hoped to pick up another 500 settlers in Barbados and the Leewards; 3 Apr. 1661, Adm 2/1745, 37*b*.

[1] The Council recommended a grant of land to settlers rent-free for seven years; 27 June 1661, CO 1/15, No. 68. The Committee did not.

[2] 10 June 1661, Egerton MS. 2395, f. 301. Povey had got on friendly terms with Windsor, hoping to be the latter's agent; cf. T. to R. Povey, 14 July 1661, Add. MS. 11411, ff. 33–34.

[3] Cromwell's Proclamation, 1655, Add. MS. 38350, ff. 205–12. Povey's ninth 'Overture' makes the point persuasively: '. . . As many Imunities from Customes and a free Trade and such other matters of encouragement [should] bee allowed as may stand with the generall Policie of Trade. And although something may seeme to bee as it were thereby given (by being forgiven) out of the Publick Treasure, it will infallibly instently fill . . . and inrich that Collonie by the necessary access of Numbers of Stock, of Industrie, & of generall Trade whereby it will become not only strong enough to withstand the greatest Conjunctions the Spanyard cann be able to make, either out of Europe or America, but will render

Merchants had imagination; the politicians had fears. The Jamaica Committee, where no merchant came, would not make a breach in the 'general policie of Trade' for the sake of any one colony, however deserving. Surinam could be considered a special case; and so, of course, could Tangier, entrepôt on the highway of Mediterranean commerce. But exploitation in Jamaica had to be cut to pattern. Since the object of settling the Island at all was to reap a profit, the politicians could not be persuaded to take a step that, in their view, would make all profit impossible. The most that the Committee would recommend at this time was the retention of D'Oyley's twelfth instruction concerning trade: Jamaican goods should be exempted from duty for a period of seven years, thereafter paying a 5 per cent. duty to the King. But they took away with one hand what they gave with the other, for the goods of Jamaica so exempted were not to include sugar, tobacco, indigo, and cotton—in other words, those very commodities that the Island, when once settled, would be expected to supply in abundance. That the Administration took Povey's lecture on the evils of parsimony more to heart than his observations on the principles of sound commerce is, however, illustrated by the munificent settlement of £21,200[1] that was shortly afterwards granted to Lord Windsor, over and above his stipulated salary as Governor of £2,000 per annum.[2] Coached so long and so well by the mercantile interest, the politicians had at last reached the conclusion that money spent on the good grounding of plantation and settlement was money well spent, bread cast upon colonial waters, which would assuredly return in time as revenue to the ports of England.

In July 1661 the Jamaica Committee (to which Clarendon, Saye and Sele, and Holles were now added) set to work to frame a new form of government for Jamaica.[3] By 2 August they had prepared Lord Windsor's Commission. Windsor himself, however, was in no hurry to take up his new Government until

---

him less Potent in his own Dominions, and make it hard, if not impossible, for him to withhold us from Tradeing with his Subjects there, and make it easy for us either to Invade his Townes or interrupt his Trade.'

[1] Of this £12,274. 0s. 2d. was distributed as the King's 'donative' to the soldiers, in October 1662; Edward Long, *History of Jamaica* (London, 1774), i. 614.
[2] D'Oyley's salary as Governor (if he was ever paid it) was £800.
[3] 3 July 1661, APCC, i. 522.

he had settled the matter of his 'pension' to his satisfaction.[1] Jamaica heard the news of his appointment in October when Middleton's *Charity* arrived. In December 1661, on the urgent representations of the Council of Plantations, whose mercantile members were aware that too much delay might be dangerous, a Royal Proclamation was issued in the Island.[2] It announced the impending arrival of a new royal Governor, and listed the improvements his coming would set in train. All Jamaicans might be assured of their future, for His Majesty and his Councillors, reaffirming their belief that possession of the Island was in every way an asset to the realm, asserted their anxiety to aid the work of settlement by every means. To this end they had decreed that, for the next two years, 30 acres of land should be allotted to every adult person who wished to settle in Jamaica, and who should make an application to that effect within the next six months. The sole obligations on the settler in return should be to plant, to prosper, and to serve in arms in case of emergency. Children henceforth[3] born in Jamaica should be 'free denizens' of England, and should enjoy 'the same Privileges to all intents and Purposes as our free born Subjects of England'. Everyone was free to go to Jamaica at once.

As few in fact were economically free to do anything of the sort, potential settlers placed themselves at the disposal of English capitalists, who 'set them out' as a Jamaican investment.[4] Merchants and grandees were eager to supplement the official propaganda by playing an active part. Of the passengers who made ready to sail with Windsor in the fleet that was preparing for him between January and March 1662, Clarendon, the Earl of Carlisle, and Sir Charles Lyttelton each fully accoutred 20;[5] while Lord Willoughby, not yet established as

---

[1] He attended meetings of the Council of Plantations, to which he had been added on 5 June, ibid., p. 516.

[2] 'The King's Proclamation for the encouraging of planters in Jamaica', 14 Dec. 1661, CO 1/15, No. 94. It was on the recommendation of the Council that the clause 'that they shall be governed by the laws of England' was added to the Proclamation; 1 July 1661, CO 1/14, No. 59, 33–34.

[3] Thus, children born between 1655 and 1662 (and their descendants) were, by this wording, not 'free denizens'; cf. E. Bridges, *The Annals of Jamaica* (2 vols., London, 1828), i. 425.

[4] For a full study of this regular practice, see A. E. Smith, *Colonists in Bondage* (Chapel Hill, N.C., 1947).

[5] Cf. The King to York, 7 Apr. 1662, CSPC 1661–8, 277; Admiralty orders, Adm 2/1745. The *Griffin* was to be lent to Windsor for two years, and was to carry

royal Governor in the 'Caribbees', showed his devotion to the royal purposes by equipping no less than 80—who might better have served his own interests in Barbados or Surinam. Windsor himself set out 40. Jamaica thus now lay full in a royalist limelight, 'a most hopefull Plantation'.

There were, however, some evil elements to be purged before Royalism could feel thoroughly at ease there. It is no paradox, therefore, that Willoughby (Governor-elect of Barbados) was instructed to afford Jamaica every assistance against attack, while Windsor (Governor-elect of Jamaica) was ordered to disband the Army there save for 400 foot and 150 horse;[1] an establishment that the Council of Plantations, after some second thoughts, had assessed as at once the minimum required to maintain internal security and to cope with external danger. For Jamaica's soldiery, despite its protestations of new-found loyalty, was but Cromwell's spawn; no Royalist could consider it a sure buckler for the Island's defence. Better, then, to put arms in the hands of a possibly inept militia of gentleman-planters than to trust soured professionals, who were exiles from another age.

In duty bound, Willoughby forwarded these royal commands concerning Jamaica's welfare to Walrond and the Council in Barbados.[2] The latter also judged it politic, despite their private conviction that for the future prosperity of Barbados Jamaica were better at the bottom of the sea, to earn both the royal approval and Willoughby's favour by a ready compliance. Their previous attempt to drive a bargain with the Council of Plantations had failed; for no answer had been made to their petition for an annual supply of 3,000 white servants, in return for which Barbados would willingly furnish Jamaica 'with a suitable number of Freemen'. The aversion of Barbadian magnates 'from acting anything to the good of Jamaica'[3] was, however, already known in London. The Lords of the Admiralty

6 ministers, 15 of their families, and Windsor's and Lyttelton's contingents. Victuals went on board *Centurion*, *Beare*, and *Westergate*, with Clarendon's and Carlisle's people as well as 12 planters of Sir Thomas Whetstones'.

[1] The King to Willoughby, 14 Apr. 1662: 'Jamaica being [His Majesty's] frontier plantation in America'; CO 1/16, No. 45; Additional Instruction to Windsor, 23 Apr. 1662, CO 324/1, 33–36.

[2] Willoughby to Walrond, 12 May 1662, CO 1/16, No. 52.

[3] Cf. reports of Captain Whiting of the *Diamond*, 3 Feb. 1662, ibid., No. 12.

warned Windsor before he set out with his fleet that he would find Barbadian enthusiasm for the settlement of Jamaica at a low ebb. They instructed him accordingly that he was to 'endeavour the settling of the busyness in such a way as that there may be noe Obstructions in the same for the future'.[1]

In consequence, when on 10 July 1662, he arrived at Barbados *en route* to Jamaica, Windsor at once issued a Proclamation of his purposes,[2] and began to recruit for Jamaica without concerting with the Barbadian political chiefs as to the proper procedure. He hurried a motley contingent aboard his ships, and sailed from Barbados after a stay of only three weeks. The main grievance of Walrond and the Council—apart from natural feelings of wounded *amour-propre*[3]—centred on the point that Windsor had made off with a large number of debtors, 'to the greate Dammage of many of the Inhabitants' of Barbados.[4] A detailed report of Windsor's activities was accordingly sent off to Secretary Nicholas.[5] It was discussed in the Plantations Committee, and then quietly shelved. The promotion of settlement in Jamaica was of more importance than analysing yet another tale of woe from Barbados.

Lord Windsor reached Jamaica on 11 August 1662.[6] The long period of martial law was ended; genuine civil government was to begin. The garrison was to be transformed into a colony.[7]

[1] 10 Apr. 1662, Adm 2/1732, 176a.
[2] 'Declaration of Lord Windsor, Governour of Jamaica, at Barbados', 11 July 1662, CO 1/16, No. 72.
[3] Walrond and the Council had already publicized the Jamaica venture in Barbados, stressing that those who were servants when they left Barbados were not debarred from attaining a freehold in Jamaica when the period of their service had expired, and that the government of Jamaica would be 'administered agreeably to the Laws of England, or such Laws, not repugnant to, as shal be enacted by Consent of the Freemen of the Island'; Minutes of the Council of Barbados, 14 Aug. 1662, ibid., No. 89.
[4] 'A Record of the whole Proceedings between the President and Councell of Barbados and Lord Windsor, Governour of Jamaica', 21 July 1662, CO 31/1, 65–72.
[5] Cf. Walrond to Nicholas, 21 Aug. 1662, CO 1/16, No. 97.
[6] On *Centurion*, commanded by Captain Christopher Myngs. Sir Charles Lyttelton was also aboard. The cargo included, besides the usual complement of strong liquors, a Public Seal, and a mace for use in the projected Assembly. D'Oyley, to whom Windsor was barely polite, left on 10 Sept. aboard *Westergate*, which took 18 months to get back to England; Beeston's *Journal*, loc. cit.; Add. MS. 12408, f. 1.
[7] A report of 31 Dec. 1661 reckons the population at 2,956 white people, and 514 blacks. 2,558 acres were planted; CO 1/15, No. 98; MS. Rawl. A. 347.

At the head of this small community, with a title that no one—other than the King of Spain—could dispute, stood His Majesty of England, represented by his appointed Governor. Like D'Oyley before him, Windsor had orders to publish at large the terms of his Commission.[1] In the main, it was a formal instrument, containing, however, yet another variation on the theme of the 'laws of England': Windsor's actions in government should not be 'repugnant, but agreeing thereto, as neare as the condition of Affaires will permit'—a sensible qualification, but one whose magnanimity was later to perplex a narrower-minded Committee of Plantations.

His Instructions, dated eight months later than the Commission, were more precise, although ambiguity was not absent. Both instruments of Windsor's Government speak in confused terms of the nature of the Council in Jamaica. His Commission remarks that a Council of 12 members shall be elected 'as shall be appointed in our Instructions'.

The second clause of the Instructions,[2] however, merely orders Windsor to appoint a Council 'according to your Commission and Instructions'; while in other clauses the Council appears, as if already constituted, as giving advice on certain measures. The twentieth clause, however, breaks fresh ground, and bears signs of having been grafted on as an appendix. Windsor is granted power

with the advice of the Councell to call Assemblys togeather, according to the Custome of our Plantacons, to make Lawes and uppon Eminent Necessityes to leavy Moneys, as shall be most conduceable to the Honour and Advantage of our Crown and the good & wellfare of our Subjects, provided they be not repugnant to any of our Lawes of England

with the important new proviso that 'such Lawes shall be in force for two yeares and noe longer unless they shall be approved and continued by us'.

But in all this there is still no mention made of the manner in

---

[1] Commission, CO 138/1, 9–12. It granted to Windsor a wider area of authority than D'Oyley's, extending the rule of the Governor of Jamaica over the adjacent Cayman Islands, Goat Island, Pigeon Island, and numerous cays. The buccaneers' headquarters, Tortuga, was not included, as an Instruction already issued to Windsor (19 Feb. 1662) had charged him to reduce that Island and its renegade French Governor to obedience; CO 1/16, Nos. 19–20.

[2] Windsor's Instructions, 21 Mar. 1662, CO 324/1, 37–56; CO 138/1, 13–19.

which the Council itself is to come into being. Yet, as the elective principle had been recognized in the granting of the power to call an Assembly, it is extremely unlikely that the Crown intended it to extend farther into the Jamaican Executive. D'Oyley's Council had indeed been elected, but then D'Oyley's Council had also fulfilled the function of an Assembly. Certainly Windsor took his orders to mean that he should appoint his own Council, and no objection was raised at home. He had, of course, been present at many meetings of the Council of Plantations while the terms of his Instructions were under discussion, and must have known well enough where his own powers lay.

Windsor's civil powers were extended beyond those granted to D'Oyley, as was to be expected. He was to appoint judges, justices, and sheriffs (but this time under the Public Seal of the Island) and to pay them 'after the manner of Barbados and Virginia, or one of them'. He retained a right of pardon. He was to press on with the work of fortification, whose cost, should it prove too great for the Island to pay, might be put on the King's charge. 'For the bearing of such like Expences' he should set aside 400,000 acres (100,000 in each quarter of the Island) as a royal demesne, 'as for a Mark of our Soveraignty in and over' Jamaica.[1] Windsor might take up to 50,000 acres for himself, and allot land in free and common socage at a rent which he and his Council should decide. As Commander-in-Chief of all shipping, he was empowered to erect a Court of Admiralty, but this time it was distinctly stated that the judges of that Court must be commissioned by the Duke of York.[2] Other maritime matters were, however, left less precisely governed. Windsor had power, as Governor, to grant private commissions and letters of marque to shipping 'for the subduing of all our Enimies by Sea or Land, within and upon the Coasts of America' —but nevertheless it would be deemed piracy if any ship

---

[1] This scheme never came to fruition. Despite Lyttelton's opinion that 'it will take away all doubts and jealousies of rumours too frequently spread, of His Maties redelivering the Island to the Spaniards, which have been hitherto a main obstacle to the settlement of it' (3 Oct. 1664, CO 1/18, No. 113), Governor Modyford was instructed to suspend the allotment and grant the area in 'parcells' to anyone who would plant it within five years; Barham's 'Account of Jamaica', Add. MS. 12422, f. 63.

[2] 10 Apr. 1662, Adm 2/1732, 174a. Jamaica's was thus the first official colonial Vice-Admiralty Court.

molested or impounded any enemy vessel without a commission to do so from the Duke or from the Commissioners of the Admiralty in England. The Lords of the Admiralty doubtless had colonial prize, and its proper destination, in mind; but the clauses as they stood were ambiguous, and Windsor's successor as Governor of Jamaica, whose mind did not lack precision, was to turn this ambiguity to his own good account. In the final clause of Windsor's Instructions, Povey's principle of the 'loose rein' was adhered to, sensibly phrased—'there are many things in so Remoat a Place which will bee Omitted & not Foreseene and necessarily must be left to the Prudence of our Lieutenant or Governor to use his best Circumspection'—but this clause too was eventually to have a curious interpretation placed upon it.

Stress has been laid on the reservation that always accompanied the grant of executive authority to a colonial Government: the recurrent proviso, and its variants, that such an authority must institute nothing that was 'repugnant to the laws of England'. These words were not intended to support the interpretation afterwards placed on them by the settlers of Jamaica: that the laws of England henceforth governed all civil situations in the Island, and that if any local enactment or procedure clashed with some verifiable principle of English law, it was on that ground alone void and non-applicable. Bryan Edwards in his *History* expresses the colonial point of view in this way:

It appears to me to be clear and uncontrovertible, that the royal proclamations and charters which guaranteed and confirmed to the first planters, emigrating to America and the West Indies, all the liberties, franchises, and immunities of free denizens remaining within the kingdom, were, and were meant to be, *declaratory only of ancient rights; not creative of new privileges*. They were nothing more than royal recognitions, expressive of a reciprocal relation between the Sovereign and his subjects . . . assuring them, expressly, or by evident implication, so long as they preserved their allegiance, the full and undisturbed enjoyment of those inherent rights, which no climate nor compact can take away or diminish.[1]

But this was never the language of the English Government, or of English lawyers. To them it seemed clear that in Jamaica

---

[1] Edwards, op. cit. ii. 416. His italics.

English law had, by the terms of Windsor's Commission, replaced the existing (and illegal) martial law: but this sub-
stitution was an act of the royal grace, as indeed was the issue
of royal Commissions to D'Oyley and to Windsor himself.
Although Englishmen delighted to call themselves freeborn, this
was so much rhetoric; the laws of England held that they were
all born subjects of the King. The clause in the royal Proclamation of December 1661 that concerns the denizenation of
children born to Jamaican settlers states that such shall have
the same *privileges* as Englishmen, indeed, but it makes no
mention of rights, nor does it appeal specifically to the laws of
England at all. The point went unnoticed at the time, for these
nice legalisms were not then of great importance.

Furthermore, in Jamaica the authority of the King, in whatever form he chose to pronounce it, was doubly unquestionable,
because he had acquired the Island by conquest (were it only
at second-hand). In a conquered country 'the laws of England
do not take place there until declared by the conqueror'.[1] The
King never did so declare. Of course he could not attempt to
govern Jamaica by Prerogative alone, for practical reasons: the
business of settlement would never have gone forward at all
had not Windsor's Instructions, and his propaganda in Barbados, contained assurances that all Englishmen going to
Jamaica would find there a society with whose ethos they were
already familiar, and where they would receive their accustomed
protection of English law. But Windsor's statement that it was
the intention of the Crown that the Island should be governed
according to the known laws of England as far as was possible,
set no legal bond upon the Crown. The King might disallow
and order repealed any colonial enactment he took exception to.
It was therefore he alone, and not his subjects, who had proper
right of appeal to the 'laws of England' as a yardstick of conduct.
A Governor had no power to pronounce these laws 'in force',

[1] Cf. the opinion of Solicitor-General Richard West in 1720, in Chalmers,
Opinions, i. 195: 'The common law of England, is the common law of the plantations, and all statutes in affirmance of the common law, passed in England, ante-
cedent to the settlement of a colony, are in force in that colony, unless there is
some private act to the contrary, though no statutes, made since those settlements,
are there in force, unless the colonies are particularly mentioned. Let an Englishman go where he will, he carries as much of law and liberty with him as the nature
of things will bear.'

unless explicitly authorized to do so. Windsor's Instructions were comprehensive, but they did not include any such authority.

Still his powers were real, and the best thing he could have done for Jamaica was to stay there, to supervise not only the inauguration of the new government but its operations as well. This he did not choose to do. He left the Island after ten weeks' stay.[1] Not wishing to be burdened with an Assembly, he performed a great many valuable actions in a tearing hurry. He disbanded the Army, reconstituting the permitted quota of troops 'under the soberest men that could be found'.[2] He erected courts and appointed court officers. He lavishly alienated land, and confirmed settlers in the tenure of their properties. He regulated prices, fixing the rate of sugar and tobacco at 3*d.* per lb. and cocoa at 4*d.*[3] He called in the commissions of the privateers, most of which were out of date where they were not fictitious, and gave them in lieu new commissions 'to take Spanyards and bring them for Jamayca, there to come to Judicature, and pay their Publique dues, being the Tenths & fifteenes' in the Admiralty Court. Now this was, of course, a great boon to the rovers.[4] It increased their numbers, broadened their horizon, and inflated their *esprit de corps.* They could now reckon themselves servants of the civil Government; for Windsor employed 1,000 privateers, under the command of Myngs and two frigates of the Royal Navy, in plundering expeditions to Cuba and Campeachy.[5] Spain's role in America was to provide prize for the needy: this view, always popular in the Indies,

[1] A royal letter dated 3 May 1662 allowed him 'to resort in person to our royal presence, either to informe us of the grounds and probabilities of future designs for the good and advauncement of our Dominions there and to take our commands and directions thereupon or to solicite & procure such other supplyes and necessaries as occasion shall require'; CO 138/1, 20. Richard Povey said Windsor was ill (Long, op. cit. i, 216), Pepys that he was lazy.

[2] Eighty-four officers of the militia testified to their continuing sobriety by sending a fulsome letter to the King, thanking him for allowing his clemency to extend 'into another world', by owning them, unworthy as they were, as his subjects and servants; 25 Feb. 1663, APCC, i. 586.

[3] For Windsor's work, cf. Minutes of the Council of Jamaica, CO 140/1, 55 et seq., and 'The condition of Jamaica at Lord Windsor's departure on 20th October 1662', CO 324/1, 258-9.

[4] The Vice-Admiralty Court was very busy in Jamaica from 1662 to 1664; cf. Crump, op. cit. 106 et seq. As late as 1675 privateers turned pirate were in seeming innocency producing these commissions of Windsor's to the baffled inspection of Lord Vaughan.

[5] See Chapter III, *infra.*

was now given the official sanction of Government, and although
the English Administration shortly changed its mind and its
Instructions with regard to relations with Spanish America,
the damage had been done.

In the Caribbean privateering remained the ever-present
alternative to a life of hard work in a hot climate; at once a
convenient refuge from a pursuing creditor, and a good opportunity for a poor man to win with a sword in an hour what
years of servitude for a master would never gain him. Could
planting in Jamaica thrive under such conditions? Would His
Majesty's 'frontier plantation in America' ever cease to be 'more
a place of soldiery than of planting'?[1] The Administration had
authorized a new government, and its accredited Governor had
set it up; but it was clear that its work was not done. Windsor's
régime certainly drew up plans for a new structure of administration in the Island, but the task of building on the foundations remained the duty of the inhabitants. If left to themselves,
they would not bother; obviously then, they required not only
the benevolent protection of the distant Government in London,
but strict discipline from a strong local authority. All reports on
Jamaica that came to hand were agreed on this.

General D'Oyley presented one such report to Clarendon,
when he at last arrived in England in the spring of 1663.[2] No
longer wrapped in the warmth of his brief authority, D'Oyley
returned with some relish to his role of Jeremiah. Refusing to
'hyperbolize' on his subject (as had many who should have
known better), he laid his humble opinion on the Island's
prospects before the Jamaica Committee. All the tales current
of the unparalleled richness of the Jamaican soil might be discounted as fantasy, for in fact it was much inferior to that in
Barbados and the Leewards: Jamaica was then producing one-
third less sugar per acre than Barbados, and one-half less per
head of tobacco than St. Christopher. The much vaunted drugs
and dyewoods had no great future that D'Oyley could see. The
climate was too unhealthy for a white man to work in. Nor
would any sensible white man want to work in it—for if he
was not stricken by sickness he was oppressed by poverty.

---

[1] Thomas Andrews to the Earl of Winchilsea, 8 Apr. 1664, HMC Finch, i. 306.
[2] Bodl., MS. Rawl. A. 347: 'The relation of Col. D'Oyly upon his return from
Jamaica to the Lord Chancellor.'

Desertion was frequent. Owners of plantations had learned to dread the arrival of any of the King's ships, for these provided a route of escape to their white hands, and captains whose ships were always undercrewed were prepared to welcome these fugitives without asking questions. From the first rumour of the frigates' coming, which was often current six to eight months in advance,

no man will be hired but from week to week, so that those who would Plant dare not, lest when their Cropp becomes ripe & fitt for inning they faile of Hands, which certainly they do if ships come, and so are discourag'd in their labour.

The equipping of the Cuba and Campeachy expeditions had denuded the plantations and caused heavy loss to many planters, who had had to burn their crops for want of white labour.[1] Other owners, either in exasperation or in greed, had sold their estates and joined the expeditions themselves, marketing their expectations of Spanish loot as credit in the taverns—and, of course, had had to flee their debts when the day of reckoning came. Thus Virginia had become a bolt-hole for Jamaican debtors just as Jamaica had absorbed those of Barbados.

D'Oyley also had some harsh words to say of the habits of merchants trading to Jamaica. These people, who 'where they bring in £100 in any necessary goods they bring in £500 in drink' would not consent to traffic in anything so unprofitable as a white servant, though they were early enough to appreciate the market value of a black. He asserted that when he was Governor he had tried to put a stop to this practice, by bringing in a law prohibiting merchants from retailing liquor in Jamaica unless they also settled a plantation there, and from importing so much as a tun of wine unless they brought in a servant with it; but this had aroused such a storm of opposition that he had had to rescind it. And yet these were the very persons who continually 'cried up' trade and asserted that their views about settlement and plantation were worthy of greater consideration by the home authorities than were those of the Governor on the spot!

[1] D'Oyley himself had mounted just such an expedition to Tolu on the Main, in 1658. Myngs, then commanding the *Marston-Moor*, had been its leader; Bridges, *Annals*, i. 233. D'Oyley had left Jamaica when the Cuba and Campeachy expeditions were mounted; so his graphic description was second-hand.

This may have seemed to some more of a sketch in chiaro-
scuro than a detailed portrait of Jamaican conditions, but the
Committee was soon able to collate it with Sir Charles Lyttelton's report on the Island, presented that October.[1] Here the
shades were as dark, although Lyttelton's commentary was
mild where D'Oyley's was bitter. The fortifications were still
half-finished and their cost mounting; there were now better
provisions available and prices were lower, but only 200 new
settlers had arrived that year; there was still too much sickness,
too much privateering, too many 'discouragements given at the
Windward Islands'. Although an Assembly he had summoned
had passed a code of laws, 'as sound and serviceable as could
be reasonably expected',[2] Lyttelton urged that some further
encouragement from the English Government was essential.
Jamaica plainly needed some capable man to keep it in order,
to keep government alive and active—some energetic planter
and promoter in one; a man who was content with a West-
India career, and not one whose heart remained in London and
whose footsteps would take him there as soon as possible.
Lyttelton himself, an able man enough, was not of the required
stamp. Like Windsor before him, he preferred to 'show his
loyalty' to His Majesty by repairing in person to the gracious
presence. He left Jamaica in May 1664.

His views were, however, carefully considered. Interest in
colonial affairs was still running high among the Privy Councillors. The project for a settlement in Carolina was afoot, and
the eight Councillors who had been constituted Lords Proprietor
of that area by the Charter of 24 March were busy (in concert
with their allies in the venture, the planters and merchants of
the West-India Interest), drawing up schemes of settlement
that should lead them all to fortune. Accordingly, despite the
gloomy reports of existing conditions, the optimism about a
successful future for Jamaica did not diminish. Writing to
Willoughby in Barbados, the King emphasized, rather tact-
lessly, that he had very good hopes of the Island's prosperity—
'Their hearts are still set on Jamaica', William Willoughby

---

[1] Written 2 May. CO 138/1, 21–23; CO 1/18, No. 111; MS. Rawl. A. 347.
Cf. also Lyttelton to Bennet, 15 Oct. 1663, CO 1/17, No. 80.
[2] Cf. Bridges, *Annals*, i. 258. MS. Rawl. A. 347 contains 45 Acts of Lyttelton's
Assembly, which must have therefore come to Clarendon's notice.

wrote his brother in exasperation.[1] These hearts were moved by
its plight, and there was a further dip into the imperial pocket.
The Treasury found another £3,000 for the use of the Island
in December,[2] but it was careful to take the occasion to draw
up an establishment for Jamaica in proper form. Its expenditure
was not to exceed an annual amount of £2,500. From this sum
the Governor should draw a salary of £1,000, his Deputy £600,
and the Major-General—the officer in charge of the forces in
the Island—£400. To the officers and soldiers went the remaining £500 in pay. These might seem large sums in London, but
they did not go far in Jamaica, where, as Lyttelton testified, a
Governor might spend as much as £600 a year on his own table
and household. However, the fact that the Administration had
now officially 'established' Jamaica—given it a Government,
a Treasury, and a budget—made it the more essential that a
firm control over its investment there should be ensured. The
English Exchequer had now a definite stake in Jamaica's success. Whitehall agreed with Lyttelton that what the Island
needed besides State-aid was an enterprising Governor who
would remain at his post and not protest himself out of office at
the first signs of difficulty. In January 1664 its choice fell on one
who had always thrived on difficulty—the redoubtable Barbadian magnate, Colonel Thomas Modyford.[3]

The entire Modyford clan was by this time finding life in
Barbados, where it was perpetually enmeshed in faction, somewhat cramping to its initiative and zeal for self-improvement.
Modyford was very active in the Carolina project;[4] while his
brother, Sir James, had already made a voyage to Jamaica,
and made a note of its potentialities.[5] Given 'solid' planting, the
Island was bound to prosper—and there were many solid
planters in Barbados and the Leewards, men who owned small
estates and whose livelihood was accordingly precarious in these
tight little islands where the grandees ruled. Sharing this view,

[1] 13 Jan. 1664, HMC Portland, iii. 279.
[2] This was paid to Colonel Edward Morgan, 11 Dec. 1663, CSPC 1661–8, 602;
and cf. Bennet to Southampton, 7 Dec. 1663, CO 1/17, No. 98.
[3] The King to Modyford, 11 Jan. 1664, CO 1/18, No. 7.
[4] The magnates of Barbados were eager to promote Carolina settlement so long
as no sugar was planted there; cf. Sir R. to Sir E. Harley, 3 Nov. 1662, HMC
Portland, iii. 268.
[5] 'Description of Jamaica, surveyed by Sir James Modyford', 1663, CO 324/1,
253–8.

Modyford put many recommendations to Secretary Bennet on Jamaica, using Kendall as his intermediary. He asked for the immediate dispatch of shipping and stores; a free passage should be granted to the first thousand settlers for Jamaica. Future planters should be gentlemen—that is, freemen, fit to vote in Assembly for the defence of their property. Civil liberties, including liberty of conscience, should be publicly announced, and if the Island were granted a 21-years' freedom from duty on its trade, settlers would flock in. The privateers, the bane of prosperity, should be called in and an admiralty firmly settled. Modyford, asserting that 'Barbados cannot last in a height of trade 3 years longer', and that then its crowded population must find a land-outlet, remained their Lordships' obedient servant.[1]

The decision to make him so in fact and appoint him Governor of Jamaica was taken in England only after hesitation. Great men, such as the Earls of Craven and Marlborough,[2] were interested in the post. A prize such as Jamaica was reputed to be surely warranted the rule of someone more important than a mere planter, one, moreover, whose political record was, to say the least, dubious. Yet, after all, whose was not, if closely scanned? The practical good sense of Modyford's 'Overtures',[3] the energy he displayed in promoting the Carolina project, his known competence as a factor in Barbados for the Royal Company of Adventurers trading into Africa, and of course the support of Albemarle, combined to turn the scale in his favour. A 'person of honour' had already been sent to govern Jamaica, anyway—and he was back in London before his friends had missed him. A formal Commission was therefore issued to Modyford as Governor on 15 February 1664,[4] embodying most

[1] Cf. CSPC 1661–8, 629–32.

[2] Cf. Williamson to Fanshawe, 14 May 1663, HMC Heathcote, 89; CSPD 1661–2, 71; HMC Hastings, ii. 143; Cal. S.P. Ven. 1661–4, 347.

[3] The Committee later dealt with his 'Overtures' in detail; 'Report on the 9 articles of Proposalls by Governor Sir Thomas Modyford', 10 Aug. 1664, CO 1/18, No. 93. His plea for the removal of restrictions on Jamaica's trade was better satisfied than Povey's earlier petition on this point. Imports into England from Jamaica were freed from duty for five years from 18 Feb. 1664; imports into Jamaica from England were to be free for 21 years. The Plantations Council of 1670, however, rescinded this. Cf. Modyford's report, Dec. 1671, answer to Question 22: only wines and strong liquors paid duty, every English ship paid 1s. and every foreign ship 2s. per ton; CO 1/27, Nos. 96, 119.

[4] Commission, MS. Rawl. A. 255, f. 7. This volume also contains his Instruc-

of his own ideas as to what his powers should be. He had the right to make laws,[1] with the consent of an Assembly. He was to prohibit the issue of letters of marque. And, best of all, he was given discretion of action, in ample degree: the Governor had 'power to act in all things not mentioned in these Instructions'.[2] What further power, after all, could a resourceful Governor want?

Colonel Edward Morgan, with the Treasury's £3,000, had arrived at Barbados in April 1664, to find the new Governor of Jamaica caught up in a whirl of activity. Having already notified the Spanish Governor of Santo Domingo both of his own appointment and of His Britannic Majesty's pacific intentions towards Spain, Sir Thomas Modyford[3] was busily contracting to transport close on 1,700 people from Barbados—those 'solid' small planters whose potential utility in Jamaica his brother had already assessed. The fact that Sir Thomas, so renowned in Barbados for his wealth, his energy, and his dexterity, was cheerfully pulling up his roots there and committing himself to a Jamaican future, infected this class of colonist with his own enthusiasm. The Barbadian magnates served him amiably enough as contractors. They were not sorry to see the last of the Modyford family. Nor did they object to the removal from their ken of so many of those people who cluttered up good land and got in the way of large-scale capital development, men of inferior social and economic status, who were unlikely to contribute anything to a planters' society except trouble.

Modyford, moreover, had the tact and address that Windsor had so signally lacked. Although he and Willoughby were on cool terms, the latter put no obstacles in the way of his recruitment. Willoughby had already sent home his opinion of Jamaica: it was only good as a 'garrison place for men-of-war and a curb upon the Spaniards',[4] and hitherto it had only robbed the other colonies of people. But he deserves credit for his amiable behaviour, the more so as his letters home after

tions, 18 Feb. 1664 (f. 1); Colonel Morgan's Instructions, 27 Feb. 1664; and the revocation of Modyford's Commission, 5 Jan. 1671 (f. 156).
    [1] Such 'to be transmitted to us, and such of them as shal bee by us or our Privy Councell disallowed thenceforward to cease and determine'.
    [2] Instructions, 18 Feb. 1664, in CO 138/1, 29–35; CO 1/18, No. 26.
    [3] His baronetcy was gazetted on 1 Mar. 1664.
    [4] Willoughby to the King, 4 Nov. 1663, CO 1/17, No. 89.

Modyford had sailed from Barbados with a first instalment of 987 settlers[1] showed that his opinion had not changed. He urged that no more Instructions to aid the plantation of Jamaica to such an extent should be sent him, 'for it is not beginning at the right end to improve His Matie's interest in these partes, for he doth but take out of his right pocket to put into his left'.[2] Willoughby had already dipped his hand sufficiently in his pocket to aid Modyford and his friends to settle Carolina.[3] So let the countries of Europe rather than other English colonies be scoured in future for Jamaica's settlers.

Modyford himself was in simultaneous dispatches taking a longer view than his *confrère*. He had certainly no objection to the importation of foreigners, for foreigners had two hands to work with like anyone else. Jews henceforth found a welcome in Jamaica which was denied them in Barbados;[4] and Modyford would have made room for the Dutch themselves had he been allowed to. At any rate, he urged, let land in Jamaica be reserved for all those who promised to bring out and set out other settlers. And if the Englishmen in the Leeward Islands wanted to better their condition, why should they not? To encourage them, they should be granted their passages free. Modyford even spoke in an unguarded moment of granting 30 acres per head not only to white but to black men. But the negro was not a servant whose period of service eventually expired; the Royal Company of Adventurers, as Modyford himself had good reason to know, dealt not in indentured apprentices but in slaves. Collecting his thoughts, he urged instead that if the Royal Company wished to build Jamaica into a profitable market, it should show early wisdom by allowing easy terms for negroes to the inhabitants of Jamaica while plantation there was in its infancy. In sum, let every sensible step be taken towards the improvement of the Island's condition, for the 'Design' was a great one indeed. It was Modyford who had helped to inspire

[1] 'None in debt'; Modyford to Bennet, 20 June 1664, CO 1/18, No. 83.

[2] Willoughby to Arlington, 29 June 1664, ibid., No. 81.

[3] Cf. also Albemarle's letter to Willoughby of 31 Aug. 1662, advising him of his own, York's and Clarendon's desire that he should aid the Carolina project, CO 5/286, 9; and the King's warrant to Willoughby to hand over £1,000 in sugar to Modyford to finance the completion of 'The Great Fort' of Jamaica; CO 1/18, No. 35.

[4] The first seem to have arrived on 31 Mar. 1664; Add. MS. 12408, f. 6. Denizenation cost a Jew £120.

Cromwell's decision to intervene in this Western world; it was he again who now reminded King Charles of an imperial destiny. 'Princes', he warned, 'that goe not forward goe backward, and theyre royall Groweth is safest when least perceptible: the well-filling this Navel (as the Spaniards call it) of the Indies may notably further their Groweth'.[1]

In Sir Thomas Modyford, therefore, the Administration felt they had indeed found a man who could be trusted to put the work of Jamaican settlement in hand. He might therefore be left to manage these matters alone—and the same went for Willoughby in Barbados.

Thus, the West-India policy of the Administration at this time may be resolved: to make a profit in the 'Caribbees', and to invest for a profit in Jamaica.[2] By their own efforts the plantations should maintain themselves. Everything had been done to start them on the right road to success: the royal authority assured, English law confirmed, representative Assemblies allowed, good Governors installed, protection for commerce and shipping bestowed, assistance in settlement granted, and capital investment encouraged; what else was there to do?

It would have been more to Willoughby's taste if the voice of the imperial authority had been oftener raised. He did not share the Government's view, that a man might be turned loose in the Indies and there forgotten so long as he kept his plantation accounts in order. For one thing, there was the problem of French encroachment; for another, the continual rumbling of disaffection among the colonists themselves. Truculence often seemed to Willoughby the cloak of treason, and the troubles of Francis Cradock over his disputed office of Provost-Marshal can be attributed in part to his gift of too ready repartee. Humphrey Walrond and Sir Robert Harley the Governor dubbed knaves,[3] and his deportation of both to England made him

---

[1] Modyford to Bennet, 10 May 1664, CO 1/18, Nos. 65 et seq. This echoes his advice to Cromwell in 1655: 'If this place be fully planted, His Highness may doe what he will in the West Indyes.'

[2] 'Its a hard chapter', remarked Joseph Williamson, 'to be at expense here upon the Plantations'; CO 1/18, No. 169.

[3] Willoughby issued three warrants against Walrond in Oct. and Nov. 1663, ostensibly for having sequestered money paid by Spanish traders, due to the King; CO 1/17, Nos. 83, 87, 90. Walrond quit Barbados in haste at the end of November. Harley, Keeper of the Seal, was arrested on 11 Feb. 1664 for 'insubordination';

more enemies both in the Island and at home.[1] His heavy hand
fell also on Samuel Farmer, Speaker of an Assembly he was
compelled to call to raise money for the Island's defence. Under
Farmer's guidance, the Assembly refused, saying that they had
already voted the $4\frac{1}{2}$ per cent. for this very purpose.[2] To Willoughby this forthright stubborn man was John Cade himself,
'a great Magna-Carta Man & Petition-of-Right-maker', he
rumbled, 'the first that started up that kind of language here',
a man who had already influenced his fellow Assembly-men 'to
dance after the Long Parliament's pipe'. There ought to be no
truckling to such—but the trouble was, he must have the money
for defence, and not a pound of the sugar currency could be
raised without the consent of the freemen of the Assembly.
(Here was the dilemma that was to perplex generations of
colonial Governors with masterful minds of their own.) For his
part, Willoughby hoped that once the Dutch threat was removed, he might be given leave to come home to set out his
ideas on 'the right regulation of Barbados, which is a master-
wheel'.[3] One may hazard a guess on what exactly constituted
that 'right regulation', but these plans he did not live to pro-
pound.

Jamaica, where the impetus towards settled government had
been so royally marked, retained its political importance.
Moreover, in addition to an extensive programme of land
alienation, Sir Thomas Modyford evolved a foreign policy of

CO 31/1, 82-83: HMC Portland, iii. 280. Henceforth Willoughby kept the Seal
himself; Willoughby to the King, 18 Feb. 1664, CO 1/18, No. 28; and to Bennet,
ibid. No. 29. Harley was home 'with the belly-ake' in April 1664.

[1] There his stock was none too high anyway. The Earl of Carlisle's creditors
were impatient for that golden revenue, and the stockholders of the Royal Company of Adventurers trading into Africa had a debt on their books of £40,000
chargeable to the planters of Barbados. The Barbadians themselves took advantage
of Willoughby's absence in Surinam—where he found another political hornet's
nest and a would-be assassin's knife—to present a formidable list of his offences to
the King-in-Council; 15 May 1665, CSPC 1661-8, 989. This included Willoughby's
embezzlement of the liquor duty and prize money; his false expense account; his
disregard of breaches of the Acts of Trade when these were made by his own
friends; his habit of forcible disseisin and unlawful imprisonment; his disrespect
for the King's name; and his liking for Jews—all of which proves little enough, save
that the Governor had managed to get himself disliked by every class of citizen.

[2] Farmer had also objected to Willoughby's overruling of the Assembly's petition
against summary banishments; HMC Portland, iii. 292-3; and cf. APCC, i. 665,
671.

[3] Willoughby to the King, 8 Aug. 1665, CO 1/19, No. 92.

his own, which deserved (indeed demanded) the attention of
the Administration. The latter was, however, unable to think
of a better, or at any rate of one that promised more profit.
Expediency thus required it to wash official hands of Modyford's private war against Spain which succeeded England's
public war against the Dutch in the Caribbean, and it was
therefore debarred from owning to too detailed a knowledge of
Jamaican conditions. The result was that Jamaica continued
to regulate her own manner of life, and thus earlier even than
the English colonies in Continental America developed that
independence of mind and outlook so often attributed to the
'frontier'. No royal frigates yet came to take a view of Jamaica;
few slave-ships yet looked for a market there; and when in 1666
war came to the Caribbean, it was not Jamaica but Barbados
and the Leeward Islands that was the centre of official attention. These years of ruin for the old 'Caribbees' were years of
rising, if deceptive, prosperity for the new English colony in the
Antilles. While the English in the Leewards sought desperately
and unsuccessfully to get the measure of the French, Governor
Sir Thomas Modyford and his aides, the privateers of Jamaica,
capitalized on the weakness of the Spaniards. Port Royal rang
with tales of derring-do and its tavern counters with pieces of
eight. To see how this came about, it is now necessary to consider Jamaica as a factor in the relations between England and
Spain after the Restoration.

III

JAMAICA AND ANGLO-SPANISH RELATIONS
1660–71

THE imposition of the Crown's authority upon Jamaica involved one factor that had not complicated the settlement in Barbados and the Leeward Islands. This was the hostile attitude of a foreign Power. There was no blinking the plain fact that Jamaica had been wantonly filched from Spain by rebels to the English Crown. That Crown, now happily restored, had no possible justification for retaining the illegal conquest. To a Spanish mind, the issue was no sooner stated than solved.

The English opinion, however, was somewhat more flexible. Charles II's Restoration took place while Cromwell's war with Spain was still in being; but in the resultant new situation it suited neither Power that hostilities should continue, and negotiations were quickly begun for a mutual cessation of arms. Charles was prompt to assure Don Luis de Haro that any such cessation should apply on both sides of the 'Line',[1] and an amicable arrangement was made that a Proclamation to that effect should be issued simultaneously in both England and Spain. By August 1660 Henry Bennet was back at his old post at Madrid, enjoying exceptional honours and 'making no difficulty about Dunkirk and Jamaica'. (His colleague the Venetian envoy reported that the Spanish Court was building high hopes on this foundation.)[2] And shortly afterwards, on 10 September, the cessation of arms was published in the Spanish capital, in an instrument that also permitted the re-entry of English merchants and their goods into the ports of Spain, Italy, and

[1] On 20 July 1660 S[tate] P[apers], Foreign, Spain], 94/44, 4, 8, 9. Don Luis, however, told the Venetian envoy the following November that to get both Dunkirk and Jamaica out of English hands Spain would have to pay 'many thousands of doubles'; Venetian envoy in Spain to his Senate [hereafter VS], 3 Nov. 1660, Cal. S.P. Ven., 1659–61, 229.
[2] VS, 11 Aug. 1660, ibid. 168, 196.

Flanders.[1] The next day a like Proclamation was issued in England. No mention was made in either of these instruments of Dunkirk, Jamaica, or the Indies,[2] but Spain was as yet confident in the honourable intentions of the English Crown.

This belief Charles took every opportunity to foster in conversations with the Spanish Ambassador, Batteville. He ever found it easier to be pleasant than otherwise, and until he had found a friend Charles could not afford to make an enemy. It was true that in the days of his exile, in 1656, he had signed a Treaty with Spain that had heavily committed him. He had promised that from the day of his Restoration to his throne Anglo-Spanish aims should march in harmony. England would assist Philip IV to regain Portugal, and would break off all relations with the Braganzas of that country. She would forbid her subjects to occupy or settle any place either in the West Indies or on the mainland of Spanish America; and, of course, she would restore Cromwell's two conquests of Dunkirk and Jamaica. But this had all been conditional on Spanish aid for his return to the English throne—and as it had turned out it was the Army not of the Dons but of George Monk that accomplished the great task. Thus this Treaty of 1656 was, in King Charles's eyes, a dead letter, even although it was not politic to say so outright.

The joint cessation of arms was a step generally welcomed. In Jamaica the hard-pressed General D'Oyley, for one, hailed the end of an 'unsuccessful war' with a momentary lightening of his despondency.[3] For a time indeed it seemed likely that more would be made of the Anglo-Spanish *rapprochement*, for many of Charles's principal advisers, in particular Clarendon, Ormond, and Nicholas, were firm in their distrust of the policy of France, which was now passing through domestic strife from the control of a Cardinal to the control of a King. But although friendship with Spain was serviceable to England, it was clear that it would never be very profitable; and it was the profit-motive that caused the contortions of foreign policy no less than

[1] 10/20 Sept. 1660, SP 94/44, 56.
[2] As Spanish and English records of the day refer both to Spanish America and the Caribbean Islands as the 'Indies', I follow this custom in this chapter.
[3] D'Oyley to the Commissioners of the Admiralty, 26 July 1660, CSPC 1574–1660, 26, p. 485.

of domestic in the Restoration era. There was already a more promising ally available in Portugal—prey just then both of Spain and the United Provinces; the Power that still held the East in fee, but which could not, in the shrewd opinion of many an English merchant, hold it long. And what, too, might not be the future of Portugal's great American territories in Brazil? England was here taking a long view, indeed; but on her side Portugal could not afford to scrutinize other people's motives, or to take any view but the short. Since her national existence in Europe was in hourly danger from Spain, and her eastern empire under pressure from the Dutch, she welcomed the first tentative English advances with a relief that turned rapidly to enthusiasm. For England's aid against her enemies, for the arrangement of peace between Holland and herself, for recognition of the Braganza as a brother sovereign, she would certainly support the English disinclination to return Dunkirk and Jamaica to Spain. With this the English Court was greatly attracted, the more so as support for the cause of Portugal would bring in its train the approval of France.

France was already bidding for the friendship of the King of England, the most eligible bachelor in Europe. Charles was not averse from knitting closer the ties of his House with the Bourbons. But he had his price: he refused the hand of the Mancini, Mazarin's niece, as being beneath his royal dignity to accept (reserving her thereby for a less formal relationship in the future). This disappointed his mother, Queen Henrietta Maria; but her vexation was largely healed by the credit she gave to her own influence in the promotion of the match between Charles's sister and Louis XIV's brother. But Spain meanwhile had also entered the marriage market, and that summer of 1660 brought off a tremendous *coup*, for she married an Infanta to Louis himself on 9 July. She designed another Spanish princess, in duty and custom, for the Emperor, to cement further the Habsburg tie. What had she to offer the King of England? Unfortunately, nobody: Spain, though she had many protégées on call, had only two daughters, and Charles would not consider lesser candidates, buxom as the signorinas of Parma might be. It was in vain that Spain assured him that, for the restitution of Dunkirk and Jamaica, the lady of his choice would be promoted to a full daughterhood of her Crown, with the tempting dowry of half a million gold crowns.[1] Charles was no longer listening to Spanish voices. Portugal had a better daughter, a bigger dowry—and so the English wooing of the Braganza princess and the Portuguese alliance began on these strictly practical lines. The intricate diplomatic negotiations that occupied the months between August 1660 and May 1661, marched in step with those long debates in Committee of the Privy Council that argued the type of Commission and tenour of Instruction that should be issued to Lord Windsor, the 'person of honour' now going Governor to Jamaica to give that disputed Island His Majesty's seal of recognition.

Spain naturally watched this course of events in a dubiety that, kindling to suspicion, finally burst into a flame of resentment. To Batteville in London,[2] Charles represented that his hand in this matter was being forced by Parliament, which had to be placated. The Ambassador for a time believed this, as it agreed with his own opinion that 'Parliament only serves as an obstacle and embarrassment to all private affairs, especially foreign ones'.[3] He therefore waited in the hope that the dissolution of the Convention Parliament and the summoning of its successor would bring some beneficial change; in a new assembly there would probably be fewer whigs and heretics about shouting their low-bred opinions into the King's ear. Spanish gold began to vie in London with the *cruzados* of Braganza, for it was the experience of European envoys that money could buy anything in England, not excluding her foreign policy.[4] They did not as yet comprehend the breadth of the English spirit of compromise: that Parliament-men would take money cheerfully from all parties but act as they saw fit.

Yet the reinforcement of Jamaica with stores, provisions, and settlers in February 1661 seemed, even to the optimistic Batteville, a strange preliminary to its restitution to his master.[5] He found his protests disregarded, while England continued down her chosen path. The English Princess Henrietta married

---

[1] *VS*, 27 Apr. 1661, Cal. S.P. Ven., 1659–61, 331.

[2] The Venetian envoy in England [hereafter *VE*] states that Batteville had Charles's promise that neither Dunkirk nor Jamaica would be incorporated in the Crown. Jamaica, however, was the Spaniard's main point; 3 Dec. 1660, ibid. 242.

[3] *VE*, 24 Dec. 1660, ibid. 601.

[4] Cf. *VS*, 8 Dec. 1660, who states that Braganza had 'squared' General Monk; Cal. S.P. Ven. 1659–61, 245.   [5] *VS*, 22 Feb. 1661, ibid. 288.

Orleans on the last day of March. Louis continued to abet Charles in his Portuguese project. Louis's Ambassador d'Estrades was now at Charles's side, beguiling him with rich dreams of a golden harvest, of Bombay as the mart for the trade of all India, of Tangier as a centre for the commerce of the Mediterranean, and of Jamaica as the key that would unlock to England the great Spanish treasuries in America. The promised dowry from Braganza of two million *cruzados* hardly required so distinguished an advocate, or even the firm support which Clarendon himself so eagerly contributed.[1] There were, however, some murmurs in English commercial circles against this new attachment and the Chancellor's promotion of it, for although the London mercantile interest as a whole made a show of welcoming the Portuguese match, there were a number who had their doubts.

Foremost among these were the traders to Old Spain. Spain was and had always been a fine, safe market for English goods, and better far than Portugal: surely, then, it was folly to tamper with these sure prospects of prosperity for the sake of chimerical hopes and three encumbrances: a plain bride like Braganza's daughter, a pirates' paradise like Dunkirk, and a fast-sinking hulk like Jamaica? But these voices were not strongly raised, for the gentlemen of the Privy Council, though now perforce suffering merchants as their colleagues in committee, were not prepared to take their lead in policy. Moreover, men who came to affairs of State fresh from the Committee of Plantations, where so much evidence of Spanish arrogance in America came before them, inclined in consequence to the firm view that Spain was the natural enemy of the expansive aspirations of England. They therefore held out stoutly against Batteville's threats of extreme Spanish displeasure, and on 9 May 1661 agreement on the terms of alliance with Portugal was reached in Council. After both Houses of Parliament had approved it, the marriage articles between the King of England and Catharine of Braganza were signed in June. It was fitting that, amid these ceremonies, Charles did not omit to write to his good friend Philip IV of Spain how averse he was from the whole project.[2]

[1] Clarendon, op. cit. i. 151–2 et seq.; ii. 183: 'Whosoever is against the match with Portugal is for the delivery of Dunkirk and Jamaica'; and *Parl. Hist.* iv. 182 et seq. [2] *VE*, 3 June 1661, Cal. S.P. Ven., 1659–61, 383.

Batteville thereupon withdrew to his tent, deaf to all overtures from the mercantile interest, chiefly the traders to 'Old
Spain', who feared that this time the politicians had gone too
far. His anger also alarmed Charles's Ministers; but their alarm
was nothing to the 'great passion'[1] news of the match aroused
in Madrid. Yet Spanish pride had to swallow the insult; with
the policy of France towards her undefined but ominous, Spain
could afford an open breach with England no more than
England could with Spain. Batteville was accordingly instructed
not to leave England, as he desired, 'as it behoves this government to adapt its policy to its strength'. His temper continued
to deteriorate, involving him in December in a first-class row
over precedence with the French Ambassador in London, and
losing him thereby any influence that remained to him. A
certain element of the ridiculous seemed fated to contaminate
this matter of high policy. English merchants, for example, were
on tenterhooks lest the powerful fleet that had sailed in the
summer to collect the Portuguese bride would put Anglo-
Spanish relations to the touch, and waylay the Spanish plate-
fleet homeward bound from the Indies: and their sigh of relief
when this did not happen was as strongly echoed by the
Ministers of Spain.[2]

In one sense England and Spain shared the same dilemma.
Neither had the resources necessary to play off one Power against
another with complete success. Restoration England enjoyed
neither moral nor financial security. If, therefore, the history
of her policy is mainly a record of scrambling from one camp
to another, of exchanging some positions built on sand for
others of the same, the cause is not hard to discover, nor particularly difficult to excuse. Her many domestic preoccupations
did not even allow England time to assess the situation in
Europe with a clear eye. In 1660 it was nearly twenty years
since France had first taken the military measure of Spain at
Rocroi; and but one since she had humbled that great Empire
at the Peace of the Pyrenees. But a belief in the strength of
Spain was to prove one of the most prolonged of European
superstitions, and England was slow to comprehend that the
Bourbon might prove at the last a greater rival to her interests

---

[1] VS, 15 June 1661, Cal. S.P. Ven., 1659-61, 386.
[2] VE, 22 June 1661, Cal. S.P. Ven., 1661-4, 20.

than the Habsburg, the traditional enemy. Certainly in the early 1660's the temper of Louis XIV was not yet the barometer of Europe. But the wealth and grandeur of his France were tangibles for which England, from the first, had a marked respect. The French Monarchy was a success because the King of France had money. To King Charles, not a moral man, the moral of this lesson was plain. Though it galled national pride and irritated Charles himself, it was a fact none the less that England was unable to implement the terms of her brand-new alliance with Portugal, could not equip the necessary frigates nor muster the stipulated number of troops, without recourse to a loan from France. Only two years elapsed before profitless < Dunkirk, so staunchly refused to Spain, was sold by King Charles for cash down—and not to King Philip, its rightful owner, but to King Louis.[1] Since the King of England had an empty Treasury himself, his own well-being and the security of his country demanded that he should keep in close contact with the one man in Europe who owned a full one. But as Louis was not disposed at this stage to be Charles's paymaster, England had to temporize with Spain on the one hand and set out deliberately to provoke the rich merchants of Amsterdam on the other, just because she was uncertain of the intentions of the French Crown. If profit had to be made in a hurry on a national scale, it could be made only from Holland. It could not be made from Spain. 'Beyond the Line',[2] (behind God's back) some small change might be picked up, and the old goal of open trade to the ports of the Indies should certainly be pursued—but beyond that, caution was the English watch-word. For England to pursue a forward policy, assured and independent, in either hemisphere, was to deal in luxuries she could not afford.

It was well known in England 'with what jealousie and offence'[3] the Spaniards watched the settlement of Jamaica following on its unlawful seizure. English statesmen therefore were at one in deprecating the rash provocations which English-

[1] This despite Parliament's bill to annex not only Dunkirk but also Jamaica to the Crown.

[2] i.e. west of the longitude of the Azores, south of the Tropic of Cancer: 'les lignes de l'enclos des amitiés.'

[3] The King to Lyttelton, 28 Apr. 1663, CO 1/17, No. 23.

men in the Indies seemed only too ready to give in their dealings with their Spanish neighbour. In England, Spain was still accepted at her own well-publicized valuation; for although in private council the Court of Spain might chafe in the awareness of its own weakness, abroad it continued to carry matters off with all the traditional high pride of the grandee. She could afford no other course, knowing well that once the world realized that Spain 'was indeed in a state to receive and not to inflict injuries',[1] she was lost indeed. But the English in America came earlier to a better appreciation of the Spanish dilemma than did their kin at home. (A superstition is stated not to be able to cross running water; the fate of this one seems to prove the saying true.) Cromwell's famous 'Western Design' had been Elizabethan in conception if not in execution, and for long something at least of the spirit of that age, its colour and its confidence, seems to attend the activities of Englishmen in the West Indies. In a memorandum written probably in 1660, setting out 'some reasons to justifye the first designe in the West Indies', appears a terse and ringing dismissal of all Spanish pretension there, to wit: 'The popes Donation is of little validitie for hee hath given to the Spaniard the Crowne of England, which hee may more legally doe than give him the Indies, the English having been subject to his power, the Americas never'[2] —before it goes on to urge the King to redeem the dishonour of the first 'Western Design' by carrying it to a successful conclusion. Jamaica was one of the most vital colonial issues of the day; and no one could consider Jamaica for a moment without remembering its Spanish past or fearing that it might possibly have a Spanish future. The island was easy of Spanish access, lying as it did in the very mouth of all the Spanish dominions in America. (The same was said of Bermuda.) Its position made it 'the navel of the West Indies' and 'a window on the power of Spain'. It was possible to see it both as a bastion of the existing English empire in America, and as an advanced post from which sorties might easily be made upon lands thought to be but slackly held by indolent governments. If it were well reinforced by the English Government, Jamaica would become

---

[1] *VS*, 10 May 1662, Cal. S.P. Ven., 1661-4, 181.
[2] 'Consideracons relating to the English affaires in America', Egerton MS. 2395, f. 614.

not only strong enough to withstand the greatest conjunctions the
Spanyard cann be able to make either out of Europe or America,
but will render him less potent in his own dominions, and make it
hard if not impossible for him to withhold us from tradeing with his
subjects there, and make it easy for us either to invade his townes or
interrupt his trade.

This sort of language filled the petitions that were presented
to the King on his return to England in 1660. To give up
Jamaica for any pretended reason of state, for any narrow
consideration of European affairs alone, would be folly—however much Spain was willing to pay. 'It would be much more
honourable', says one such petition, using the word loosely, 'to
preserve it, for a better opportunitie of making peace or inforc-
ing warre.'[1] The story that Charles was preparing to barter all
his Caribbean possessions for a Spanish alliance was widely
believed, and its currency accounts for the unusual vehemence
of many of these petitions. Prior to the Restoration itself the
Presbyterian merchant Thomas Middleton had made it his
business to spread the tale in London that the arrangement
made in 1656 between Charles and Philip IV included the
handing-over of Barbados and the other West Indies to Spanish
rule, and that the Duke of York in command of a Dutch fleet
was about to set out on this commission, calling at Spanish
ports for a reinforcement of 5,000 troops.[2] By the summer of
1660 this story, which was not entirely far-fetched, had spread
rapidly throughout the West Indies and had half-convinced
General D'Oyley for one. It was scotched only by the royal
Proclamation of September, and by the vote of the Commons
that month that Jamaica and Dunkirk should be declared
annexed to the English Crown. It was well known, however,
that Spanish money continued to find ready takers in London.
Batteville wrathfully reported in February 1661 that the venality
of Ministers of State had reached such an insufferable pitch that
they were barefacedly demanding money to sell their votes and
support the restitution of the two Cromwellian conquests. It
was because the lure of Spanish gold so powerfully attracted the
politicians that the merchants and planters continually pressed
Charles to stake out a definite area in Jamaica as a royal

[1] 10 June 1661, Egerton MS. 2395, ff. 241, 301.
[2] Middleton to Governor Daniel Searle (Barbados), 26 Mar. 1660, CO 31/1, 1–2.

demesne, thus committing the Crown to the maintenance of
the Island. Certainly the sale of Dunkirk (despite the King's
repeated denials that this would never happen) dismayed both
the colonizers and the promoters of colonization in Jamaica.
Thereafter any alarm at home raised the spectre in the Indies;
as late as 1679 Jamaicans could thrill to the rumour that a
measure of Danby's iniquity was his desire to sell the Island to
Spain.[1]

For the moment, however, the September proclamation
calmed these fears. In February 1661 D'Oyley was recom-
missioned as Royal Governor in Jamaica, but he received no
orders from home how he should comport himself towards
Spain. Only from Bennet, who as Minister in Madrid was working hard and successfully to gain himself a reputation for states-
manship, did he receive notification of the Spanish declaration
of a cessation of arms, together with the injunction that he
should publish this in Jamaica.[2] D'Oyley complied; but a month
later he had come to the conclusion, which he announced to
an approving Council-of-war, that the peace 'did not concern
this side of the Line', and proceeded to issue commissions of war
against Spanish shipping in the Indies. That was the best way,
obviously, to 'indeavour a trade' with the Spaniards. No one
gainsaid him. Spain had always refused to recognize the English
possessions in the Indies, and even the presence there of Englishmen. How then could her Ambassador logically complain of
depredations there, carried out presumably by phantoms?
Confronted with such an argument, it is small wonder that the
choleric Batteville was remarked to be 'very high'.[3]

The point raised was a nice one indeed. Spain's devotion to
a legal fiction was to cost her dear. It allowed England to pro-
fess friendship for Spain in Europe while disavowing responsibility for the hostility her subjects showed towards the Spaniards
in America. From the English point of view, although there was
always a danger that Spain might be goaded to retaliatory
action in American waters, this was a sound policy. No Englishman saw anything amiss with it. Sir Richard Fanshawe, who if
not a competent diplomat was certainly a scrupulous and high-

[1] Cf. CO 138/1, 112.
[2] Minutes of the Council of Jamaica, 5 Feb. 1661, CO 1/15, No. 37.
[3] Anthony Isaacson to the Earl of Winchilsea, 8 July 1661, HMC Finch, i. 135.

minded man, could write in these terms to Clarendon without a qualm of conscience: 'I know many wise men think it would be better for our King to await the death of the King of Spain, and then do what we like in the West Indies while the Spaniards are at broils amongst themselves.'[1]

And for once Fanshawe's diagnosis was not mistaken. There were indeed many of these 'wise men' to be found in the highest places at the English Court and in the Privy Council; nor were there lacking men who thought along these lines in the innermost counsels of the King of France.

Fanshawe wrote these words from Lisbon, where he was then Minister, in the autumn of 1662.[2] The year had seen a hardening of the English attitude towards Spain in America. In March the Committee of Jamaica, working with the Council of Plantations, finally finished drafting the official Instructions for Lord Windsor. Their ambiguous language has already been noted. The Governor of Jamaica was to foster good commercial relations with the Spanish colonies; but at the same time he was to press on with the work of fortification, and to ensure that new plantations were laid out contiguously along the coasts, the better to co-ordinate the Island's defence. At all times he was to 'keepe a very circumspect eye' on the Spaniards, 'in case matters should not go well 'twixt us and Spain'.

Matters did not go well; the scale tipped; and on 8 April Windsor, about to leave England, received an additional instruction.[3] He was still to try to arrange a peaceful commerce with the Spanish colonies: but, if the Spanish Governors would not countenance this, then he must take steps to 'settle such Trade by force, and by doing such Acts as the Councell [of Jamaica] shall judge most propper to obleige the Spaniards to

---

[1] Fanshawe to Clarendon, 21/31 Oct. 1662, HMC Heathcote, 39. Clarendon is certainly 'the very great Councellor in England' who agreed with this view referred to in Fanshawe's letter to Bennet, 13/23 July 1664, SP 94/46, 129–30.

[2] He was under instruction to find out details of the Portuguese administration in Brazil, how they ordered the raising and distribution of sugar, how much was annually imported, and what duties it paid. He was to 'make himself marvellously learned' in all these matters so that a calculation might be made whether it was possible for England to engross the Portuguese sugar-trade, by acting as Portugal's carriers and distributors in place of the Dutch. Cf. The King to Fanshawe, 23 Aug. 1661, HMC Heathcote, 19; Clarendon to Fanshawe, 6 Dec. 1661, ibid. 23–24.

[3] CO 389/5, 57–58. The Court of Spain was anyway greatly alarmed at the number of frigates—four, rumoured in Madrid to be fourteen—that were detailed to accompany Windsor to Jamaica; VS, 21 June 1662, Cal. S.P. Ven., 1661–4, 203.

admitt them to a free trade'. On his arrival at Barbados in
July, Windsor roundly declared that it was not only probable
'but by intelligence known' that the Spaniards had a design
on foot for a descent upon and the recapture of Jamaica.[1] He
dispatched the *Griffin* frigate from his fleet to inquire of the
Governors of Porto Rico and Santo Domingo how far they
would co-operate in encouraging an Anglo-Spanish trade in
the Indies, which he was pledged to obtain. But to ask for freedom of trade in these waters was still to demand the other eye
of the Spanish King. The Governors could only return one short
and dignified refusal, which arrived at Jamaica simultaneously
with Windsor and his entourage. The Council which he quickly
appointed was therefore decidedly eager to implement the trade
'by force'.[2]

Thus in September Jamaica was a scene of brisk action.
Expeditions were busily equipping, with designs on St. Jago
de Cuba, on the Moskito Coast, and on Campeachy. A plan
to reduce the pirate haunt of Tortuga to the obedience of the
Governor of Jamaica, for which royal authority had been given
in February, was speedily pressed forward. The manning of
these projects helped to remove the soldiers' disgruntlement at
General D'Oyley's removal, and to put point and purpose into
the life of the Island at a critical moment. Captain Christopher
Myngs in His Majesty's frigate *Centurion*, commanding a fleet
of 11 ships and a force of about 1,300 men, set sail for St. Jago
de Cuba on 21 September, returning a month later with considerable booty, a rousing tale of success, and encouraging
evidence of Spanish decay.[3]

Although Windsor himself quitted Jamaica for good on 28
October, the commissions he had issued to the private men-of-
war ensured that the policy of singeing the King of Spain's
beard in the Caribbean went on. But there were no more
spectacular victories. The privateers perforce took to casual
roving, and the rovers took to alliance with the French buccaneers of Tortuga and Hispaniola. On 12 January 1663 *Centurion* sailed in command of another fleet of privateers to Cam-

---

[1] 'Declaration of Lord Windsor, Governor of Jamaica, at Barbados', 11 July
1662, CO 1/16, No. 73.

[2] Minutes of the Council of Jamaica, 29 Aug. 1662, CO 139/1, 17.

[3] Cf. C. H. Firth, 'The Capture of St. Jago de Cuba', *English Historical Review*,
xiv. 536-40.

peachy. There Englishmen first introduced themselves to the cutting of logwood and penetrated the thick jungle hinterland of the coasts. But there was no profit to be got, nothing but blows; the Spaniards had had wind of their coming, and awaited them with a strong force. And the privateer fleet was absent until April, to the great unease of Lyttelton and the Jamaicans. Captain Abraham Langford failed miserably in a private design against Tortuga, and the men he had mustered scattered thereafter on their own business. In June Captain Sherdick and another fleet went off to take St. Thomas in the Virgin Islands. They were successful in this, but they did not choose to return to their base until March 1664, profitably employing the intervening months in piracy. Views on the usefulness of the privateer's trade, both in Jamaica and in England, began to change. It was one thing to distract an unruly soldiery with warlike exploits, but it was quite another to denude a struggling colony of its strongest right arms at a time when it was their work alone that could make its future secure. In 1663 it was calculated that Port Royal and Tortuga could between them raise and equip 15 private men-of-war and nearly 1,500 men to crew them, 'desperate people, the greater part having been in men-of-war these twenty years'.[1] Every proposition put forward by both merchants and planters for the attention of their colleagues on the Council of Plantations insisted that if privateering continued as the staple industry of Jamaica, it could not fail to ruin and depopulate the Island before very long. The traders to 'Old Spain', and the English merchants in Cadiz and Seville, testified that England's commerce and reputation were being greatly damaged by these wild activities in the West Indies.[2] And when the reports that both D'Oyley and Lyttelton presented to Clarendon that year urged that no further encouragement should be given to the privateers, the English Administration very sensibly decided that there must be no further private expeditions on the lines of that to St. Jago de Cuba.

There was another reason for this decision. On 10 January 1663 the 'Royal Company of Adventurers Trading into Africa' was constituted in England, with a list of stockholders that included every major figure in the Court and in the Administra-

[1] There is a list of these ships and their captains in CO 1/17, No. 112.
[2] Cf. Williamson to Fanshawe, 14 May 1663, HMC Heathcote, 88.

tion, as well as every moneyed man in London and Bristol.[1] Spain, the only colonizing country that had no *point d'appui* anywhere on the West African coast, could not supply her own plantations with negroes, and so must turn to a middleman who could.[2] In March 1662 Modyford had urged the King to grant a licence to Spaniards to trade for slaves at Barbados and Jamaica; for experience showed that illicit traders from Carthagena were prepared to pay up to 220 pieces of eight per negro head. Here was a strong argument for making a breach in the terms of the Navigation Act, and so in February 1663 the licence was granted: Spaniards might henceforth buy negroes at the 'Caribbees' and Jamaica, with 'such other European comodityes as their own plantacons may want'.[3] Now, this was a trade peculiarly ill-adapted to a prosecution by force; from this time forward, therefore, Whitehall was distracted by double vision when it looked upon the Spaniard in America. In one view, he was a good customer:[4] in the other, a rapacious miser ripe for pillage.

[1] For comprehensive lists, cf. CSPC 1661–8, 408; CSPC 1669–74, 934.

[2] 'More than any other one factor, the need for negroes eventually ended Spanish control of her own markets'; Elizabeth Donnan, *Documents illustrative of the History of the Slave Trade to America* (4 vols., Washington, 1930), i. 104.

[3] Modyford to Sir J. Modyford, Mar. 1662, CO 1/17, Nos. 7–9; the King to colonial Governors, 13 Mar. 1663, CO 389/4, 11.

[4] Considerations of space prevent a full examination of this traffic in slaves. In 1664 Sir Martin Noell arranged a contract with Domenico Grillo, Spain's Genoese *asientisto*, whereby the Royal Company of Adventurers undertook to supply him annually with 3,500 slaves for the Spanish plantations (SP 94/46, 3, 101; Donnan, op. cit. i. 108; Company Minutes, 20 June 1664, T 70/75, 16). Barbados was to be the base of this trade (T 70/75, 5); but the Company was unable to make good its contract, and the Spaniards thereafter dealt with the Dutch West-India Company at its base, Curaçao—'several thousand yearly, a vast trade', wrote Governor Byam of Antigua to Willoughby in 1670 (CO 1/38, No. 65). After the Madrid Treaty was signed (1670) Lynch hoped to make Jamaica the base of an Anglo-Spanish trade (Add. MS. 11410, f. 490; Egerton MS. 2395, f. 501), and the new (1672) Royal African Company sent agents to Seville in 1676 to make a fresh contract (T 70/77, 63b). But the Lords Committee of Trade considered that slaves were commodities within the meaning of the Acts of Trade, and therefore could not be imported into English colonies save in English ships (22 Jan. 1678, CO 391/2, 211). The Spanish Government had simultaneous misgivings: the *Consulado* of Seville would not permit Spaniards in the Indies to buy slaves from Englishmen (or Dutchmen) for fear that other goods would be traded too.

The traffic, however, continued spasmodically, and many Spanish ships called at Port Royal in the 1680's in the hope of picking up a slave cargo (Lynch to Lords Committee, 28 Feb. 1684, CO 138/4, 246). When Hender Molesworth took over the Government he asked for an official ruling on this trade. The Lords Committee, acting on the Customs Commissioners' advice, decided to permit it (the King to

It was the first image that now came sharply into focus. Charles II assured the Duke of Medina in April 1663 that he entirely disapproved of what had been done at St. Jago de Cuba. When news came in May of the Campeachy expedition, Charles was as quick to disavow that.[1] Medina did not believe him; but the fact that a new weapon had been forged against Spain in the Indies, which might easily be perfected and constantly employed, did not fail to make its impression at Madrid. When June brought a victory of Anglo-Portuguese arms over Spanish forces at Evora, Spain felt her position as precarious indeed. How much longer could she dissemble her weakness? The English had struck at her successfully from two sides, in the Indies and in Portugal, without any declaration of war,[2] but she could do nothing in her own defence. Medina himself inclined to the opinion that it would be better to allow 'the nations of the North, attracted by trade and intent on business', careless about the acquisition of territories so long as they might exploit their commerce, to trade freely in Spanish ports, whether in America or elsewhere. He again stressed the melancholy truth that it was pointless to betray resentment, as there was no means of exacting vengeance.[3]

This conciliatory attitude that Spain now adopted (together perhaps with the rumour that 200,000 Spanish crowns were ready to buy goodwill in London),[4] encouraged the English Administration to hope that times of profitable amity lay ahead. Orders to stop all further hostilities against Spanish possessions in the West Indies arrived in Jamaica in July 1663. The King wrote to Lyttelton that, while he approved the dash and efficiency of Myngs's expedition to Cuba, he felt nevertheless that no lasting benefits to his service had resulted from it. Designs of this type might gain some transitory success, but Jamaica would inevitably be weakened if its most able and vigorous inhabitants thus dissipated energy and resources that were better applied to the more humdrum, but in the long run

---

Molesworth, 30 Nov. 1684, CO 138/4, 278-9); and an Order-in-Council to that effect was issued on 29 Apr. 1685 (APCC ii. 81).

[1] *VS*, 28 Apr. 1663, 30 May 1663, Cal. S.P. Ven., 1661-4, 317, 327.

[2] Venetian envoy in France [hereafter *VF*], 24 July 1663, Cal. S.P. Ven., 1661-4, 338.

[3] *VS*, 30 May 1663, ibid. 327, 381.

[4] *VF*, 6 June 1663, ibid. 328; 3 July 1663, ibid. 331.

more profitable, ventures of planting, settling, and cultivation.[1]

Yet even now the Administration did not definitely commit itself to a prohibition of privateering. The argument, hollow though it eventually rang, that the privateers' force was the only sure means of defence the Island possessed, could not at this time be rejected. William Coventry wrote to Lyttelton privately that he might continue to employ the privateers; and so the Deputy-Governor (who had intended to call them in though doubting his capacity to do so) left them out,[2] it appears in some natural bewilderment. The King himself was a little more definite, though not much. He pointed out that he had no objection to the employment of naval frigates or private men-of-war, provided always that the profit and prize resulting from their activities were legally declared in the Admiralty Court, where the royal dues of tenths and fifteenths might be properly assessed. His proviso was, that such ships should not be permitted to recruit their crews from among the soldiers and other inhabitants of Jamaica. (Where else His Majesty expected these ships to recruit themselves can only be surmised.) Thus it is not surprising that Jamaicans in general had no idea whether privateering was officially prohibited or not, and not unnatural that they inclined to enjoy the benefit of their own doubts.[3] Spanish prize therefore continued to be made welcome in Port Royal, and Lyttelton continued to report the consequent Spanish reprisals at sea as 'insolencies', and to record Jamaica's righteous indignation at such disgraceful conduct.

Nevertheless, Medina's belief that England preferred trade to war was correct, so far as it went. She had now displayed her strength in the West Indies, and frightened the Spaniards. Now she was prepared to meet conciliation half-way. Peaceful methods had obtained great commercial advantage for England from the Portuguese in the East Indies: why should not similar means bring about a like result from the Spaniards in the West?[4]

[1] The King to Lyttelton, 28 Apr. 1663, CO 389/4, 13–14.
[2] Lyttelton to Bennet, 18 Oct. 1663, CO 1/17, No. 80.
[3] Extract of a letter from Jamaica: 'Nor is it well understood whether His Majesty's order applies to commanding under Lord Windsor's commissions, or prohibiting only wild excursions by the inhabitants, for since then a letter from Mr. Wm. Coventry enjoins the Gov. to take care of HRH's dues from the men-of-war'; CSPC 1661–8, 811.   [4] VS, 2 Apr. 1664, Cal. S.P. Ven., 1664–6, 6.

Accordingly, the instructions issued to the new Governor of
Jamaica, Sir Thomas Modyford,[1] enjoined him to restrain all
English subjects from molesting the property or invading the
territories of His Catholic Majesty in America, and to prohibit
the further issue of letters of marque.[2] All Spaniards were to be
treated by the English as friends and allies. Prize was not to be
made of Spanish ships and goods by colour of any commission
that privateers might still have under the signature of previous
Governors. One of Modyford's first acts was therefore to send
from Barbados an embassy to the Governor of Santo Domingo,
informing him of this new outburst of friendship: the embassy
was led by two Quaker gentlemen to make it more convincing.
They were instructed to treat 'very warily'[3] for a trade, especially in negroes. The Spanish Governor was reserved about this,
as well he might be, and would give only a formal permission
for English ships to water and careen in case of necessity in
Spanish ports; this, of course, was all he could lawfully do. The
point of trade was not touched on. As Colonel Thomas Lynch
wrote to Bennet (now Secretary of State in Nicholas's place,
rising high in Court favour and taking his pro-Spanish policy
up with him) there had been 'too many mutual barbarisms'
between the two nations in the Indies for friendship suddenly
to flourish merely on orders from London and Madrid.[4] The
sudden English enthusiasm for it was too patently suspect, as
its consummation could only bring all the profit to the Englishman and give nothing at all to the Spaniard. Jamaica did not
attract Spanish merchants, even if there were any bold enough
to venture their ships anywhere near Port Royal. There were
no negroes there, nor even an agent of the Royal Company.
Spain's Genoese contractors, the Grillos, had made the Dutch
island of Curaçao their 'factory' for the distribution of slaves to
the Spanish Indies. In these circumstances, clearly Spain had
no reason to seek a trade with the English. There was nothing to
be gained by it; on the contrary, a great deal might be lost.

[1] The Spaniards, watching Modyford's busy recruitment of men in Barbados,
wondered whether these were going to Jamaica as planters or as privateers; *VF*,
noting news from England, 6/16 June 1664, ibid. 39.

[2] The King to Modyford, 15 June 1664, CO 1/18, No. 73.

[3] Modyford to Governor of Santo Domingo, 10 May 1664; and Commission to
Cary and Perrott, in CSPC 1661-8, 739, i, ii.

[4] Lynch to Bennet, 25 May 1664, CO 1/18, No. 68.

The sanction to Windsor to pursue a trade by force was not so easily forgotten either by Englishman or by Spaniard in the West Indies.

It was early evident, moreover, that the problem of the privateer was not to be settled by a mere stroke of the administrative pen prohibiting his existence, or by any firm words in the Commission of a Governor of Jamaica. As Lynch pointed out, 1,500 independent seafarers perforce suddenly grounded on Jamaica would prove as great a menace to the English settlers there as ever they had been to Spanish ships at sea. Only a strong force of frigates could make them come in if they did not feel so inclined. Nor had the English any reputation to gain by meticulous conduct in this matter; for the Spaniards called every rover an Englishman whether he was one or not. A privateer who was denied an English commission would have no qualms about taking a French one. In June 1664 Colonel Edward Morgan warned Bennet that the suppression of privateering would inevitably bring about an increase of indiscriminate piracy.[1] Now the Colonel was impressionable, for his new chief was already, after only four weeks' acquaintance, 'our incomparable Governor'—so the voice was probably Jacob's. For Modyford early impressed this same argument on the Government at home.

He insisted on the distinction the seafarers themselves made, that privateering was a respectable occupation and that piracy was not. The privateer patrolled the seas by virtue of a lawful commission,[2] which was his hire and his salary too—for he met his own expenses on the system of 'no purchase, no pay'. A rough diamond, perhaps, but by no means an outlaw; certainly a man trained in a skill and bred to a trade that could do the King great service. For to whom else in the Indies could planters, settlers, and honest traders look for their defence? Militia and muster was all very well, but in truth the front line of Jamaica lay under the guns of Carthagena and over where the wind whipped the cliffs of Hispaniola. The privateer was the shield of Jamaica; as for his employment as such, did not Sir Thomas's Commission as Governor empower him 'on extra-

---

[1] E. Morgan to Bennet, 28 June 1664, CO 1/18, No. 82.

[2] Worth £20 to the Governor who issued it—according to Charles Modyford, testifying on his father's behalf in 1671; CO 140/1, 226.

ordinary cases, by the Council's advice, to use extraordinary remedies'?

From the outset, Modyford assumed that the normal political climate of Jamaica was a state of emergency. It was his watchword therefore to act to the letter of the comfortably loose 'discretionary clause'. He arrived on the Island on 1 June 1664, and proclaimed the cessation of hostilities against Spain on 16 June. But he reported to Bennet on the last day of the month that in the matter of revoking the commissions of the privateers, he now considered it more prudent to do by degrees what he had originally intended to do outright. He hoped that he would be excused this 'somewhat dispensing' of the strictness of his instructions on the point, which bade him subject all that fraternity to condign punishment.[1] He assured Bennet that it was not for the privateers' own sake that he took this step, reminding him of the abhorrence of privateers he had so often expressed when in Barbados. It was therefore with considerable gratification that he received Bennet's permission in November to employ this 'gentle usage'.[2]

Although Bennet was never at home with West-India affairs —disliking their anti-Spanish content—he could not just then ignore them.[3] de Tracy had now gone as *Surintendant* to Martinique, and the shadow of Colbert daily grew longer in the Caribbean. Moreover, the Dutch—already marked down in Court policy as the enemy—were still everywhere to be found, and everywhere in the way; battening on the negro trade in Guinea and in the West Indies, accepted as a valuable middleman by English and Spanish colonists alike. Modyford early worked out a plan for the extirpation of the Dutch strongpoints, which Bennet was glad enough to endorse as 'the best in those parts'.[4] Following this lead, the Jamaica Committee urged that the privateers should be diverted from their pursuit of the Spaniards to the hunting of the Dutchmen.[5] They also thought up an odd solution to the problem of the privateers' future:

[1] Modyford to Bennet, 30 June 1664, CO 1/18, No. 83.
[2] Bennet to Modyford, 12 Nov. 1664, CO 1/18, No. 113.
[3] A plan by Abraham Langford to seize Curaçao was already in Bennet's file; cf. CO 1/19, No. 25. The King later asked Modyford's opinion on it, ibid. No. 26.
[4] Modyford's 'Proposition', ibid., No. 29; and 'Propositions of Mr. Kendal concerning the Calling-in the Privateers of Jamaica', Nov. 1664, CO 1/18, No. 137.
[5] Jamaica Committee to the King, 7 Nov. 1664, ibid. No. 133.

once the Dutch had been successfully routed in the Caribbean, the rovers should return to serve the King in home waters. The Duke of York was asked to put this view to Modyford, which he did with apparent conviction,[1] the more willingly as the English navy was then desperately short of men;[2] but there is no record of any Caribbean privateer forsaking his natural environment for the doubtful privilege of joining His Majesty's Navy and serving in a highly dangerous war wherein there was likely to be neither 'purchase' nor pay.

While the new Governor of Jamaica was making a genuine effort to distract privateers from harrying Spanish shipping, the politicians in London and Madrid continued to debate the advantages or otherwise of promoting Anglo-Spanish trade in the West Indies. The merchants of Seville and the *Casa de Contratación*, of course, urged that the traditional Spanish exclusionism must stand. Both the Council of the Indies and the Holy Inquisition were horrified at the idea of permitting any sort of traffic with the English in those seas, the former because of its commerce, the latter because of its faith—for the Church was not disposed to forget that all *corsarios* were by tradition *luteranos*. The Court at Madrid had a divided mind on the matter. Medina was still a stronger influence on policy than the stubborn Penaranda, and he had long believed that some measure of appeasement was necessary. Was it not better 'to agree decorously to what they could not persist in refusing'?[3] The Caribbean could only be cleared and regulated by strong naval forces. These Spain simply did not possess, nor had she the financial resources to obtain them. The sea-Powers dominated the Caribbean, no matter what the law said, and therefore, as a matter of common sense, must be placated. But although Medina had power to make himself heard, he could not surmount the inertia around him; for the Court of Spain, as Clarendon tells us, was 'irresolute and perplexed in their own affairs, as the counsels of Madrid were in the last years of the King'.[4]

[1] York to Modyford, 17 Nov. 1664, Adm 2/1745. York did not, however, think it fit to write to the privateers themselves, 'for they are of all men the most libertine & dissolute, and may make ill use of a letter from the Duke, challenging it as a right to have commands in the Kings shipps, tho' the least fit for it'.
[2] Cf. Tedder, op. cit. 109.
[3] *VS*, 26 Nov. 1664, Cal. S.P. Ven., 1664–6, 92.
[4] Clarendon, op. cit. ii. 761.

So there was no decision. But delay came naturally to Spanish diplomats, and Medina, although dealing almost daily with Fanshawe, allowed no hint of his own feelings in the matter to colour the formal tone of the transactions—or, if he did, the Englishman did not perceive it.

Fanshawe's own Instructions were framed on an ambitious scale. After emphasizing the Spanish weakness in the Indies and the English strength there, he was to proceed to arrange a Treaty of peace and commerce. He was to obtain for England an open trade in the Indies, 'at least for a certain number of shipps',[1] as well as Spanish consent to the Royal Company's contract with the *asientistos*, to supply negroes for the Spanish plantations. For this, and for other services in Europe, England would pledge herself to aid Spain in counteracting the intrigues of Louis XIV. Medina adopted a position of dignified immobility. He stood by the old Anglo-Spanish Treaty of 1630, which stipulated a peace beyond the Line—and beyond that he would not go. This perplexed Fanshawe as a 'brick wall', but it did not seriously incommode Bennet, who in London was quite prepared to accept the argument of the Spanish agent, Moledi, that no Treaty existed that specifically governed the relations of England and Spain in the Americas. Moledi said that this meant that England had no legal right to be in the Indies at all. Bennet answered that it also meant that Spain had no legal basis for grievance.

It was a good answer. The Law of Nations was silent concerning the 'Line', and it was this silence that allowed England to seize the initiative, and to regulate her actions in America on the ground of expediency alone. Spain on her side had to adhere to the terms of a Treaty she knew to be outmoded, because she knew well that to open the door of commerce in the Indies would be to unlock the last treasury that remained to her. By the Treaty of Munster in 1648 she had accorded valuable recognition to Dutch traders in the West Indies, and to this Treaty England constantly made irritated reference; but in the Spanish view there was an obvious distinction to be made between England, a territorial power in America, and the United Provinces, whose empire was founded on the exploitation of the world's commerce. Fanshawe's terms were too extra-

[1] Instructions in SP 94/46, 129–30.

vagant: England would agree to formal peace in the Indies only
if Spain would allow her to trade there, and Spain must also
make a truce with England's ally Portugal. Spain was not yet
prepared to shop in that market; and nothing, as Fanshawe
himself realized, would induce her to do so but 'invincible
necessity, as the only jewell that can purchase peace there'.[1]
Spain's necessity, though severe, had not yet conquered her—
but time was on the English side.

It certainly seemed so in the spring and summer of 1664.
Spanish ships continued to be seized for English prize in the
Indies. Moledi in April presented a formidable list of demands
for restitution and reparation, asking also for the punishment of
the Governor of Jamaica who permitted such flagrant breaches
of the peace between the two nations.[2] His insistence that the
Treaty of 1630 had arranged for a peace on both sides of the
Line was in fact upheld by the Crown lawyer Dr. John Exton,
who ruled that some Spanish ships seized in Jamaica which
were now lying in the Thames were not lawful prize.[3] But
although the King made a favourable impression on Moledi
by instructing Modyford to suppress these depredations and
restore any goods already taken,[4] July saw the privateers still
busily about their business, and their profit accumulating in
Port Royal. Secretary Bennet was now reluctantly coming to
the conclusion that tolerance of privateering was after all a
strong card in his diplomatic hand,[5] and, supported for once by
Clarendon's firm antipathy to Spain, he preferred to 'lett things
passe quietly on' in the Indies until Fanshawe worked a miracle
in Madrid. The day was distant: Moledi in London and Medina
in Madrid grew steadily more bitter at the English dissembling.
Moledi, with scathing reference to Exton's judgement—of which
no more had been heard—demanded the apprehension of Sir
Charles Lyttelton when the latter returned from Jamaica in
August 1664:[6] but he was careful to do so not on the ground

[1] Fanshawe to Bennet, 23 Mar./2 Apr. 1664, SP 94/46, 7-8.
[2] Moledi to Bennet, 26 Apr. 1664, ibid. 36.
[3] Exton to Bennet, 15 June 1664, ibid. 90.
[4] Minutes of the Council of Jamaica, 19-22 Aug. 1664, CO 1/18, No. 73;
CO 140/1, 121-3.
[5] There are 'Reasons for continuing the private men-of-war in Jamaica', probably by Lyttelton, dated Aug. 1664, in SP 94/46, 224-7.
[6] Moledi to Bennet, 20 Aug. 1664, ibid. 196.

that Lyttelton had broken the articles of peace (which Spain could not afford to admit) but that he had disobeyed the Proclamation of the cessation of arms, to which both Governments had agreed.[1] Lyttelton avoided the charge by putting the responsibility for the recent actions of the privateers on the commissions and letters of marque that Lord Windsor before him had so readily issued, 'for which I assume he had Your Majestys order'.[2] Whether Lyttelton was as guileless as he made out, this defence could not be impugned. The English monarchy could hardly pretend to any strong moral standing here, and it did not. It was indeed this attitude of frank cynicism that appalled Spain more than anything else. Last of all the great European powers, she still retained a simple faith in the validity of diplomatic instruments and in the honour of a Crown. But Charles and Louis were both strangers to such a belief; and it was the eventual realization that this was so that helped bring Philip of Spain to his despairing end. It is therefore not surprising that Fanshawe's draft for a treaty found little favour with Medina, that Medina's arguments made little impression on Fanshawe, and that both Courts expressed impatience while the 'mutual barbarisms' continued in the Indies, poisoning any possibility of rapprochement.[3]

It was thus with enormous relief that Spain saw the sea-powers turn on one another, both in Europe and in the Indies—while France, perplexed, held the ring.[4] In January 1665 the Duke of York authorized all the English colonial Governors to grant letters of marque against Dutch shipping.[5] Good news for Spain: let Englishman broil with Dutchman, let de Ruyter sweep him from the Caribbean as Tromp had once swept him from the Channel. Inflated reports of de Ruyter's success in the Indies cheered Madrid immensely.[6] With further satisfaction she heard of a French fleet setting out, in April 1665, for West-India waters. Thus was the fire kindled in the house of

[1] Cf. Fanshawe to Bennet, 14/24 Sept. 1664, SP 94/47, 26.
[2] Lyttelton to Bennet, 23 Aug. 1664, SP 94/46, 203.
[3] Cf. Fanshawe to Bennet, 8/18 Nov. 1664, SP 94/47, 113; an account of the English raid on Santa Marta, ibid. 151; and 'A relacon from the Viceroy of New Spaine', recounting further English raids on Campeachy, SP 94/49, 133–5.
[4] Cf. VS, 28 Jan. 1665, Cal. S.P. Ven., 1664–6, 123.
[5] 9 Jan. 1665, CSPC 1661–8, 910.
[6] Letters from The Hague, 18 Dec. 1664, Cal. S.P. Ven., 1664–6, 107.

others, indeed.[1] Preoccupied with these formidable foes, England must stop her aggression in Spanish America and end her aid to Portugal. England would no longer be able to treat Spain with contempt, and to blackmail her with the threat of further privateering in the Indies.

In April the Count of Molina, Spain's first official Ambassador to England since the disgusted Batteville had quit in 1662, arrived in London. A special Committee of the Privy Council, consisting of four major figures of the Administration (Clarendon, York, Southampton, and Bennet, lately created Viscount Arlington) was convened to deal with him. As yet no one was in any hurry. Fanshawe's draft Treaty was under inspection, and generally disapproved of as being too full of half-measures. The English Government wished to await the outcome of the Dutch war before they came to any conclusive arrangement with Spain, and indeed that spring the war gave promise of being as beneficial to English interests in every respect as its propagandists had claimed. And of course the longer England was engaged in warfare, the better Spain was pleased. But the resounding success of the Anglo-Portuguese forces at Villa Viçosa on 18 June was at once a setback to Spanish confidence and an affront to Spanish pride; and while Molina was fencing amiably enough with the Committee in London, Medina was again taking a high tone with Fanshawe in Madrid, reverting in August to the old, full claim for Tangier[2] and Jamaica—the latter place being still, as Fanshawe reported, 'situated in the Apple of their Eye'. It was clear they would never concede open trade to England in the Indies 'unless the skye falls'.[3] In September, however, all was changed: Philip IV died, leaving his Court split into faction, leaving his inheritance to a sick infant, and leaving to the Powers of Europe that celebrated problem of the Spanish Succession which was to poison all their diplomacy for the next fifty years.

It was a moment for decision. England knew that France's hostility to her was growing. In November the committee of Privy Councillors began to put pressure on Molina, using Fanshawe's draft treaty as a basis for further negotiation. New

---

[1] The expression of the Venetian envoy in France; 31 July 1665, Cal. S.P. Ven., 1664-6, 228.

[2] Tangier was Portuguese property, but Spain regarded Portugal as a vassal.

[3] Fanshawe to Arlington, 2/12 Aug. 1665, SP 94/49, 57.

articles included an English pledge to induce Portugal to make peace with Spain, an undertaking by Spain to yield her claims to Tangier and Jamaica, and a joint decision to make a mutual offensive and defensive alliance. On the commercial articles, however, the deadlock would not break. It was then arranged that the Earl of Sandwich (just then something of an embarrassment in Government circles) should go to Madrid with the English proposals for commercial amity, and there, in conjunction with Fanshawe, negotiate further with the Spanish Court. Arlington wrote at length to Fanshawe explaining all this, and asking him to prepare the ground with Medina. The letter was mislaid, and never arrived at its destination.[1]

This was singularly unfortunate, for Fanshawe, aware that the death of Philip IV had shattered all Spanish confidence, had resolved to make the sky fall that year. If Anglo-Spanish deadlock was ever to be broken, surely it was now. So he pressed on and came to terms with Medina, reviving the Treaty of 1630 and adding new clauses that involved Spanish recognition of the English position in the Indies, privileges of trade such as Spain had already granted to the Dutch in the Indies by the Treaty of Munster, and the adjustment of a 30-years, truce with Portugal. He signed this instrument on 7/17 December 1665, and sent it home. It was its timing rather than its terms that dismayed his Government; the latter were indeed later made the basis for the Treaty made at Madrid in 1667, which drew general approval. At this moment, however, England had not decided to abandon the goal of an open trade in the Indies, nor that of a full peace between Spain and Portugal. Fanshawe's treaty was not ratified; and the Earl of Sandwich, originally designed to assist Fanshawe, went out to Madrid with Sir Richard's revocation and broke the good man's heart.

In the meantime war in the Caribbean had naturally revived the privateers and made them respectable servants of their country. No ships could be spared from home waters, where the English navy was locked that summer in battle with the most formidable naval force in Europe; so Modyford had turned, as he had always known he must turn in emergency, to use the only instrument that lay ready to his hand. Now at last had

---

[1] On this, cf. H. C. Fanshawe, *Memoirs of Ann Lady Fanshawe* (London, 1907), appendix ii.

come those 'great occasions' for which the privateers had always seemed to him to be designed. Now he could safely 'change his copy',[1] cease to hang useful seamen as pirates, give them letters of marque, make them privateers, and send them out on the King's business. The scheme he drafted followed the lines of that already endorsed by Arlington. In April 1665 he sent ten ships and 600 men to fall on the Dutch islands of Saba, Statia, and, if possible, upon Curaçao, the grand prize of all. All this, he was confident, would soon cause the very name of Dutchman to be forgotten in the Indies in a short space of time. And it would cost the King nothing, for everything was on the rate of 'no purchase, no pay'. Some of the privateers were no doubt reclaimable to the ways of humanity and order; but for the rest, Modyford argued, it were better for everyone's peace of mind that they be kept in full employment, cutting, thrusting, and looting for purely patriotic reasons.[2]

Spanish America could not hope to escape scalding while the Caribbean boiled. The privateers who had come in 'from Spanish quarters' Modyford had left unquestioned, in order to mount them without delay for the attack on the Dutch. Perhaps he had no need to question them, anyway. Certainly that year the privateers in Spanish quarters had hardly had an idle moment. In January they had made a sortie on Tabasco. In February they had made off with 50,000 pieces of eight from Santa Maria de la Victoria. They had plundered Truxillo. They had captured two rich ships off Campeachy, and ravaged the Moskito Coast. They had ventured as far south as Reseado in Guiana. And the story went that about all these exploits Modyford was not so blandly ignorant as he professed. For example, one raid on Cayou in Cuba had been particularly savage. The Governor of Havana reported that the town had been sacked, the churches despoiled, by a force of 700 men,

with the consent of the Governor of Jamaica, who would answer claims for restitution that he had no controul over pirats, but 'tis wel knowne that this is a simulation, for the prisoners doe al depose that the prizes are divided, and that they send to the Governor of Jamaica a share of them.

[1] Modyford to Arlington, 20 Feb. 1665, CO 1/19, No. 27.
[2] The King to Modyford, and Modyford to the King, both dated 16 Nov. 1665, CO 1/19, Nos. 126–7.

Rumour also said that Modyford's share of the proceeds of Mansfield's raid on Nicaragua was no less than 12,000 pieces of eight.[1]

Yet however obtained, and however distributed, Spanish gold was the making of Port Royal, filling it with hope and confidence as well as loot. Accordingly the privateer could not be drawn off his natural prey. He showed little enthusiasm for fighting the Dutch, once he had accepted the badge of patriotism his letter of marque gave him. The first expedition did take Saba and Statia, but it thereafter foundered on the rocks of private enterprise, and never got as far as Curaçao; although Jamaican rovers annoyed Lord Willoughby considerably by 'rambling' as far as Tobago, thus forestalling a force that he had sent to win that Dutch prize for Barbados.[2] For privateers had no zeal in the pursuit of Dutchmen, the commercial travellers of the Indies, who had always supplied them with their necessities and driven a fair trade. It was only from a Spanish foe, not from Frenchmen or Hollanders, that they could obtain sufficient 'purchase' to pay for their new sails and rigging.

Thus, not many ships of the original expedition chose to return to Jamaica. Captain Mansfield, who had a blood-feud with Spain, sailed south-west to capture Providence at the close of 1665,[3] and thereafter went downwind to the coast and sacked Granada. Jamaican privateers were soon back at Campeachy; riding off Havana as of old; making common cause once more with the French *frères de la coste* of Hispaniola.[4] The only inducement Modyford could hold out to them to return to Port Royal was to promise them letters of marque against the Spaniard, as Windsor had done before him. For this step he had his authority—an authority of connivance, if not of consent. Albemarle, in a letter of 30 May 1665, gave his cousin ✓ discretion to grant such commissions against the Spaniard 'if necessary'. This was (it appears) sent by a private channel: Sir

---

[1] Accounts of these affairs are in SP 94/49, 133 and SP 94/51, 80–82. The piece of eight was worth about four shillings and eightpence, in contemporary values.

[2] Willoughby had raised 6 ships and 350 men for this expedition; Willoughby to the King, 29 Jan. 1666, CO 1/20, Nos. 5–6.

[3] A narrative of this exploit is in CO 1/20, No. 21. Mansfield (Mansvelt) had a Portuguese commission—so he said.

[4] For these activities, cf. C. H. Haring, *The Buccaneers in the West Indies in the 17th Century* (London, 1911); Violet Barbour, 'Privateers and Pirates in the West Indies', *American Historical Review*, xvi. 529–66.

James Modyford forwarded it to his brother on 1 June. It did not reach Sir Thomas until the following March.[1] He used this 'discretion' immediately (although he afterwards laid emphasis on his long forbearance from doing so).[2] And the moment he did so, the initiative in Anglo-Spanish relations fell into his hands. There it was to remain for nearly five years.

The Governor of Jamaica became a man of international significance at a peculiarly awkward moment. In January 1666 Louis XIV had declared war on England. This he did reluctantly, as his previous commitment to aid Holland now impeded the design he had formulated against the Spanish Netherlands. The war in Europe was thus a half-hearted business, a mannered performance, all feint and manœuvre. In sharp contrast was the ferocity of the West-India campaign.[3] France attacked ruthlessly in the West Indies, and the English plantations in the Leeward Islands were her first victim; but it was by no means likely that they would be her last. Would France ally with Spain to drive the English out; or with England to break for ever the Spanish power in America? No one knew: but whatever the plans of Louis, from England's point of view it was clearly no moment to continue the quarrel with Spain. The French envoy D'Embrun was already winning dangerously golden opinions in Madrid. In August the Braganza's French bride arrived in Portugal. The time had again come for the employment of delicacy and diplomacy, the call was already out for the exercise of all Arlington's tact and skill. He squared himself to the problem, only too well aware that a gang of ruffians who had tasted blood in the Indies might at any moment nullify months of work and all his hopes for the future. He had broken Fanshawe for his haste and enthusiasm; but the privateers were out of his reach, and they were nothing if not hasty and enthusiastic. The dispatch of the strong naval squadron of Sir John Harman to the Indies in March 1667 however gave clear indication that England had stopped relying on the old argument

[1] Cf. Modyford to Albemarle, 1 Mar. 1666, CO 1/20, No. 24. Albemarle's own letter of 30 May 1665 does not appear to be in existence, which is not surprising, nor is it likely that a copy was made. Modyford later forwarded it (he says) to Arlington.

[2] Modyford to Arlington, 21 Aug. 1666, No. 134.

[3] VF, 15 June 1666. In particular in St. Christopher had 'a tragic scene of inhuman barbarity been disclosed'; Cal. S.P. Ven., 1666-8, 11.

that the privateers were the surest buckler for the defence of the Caribbean. It now became necessary for the English Government to disown that fraternity, and to stand publicly aghast at the scope and efficiency of its activity.

From May 1666 the Earl of Sandwich was in Madrid, hoping to attract a Spanish alliance by laying the blame for the sins of the past on the unbridled licence of the corsairs.[1] England saw that year out in a chastened mood. The war against the United Provinces, started amid such high hopes of quick profit, had proved bloody and costly. The French intercession at the side of Holland might yet be fatal. Plague in 1665 and fire in 1666 had quenched the original enthusiasm of mercantile London. English hopes of gaining access by aggression to the national wealth of the Dutch had now faded, and negotiations for peace were instituted by Charles II himself in October. Thus, as she watched English confidence wane and English difficulties increase, Spain felt she might now resort again to a high tone of offended rectitude. How, for example, did the Earl of Sandwich propose to explain or excuse the capture of Providence Island? How dared England ask for the friendship of Spain in Europe when she had so often proved herself the firm enemy of Spain in America?[2] Sandwich endeavoured to treat these questions as rhetorical (as indeed in one sense they were), but 'he was in playne terms . . . told that without the restoring [Tangier and Jamaica] and renouncing any friendshipp with Portugall, there would be noe progresse made in any Treaty'.[3]

To all his assurances that the rovers in the Indies were out of control, with the bit between their teeth, Medina made the strong reply that that state of affairs did not diminish the responsibility of the English Government, which had been only too ready to throw the reins on to the horse's back.

But time, once again, was on the side of the English in these negotiations. The European settlement of the Dutch war might be slow in coming, but at least it was in sight: King Louis was no more anxious for the continuance of useless hostilities than King Charles. Even the circumstance that the negotiations with

[1] VS, 3 Nov. 1666, ibid. 100.
[2] Cf. VF, 14 Dec. 1666, Cal. S.P. Ven., 1666-8, 120.
[3] Sandwich to the King, 14 Sept. 1666, SP 94/52, 37a.

Spain were being conducted in Madrid and not in London worked to England's advantage. If Sandwich was content for the moment to mark time, his hour would strike. Indeed, by March 1667 he was able to abandon the defensive.[1] He began to threaten darkly that once peace was assured in Europe the Spaniards would have both the French and the English to contend with in the Indies, conjoined to accomplish their destruction; and what chance would they have against that combined might, when all their boasted power in America could not even take the measure of a handful of ruffian buccaneers?[2]

It seemed no empty threat. That spring the King of France was plainly clearing decks for action—binding Portugal fast in a formal alliance at the end of March, while stimulating Holland and England to an amicable peace. By April his plans for war on Spain were fully matured, and to these the King of England had acquiesced. The royal cousins made a private agreement not to enter any alliance that was opposed to the interests of the other. Once he had promised to return English St. Christopher to English hands, together with the other captured Leeward Islands, in return for an English pledge to restore Acadia, Louis turned his back on the West Indies and their affairs. May saw him commence his celebrated 'journey' into the Spanish Netherlands, claimed in right of his Spanish wife: the opening move in the long political game that was to decide the fate of the succession to the Dominions of Spain. Now also Louis openly courted a firm alliance with England, offering generous terms that included assistance in attacking Spain in the Indies, and the division with England of the rich Dutch commerce in those seas. All this was tempting indeed. But Charles was embroiled more than ever that spring in domestic difficulty. He had to cope with an empty treasury, an angry Parliament, a national scandal, a naval fiasco, a witch-

---

[1] He was much irked by having to witness the rejoicing in Madrid in February over the news that Spanish troops had recaptured Providence Island the previous August, and had put all the English they found there to the sword—on the ironic ground that such Englishmen, trespassing on Spanish soil, could not be subjects of a friendly king, but pirates, who could claim no protection from any law; cf. Sandwich to Arlington, 28 Feb. 1667, in *Original Letters and Negotiations of Fanshawe, Sandwich, Sunderland, and Godolphin, with answers of Hyde, Arlington, Coventry, Williamson, etc., 1663–1678,* ed. T. Bebington (London, 1701), 9; and Sandwich to the King, 7 Apr. 1667. SP 94/52, 170.

[2] *VS,* 16 Feb. 1667, Cal. S.P. Ven., 1666–8, 146.

hunt, and a family row. He had necessarily to play a cautious role on the European stage. Moreover, in the bright glare that now beat upon the French Court it was sometimes impossible to see what Louis was doing. France's ambassador in London might use honeyed words, but France's ambassador in Lisbon was a dangerous nuisance, for he was stiffening the Portuguese against any implementation of that truce with Spain which was the one good thing Fanshawe had accomplished, and which Sandwich was instructed to pursue.

Still England's problem was nothing to Spain's, the sands of whose hour-glass now ran out. Spain agreed to sign the commercial treaty if a separate article was inserted that neither Power would aid the enemies of the other—and did so, on 3/13 May 1667, two months before general peace was concluded at Breda. England now got from Spain what the Dutch had got at Munster. Here was a wedge inserted that might yet prise open the jealously guarded door of the Spanish Indies; and although the treaty did not mention any English rights in America, both Sandwich and his Government had reason to be pleased with it.[1] Fanshawe's treaty had miscarried; but here was the fruit of his labours delivered at the proper time. Sandwich wrote home that it was for Arlington to decide how far it would be fitting and useful to inform the English in the West Indies of the spirit and letter of this new arrangement,[2] adding however his own opinion, that the depredations already connived at by the English Government there had reacted unfavourably to the honour of the nation. (Reports from Tangier that many good traders were now avoiding the Caribbean entirely helped convince him of this.)[3] With this Treaty signed, there was now no reason to continue the support of buccaneering as an integral part of England's foreign policy in that area. Since the Treaty of Munster the Dutch had received 'not one spoyle' from Spain in the Indies; why should not the new

[1] Cf. F. G. Davenport, *European Treaties bearing on the History of the United States* (Washington, 1929), ii. 94–109.

[2] The Venetian envoy in Madrid, reporting the conclusion of this Treaty, commented that 'the confirmation is to come from England and with it the opinion whether they should set a time limit for the Spaniards to recover Jamaica in return for a payment of 500,000 pieces'. Rumours of this apparently reached Jamaica, but whether they had any foundation I cannot say; 28 May 1667, Cal. S.P. Ven., 1666–8, 193.

[3] SP 94/51, 148.

Treaty of Madrid bring about as good a harmony between Englishman and Spaniard?[1]

But events in Europe continued to find only distorted reflections in the waters of the Caribbean. The year 1666, precursor in Europe to a general *détente* in the relations of all the combatant powers, had been one of mounting fury in the West Indies. There the French had a more forward policy than King Louis himself; there the English still believed themselves on a tide that would carry them to fortune. Jamaica, not beset by the French problem, pursued an undistracted enmity of Spain. It was on 22 February that Sir Thomas Modyford took his decision to grant letters of marque against the Spaniards. His Council needed no persuasion. To them it was the obvious step to take.[2] Spanish prize furnished Jamaica both with the means to buy many necessary commodities at easy rates, and with valuable cargoes of the commodities themselves. So rich a store of goods, so simply replenished, would continue to attract New England men there to barter their provisions, would swell the prosperity of Port Royal, and would bring to Jamaica further settlers from the Windward Islands. Tilting at the Spanish foe would so occupy the minds and time of the buccaneers from Hispaniola, Tortuga, the Bahamas, and the Caymans that there would no longer be any danger of their harassing Jamaica herself for want of steadier employment. And had not the exploits of these rovers against the Dutch, which the King himself had been kind enough to commend, proved conclusively that the best form of defence was attack? Only by using such measures, it was evident, could they ever force the Spaniards to a free trade, as 'all wayes of kindness' had produced 'nothing of good neighbourhood'. All Spanish Governors in the Indies held as dogma the opinion that the Englishman was an illegal intruder whom, in God's good time, Spanish arms would drive for ever from those seas. They did not seek to disguise this attitude. Everyone knew it. Was it reasonable, then, 'to lett them quietly grow upon us, untill they are able to doe it?' See how the rogues had taken advantage of the English preoccupation with the French in the Antilles to seize and hold Providence. What they had done there they would do again in Jamaica if a favourable day dawned.

---

[1] Sandwich to Arlington, 14/24 May 1667, Bebington, op. cit. 13.
[2] Minutes of the Council of Jamaica, 22 Feb. 1666, CO 140/1, 143-7.

It was indeed fortunate that d'Estrées's powerful French fleet was the enemy and not the friend of Spain—but for all Modyford and his Council knew, that attitude might change any day, and then the English in the Indies would need at the last all the courage and skill of those stout men-of-war that plied in their own colours on those seas.

It must bee force alone [Modyford insisted] that can cut in sunder that unneighbourly maxim of their government to deny all access of strangers: which if His Matie pleaseth to permit this small Collony to continue to use, will in a short time shew its effects, to his great Honour and the comfort of all his Subjects.[1]

None of these arguments could safely be dismissed as negligible that summer of 1666. The Spaniard had proved himself an able opponent in the game of diplomacy, skilled in the tactics of delay, always ready with the indignant counter-charge. But the Indies were his heel of Achilles; there he was exposed as both weak and wealthy, a juxtaposition of attributes that in an age of *Machtpolitik* bordered on the scandalous. It was chiefly in letters to his patron and kinsman, the Duke of Albemarle, that the Governor of Jamaica canvassed his point of view. Albemarle was Lord-General, and Jamaica was a frontier-post; so it was natural enough that it should be from Albemarle that Modyford received the precious permission to use his own judgement in regard to that purely military matter, the granting of commissions against Spain. Arlington, in contrast, kept his hands officially clean of this business. No letter signed for the King by his Principal Secretary of State ever instructed the royal Governor of Jamaica to wage war on a neighbour with whom England was at peace. Arlington, of course, knew well enough what was going on in the West Indies; for the shrewd Modyford, aware his policy did not lack critics at home, was careful for the sake of his own security to keep the Secretary informed, as in duty bound a colonial Governor must do.[2] It

---

[1] Modyford to Arlington, 21 Aug. 1664, CO 1/20, No. 134.

[2] Arlington did not often answer Modyford's letters, but in one he referred him to Albemarle for further instructions; ibid., No. 27. Arlington may genuinely have considered that Jamaica, a military garrison, was in the Lord-General's 'department', at least to begin with; but the Commission to Sir James Modyford as Governor of Providence Island, issued on 10 Nov. 1666—three months after the Spaniards had recaptured the place—certainly passed through the Secretary's hands.

was natural, therefore, that the Governor should attribute his fall, when it came, in large measure to Arlington's double-dealing.[1] He could not fail to believe that he had been sacrificed to save an official face at Court. But so long as his patron Albemarle lived, Modyford was confident of support for his policy in Jamaica.

It was known that both the King, always easily impressed by the spectacular and the flash of gold, and the Chancellor, gratified by evidence of the growing prosperity of the Island and the careful husbandry of its Governor, agreed with Albemarle that 'connivance' beyond the Line was still their best tactic. Modyford was careful not to compromise them. He assured Arlington that he had done all in his own name in the matter of granting the privateers' commissions, so that England's diplomacy in Europe might not be embarrassed, for he well knew that diplomacy there wore a different face and spoke in words other than those that were the mode in the Indies. (For this finesse, this forbearance, he was later to be regretful: he was left saddled with the responsibility he had claimed.) But meanwhile his policy enabled him to entice the English buccaneers from Tortuga and Hispaniola back to Jamaica, and Albemarle congratulated him. Even during the protracted negotiations that preceded the Anglo-Spanish treaty of May 1667, the Duke continued to write to the Governor that 'he might still employ the privateers as formerly, if it be for the benefit of His Majesty's service'.[2] It was shortly to become only too clear to Spain that England had no subjects in the Indies more thoroughly devoted to King Charles's service than the freebooting fraternity between 1667 and 1670.

---

[1] Cf. Modyford to Arlington, 1 Oct. 1669: 'Since His Lordship referred him to the Lord General's directions touching the privateers of this port, he has corresponded with His Grace about their motions and the powers he gave them, which His Grace in all his returns approved of; and had the same been remembered by His Lordship, he [Modyford] should not in the late debates touching these matters be thought so imprudent as he hears he has been'; CSPC 1669-74, 41-42. In 1674 Modyford was very active in supplying the materials for Arlington's impeachment; cf. VE, 2 Feb. 1674, Cal. S.P. Ven., 1673-5, 275.

[2] There is, again, only Modyford's word for this; cf. Modyford to Arlington, 21 Aug. 1666, CO 1/20, No. 134. But he purports to quote Albemarle's actual words in a letter of 2 Feb. 1667: 'and for your giving commissions to the privateers (against the Spaniards), I think you have done pursuant to your own instructions and orders sent you, until there shall be some other alternative of these orders'; CO 1/24, Nos. 11-12.

Naturally it was with great dismay and high indignation that
Spain discovered that alteration in her European policy towards
England had no effect in America. There it seemed that the
Treaty of Madrid might not have been made. The scale of
warfare between the two nations in the Indies did not at once
dwindle and diminish to nothing—rather it increased, breaking
fresh ground. There is no evidence that either the Madrid
Treaty of 1667 or that of Munster to which it referred was ever
forwarded to Modyford at all. Modyford himself declared that
he had not read the Treaty of Munster, and could therefore
hardly consider it binding on his actions. It is possible that
Arlington was bearing in mind the hint Sandwich had given
him, to keep Jamaica in politic ignorance of Anglo-Spanish
diplomacy in Europe. The Administration's confidence was
certainly increased by the news of Harman's naval victory in
June 1667 over the French in the Leeward Islands, too late
though this came to save the English plantations there from
devastation. Molina in London, still protesting about the continuing seizure of Spanish shipping in the Caribbean, had now
to 'quiet down' his indignation, for the English were now openly
claiming that beyond the Line no law ruled save that of force.[1]
Here the tables were fairly turned. This was a cry that had once
been Spain's; Englishmen of Elizabeth's and James I's day,
harried and outnumbered in the West Indies, had sought peace
beyond the Line from Spain and were refused it. The Spaniards
now regarded the 1667 Treaty as their last line of retreat: but
the English interpreted it as a first step to the goal of open trade
in the American seas. From English depredation at sea it was
literally but a step to expeditions on land. It was just possible
for Spain, anxious to save face, to see in the Darien raid of 1667
a fair reprisal for her own recapture of Providence; but what
excuse could shrug away the English expedition to Puerto
Principe in Cuba in January 1668, with 10 ships and 500 men
under Henry Morgan's command? And his attack on Porto
Bello in June, at the height of the Fair, was a plain act of war—
it deserved no other name.

Modyford's answer to the first charge was that Morgan had
been sent to Cuba to bring back definite intelligence of a Spanish
design against Jamaica. Not surprisingly Morgan found suffi-

[1] *VE*, 31 Aug. 1668, Cal. S.P. Ven., 1666–8, 333.

cient evidence of this—for there was always an intention, at least, in the mind of every Spanish Governor in the Indies to sweep the English from the Caribbean as soon as an opportunity arose—to give his tolerant conscience adequate excuse to plunder and pillage. But on the exploit at Porto Bello even the nimble wit of Sir Thomas Modyford was put to it for a ready reply. He had himself, he said, chid Morgan, for the letters of marque were valid only against Spanish *shipping*. He managed to find some extenuating circumstances, drawing attention to the skill, the daring, the *élan* of the English attack. He deprecated the inflated reports of the extent of the booty the English had gained—each privateer, by his reckoning, had cleared only £60 profit.[1] It was, of course, to Albemarle that the Governor forwarded the most favourable narrative of this expedition, to warm that veteran's blood perhaps for the last time before he died. But Modyford was well aware that the magnitude of the success of this last exploit—and it showed through all attempts at concealment or minimization—was bound to swing official sentiment against him, and make him a scapegoat for Spanish wrath. He begged Albemarle to 'present his behaviour' as well as possible, 'that no sinister construction may be put on his actions'.[2] He had passed the limit even of connivance, and he knew it. The only thing he could hope for now was that a corresponding anti-Spanish policy should shape itself in England.

As only a very rash man would have been prepared in 1668 to stake what the political situation in Europe would be even two years hence, Modyford may well have considered he was taking a fair risk. Since the conclusion of the Treaty of Madrid the previous year, the Court of Spain had perforce kept on amiable terms with the Earl of Sandwich. Spain swallowed a great deal, if not all, of her resentment at the continued provocations in the Indies, for she was looking desperately for an offensive and defensive alliance with someone—anyone—to protect her European territories from the rapacity of the King of France. In vain had appeal been made to her natural protector, the Habsburg Emperor in Vienna. Leopold hearkened

---

[1] But cf. memorial of Molina to the King, 7/17 Jan. 1669. Every soldier had 600 oz. gold at half a crown an ounce, 'whence it may be guessed what quantity the officers, Governor, and their confidants had'; CO 1/24, Nos. 1-2.

[2] Modyford to Albemarle, 1 Oct. 1668, CO 1/23, No. 59.

not to the heart-cries from Madrid but to the siren song of
Louis. For in October 1667 Habsburg and Bourbon began to
discuss amicably together not only the present predicament of
Spain, but the future partition of her dominions when the
Spanish King went to his eagerly awaited end—'which God
prevent'. In secret the two monarchs signed an agreement on
20 January 1668, wherein the Spanish Indies were allotted to
the Habsburg; a bizarre bequest, which the Austrians themselves thought rather ridiculous, although they later perceived
its less comical aspect. This was one of Louis's personal arrangements: certainly Colbert, the founder of the Company of the
West Indies, the man who had ensured that the Caribbean was
included in all considerations of French naval strength and
strategy, would never have consented to it.

Spain, although she could not know the extent of the Austrian
defection, remained uneasy. It was again time for her to catch
at straws, and so again she looked on England and the English
commercial terms of alliance with a less baleful eye. Sandwich
since the departure of d'Embrun from Madrid in July had been
doing a fair amount of thinking aloud in Medina's presence.
The *asiento*, now; might not that new seven-year contract for
the delivery of negroes that Spain had just concluded with the
Grillos be somehow displaced in the Royal Company of Adventurers' favour? Or perhaps a monopoly of the trade in
Campeachy logwood?[1] Medina seemed glad to encourage this;[2]

---

[1] F. R. Harris, *The First Earl of Sandwich* (London, 1912), ii. 111; Sandwich's
'Discourse of what advantages His Majesty may farther have from Spain, by a
nearer league', in Bebington, op. cit. 97–105: 'The monopoly of the Campeche
wood is of considerable profit. . . . Of Campeche wood there is occasion to spend,
as they tell me, about 20,000 quintals every year in England, Holland, France,
Flanders, Genoa, Venice, Smirna & Turkey and also in Muscovia. I understand
the Spaniards do now bring in not above 15,000 quintals, or 500 tun, every year.
. . . The Campeche wood, they say, is worth each quintal at

London	40 sh.
Amsterdam } about 80 florins.	
Sevil	8 pieces of eight.

I am told every year that a ship of 600 tuns, and a *patache* of 300 tun, will be
sufficient for the trade.'

[2] Harris, op. cit. ii. 113; Sandwich to Arlington, 11/21 Oct. 1667, SP 94/53, 56–
57: '[Medina] enquired if it would not be a thing esteemed by the King my master
to have the sole emption of the Campeche-wood in the West Indies. . . . In general
I judge it to bee of good advantage if an understanding merchant had the handling
of such a monopoly, and perhaps be worth 30 or 40,000 pieces of eight per annum.'

he did not even reject the possibility of allowing to England the use of a 'free port' in Spanish America. Sandwich quickly suggested Rio de la Plata, or Carthagena, or Vera Cruz. Given such a port, England would of course reduce her demands for an entirely open trade. What, too, were the chances of sending an English ship annually to the Philippines, or perhaps three to Buenos Aires, or two maybe with the galleons to Porto Bello, and two for good measure with the *flota* to Mexico?[1] The English would, of course, require security from Spain for all their present possessions in America. And if Spain made any new conquests in America or in Africa, the English there were to have a licence for equal trading rights.[2]

[1] Sandwich's 'Discourse', loc. cit.: 'I believe also the Spaniards (though they will not admit a general trade) may without much inconveniences give leave every voyage for 2 or 3 English ships to go with the Flota from Sevil to the Indies, and trade, and return in company with the Flota to Sevil again. . . . The best information I have yet of this . . . is that the Merchants of Sevil might buy such a licence at 100/000 p/8, but this is a rude guess.'

[2] Rumours of this negotiation reached the ears of West-India merchants. Sir James Modyford wrote from Port Royal to Sir Andrew King in London, 11 May 1668:

'. . . But if your newes concerning ye opening to us a trade with ye Spanish dominions here prove true . . . I shall as breefly as I can give you my brothers and my replie & resolutions about it as ffoll: imp. That you take for an assured conclusion, yt noe trade can be obtained in ye Indies by us or any other forayners but by orders directly from Spaine; all ye obleiging & artifitiall wayes possible having been tryed to noe purpose about it; & therefore never thinke farther of it, unless yt which you last writt of tradeing to all but foure places be fully agreed on.

'Item. In such case it is certain yt Sta Martha is ye properest place for our trade wth ye Spanyard, ye same being directly South from this place [Jamaica] . . . whereas Compeach lies due west, & ye retourne from there hither may cost us 3 months (I say) 3 months voyage & sometimes more, & not above 7 dayes to Sta Martha.

'. . . Item. Upon ye whole our advise is yt if ye sd. permission will certainly be granted to all partes except foure, yt in such case you doe informe yourselfe well of ye comodities fitt for SM & ye Maine, wch lies to windward of Cartagena, & buy in assortement of them to ye value of ten thousand pounds sterling, & put them in a good ship of 26 guns att least & send her away with speed—but not unlesse you be verie certaine of ye permission from Spaine, & yt ye shipp touch here att Jamaica first, & yt shee bring wth her authentique copies of ye Capitulations, & if possible a notification thereof from ye King or Contrataction House to the Governour of Sta Martha, comanding him to observe the same—all wch is absolutely necessary, for wthout it, the Spaniard will be apte to putt many [?] on us. That in such case my brother & myselfe will goe halfe of both ship & cargoe. . . . You must be very vigilant in observing wt adventurers are gon before us, if any . . . for it is certainly to be expected yt every marchant will be greedy of this trade, but then I believe few or none will thinke of their markett at Sta Martha. . . .' Westminster Abbey Muniments, 11917-18.

But for Spain, this was not a straw to catch at, but a rope to hang herself. She decided to cut her losses in Europe rather than incur worse in America. She began negotiations with France in the spring of 1668, and concluded the peace of Aix-la-Chapelle on 22 April/5 May.

Just prior to this the solidarity of English policy had dissolved, for her domestic frictions now made nonsense of her diplomatic engagements. Parliament and the mercantile interest, acutely suspicious of French ambitions, compelled the King to reverse his policy in Europe. Sir William Temple set out to make his Triple Alliance with Holland and Sweden, and concluded it on 28 January 1668, three days after Louis had made common cause with the Emperor. True to this new anti-French course, Sandwich was now instructed to carry through that peace between Spain and Portugal that had for so long been on the agenda. Despite protest and obstruction from France's envoy at Madrid, he successfully accomplished his task (13 February). The Portuguese goad at last removed from her side, Spain was prepared further to improve her relations with England, though not of course on those overweening terms with which Sandwich had plagued her in her hour of darkness. Although the peace at Aix had closed one chapter in her relations with the French monarchy, she was quite correct in fearing that the volume retailing the history of the Spanish Succession was still in process of publication. She therefore turned eagerly to this new Triple Alliance—which when viewed from the front looked solid enough, and which was known to be a source of acute embarrassment to Louis—to obtain from it a guarantee that the terms of Aix would be respected, that Spanish territories would no longer be at the mercy of French ambition. This was clearly the commonsense step to take. Even Molina, although busy making representations in London that His Majesty's subjects in the Indies were still not making good His Majesty's royal intentions of peace and goodwill,[1] was of opinion that the Frenchman was potentially a more dangerous foe in those seas even than the Englishman. It was well known that you could buy an Englishman out if you made it worth his while. If then a load of logwood and a chest of Spanish crowns would placate the English merchants and win Charles away

---

[1] Sandwich to Arlington, 23 Sept./3 Oct. 1668, SP 94/53, 317.

from his French attachments, Spain should hand them over and consider it a reasonable bargain.

But Louis was not the man to wait while Spain geared herself to make so painful a decision. His hands free after he had secured the friendship of the Emperor and settled his first account with Spain, he turned quickly to demolish the irksome Triple Alliance at its shaky foundations, and with it Spain's reinsurance for the future. He sent Colbert de Croissy and a splendid embassy to London in August 1668. The French gentlemen talked in public about commercial matters to keep the Parliament-men sweet, and in private to King Charles about what King Louis could offer him. Charles, who disliked the Triple Alliance even more than did Louis himself, listened to them eagerly. Into the scales that France was now dangling before him he threw a demand for Spanish America, which would certainly have gladdened the heart of his Governor of Jamaica, had that anxious officer known of it. Louis had his hands tied in this matter by his curious promise to the Emperor, and he could not go all the way with Charles. But he persuaded him to agree to raise this and kindred problems later, on a promise that any further action he took with regard to the question of the Spanish Succession would not ignore the claims of England. European problems delayed the consummation of this agreement for over a year, but these terms of settlement *vis-à-vis* the Indies had not changed when the Secret Treaty between the two kings was signed at Dover on 22 May/1 June 1670.

All this was secret policy: but it was as hard to tell what policy the nations were prepared to own to in public. England had still not got what she wanted from Spain. She was still prepared, therefore, to frighten the Spaniards into acquiescence with the spectre of plunder in the Indies. The time was propitious. English privateers were back at Granada in 1669, while d'Estrées's fleet was harassing the Spanish Indies, plundering Cuba and Santo Domingo, as disregardful of the peace of Aix as were the English of the Treaty of Madrid. Ralph Montagu, the English agent at Paris, reported to Arlington in December that the French were 'mightily set' at being strong at sea, the King being much encouraged in this by Colbert. They had declared that every summer henceforward they would have

between 40 and 50 ships at sea.[1] Spain could guess well enough
how many of these would employ their time. But this French
incursion gave England pause also. Arlington had been listening
to the advice of Dr. Benjamin Worsley, the secretary of the
Plantations Committee and an ardent Francophobe, who put
forward all the usual arguments why the English privateers
should be supported, together with a strong reminder that the
French were growing ever stronger in the Indies. There were
already signs that they would either attract or compel the buccaneers into their service, and if that happened the whole problem of lawlessness in the Indies would increase tenfold.[2] It was
no time, therefore, to suppress the English rovers.

The common sense of this could not be gainsaid; and so the
English Administration did not disown, as Modyford feared,
Morgan's exploit at Porto Bello. Arlington found himself mini-
mizing the matter much in Modyford's own manner, insisting
to the infuriated Molina that these distressing ruptures would
not occur if the open trade for which Sandwich was still pressing at Madrid were granted. Moreover, in March 1669 the
High Court of Admiralty announced its judgement that what
had been taken at Porto Bello was good prize. The Duke of
York, whose tongue was loose, added insult to this injury (for
which as Lord High Admiral he was nominally responsible) by
the remark that the Spaniards had only themselves to thank.

Spain rightly believed that all this indicated that the policy
of Modyford and Morgan in the Indies would be underwritten
in England so long as Spain refused to meet the English terms
for a settlement: if Spain would cease to claim Jamaica, and
permit an open trade in the Indies, there would be peace beyond
the Line. Spain had therefore to go farther along the road sign-
posted by the 1667 Treaty of Madrid. Molina reiterated that
Porto Bello and the pillage elsewhere were breaches of a solemn
engagement not yet two years old: if the Treaty meant anything
at all, it had decided for a mutual cessation of hostilities between
the subjects of the one signatory and the subjects of the other.
And even if the Spaniards, living perpetually on their nerves in
the Indies, had indeed provoked the English into these new

[1] Montagu to Arlington, 21–24 Dec. 1669, HMC Buccleuch–Whitehall, i. 455;
VE, 4 Jan. 1670, of 'great searching of heart' at this news in England; Cal. S.P.
Ven., 1669–70, 2.   [2] Dec. 1668, MS. Rawl. A. 478, f. 53.

outrages, as York claimed, still the Treaty had laid down a machinery by which legal recourse could be obtained. Local reprisal was a breach of this article. He insisted bitterly that the English Government's attitude was not merely dishonourable, but incomprehensible—for the English were claiming liberties in the house of others which they refused to allow in their own.[1] Every colony England possessed was confined in the commercial swaddling-bands of her Acts of Trade: what right then had she to object to the similar policy of the Spanish empire?[2]

The King of England's only answer was a repetition of the earlier excuse that he was unable to stop the privateers.[3] If he antagonized them with proscription and punishment they would assuredly take out French commissions, league with the buccaneers, and continue their hostility to Spain from that quarter. (The language was Modyford's own, as Molina plainly recognized, for he at once mooted the recall and punishment of the Governor of Jamaica, as a salutary warning to all the privateers.) York was at one with the King in this matter. Prince Rupert was all for combining with France and driving Spain from America entirely. To put this idea into words was of course 'an extravagance', but the threat was real enough— indeed, it was already mooted in Charles's bargain with Louis— and Spain could not ignore it.[4]

But fortunately for her, the policy of the English Court had already diverged from that of the politicians. The spring of 1669 saw paradox at work. On the one hand Charles was negotiating with Louis to sap the Triple Alliance and weaken Spain further. On the other, Arlington was trying to bring the Triple Alliance Powers to a joint guarantee of the security of all the Spanish dominions. The latter task was brought to a successful conclusion on 7 May at The Hague, just a twelvemonth before equal success crowned the efforts of the former at Dover.

Meanwhile Morgan had capped his achievement at Porto Bello. In October 1668 he was at Caracas with 10 ships and

---

[1] *VE*, 8 Mar. 1669, Cal. S.P. Ven., 1669–70, 24, 29, 38.
[2] *VE*, 15 Mar. 1669, ibid. 35.
[3] Cf. a letter of 21 Aug. 1669 in HMC Report vi (Ingilby), 367a: 'The King on Thursday last had news by letter from Jamaica [of Morgan's exploits]. This I had from the King's own mouth, who says it shall not be printed, lest its by reflecting too much on the Spanish bravery should provoke them to a revenge.'
[4] *VE*. 3 May 1669, Cal. S.P. Ven., 1669–70, 60, 73, 77.

800 men. On the 14th one of the King's frigates, *Oxford*, arrived at Jamaica. Modyford had asked for it to be sent on the old excuse that a ship of countenance was necessary to control the privateers, and Albemarle had procured it for him from the Duke of York on that understanding.[1] The Governor had the temerity to make a privateer of it. He put it under Morgan's command, sending it off to join him at Isle la Vache, north of Hispaniola, in December. On 2 January 1669, while there was a conference proceeding on board how best to tackle Carthagena, *Oxford* blew up, causing heavy loss of life and filling the Count of Molina, when he heard of this, with joy that God had at last punished those who had committed the great crime at Porto Bello.[2] But Morgan's own angel had not deserted him, and, safe and sound, by mid-March he was gone to Maracaibo, a savagely successful expedition. He arrived back in Port Royal on 17 May, seven days after the guarantee of Spanish territory had been signed at The Hague, and just after Arlington had at last been able to write to Modyford ordering him to put an end to hostilities.[3]

Modyford, who would not disobey an order when one was given him, called in all commissions against the Spaniards at once, although he continued to issue 'let-passes' to private ships. On 14 June 1669 he proclaimed that Jamaica was now at peace with Spain. He sent letters to the Governors of the Spanish plantations that their troubles, which had of course been brought upon their heads by their own unseemly conduct, were now at an end. He sent a similar communication to the Count of Molina himself, which can only have made that grandee the more assiduous in his pursuit. This letter, showing as it does Sir Thomas Modyford in his best vein, deserves quotation.

Sir, [says he]
  You cannot be ignorant how much your whole nation in these parts did applaud my justice and civility to them at my first coming to this government, which (notwithstanding the small returns I received) I should have continued to this day, had not an invincible

---

[1] CO 1/21, No. 51. Both Beeston (*Journal*) and Long (Add. MS. 12408) state that *Oxford* brought instructions 'countenancing' war with the Spaniards, but I am unable to verify this.

[2] *VE*, 12 Apr. 1669, Cal. S.P. Ven., 1669–70, 48.

[3] On 11 May. The letter is referred to by Modyford, but I have not been able to trace it.

necessity compelled me to allow our privateers their old way, that
I might keepe them from joyning with mine and your Masters
enimies [the French] . . . to which I find them too much inclin-
able. . . .

. . . I know and perhaps you are not altogether ignorant of your
weakness in those parts, the thinnesse of your inhabitants, want of
hearts, arms, and knowledge in warr, the open opposition of some
and doubtfull obedience of other of the Indians, so that you have no
towne on this side the Line but that my masters forces would give
him, did not his signal generosity to yours restrain them. What wee
could have done, the French will doe, unlesse these men by your
intercession be brought to serve your master, and then you will be
soe sensible of their usefulness that you will no longer maligne me for
the evills they have done the vassalls of your prince. . . .

Its possible this franke discovery of my knowledge in your affaires
will invite you the more earnestly to indeavour my oppression,
but I am secure in the goodnesse and wisdome of my sovereigne
lord. . . .[1]

So, at any rate, he hoped. But Modyford did not know when
he wrote this that two months previously the Queen Regent of
Spain had issued a royal *cedula* ordering her Governors in
America to proclaim war against all the English south of the
Tropic of Cancer, with permission 'to seize upon all English
ships in the Indian Seas'.[2] In the autumn Spain equipped a
small fleet and sent it out to concert action against the English
with the Spanish Governors in the Caribbean. The issue of a
proclamation of war in February 1670 by the Governor of
Carthagena, and a study of the language of the royal *cedula*
itself (which came to hand in Jamaica only that June),[3] forced
Modyford's hand. A Spanish raid on the north coasts of the
Island made a renewal of the war inevitable. Modyford called
in all the privateers who were still roaming—most of them on his
own let-passes—and grouped them as a fighting force under
Morgan.[4] To Morgan he gave the title of Admiral and orders
to 'attaque, seize, & destroy all the enemy vessells that shall
come within his reach . . . to doe & performe all maner of

---

[1] Modyford to Molina, 15 June 1669, CO 138/1, 41.
[2] CSPC 1669–74, 149.
[3] It was sent to Modyford by the Dutch Governor of Curaçao.
[4] Morgan finally had under command 36 ships with 1,846 men, 8 ships and 520
men being French; Livingstone, *Sketch Pedigrees of Some of the Early Settlers in
Jamaica* (Kingston, 1909).

Exployts which may tend to the Preservation and Quiett of Jamayca' and to divide the spoil 'according to their usual rules'.[1] A vein of irony permissible in a communication from one old friend to another is prominent in the terms of the actual commission of war.

You are to inquire [Sir Thomas instructed his Admiral] what Usage our Prisoniers have had & what quarter hath been given by the Enemy to Such of ours as have fallen under theyr Power; and being well inform'd you are to Give the Same, or Rather, as our Custome is, to exceede them in Civilitie and Humanitie, indeavouring by all meanes to make all Sortes of People sensible of your Moderation & good nature & your inaptitude & Loathnesse to spill the Blood of Man.[2]

On 2 July, therefore, the struggle recommenced: and Henry Morgan geared himself for his greatest exploit in the Indies.

Meanwhile in Europe the guarantee at The Hague had naturally committed England, as the originator and moving force of the Triple Alliance, to a policy of friendship with Spain. Sir William Godolphin went out to Madrid in the autumn of 1669, to act on instructions that had been drawn up the previous February. His fifteenth instruction was more explicit than any previous order governing the conduct of English ambassadors who would negotiate on America. To the expected outcry from the Spaniards about the continued depredation on their territories by the privateers of Jamaica, Godolphin was to reply that the extent of the lawlessness rife in the whole area only served clearly to prove how essential it was to arrive at some definition of rights and interests in America, both Spanish and English, in order that friendship and good neighbourhood between the two nations might be based on certain and accepted ground. To this end, then, he was to proceed to negotiate a Treaty that would prohibit all acts of hostility in the Indies. If the Spaniards raised their time-honoured objection to the principle of open trade as applied to the commerce of America, Godolphin was not to protest on that score, but to ensure instead that each contracting party might have provision made for

---

[1] Minutes of the Council of Jamaica, 29 June 1670, CO 140/1, 196-200; Add. MS. 11268, f. 66.
[2] Commission to Morgan, 22 July 1670, Add. MS. 11268, ff. 68-70.

'wood & water' in the ports of the other, together with an amnesty for all past offences, and the release of prisoners on both sides. If they doubted the integrity of Godolphin and his Government on this matter (as no doubt they would in the belief that the whole discussion was designed by the English to gain them time to bring off some new *coup* in the Indies), he was to assure them that a provisional order would be sent to the Governor in Jamaica to cease all hostilities and call in his privateers.[1] In this, as has been noted, the English government was for once as good as its word, and the order went to Mody-ford that May.

Bred in Arlington's own tradition of dexterous diplomacy, Godolphin was confident that he could carry out his instructions and gain even more than he was asked. He had the charm that both Fanshawe and Sandwich before him had conspicuously lacked, and with its aid he early established amicable relations with Medina, Penaranda, and the other grandees of the Spanish Court. It was clear to him that the legal fiction to which for so long Spain had so devotedly clung, that there were no rights in America but her own, must now be abandoned by her—but if that could be done without insult to her pride or injury to her possessions then it should be. Nevertheless, he did not forget what Spanish statesmen, obsessed with the non-essentials of diplomatic usage, so frequently forgot: that England held the initiative in the Indies, so long as Modyford and his buccaneers were held in leash. His best policy was therefore to wait until the Spanish Court had come to recognize this fact and all its implications of its own accord. Then England might 'consent and condescend to an adjustment of matters in the Indies rather than to sollicite it'.

The opposition to any formal recognition of the position and possessions of England in America still came, as was to be expected, from the 'Galleon Generalls' and the Council of the Indies. In their view, persons who came to wood and water in Spanish American ports might very well stay to trade with inhabitants who, as Madrid well knew from a century and a half of colonial experience, would not be unwilling to welcome them. They thought a Treaty too binding an instrument: a mere *cedula* or permission would do well enough, for this could later

---

[1] Instructions to Godolphin, 24 Feb. 1669, SP 104/174*b*, 183–5.

be ignored or even rescinded without fuss.[1] Godolphin realized how deeply ingrained in Spanish minds this opposition was. 'The very name of this Treaty', as he wrote later, 'peerceth generally the hearts of this people, having never yett made any particular one on this subject, nor indulged in any negotiation approaching thereunto.'[2] He assured Arlington that ever since he had been told of the King's earnest expectation of an early settlement, he had not had 'one quiet hour, running up and downe from morning to night from 1 Councellor to another and sustaining all the froward arguments imaginable relating to the Indies'. The Court of Spain, equally anxious for a solution but worried as usual by the responsibility of taking a decision, called in the services as mediator of Molina himself, who had quitted his London post in May. On 13 July Godolphin was able to write home announcing the success of his mission. 'After many contests and strong opposition, my American Treatie is signed and sealed by mee and the Conde de Peñaranda on Fryday last.'[3]

An able observer in Madrid, the Venetian Ambassador, has more to say on this point than the rather self-satisfied letters of Godolphin choose to reveal. His letter to his Senate in August deserves study:

That which the Count of Molina was unable to achieve during the time of his lengthy embassy in London he has concluded in a few months of negotiation at the Court of Madrid, having made himself a mediator between them and the English minister Godolphin upon the questions of America. . . .

Knowing from experience that they would always turn a deaf ear in England to such remonstrances, Molina applied himself to procure quiet for America in another way. He suggested to the Council there that they should grant the English the title of the conquests made from Spain, so that by bringing them amicably to a fresh peace agreement in which things can be better specified for the future, and by giving up only in name what has already been lost, they need not quarrel over the rest or expose that most important trade to further risk. Thus the urgency and the hope of Spain to

---

[1] Godolphin to Arlington, 4/14 May 1670, SP 94/56, 23; 28 June/8 July 1670, ibid. 34.

[2] Godolphin to the King, 19/29 July 1670, HMC Downshire, i. 5–7.

[3] Godolphin to Arlington, 28 June/8 July 1670, SP 94/56, 201; 13/23 July 1670, SP 94/57, 133.

have those Seas and countries in peace once and for all has brought them to-day to strip themselves of their claims to the territories lost.

England was unable to promise less than peace in order to obtain confirmation of the lawful possession of Jamaica and of the other conquests in America, especially as the ships of this nation are to be admitted to all the Spanish ports for their requirements. Upon the point of trade there is not a word in favour of the English, but whereas hitherto they have profited by reprisals, carried out by armed force, they will in the future introduce themselves quietly into the ports and little by little into the trade. Spain will have purchased a peace that may possibly bring her no more advantage than the wars might have done her mischief.[1]

This second Treaty of Madrid, which bears the date of 8/18 July 1670, was to regulate the relations between England and Spain until the Treaty of Utrecht. It confirmed the earlier arrangement of May 1667. It promised the cessation of hostilities between the two nations in America, and looked forward to the growth there of peace and friendship. The commissions of war that had been issued on both sides were to be called in forthwith. Prisoners would be released. There had been much ado about the seventh clause—from the English point of view the key to the whole thing, before it ran in this form:

All offences, losses, damages, and injuries which the English and Spanish nations have, for whatsoever cause or pretext, suffered from each other at any time past in America, shall be buried in oblivion and completely effaced from memory, as if they had never occurred. Moreover it is agreed that the Most Serene King of Great Britain, his heirs and successors, shall have, hold, and possess for ever, with full right of sovereignty, ownership, and possession, all the lands, regions, islands, colonies, and dominions situated in the West Indies or in any part of America, that the said King of Great Britain and his subjects at present hold and possess; so that neither on that account nor on any other pretext may or should anything ever be further urged, or any controversy begun in future.[2]

The eighth clause stated flatly that the subjects of the two Crowns would maintain no trade with one another in the West Indies, but the ninth 'left a door open',[3] as it permitted licences to do so to be issued in the future. The tenth clause allowed the ships of both nations to enter each other's ports when under

---

[1] *VE*, 22 Aug. 1670, Cal. S.P. Ven. 1669–70, 284.
[2] Davenport, *Treaties*, ii. 187–96.
[3] Godoplhin to the King, 19/29 July 1670, HMC Downshire, i. 5–7.

stress of weather or shipwreck, or to repair, refit, and revictual. The twelfth warned them that no untoward delay should be pleaded even for these necessary reasons. The fourteenth clause insisted that demands for reparation for damage should be promptly attended to by both sides. The fifteenth was the usual 'saving clause', though what precisely it saved and for whose benefit was a matter on which there was later to be much serious difference of opinion. The clause stated, but did not synthesize, the Spanish and the English claims. It laid down that

This present Treaty shall in no way derogate from any pre-eminence, right or seigniory which either the one or the other allies have in the seas, straits, and fresh waters of America, and they shall have and retain the same in as full and ample a manner, as of right they ought to belong to them.

This was Spain's opinion. But the clause ended with the English view:

It is always to be understood that the freedom of navigation ought by no manner of means to be interrupted, when there is nothing committed contrary to the true sense and meaning of these articles.[1]

Thus, then, was a long controverted business brought to a temporary conclusion, signed and sealed in a moment of mutual difficulty, unaccompanied by any genuine trust. The door was indeed open; but both the custodian and the caller had their foot in the jamb.

But to the English just then its conclusion looked like a major diplomatic triumph. 'I am verily persuaded', Godolphin expansively informed the King,

if wee can once demonstrate to the Spaniards our capacity of liveing like good neighbours near them in America . . . we may afterwards in a short time improve the present concessions into whatsoever degree of farther libertyes in those Indyes our interest may prompt us to desire.[2]

---

[1] Cf. R. Pares, *War and Trade in the West Indies* (Oxford, 1936), 30; and his comment, 37, on Anglo-Spanish relations in 1738: 'The dispute between England and Spain was about a rule and an exception. Spain asserted that the Spanish sovereignty of the Indies was the rule and the English right of navigation was the exception; England retorted that the natural freedom of navigation was the rule . . . for we allowed Spain no extraordinary sovereignty in America or anywhere else.'

[2] Godolphin to the King, 19/29 July 1670, SP 94/57, 36–37; HMC Downshire, i. 5–7. Godolphin considered that the English Acts of Trade were an obstacle to the full exploitation of his achievement; SP 94/57, 17–21.

Very many believed this. Arlington sent his ratification and warm approval to Godolphin on 19 August.[1] The English Court was highly content. Everywhere great hopes of the outcome of this new Treaty were confidently expressed, so much so indeed that the Dutch envoy in London grumbled that Spain ought in all fairness to grant the same facilities to Dutch as to English shipping.[2]

It remained for Admiral Henry Morgan to write the codicil to this international testament. A month before Godolphin announced his achievement, Arlington had written again to Modyford in Jamaica. He knew his man, and dreaded lest some sudden explosion in the Caribbean shattered the harmony that was slowly being composed in Europe. He reminded Sir Thomas that the difficulties Godolphin was meeting at the Court of Madrid were largely attributable to the natural resentment felt by the Spaniards at the doings of the privateers in America. It was, accordingly, His Majesty's pleasure that the Governor of Jamaica should retain his privateers in whatever state the receipt of this present letter found them—in other words, in a state of peace with Spain. The King had come to the conclusion that 'this way of warring' was neither honourable to the nation nor even profitable to the revenue. He wanted accordingly to put an end to it. If, however, Modyford had any suggestions to make how best to dispose of the privateers, admittedly a valuable body of men, he should forward them so that they might be considered. A new Council of Plantations was just then being designed for the better care of colonial affairs, and an era of peace, said Arlington with emphasis, was looked forward to in the Caribbean as elsewhere in America.[3]

This dispatch did not reach Jamaica until 13 August, by

---

[1] Arlington to Godolphin, 19 Aug. 1670, SP 94/57, 85.
[2] VE, 29 Aug. 1670, Cal. S.P. Ven., 1669–70, 296. The English from the outset read more into this Treaty of Madrid than its terms warrant. As an example, the Lord Keeper's announcement to the Commons on 24 Oct. 1670 may be cited. Explaining the Treaty, he commented that in it Spain had ceded all her pretensions to Jamaica 'and other the islands and countries in the West Indies in the possession of His Majesty *or his subjects*'; *Parl. Hist.* iv. 458; *Lords Journals*, xii. 352–3. The Treaty does not of course mention Jamaica by name, or yield any of the Spanish claim to sovereignty—nor was Spain prepared to allow English subjects to occupy Spanish lands, as, for example, in Campeachy and other logwood-settlements in Yucatan.
[3] Arlington to Modyford, 12 June 1670, CO 140/1, 42–43.

which time the privateers were in a state of war, at sea under command of Morgan. So Modyford followed the letter of his instruction, and left them 'as they then were'.[1] His dilemma was none the less acute. He knew that, even prior to his own declaration of war against the Spaniards, the Earl of Carlisle had been chosen to succeed him as Governor.[2] He knew too that Albemarle's death had removed the only sure aid he had at Court. But he was not the man to turn back. Never had his forensic skill been so assiduously employed as in the summer and autumn of 1670. He at once found out who were the important figures on this new Council of Plantations Arlington had spoken of. His son Charles in London began acting as his intermediary with Ashley.[3] Sir Thomas himself, knowing well the great respect Ashley had always borne righteous causes, implored His Lordship's countenance and assistance for this one.[4] He branded the Spaniard as the aggressor in the Indies, and to prove his point forwarded copies both of the Regent of Spain's *cedula* and the commission of war against the English issued by the Governor of St. Jago de Cuba.[5] He pleaded that he could not afford to wait up to nine months while instructions how to deal with this new state of affairs were being sent from England, for Jamaica might have been ruined by invasion in the interval. It was to avoid this that he had given orders for the immediate reopening of hostilities.[6] He listed 13 other reasons for this action, as solid and convincing as he could make them. He again stressed that the Governor of an outlying colony must have full discretionary power, such as 'the wise Romans gave their generalls, *"invideat ne insula nostra Jamaica aliquid detrimenti accipiat"* '. Arlington's letter had most unfortunately arrived the day after Morgan had set off, so Modyford had had to content himself with sending a courier after the Admiral to warn him 'to behave with all moderation possible in carrying on this war'. He was aware, of course, that the privateers would

---

[1] Modyford to Arlington, 20 Aug. 1670, CO 1/25, No. 55.
[2] Cf. *VE*, 27 June 1670, Cal. S.P. Ven., 1669-70, 235.
[3] Cf. petition of Charles Modyford, 28 Sept. 1670, CO 1/25, Nos. 66-67, 107.
[4] Cf. Modyford to Ashley, 6 July 1670, CO 138/1, 49-51.
[5] There is a copy in CO 138/1, 46.
[6] Modyford to Ashley, 24 June 1670, 31 Aug. 1670; CO 140/1, 196-200, 203; 'Considerations from Sir Thomas Modyford', CO 138/1, 136-7; Modyford to Arlington, 20 Aug. 1670, ibid. 51-53.

plunder, but that was inevitable. Had not the late Lord-General's advice always been that the soldier should 'looke on the enemy as the surest pay'? Privateers had no sure source of income but this, and if they were therefore somewhat indisciplined in their actions, no 'rationall man' could really be surprised. He did not retreat from his opinion that the Spaniard in the Indies was a menace and a nuisance, who deserved all the trouble he got. He hoped in time to 'fix the war in their country'.[1] 'A little more suffering' would 'force them to capitulations more suitable to the sociableness of man's nature.' Godolphin should be ordered to include a positive mention of Jamaica in his projected Treaty, for without that there was no security, as had so often been proved. Modyford concluded his case with the stout assertion that if he had to do the same again for the safety of Jamaica, he would do it, despite all the trouble that now threatened him. But would Ashley mediate on his behalf with His Majesty?

Whether Ashley complied with this request or not is questionable, but His Majesty was not to be moved. Spain had for long made it plain that the chances of Anglo-Spanish *rapprochement* were small while Sir Thomas Modyford ruled in Jamaica. Prior to the signing of the Treaty of Madrid, therefore, new candidates for the post were being canvassed. The new Council of Plantations were told of the King's intention to remove Modyford, and asked to give advice on the kind of Commission and Instructions that should be granted to his successor. By 23 September 1670 a Commission was already in draft for Sir Thomas Lynch, who was to act as the Earl of Carlisle's Lieutenant-Governor in Jamaica. A petition from the Council and freeholders of the island on Modyford's behalf was read and rejected in the Privy Council in November.[2] On 31 December Lynch's formal Instructions were drawn up, and five days later he was given the formal instrument of Modyford's revocation, together with a letter of the King to Sir Thomas ordering him home.[3]

Lynch's Instructions, however, were not officially delivered

[1] Modyford to Arlington, 6 July 1670, CO 138/1, 43.
[2] Petition of merchants and freeholders of Jamaica residing in London to the King, 9 Nov. 1670, CO 1/25, No. 91.
[3] Ibid., No. 107.

to him until the end of February, and he did not leave England
till April. He actually set foot in Jamaica only on 25 June 1671.
Thus there was a delay of eleven months between the signing
of the Treaty of Madrid and the replacement of the guilty
Governor. At no time during that period was Modyford sent
any notification of the terms of that Treaty. Whether this was
because he was no longer regarded as the official Governor in
Jamaica, or because (as Molina suspected) the Government
intended to connive at one last crime in the Indies,[1] is open to
surmise. Governor or no, it was certainly clear that Modyford
was the one Englishman who it was essential should have known
the terms of that Treaty by heart. Modyford certainly knew
there was a treaty, for he received private information of its
terms in December 1670, but everyone knew by now what
advantage he always took of *lacunae* in his instructions, and
this was a large omission indeed. The last clause of the Treaty
spoke in clear language about due notification. Its terms were,
first of all, to be ratified within four months from the date of its
signing—that is, by November 1670. (They were actually ratified by England on 12/22 August and by Spain on 8 October.)
Eight months from the date of ratification the Treaty was to be
published 'both in the West Indies and elsewhere'. England
took the Spanish date as being operative, and Lynch in his
instructions was charged to publish it within eight months of
10/20 October 1670—that is, by June 1671. Then, and then only,
he was to revoke the commissions that had been granted against
the Spaniards by Sir Thomas Modyford. Until Lynch appeared
in Jamaica, however, none of this was officially known in the
Indies. The text of the Treaty actually came into Modyford's
hands by May; for the Governors of Porto Rico and St. Jago
de Cuba, with great profusions of cordiality, both sent him
a copy, hoping to come to some swift arrangement for simultaneous publication. Modyford was as polite in return;[2] in one
sense he could afford to be, as Morgan arrived back in Jamaica
that month, hugely pleased with himself and his winter's work
at Panama, and busy collecting addresses of thanks from the

---

[1] *VS*, 17 June 1671, Cal. S.P. Ven., 1671-2, 67.
[2] Minutes of a Council at St. Jago, 31 May 1671, CO 1/26, No. 63; Modyford
to the Governor of Porto Rico, May 1671, CO 138/1, 130; and to Santo Domingo,
ibid. 132-3.

Governor and Council of Jamaica. Far otherwise, of course, was the reaction at the Court of Spain.]

Rumours of some extensive new campaign of pillage and plunder in America had filtered through to the ears of the Count of Molina, who had been sent back to London to inaugurate the new era of goodwill in the relations between England and Spain, as early as February 1671. He was anyway uneasy to find that Modyford was still ensconced in Port Royal, and his nominated successor still in England. What could this portend? He warned his Government that if an opportunity occurred for England to make some conquest in the Indies, it would not be neglected.[1] In March Godolphin reported from Madrid that the circumstantial reports that were beginning to come in about the nature of this new campaign had put the Spanish Ministers 'exceedingly out of humour'. But by May and June, when the full story of the plundering and burning of the great city of Panama was fully known, it was not mere ill-humour that the English envoy had to contend with. The Queen, he related, 'was in such a distemper and excesse of weeping and violent passion as those about her feared it might shorten her life'.[2] Penaranda was in tears, suffering from acute remorse and shame that he had ever put his hand to a treaty with England.[3] Godolphin himself was furious. He felt his position keenly. He was the representative of an England that had just professed all friendship and promised all respect for the Spanish Crown. But Modyford and Morgan had behaved towards the latter's dominions in America like the looters of a sinking ship. He wrote angrily to Arlington that the balance of power in Europe should not be risked for the sake of stuffing rogues' pockets with pieces of eight.

Molina continued to make his furious accusation that this expedition to Panama had in fact been underwritten by the English Administration, tacitly if not overtly, as one last card to be played before the stakes were called and the Treaty of Madrid became operative in the Indies. This was how England had employed her eight months' grace! The charge rang round the Court of Spain. Godolphin felt himself on no firm ground

---

[1] *VS*, 17 June 1671, Cal. S.P. Ven., 1671-2, 67.
[2] Godolphin to Arlington, 22 Mar./1 Apr. 1671; 14/24 June 1671, SP 94/55, 104-10.   [3] *VS*, 1 July 1671, Cal. S.P. Ven., 1671-2, 84.

here. It was true that in November 1670, on his own insistence, the English Council of Plantations had recommended that acts of hostility should be publicly prohibited in the Indies even before the stipulated eight months had elapsed,[1] but he had no evidence that his advice and theirs had been heeded. He could only reiterate what Sandwich had reiterated before him: that there was no connivance, that the pirates were out of hand, that the King of England was as shocked as the Queen of Spain, and that he had already ordered Modyford to be sent home a prisoner. Godolphin with a bravado we must admire gave his personal word as a Cavalier that he served a King of so great an Empire that he did not need to stoop to 'acts of dissimulation and little plunders'. But in truth the plunder was not little: it was in the region of six million Spanish crowns: and what, he asked Arlington privately, was going to be done about that? 'God grant', he concluded with considerable feeling, 'that Sir Thomas Modyford's way of defending Jamaica (as he used to call it) by sending out the forces thereof to pillage, prove an infallible one; for my own part, I do not think it hath been our interest to awaken the Spaniard so much as by this last action'.[2]

Indeed it was not. The Duke of Medina Celi was busy that summer with plans to raise 10,000 troops, set them on 12 ships-of-the-line, and turn the lot loose under one comprehensive letter-of-marque in the Indies. These fortunately proved abortive; but in the Caribbean Panama indeed had lasting consequences. It effectively poisoned any small chance the Treaty of Madrid had of proving fruitful of both trade and friendship between the two nations in America.

On 16 May Charles Modyford, his father's proxy in many matters, fulfilled the duty again. He was placed in the Tower. The King told Godolphin in August that he might assure the distracted Queen (with whom His Majesty condoled) that he would cause the leader and author of this outrage to feel the effect of his most just indignation, by inflicting an exemplary punishment befitting the gravity of the crime.[3] The Queen retorted that the man's life—she did not make Charles's nice

[1] 15 Nov. 1670, CO 389/5, 108.
[2] Godolphin to Arlington, 28 June/8 July 1671, SP 94/58, 118–20; 14/24 June 1671, ibid. 110.
[3] VS, 12 Aug. 1671, Cal. S.P. Ven., 1671–2, 91.

distinction between Modyford and Morgan—mattered nothing to her, but that his best punishment would be to force him to disgorge the plunder taken.[1] (An inquiry into this matter was made, but Charles Modyford proved that Sir Thomas was really rather a poor man, and that in fact the King owed him several years' arrears of salary, not to mention reimbursement for the personal expenditure the Governor had incurred in keeping the fortifications of Jamaica up to the mark.)[2] The fact was, however, that Sir Thomas's life was not in danger, nor indeed were whatever doubloons he had about him. Lynch was given explicit instructions nevertheless how to deal with the incumbent when he got to Jamaica. The arrest of Modyford was to be carried through with the minimum fuss and the maximum efficiency. The Government plainly expected that the privateers of Jamaica would rally to their master's side,[3] who had anyway 400 personal servants and slaves. Lynch himself was so convinced of this that he waited three months before he moved in the matter at all; then impounding Sir Thomas in a stealthy and underhand manner that gained him no friends and a bad reputation, as he admitted later, 'at Villiers House'. But Lynch was empowered by his instructions to tell his prisoner that his life and fortune were in no danger, that he was not regarded as a capital offender, 'but there was a necessity of the King's making this resentment for such an unreasonable irruption'. Lynch it seems overdid these reassurances,[4] for Modyford afterwards expressed great resentment at being molested in any way at all. He was, however, placed in the Tower in the place of his son in November[5]—the same month as the Treaty of Madrid was at last published in Jamaica.[6]

The Treaty of Madrid of 1670, although it never fulfilled its more active pledges, accomplished two things at least. It put an end to the official English connivance at privateering, and it

[1] VE, 18 Dec. 1671, Cal. S.P. Ven. 1671–2, 133.

[2] Charles Modyford to Arlington (address, Tower of London), 28 June 1671, CO 1/26, No. 84.

[3] Cf. Instructions from York to Captain Hubbard of the Assistance, 15 Aug. 1671, CO 140/1, 225–31.

[4] Lynch to Arlington, 20 Aug. 1671, CO 1/27, No. 22; cf. Lynch to Lyttelton, denying that he had made them at all; 5 Mar. 1672, CO 1/28, No. 22.

[5] On 17 Nov. 1671, Morgan was sent home in the Welcome frigate in Mar. 1672.

[6] Cf. Godolphin to Arlington, 11 Nov. 1671, that Spanish opinion was much 'quieted' by this news; SP 94/59, 55.

brought the Law of Nations 'beyond the Line'. Between 1660 and 1670 'frontier law' had ruled there, a law of cut and thrust; and the wild doings in the Caribbean had reacted on the diplomatic arrangements of Europe, often violently, always with effect. By 1670 the English Administration had become aware, however reluctantly, of an imperial commitment in the West Indies; the area must be regarded as part of the national polity. This is not to say that any Treaty could calm the waters of the Caribbean, or that Panama marked the last occasion of a clash between the subjects of the two signatories in those seas. But although the blood of English rovers flowed as freely as ever in the Indies between 1671 and 1689, it did not flow in the service of their King. Government looked for other agents to maintain its control; the dangerous discretionary power to which Modyford had so often appealed was discarded,[1] the hotheaded independence of the colonial Assemblies curbed, the problem of a perpetual revenue faced if not solved. Men only too prone to assert their wish to live 'according to the laws of England' had in fact lived lawlessly, and a closer supervision of all aspects of colonial life by the metropolitan Power was clearly necessary. The attempts of the English Administration both to regulate the foreign relations of Jamaica by the terms of the Treaty of Madrid, and to control her domestic business by the imposition on her constitution of the Irish Poynings' Law, may properly be regarded as components of one imperial scheme.

---

[1] Cf. Lynch's 48th Instruction—he was 'not to permit or encourage reparations to be sought in any other way than what is directed and agreed in the said Articles of Madrid', CO 138/4, 33; on which he commented to Williamson on 29 Nov. 1671 that 'it will check these people mightily to know they must only fight like baited beasts within the length of their chain'; CO 1/27, No. 47.

IV

THE CONSTRUCTION OF AN IMPERIAL AUTHORITY

1667-75

HAVING traced the fortunes of Jamaica thus far, it is necessary to return to see what ravages time and chance had
scored elsewhere in the Caribbean since the outbreak of
the war with the Dutch. The English Administration was neither
materially nor morally equipped to wage a global war, and
there was no one in its ranks who might have played the role
of Chatham. But the same brash self-confidence that had induced the politicians to force a series of quarrels on their
country's chief commercial rival in Europe encouraged them
also to believe that all the English colonists in America had
much to gain from a similar policy of calculated aggression
against their neighbours. It was an ill-founded belief: to be
sure, the province of New Netherland was a considerable prize
in itself, and made a fine patrimony for the Duke of York; but
there were no comparable territorial rewards to be won in the
Caribbean, and even if there had been it should have been
obvious that the prosperity of the English economy in that area
depended on the maintenance of peace. But war seemed the
quickest road to wealth; not peace but profit was the Administration's goal.

In November 1664 York as Lord High Admiral empowered
the two Governors in the West Indies to grant letters of marque
against all Dutch shipping. He had no intention of squandering
the naval strength of England in the dispatch of valuable
frigates to West-India waters; the defence of the American
frontier should be left to the frontiersmen. Although in November 1665 a system of convoy was introduced for the better
security of home-coming merchantmen,[1] and instructions given
that such fleets were to leave West-India ports only on author-

[1] Convoy outward was also instituted, e.g. 30 merchant ships left Bristol for the
West Indies on 11 Nov. 1665; CSPD 1664-5, 98.

ized dates,[1] such convoys still had their first sight of a naval escort off the Soundings—for both to the Admiralty and to the mercantile interest the risks of privateering action in the Channel outweighed those of any similar action in the Caribbean. Moreover, Arlington had been impressed by the scheme of aggression against the Dutch bases in the West Indies that had been put forward by Sir Thomas Modyford. Modyford, as has been seen, was confident of his ability to mount a campaign in the Caribbean on the cheap, on a basis of 'no purchase, no pay', using the privateers of Jamaica as his striking force. It turned out that he was wrong,[2] but the implication of his argument—that the English in the West Indies had only to bestir themselves to reap a rich harvest there—had considerable influence on public policy at home. There was just then no great concern there about the West Indies. In February 1665 the King had indeed warned Willoughby that de Ruyter's fleet of 12 men-of-war had gone to the Guinea coast, whence it was likely he would sail to the Caribbean, with Barbados as his main objective;[3] but the outcome of the subsequent attack on that Island was much as Whitehall expected. de Ruyter was beaten off in April with great damage. To the Barbadians, however, this seemed more a proof of the mercy of Providence than evidence of their own impregnability.

Willoughby did his best to arouse the home Government to the actual predicament of the colonies in his charge, in an area where sea-power lay exclusively with the enemy. He had no money to put the defences in order. Part of the returns from the $4\frac{1}{2}$ per cent. duty had been devoted to the settlement of St. Lucia as a measure of defence, but the rest had been paid to the Earl of Carlisle's creditors, without at all satisfying them. The Royal Company of Adventurers impounded the duties on negroes. He asked for 3,000 muskets and 380 barrels of powder,

[1] The King to Willoughby, 16 Nov. 1665. The set dates were 31 Mar., 30 June, and 30 Sept. Ships from Surinam were instructed to voyage with those from Barbados and the Leeward Islands; CO 1/19, No. 124. The dates for ships to leave Jamaica were set at 24 Mar., 24 June, 24 Sept.; ibid. No. 126.

[2] In the long run. But, as John Reid (sub-commissioner of prizes and Royal Company factor) wrote to Arlington in Jan. 1666, Tobago had fallen to two small frigates and only 80 men; CO 1/20, No. 7.

[3] The King to Willoughby, 2 Feb. 1665, CO 1/19, No. 16. In Barbados there were only 63 powder-barrels in store. At Montserrat and Nevis de Ruyter did great damage.

and was told that if Barbados wanted arms and ammunition, she must buy them—she was not to expect them as a gift. Arlington told him flatly in May, a month after de Ruyter's visit, that no ship could be spared from European waters for the defence of the Caribbean.[1] Ordnance stores were grudged, and anyway the issue of a warrant for their dispatch was no guarantee that they would in fact be transhipped.[2] Watts in St. Christopher, watching the regular arrival of arms to the French part of the island, was unable to get even a pound of powder.[3] In August Willoughby asked leave to return to England to put his case in person, but although Arlington gave a careless consent, Albemarle wrote that this was no time for an officer to quit his post:[4] a view with which Willoughby's own second thoughts agreed. It was due entirely to the Lord-General's representations that two frigates were made available for West-India service in January 1666, when war with a second and more formidable enemy, France, was imminent. Even then, however, Willoughby was reminded that this was an exceptional favour,[5] not to be regarded as a precedent or a right. His agent in London, John Champante, continued to press Joseph Williamson for a regular supply of arms and ammunition.[6] For if these were not sent, how could the King's loyal subjects in the West Indies obey his confident injunction to 'root out & utterly damnify' all the Frenchmen and Dutchmen in the area?[7]

The impossibility of carrying out such an order as conditions were at present was plain to the planters from the outset, and anyway a tentative scheme to seize Saba, Statia, and Tobago from the Dutch was nullified by the action of Modyford's commissioned privateers from Jamaica. Henry Willoughby, the Governor's nephew (who was more energetic than most and who had been chiefly responsible for the rebuff of de Ruyter the previous spring) impressed on Williamson that the Island was

[1] Arlington to Willoughby, 16 May 1665, ibid. No. 57.
[2] One such warrant of Feb. 1665, for stores to be issued to Sir John Colleton, was not implemented till Mar. 1666, and even then only 30 of the stipulated 500 powder-barrels arrived; Willoughby to the King, 15 July 1666, CO 1/20, No. 120.
[3] Watts to Albemarle, 18 Oct. 1665, CO 1/19, No. 112.
[4] Arlington to Willoughby, 5 Dec. 1665, CO 389/4, 55; Albemarle to Arlington, 11 Jan. 1666, CO 1/19, No. 96.
[5] York to Willoughby, 10 Mar. 1666, Adm 2/1745.
[6] Champante to Williamson, 12 Jan. 1666, CO 1/20, No. 2.
[7] The King to Willoughby, 8 Feb. 1666, ibid. No. 11.

only capable of 'making a defensive war';[1] but it seems that no one studied Williamson's collection of *Caribbeana* but Williamson himself,[2] and he was still a dim figure in the Administration while his master Arlington held the limelight.

Lord Willoughby's exasperation at his offhanded treatment by officialdom continued to mount. Were not the lives of Barbadians more valuable 'than twenty Coasts of Guinea'?[3] As early as October 1664 he had asked Arlington that he might be sent adequate notice of the expected rupture between England and the United Provinces;[4] not so much that he feared what the Dutch would do, but because he knew that, if the French joined with them in the Caribbean, 'they would carry all before them'.[5] That year a new royal Governor, de Tracy, had been dispatched to the Islands with a squadron of seven ships, carrying close on 1,500 passengers and soldiers. The reconstituted French West-India Company had a capital fund of four million *livres* to animate its operations—vivid contrast with the notorious impoverishment of the English Government, which had to administer three kingdoms on as much. This Company was itself a branch of the French Government, Louis himself being the principal stockholder. Its task was 'to perform a national service and to make possible the success of a national policy'.[6] What that policy was, Englishmen in the West Indies had little doubt. Willoughby's jealousy of the French, of their handsome

---

[1] Henry Willoughby to Williamson, 28 Aug. 1666, CO 1/20, No. 140.

[2] He had, for example, a list of the names of the Councillors of Barbados, with comments; cf. ibid. No. 145; perhaps this information, like his geographical data, was 'from Major Scott's mouth'; cf. CO 1/21, No. 175.

[3] Willoughby to the King, 21 Apr. 1666, CO 1/20, No. 58.

[4] Willoughby to Arlington, 16 Oct. 1664, CO 1/18, No. 125. Cf. also his letter to the King of the same date, in Bodl., MS. Clarendon 82, f. 132.

[5] CO 1/20, No. 6. The French knew this too, as may appear from the dispatch of the Venetian envoy in Paris to his Senate of 22 June 1666: 'The first plans entertained by France when this war broke out, at that time between England and Holland alone . . . seem to have been to keep the fire burning . . . so that [their] attention being diverted from the commerce of the Indies, this Crown should have a free field for reaping a harvest in those parts. . . . Circumstances are certainly very favourable for this country to win advantages in trade, abandoned by the others, and to push on with their conquests, since the wealth of this Government can very easily support powerful armaments and at the same time despatch numerous fleets to the Indies'; Cal. S.P. Ven., 1666-8, 16. Cf. also a letter to the Earl of Winchilsea, dated 12 Feb. 1666, in HMC Finch, i. 412: 'Advice from Holland says [that Louis XIV] intends to land 1,200 men at Barbados, or some of the plantations: others fear the old game of Scotland.'

[6] S. L. Mims, *Colbert's West-India Policy* (New Haven, 1912), 82.

endowment of shipping, their stores of arms and ammunition, their paid and well-disciplined garrisons in every island—'all done by a Company'—was early aroused.[1] The French were naturally 'an encroaching nation',[2] and he noted the advent of de Tracy as the portent it was. 'In fine', was his prescient comment, 'the dispute will be whether the King of England or of France shall be monarch of the West Indies, for the King of Spain cannot hold it long, and this is the first year's entrance of the King of France on his own account'.[3]

But for all his warnings, he was not informed from home that France had declared war (26 January 1666). But they had the news in Martinique by mid-March[4]—and in consequence, English St. Christopher had fallen and Nevis had succumbed to the French assault by April, before Willoughby was able to move to prevent it. He made his point for the last time:

If it once come to run in a blood, God bless Barbados, that fair jewel of Your Majesty's crown. . . . I am come to where it pinches, and if Your Majesty gives not an ample and speedy redress, you have not only lost St. Christophers but you will lose the rest, I, and famous Barbados too, I fear;[5]

and, with not a little of the Roman *gravitas* that so notably invested the generation of English gentlemen of the 1640's, he took sail to defend the Leewards, and fell a victim to the hurricane.

Willoughby's death, and the ruin of the Leeward Islands,[6] gave a rude shock to the English Administration.[7] The Plantations

[1] Willoughby to the King, 4 Nov. 1663, CO 1/17, No. 89.
[2] The French complained with equal justice of Willoughby's encroachments on St. Lucia and Dominica. The French Government was anxious that the consolidation of the new Company should not be jeopardized by frontier squabbling: Colbert urged the Governor of Martinique to come to an arrangement with Willoughby if possible.
[3] Willoughby to Arlington, 5 Oct. 1664, CO 1/18, No. 119.
[4] Mims, op. cit. 124; although rumours that war was imminent had been current in Barbados since January; Willoughby to the King, 29 Jan. 1666, CO 1/20, No. 6.
[5] Willoughby to the King, 12 May 1666, CO 1/20, No. 92.
[6] Antigua and Montserrat were ravaged in Nov. 1666. The privateers were displaced from Statia and Tobago. Surinam fell to the Dutch.
[7] York ordered 6 more frigates to be fitted for the West Indies, provisioned for 6 months at least; 29 Oct. 1666, Adm 2/1745. *Hope* and *Coventry* had previously been sent, but with only 4 months' provision and very little powder; CO 1/20, Nos. 119–20. Willoughby had had to impress 8 merchant-ships to act as men-of-

Committee was galvanized into action.[1] A quartet of officials was at once appointed to govern Barbados *ad interim*—William Willoughby, his nephew Henry, and the merchants Hawley and Barwicke.[2] A Commission as Captain-General[3] was to go to William Willoughby when his brother's death was proved certain. Willoughby was granted Vice-Admiralty powers, together with the authority to impress merchant shipping for the King's service[4] that he had already asked for on his brother's behalf. (He was to find that lack of direct permission on this point had not stopped the masterful Francis from carrying out a great deal of arbitrary impressment prior to setting out on his last expedition.) At the same time Sir Tobias Bridge was commissioned as commander of a regiment of 800 men for the defence of Barbados.[5] Thus the month of February 1667 saw much activity: the arrival of four frigates at Barbados; the departure from England of William Lord Willoughby on *Colchester*, with Samuel Farmer and Sir James Modyford as his fellow-passengers; and preparations put in hand at the naval dockyards for a strong fleet of the King's ships to go out at once to the West Indies.[6] This fleet, under command of Sir John Harman, reached Barbados on 9 June, and was at once sent down to the relief of the Leeward Islands.

Willoughby himself had arrived in Barbados on 23 April. The gentlemen of the Assembly, well aware of their indispensability in such a time of emergency, were enjoying alternate bursts of patriotism and faction. Last year they had voted one million pounds of sugar to equip a new fleet of merchant ships,[7] which,

---

war, and 120 seamen; HMC Portland, iii. 301; Minutes of the Council of Barbados, 28 Feb. 1667, CO 31/1 100. Willoughby himself was lost with *Hope*, and *Coventry* was captured by the French.

[1] 12 Dec. 1666, APCC, i. 693. Twenty-three merchants had petitioned the King on 3 Dec. that William Willoughby should be sent to Barbados at once; CO 1/20, No. 188. The King later assured the Council of Barbados that 'the entire Exchange' had voted William his brother's successor; 2 Jan. 1667, CO 1/21, No. 22.

[2] Commission, 5 Dec. 1666, CO 31/1, 92.

[3] Commission, 3 Jan. 1667, CO 1/20, No. 198.

[4] Warrant of powers of impressment, CO 1/21, No. 23.

[5] Commission, CO 1/21, No. 10. The soldiers were to be paid out of the King's moiety of the 4½ per cent.; ibid. No. 24.

[6] It was the King's suggestion 'to manage the war by small squadrons, and not to commit the entire Fleet to home waters'; the King to York, 6 Feb. 1667, ibid. No. 17.

[7] They had also appointed three of their own number to administer this fund,

with the aid of the King's frigates that were promised, was to go down and recover St. Christopher and Nevis. To this they had since added a robust rider, to the effect that all laws in Barbados passed in the reign of Charles I and 'of his present Majesty' that had not been repealed, 'shall be taken to be the laws in force, and that the inhabitants shall be governed as heretofore, according to the laws of England and the constitution and laws of this Island'[1]—an assertion that was in quieter times to attract more attention at home than it now received there. However, by June the new Governor was able to tell the King that he had conquered the opposition to the name of Willoughby in the Island —principally by distributing offices open-handedly among the members of the *bloc*.[2] He made a friend of Samuel Farmer,[3] and backed the more sensible of the Assembly's opinions, in particular their objection that Barbados had no open trade to Scotland for white labour and to Guinea for black. Given three or four thousand Scottish servants, he felt sure he could 'grapple with Mons[ieu]r'. He insisted that the 'Caribbees' could not be made safe by his exertions, or by those of the inhabitants alone. The home Government must play its part: "tis not 10 times His Maties Revenue here will preserve these Islands without constant supplies from His Matie.'[4] Some people still seemed to believe that Barbados had independent resources, that it could draw a revenue from a bottomless well of gold. In fact the revenue amounted annually to some £6,000 only—and already there was more charged to its account than it could possibly discharge in five years.[5]

While Willoughby was inspecting the Leeward Islands,[6] the

because they 'would not trust the King further than necessity compelled them'; F. Lord Willoughby's Narrative, 20 Apr. 1666, CO 1/20, No. 57.

[1] Minutes of the Council of Barbados, 7 Mar. 1667, CO 31/1, 110–11.

[2] W. Lord Willoughby [hereafter Willoughby] to the King, 3 June 1667, CO 1/21, No. 54.

[3] Willoughby to the King, 7 May 1667: 'I wish Your Majesty had no worse subjects in your English Parlament'; ibid. No. 43.

[4] Ibid., No. 89; 16 Sept. 1667, Stowe MS. 755, f. 19.

[5] Willoughby to Arlington (a Commissioner of the Treasury), 26 Nov. 1667, CO 1/21, No. 149. He sent his son home with the accounts to prove his point, but neither the point nor its proof can have given much consolation to the creditors of the first Earl of Carlisle, whose claims on the revenue of 'Carliola' were by now computed to total close on £25,000; APCC, i. 737.

[6] Between Oct. 1667 and Feb. 1668. He received news of the peace signed at Breda in November, while in Antigua.

Assembly of Barbados fell to its usual pleasures of disputation and self-assertion.[1] The Governor, though much more tolerant than his late brother, was by no means a docile man, and on his return his relations with the leaders of the Assembly became more and more strained. The danger of war over, the solidarity of the Island politicians dissolved. He felt confident that he had their measure; but he was not certain how much influence their friends had in London. Many of these, he knew, had rallied to the cause of one George Marsh.[2] This absentee planter of St. Christopher, in liaison with Governor Russell of Nevis, had for some time been agitating for the detachment of the Leeward Islands from the control of the Governor of Barbados. Marsh said he spoke for the Islanders; Willoughby wrote home that this was nonsense. The Montserrat planters had told him they did not want separation; Antigua planters wanted a number of things, including a free port and relief from the $4\frac{1}{2}$ per cent.— but not separation.[3] Of Nevis, where Russell ruled, he remarked curtly that the defence of the place had cost five times its worth.[4] He remained uneasy about these machinations,[5] however, and got the permission he wanted to return home to see what exactly was going on.[6] He left Barbados in October 1668 and did not come back until four years had passed.

The Committee of Plantations was now pondering the seven-year lease of 'Carliola' held by Francis Lord Willoughby. This had been transferred to his brother, but was now due for renewal. But perhaps it should not be renewed? Was it right that the Leeward Islands should be tied to Barbados? Marsh's petition on this matter made some serious charges.[7] Barbados,

[1] It was now that the Assembly openly aired a grievance long since discovered: the passage of the $4\frac{1}{2}$ per cent. Act by Francis Lord Willoughby through an Assembly convened under the outworn authority of the Carlisle Patent. The Assembly being thus illegal, so too was the Act!

[2] He was also particularly suspicious of Edward Thornborough, secretary to the 'Gentlemen-Planters', a friend of Hawley and Barwicke; cf. Willoughby to the Privy Council, 22 July 1668, CO 1/23, No. 23; Higham, op. cit. 72–73.

[3] Willoughby to the Plantations Committee, 2 Jan. 1668, CO 1/22, No. 17; 'Proposals of the inhabitants of Antigua', 31 Jan. 1668, ibid. Nos. 19–20. Willoughby had himself a plantation in Antigua, and always spoke warmly of the Island; cf. CSPC 1661–8, 1788.

[4] Willoughby to the King, 11 Feb. 1668, CO 1/23, No. 34.

[5] Cf. Willoughby to Williamson, 11 Aug. 1668, ibid. No. 37.

[6] Ibid., No. 38. Permission had been refused the previous March; APCC, i. 763.

[7] 2 Oct. 1667, CO 1/21, No. 119.

it said, had monopolized all the war-stores[1] that had been sent
out while the fighting was on, and had selfishly left the other
Islands to fend for themselves—with what disastrous consequences all the world knew. The plantations in Nevis and St.
Christopher were now devastated. It was, moreover, certain
that Barbados would take no step to aid the work of restoration
and reconstruction necessary there, because her own sugar was
reaping and would continue to reap great advantages from this
sudden removal of the local competition. Since it was plainly
not to Barbados's interest to promote the revival of the Leewards' economy, the revival in fact would not be promoted, as
Barbadians had never yet been known to do anything for
motives of pure altruism.[2] Was it not notorious that Colonel
Lambert, the Barbadian who presided over the body of Commissioners which was now negotiating with the French for the
restoration of St. Christopher, was deliberately delaying the
proceedings?[3]

To these charges Willoughby's agent Champante put up a
stout, if not a convincing, defence. He pointed out, what was
true, that Nevis would undoubtedly have fallen to the French
with St. Christopher in the spring of 1666 had it not been for
the prompt assistance sent down from Barbados in the expedition that had cost the Governor his life. Moreover, were the
Leeward Islands to be separated from Barbados, Barbadian
debtors would thereby be provided with convenient sanctuary
on their own doorstep, very much easier of access than those
plantations in Continental America to which they were wont
to go. The agent roundly denied that any change in the terms
of Willoughby's Patent would be of service to His Majesty's
interests. He urged the Lords of the Privy Council to satisfy
themselves that this petition for separation which they had
before them was actually representative of the opinion of the

---

[1] Governor Russell of Nevis reported that he had received four of the six guns
allotted to him, but no powder; CO 1/21, No. 136.

[2] Compare the comments of Governor Sir Richard Dutton (Barbados) on 3 Jan.
1682, when asked by Stapleton (Governor of the Leeward Islands) to levy war on
the Caribs of Dominica. The people of Barbados 'are so little interested in the well-
being of the Leeward Islands, which can never be useful to them and are, as they
think, growing too fast upon them already, that they would be well content to see
them lessened rather than advanced. I do not expect that a man in the Island will
concern himself with them, much less contribute towards such a war'; CSPC
1681–5, 357.   [3] Higham, op. cit. 69.

freemen of the various Leeward Islands themselves, and was not merely a grievance trumped up by disgruntled London merchants who saw no chance under the present dispensation of ever recovering their debts from the ruined planters and owners of estates, and who objected to the inevitable preponderance of Barbados in the West-India trade as a whole.[1] Willoughby himself meanwhile arrived in England to reinforce these arguments; and as a result, when his lease expired, the Commission issued to him as Captain-General in November 1669 remained unaltered in respect of the area of his command, of which he remained Governor 'during pleasure'.[2]

Between 1667 and 1669 the Privy Councillors had of course matters on their minds of more immediate significance than these colonial questions. It was not only the West Indies that were exhausted by an unfortunate and unsuccessful war—so also was the English Administration itself. Clarendon was now made scapegoat for the shattering of other men's illusions, and there was a re-examination of that structure of Government for which he had stood sponsor.

In this process the colonies were not, indeed, entirely forgotten. The ninth 'Head' of 17 such presented by Parliament against the Chancellor accused him of introducing an arbitrary government into the Plantations. Something could be made of this, though not much. It was Clarendon who, lurking behind the façade of his son's part-proprietary in Surinam, had exempted that colony from the regulation of the Acts of Trade for the good of his private pocket.[3] Was it not also the case that, although Nevis was worth some £20,000 a year to the King, not a penny of this sum had come His Majesty's way because of some dark guile on the Chancellor's part?[4] It was Clarendon who had committed Humphrey Walrond to the Fleet prison, and who had supported Francis Lord Willoughby in his persecution of Sir Robert Harley (Buckingham's man), as well as in that of the redoubtable Samuel Farmer (the merchants'

---

[1] 'Answer of John Champante', 20 Oct. 1667, CO 1/21, No. 137.
[2] His Commission, 11 Feb. 1667, in SP 104/174b, 118–27, may be compared with that of 20 Nov. 1669 in CSPC 1669–74, 128.
[3] A letter of Thomas Kendall's of Nov. 1664 dwells on this anomaly, CO 1/18, No. 136.
[4] Sir Charles Wheler in particular laid the ruin of Nevis at Clarendon's door.

friend)[1]—although in fact it was Arlington's signature that appeared on the warrant for Farmer's arrest. The Chancellor's machinations had also blocked the petition for aid that Farmer had made to his sympathizers in the House of Commons.[2] And his foreign policy had led, in short, to the loss of St. Christopher and to the growth of French competition in the West Indies.

There was more, of course, behind these charges than mere jealousy or spleen. There was also a genuine perplexity. Who *had* been responsible for the loss of St. Christopher? Who, indeed, had 'lost the war' in Europe? It was one thing to place a prominent, disliked figure in the pillory, but it was quite another to state where exactly the remedy to prevent such disasters in the future should be applied. It irked the vigilant Commons that 'policy' should be a mystery, that foreign affairs should still be a private affair of Prerogative, when it was they who were asked to pay for the blunders that monarchy and monarchy's agents made. So henceforth they became bolder in criticism, and the Administration closed its ranks against them— or did so as far as it could while two mutually exclusive foreign policies were being pursued at once.

The Committee of Plantations was directed on 23 September 1667 to examine the terms of the Commissions of the twin Councils of Trade and of Foreign Plantations of 1660, with a view to reviving these now moribund bodies.[3] A reorganization of all the various Committees of the Privy Council and their spheres of responsibility followed at the end of January 1668. On 12 February the King announced that this reorganization would enhance the reputation of his Administration.[4] The four standing Committees he appointed included one 'for the busynesse of Trade', which also had under its charge the affairs of the foreign plantations, and those of Irish, Scottish, and Channel Islands commerce.[5] In

[1] 29 Apr. 1664, APCC, i. 619; Clarendon, op. cit. ii, § 1160; *Commons Journals*, ix. 15–16.

[2] 11 Nov. 1665, APCC, i. 665; CSPC 1661–8, 1057; cf. Clarendon, op. cit. ii, § 1739.

[3] 23 Sept. 1667, APCC, i. 720.   [4] 12 Feb. 1668, ibid. 747.

[5] 'Regulation of Privy Councell Comittees', 12 Feb. 1668, Add. MS. 38861, ff. 18–20; Andrews, *Committees*, 88–90. Its members were Buckingham, Ormond, Anglesey, Ossory, Bridgewater, Robartes, Lauderdale, Arlington, Holles, Ashley, Clifford, Cartaret, Morice, and W. Coventry. Carlisle, Craven, and Fitzhardinge were added on 10 June, and Sandwich on 13 Jan. 1669.

addition, a new Council of Trade was established in October.[1]

It was, however, on the Privy Council Committee, and not on this Council, that the burden of colonial administration continued to fall. It considered its first business in March. Willoughby was sent 'a Civill letter that may signify nothing' until such time as his superiors had got their bearings;[2] meanwhile Sir Tobias Bridge's reports on the parlous state of his troops were carefully examined.[3] Clearly the best thing to do with his regiment was to disband it.[4] A sub-committee, set up to consider how best to ameliorate the results of a fire in Bridgetown, Barbados, which had destroyed the magazine there,[5] has importance in that it brought before official notice the body that now styled itself the 'Gentlemen-Planters of Barbados in London'.[6] These Gentlemen-Planters were, of course, not strangers to the politicians, nor indeed were their views, most of which were grievances. They still put these forward as if the sense in them was self-evident, and must convince any reasonable man. The Lords Committee took a sharp tone, refusing to bandy words on general policy with merchants.

In riposte to the Gentlemen-Planters' complaints about the $4\frac{1}{2}$ per cent., they brought to the Gentlemen's attention the notoriously bad book-keeping of that duty. How could it be called burdensome, when it had been expressly designed, by His Majesty's favour, 'for the support of the Government of that Island'? Since, moreover, the presence of a regiment of the King's troops was the strongest support any Government could wish for, and since, furthermore, that regiment was in sore straits, lacking both pay and equipment, it was but the merest justice that these deficiencies (which were anyway the fault of

[1] The report on the Acts of Trade which this Council presented in December was the main justification for its existence. The proportion of 28 politicians to 19 merchants contrasts markedly with the composition of the 1660 Council. Its instigator was Ashley, its most active member his client, Benjamin Worsley, many of whose papers are included in the Shaftesbury Papers in the Public Record Office; cf. in particular 'The advantage of Trading with our Plantacons', of which there is also a copy in MS. Rawl. A. 478, ff. 57 et seq. The Council expired in 1672.
[2] Report of Committee, 12 Mar. 1668, CO 1/22, No. 52.
[3] Bridge to Albemarle, 27 May 1668, CSPC 1661-8, 1741, 1760-2.
[4] The King to Bridge, 20 May 1668, CO 1/22, No. 100; Privy Council to Willoughby, APCC, i. 775.
[5] Order-in-Council, 12 June 1668, APCC, i. 778
[6] On 16 June 1668, CO 1/22, No. 123.

the Barbadians) should be made good out of the proceeds of the 4½ per cent. duty. Orders to that effect had been given over a year ago. Barbados should look to their implementation at once. A more amiable answer was, however, returned to the request that the Island might be allowed to recruit white servants from Scotland, Ireland, Jersey, and Guernsey: this might be done, so long as no traffic in goods took place.[1]

But before the Committee would consider any further petitions it resolved to make itself better acquainted with the situation in the West Indies. Even on the most superficial inspection, there seemed to be a very great deal to put right. In Barbados there was fire-damage and war-damage to assess.[2] There was the problem of making the French pay for the ruin they had brought on the English half of St. Christopher. There was an unpaid account of some £4,500 for ordnance supplies. Disquieting reports of local cowardice during the fighting required investigation.[3] And there was, lastly, an accumulation of litigation about impounded goods and property, which had to be settled. Most of this last business resulted from the hasty action of the elder Willoughby in impressing ships, men, and materials for the preservation of His Majesty's colonies: His Majesty now found himself confronted with a West-India bill of £14,000. Every shipmaster and owner in the Caribbean who had ever lost a strand of rigging seemed determined to go to law about it at the Crown's expense, and there was no lack of 'spoiled lawyers' in the Islands to urge him cheerfully on. It was the refusal of merchant-captains to abate their claims that caused the exasperated Privy Council to pick up a cudgel of counter-attack that had too long lain unused. For when the records of these same shipmasters were examined, what a tale of unsigned dockets, forged cockets, missing certificates and falsified bonds was revealed! Was this how the Acts of Trade were administered in the colonies? Was this how the royal Governors obeyed their pledged Oath to see the laws were faithfully observed? These questions, perhaps indignantly rhetorical at first, took on a tone of honest inquiry. To the new Council of Trade this

[1] 31 July 1668, APCC, i. 792; Order in Council to Willoughby, Feb. 1667, CO 1/21, No. 24; 20 May 1668, APCC, i. 775; 29 July 1668, ibid. 790.
[2] Cf. CSPC 1661–8, 1817.
[3] Cf. report of Dr. Leoline Jenkins, judge of the Admiralty, in CO 1/23, No. 47; and Henry Willoughby to Williamson, 28 Aug. 1666, CO 1/20, No. 140.

whole matter was transferred, so that it might be passed in review.

The Navigation Act of 1660, the terms of which had been to hand in Barbados as early as 1 August of that year, had distinctly required colonial Governors 'before their entrance into their Government' to take a solemn Oath to do their utmost to enforce the Act's commands. No machinery for carrying out this requirement, however, had ever been established. Colonel Modyford, when 'planter-Governor' in the Island, had indeed taken such an Oath of his own accord,[1] but that was doubtless to curry favour with the authorities at home. In June 1663 a letter had been sent out to all colonial Governors drawing attention to the many reports[2] that were then circulating, concerning the non-observation of the Act in the colonies. In August a *pro forma* was forwarded to them, to appoint A . . . B . . . to administer the Oath to the Governor. A . . . B . . ., however, remained a phantom, despite the accompanying warning that any failure to materialize him would cause His Majesty great displeasure.[3] Even after the passing of the Staple Act in 1663 ships continued to trade direct from colonial to European ports and back, and the Dutch carrier was still sure of his welcome in the Leeward Islands. Masters of English ships were not giving the correct bonds and certificates of the goods they had aboard, where they had loaded them, whither they were carrying them. In 1665 the Privy Council had ordered that henceforward a 'perfect accompt' must be kept, and that a Governor must transmit full returns, giving the names of all ships and their masters, together with a description of their cargoes, that had traded within his particular jurisdiction. Duplicates of all bonds entered in the naval office should be sent home twice a year.[4] No Governor and no colonist, therefore, could plead ignorance of the requirements of the law, nor in fact did they:[5] the colonial point was always that the Acts

[1] CO 31/1, 22. He later asked Arlington to appoint someone to administer the Oath to him as Governor of Jamaica; Modyford to Arlington, 20 Feb. 1665, CO 1/19, No. 27.

[2] Cf. Order-in-Council of 15 Aug. 1662, referring to Downing's allegations of a trade from Barbados to Dutch ports; APCC, i. 569.

[3] Circular, the King to Governors, 25 Aug. 1663, CO 1/17, No. 78.

[4] 6 Mar. 1665, APCC, i. 649.

[5] Perhaps a Scot may comment that had the colonists been Scots, they might have pleaded the old Scots law of desuetude and got away with it.

of Trade were misconceived, not that they were difficult to understand. Even so trusty a Governor as Francis Lord Willoughby sympathized with the Barbadians' dislike of these Acts, although he conceded that Barbados and Nevis, being rich islands, could support the burden better than Antigua and Montserrat, whose petitions to 'be restored to their pristine happiness'—an open trade—he forwarded to the King with favourable comment.[1] The King in one of his replies did promise some amelioration, but none ever came. Nor, fortunately for the colonists, did any stern enforcement of the law. In 1664 the Committee of Plantations did indeed ask the Farmers of the Customs to send over agents to the colonies to see that the Acts were observed;[2] but as the Farmers were left to carry out this service at their own expense, it is not surprising that they decided that the Revenue could afford a loss by default better than they could the expense of seeing that loss recouped.

But the Farmers did not relax their devotion to the principle of confining the colonial trade, however reluctant they were to meddle in the practice, for it was they who advised the Committee during the Dutch War in Europe against allowing any relaxation of the Acts in the colonies.[3] The Committee were then considering suspending the Acts in order that English merchants might bring home their goods from foreign ports with less likelihood of capture, the merchants having asserted that they would be at a disadvantage compared with their Dutch competitors and enemies unless they were allowed to ship their goods in war-time as the property of aliens in alien ships.[4] The Farmers feared that foreign nations would profit from any such suspension, the ports of the West Indies would hum with foreign shipping and fill with foreign gold, while

---

[1] Cf. Willoughby to the King, 4 Nov. 1663: The Acts might yet 'ruin' the colony; CO 1/17, No. 89. (And so staunch a Cavalier as Sir William Berkeley in Virginia was also of the view that they were 'mighty and destructive'; Beer, op. cit. ii. 113.) Willoughby's views on the whole matter came out, however, in 1666, when he came to 'where it pinches'. 'Whoever he be who advised your Majesty to restrain and tie up your Collonies in point of trade is more a Marchant than a good subject and would have Your Majesty's Islands but nursed up to work for him and such men'; Willoughby to the King, 12 May 1666, CO 1/20, No. 92.

[2] 22 Apr. 1664, APCC, i. 618.

[3] Report of the Farmers to the Committee of Plantations, 28 Feb. 1665, CO 1/19, No. 31.

[4] Harper, *Navigation Laws*, p. 68.

English seamen—and indeed entire English colonies—would desert to the lucrative service of France. Their fears were, however, discounted by the politicians and the Acts were in fact relaxed, but enumeration, the West Indies' bugbear, remained a cardinal principle. The colonies there, as has been noted, were relegated to the back of the official mind until their hardships and misfortunes compelled a reversal of this attitude; and so, when their economic state was once more examined by the Committee of Plantations in November 1667, the Governors were chided for their neglect and non-observance of the Acts of Trade in a tone more of sorrow than anger.[1] The King, so the Committee said, was just then 'desirous rather at first to advise all of them of the neglect than to proceed vigorously against them'.[2]

The Council of Trade, reviewing this history, was, in contrast, strongly in favour of vigorous procedure.[3] It revived the idea of inspection and control as a responsibility of the Farmers of the Customs. It recommended in its report that the latter should instal and maintain 'a person' in each colony, who should concert all its commercial business under his charge, and who should also administer the required Oath to the Governor. Ships of the line should in future carry out the instructions they had for too long ignored—to impound the illegal trader in Caribbean as in all other waters, and send him home as prize.[4] This was a sensible observation enough; but obviously naval frigates could hardly do as the Council of Trade wished, since they were very seldom in Caribbean waters at all. Thus a solution to these difficulties had to be delayed until it could be concerted with that of the larger question of defence in the West Indies as a whole.

The course of the late war had served to prove one thing conclusively to the Administration: that the English islands in

---

[1] By the Commissioners of the Treasury: Albemarle, Ashley, Clifford, Coventry, and Duncombe; 12 Nov. 1667, T 11/1, 49–51.

[2] Circular from Committee of Trade to Plantation Governors, 12 Nov. 1667, T 11/1, 49–51.

[3] Report of Council of Trade, Dec. 1668, CSPC 1669–74, 1884; 20 Jan. 1669, APCC, i. 827; CO 1/23, No. 93. It is signed by Arlington, Ashley, Carlisle, Craven, and Ormond; Sirs J. Berkeley, J. Trevor, T. Clifford, W. Coventry, T. Littleton, and G. Downing; and 12 others, including Child and Worsley. Cf. Beer, op. cit. ii. 343.

[4] 27 Jan. 1669, APCC, i. 829.

the Caribbean, far from being so many redoubts from which sorties on the unsuspecting could be made, were but sheepfolds on which the wolves were only too eager to descend. The risk of losing them all must therefore not be run again. The affairs of the colonies there must in fact be regulated in that 'uniform' style that had been designed in 1660, but which had never— now that the Administration turned a suspicious eye on its own record—been given concrete expression.

In the spring and summer of 1669 the Privy Council ordered an inquiry into the state of the revenue and the general condition of the 'Caribbees'.[1] The Treasury's report on the $4\frac{1}{2}$ per cent. duty, presented in October,[2] was so depressing that the Council decided to accommodate the wishes of those who were touting for what they hoped was a safe West-India profit. The settlement of the claims to 'Carliola' so painstakingly arrived at in 1663, was now thrown overboard. It had never been honoured anyway. A suggestion to farm the Revenue had been made as early as 1664,[3] and, despite the strong objections both of William Lord Willoughby and of the Barbadians themselves, this suggestion was now adopted. The Revenue arising from the Farm was to be devoted to the support of the militia in the Islands, and to finance the work of reconstruction necessary as a result of the war.

The Barbadians were quick to voice their resentment to the King himself. In a petition of October 1670 they pointed out that the $4\frac{1}{2}$ per cent. duty had been granted by them only 'provided the Supporte of the Government & other publique charges expressed, should out of the said $4\frac{1}{2}$ per cent. bee satisfied'.[4]

It was, therefore, not an honorarium to be put in the royal pocket. On this, however, Heneage Finch the Attorney-General expressed a contrary opinion (and doubtless the King's own) in the House of Commons. The duty was in fact a tribute, paid in consideration of a free grant of the Barbadians' titles from the

---

[1] Cf. 26 Feb. 1669, 12 May 1669, APCC, i. 836, 854.

[2] Cf. Cal. T.B., 1669–72, 151 et seq.

[3] Cf. the petition of William Willoughby and James Halsall, CSPC 1661–8, 873; and a memorandum of 1664, that no account of the $4\frac{1}{2}$ per cent. revenue had yet been received in the Exchequer, 'nor ever will be'; CO 1/18, No. 158.

[4] Petition of the Deputy-Governor, Council, and Assembly of Barbados to the King, 21 Oct. 1670, CO 1/25, No. 78; Harlow, *Barbados*, p. 282.

King.[1] On 9 September 1670, therefore, the Revenue from the
4½ per cent. duty was farmed to George Marsh the petitioner,
Robert Spencer, Sir Charles Wheler, and Colonel John Strode,
at a rental of £7,000 per annum.

Strode had previously put in a bid to farm the duty in the
Leeward Islands separately, at a rental of £600[2]—thereby out-
bidding Marsh, who had the same idea. The Administration
agreed to this, and thereafter was prepared to support the
project to separate the Leewards entirely from the control of
Barbados—the more so as Sir Charles Wheler had declared
himself willing to govern the Islands without salary, provided
he secured the Farm in Barbados.[3] The new Council of Plantations continued the policy, and three weeks after the Farm had
been settled as Wheler desired, it recommended the erection of
a new Government in the West Indies.[4] Willoughby's protests
went for nothing,[5] and the drafting of Wheler's Commission[6]
as first Governor of the Leeward Islands was put in hand simultaneously with that for Lynch as Lieutenant-Governor in
Jamaica.

These two Commissions have a precision of wording lacking
in the previous Commissions issued to West-India Governors.
In Wheler's, the emergency powers of issuing Orders-in-Council,
which the Willoughbys had enjoyed, disappeared. Wheler was
not allowed to appoint what deputy-Governors he pleased in
the islands under his command, as had been the Willoughby's
practice.[7] He was to send home for confirmation all laws as soon

---

[1] 28 Nov. 1670, Stock, *Debates*, i. 369.

[2] 8 Dec. 1669, APCC, i. 878. The King-in-Council had ordered the Treasury
Lords to 'perfect a contract' on 22 Dec. 1669, with a proviso that the Crown might
resume the Farm at the end of the seven-year period; Egerton MS. 2395, f. 463;
APCC, i. 881.

[3] 'Proposals of Sir Charles Wheler', 9 Feb. 1671, CO 1/26, No. 21.

[4] Council of Plantations to the King, 22 Sept. 1670, CO 153/1, 1–3; cf. also
CO 389/5, 5, 16.

[5] Cf. Willoughby to the Council of Plantations, 29 Oct. 1670, ibid. 8–11: 'A
designe of very inconsiderable persons for their own Privat advantage'; and he
wrote darkly that these Leewards separatists would soon find that they had sawn
off the bough they sat on; Willoughby to (Deputy-Governor) Codrington, 7 Nov.
1670, CO 31/2, 21–26.

[6] Commission, 25 Jan. 1671, CO 1/26, No. 7.

[7] A later Commission to Wheler (24 Feb.), however, gave him this authority,
but instructed him to continue Stapleton as Lieutenant-Governor of Montserrat,
'for the good opinion His Matie has of his abilities'; CO 153/1, 17. Stapleton's
Commission is in CO 1/26, No. 65.

as they were passed in the Assembly. If these laws were not confirmed within two years then they were to lapse, and were not to be continued by the will of the Assembly and by that alone, as was the habit in Jamaica. The contrast here with the terms of Francis Lord Willoughby's Commission, wherein laws were only non-effective if they had been distinctly disallowed by the King, is very marked.

In the spring of 1670 the King wrote cordially to Willoughby, regretting that his time had been fully taken up with the business of Parliament and the affairs of the State—two branches of administration that Charles allowed to interlock as little as was possible. Now, however, since 'a happy conclusion'[1] to these was in sight, Barbados could expect to receive his constant attention.[2] But the royal good humour was soon to be dispelled by fresh evidence of Barbadian assertiveness. This had long been a distant nuisance, but now it became an obstacle in the King's own path.

In November he asked the Commons to raise a large supply, ostensibly to equip the fleet and maintain the Triple Alliance against France.[3] Sugar was one of the commodities on which the Commons loyally voted to raise the duty.[4] The Gentlemen-Planters were under instruction from the Assembly of Barbados to block any move on the part of the English refiners to prevent the importation of, or increase the duties upon, sugars refined in the plantations themselves. If Parliament wanted to raise any sugar duties, let it raise the 4s. impost on foreign sugars imported, particularly on the crop from Brazil.[5] But the Commons would not have this; the English manufacturing trade with Portugal was too important a national asset to be risked thus. Moreover, the merchants who traded to the American

---

[1] That summer Charles arranged his private Treaty of Dover, with Louis XIV.
[2] The King to Willoughby, 6 Apr. 1670, CO 324/2, 20.
[3] 26 Nov. 1670, *Commons Journals*, ix. 171-2.
[4] The suggestion to do this was put into the Supply Bill by the English refiners. The existing duty on unrefined colonial sugar, as laid down in the Book of Rates, was 1s. 6d. per 100, as against 4s. per 100 on foreign sugar. The duty on refined English sugar stood at 5s. per 100, as against 7s. 4d. per 100 on foreign.
[5] For this and other argument, cf. 'The State of the Case of the Sugar Plantations in America', 1 May 1671, printed in *Lords Journals*, xii. 486-7. The Customs Commissioners pointed out that it was not the duties, but over-production, that was the real core of the planters' problem; cf. Beer, op. cit. i. 165. A petition of the English refiners to the King-in-Council, dated 5 Nov. 1671, is in Add. MS. 25115, f. 300.

colonies supported the case of the English sugar-refiners because they had long nursed a grievance against the Assembly of Barbados for its regulations about debt. A brawl of argument now ensued between Portugal traders, English refiners, English merchants, and Barbadian planters.

For the latter the Gentlemen-Planters, of course, lobbied assiduously. The Earl of Sandwich, President of the Council of Foreign Plantations, was sympathetic, and was well briefed by Worsley on the national importance of sugar. Sir Robert Howard, although an auditor of the Exchequer, was mindful of his friends in Barbados and urged the planters' case in the Commons. Sir Thomas Clarges remarked mournfully there that $4\frac{1}{2}$ per cent. had lost England St. Christopher and Surinam, and would yet lose her Barbados too.[1] The English merchants and the refiners continued to assert how advantageous it was to the nation to have English plantation sugar come overseas unrefined because of the 'double navigation' involved, and were quite prepared to buy the support of other members of Parliament by a lavish distribution of cash.[2] All these petitions of the King's subjects against a tax caused Clifford the Treasurer to express his severe displeasure—'there is but one degree between petitioning and commanding'—and, given this lead, the country gentry, who saw no reason to prefer one band of tradesmen to another, saw to it that the Bill passed intact to the House of Lords (March 1671).

Their Lordships, perhaps because they appreciated the fiscal arguments of Willoughby, who was present in person to protect his planters' interests, but more likely because they were anxious to deflate the ever-increasing pretensions of the Commons, reduced the proposed duties.[3] This caused a famous resolution to be passed *nemini contradicente* by the Commons on 13 April 1671, 'that in all aids given to the King by the Commons the rate or tax ought not to be altered by the Lords'.[4] A row broke

[1] Harris, *Sandwich*, ii. 224, 226.
[2] Cf. Stock, *Debates*, i. 367–78.
[3] The Commons had voted to put $\frac{1}{4}d$. per lb. on English muscovado, $\frac{1}{2}d$. per lb. on Brazil muscovado; $\frac{1}{2}d$. on brown unpurged sugars (panels); $1d$. on English white (refined) and foreign white; $3d$. on foreign loaf, $2d$. on foreign powder, and $\frac{3}{4}d$. per lb. drawback on English refined sugars re-exported. The Lords reduced the $1d$. duty on English whites to $\frac{3}{4}d$., and, to preserve the Anglo-Portuguese trade, reduced by the same amount the duty on Portugal sugars. Cf. Beer, op. cit. i. 82–83.
[4] Stock, *Debates*, i. 385; *Commons Journals*, ix. 235.

out between Buckingham and Arlington, and relays of angry messages passed between the Upper and Lower Houses. In the subsequent clamour the King's main interest—more money—was not surprisingly lost sight of; and the Supply Bill fell. Parliament was prorogued on 27 April without any settlement of the revenue to the King's satisfaction.

The Gentlemen-Planters put it somewhat too mildly when they wrote to the Assembly of Barbados that the King was 'not over-pleased' with the planters because of the loss of his Bill over the sugar question. They advised the Assemblymen to moderate the language, and indeed the number, of their petitions to the Crown[1]—and this was sound advice, for the most recent of these, besides commenting with asperity on the 'inconveniency' of Patent offices in the Island, had gone so far as to ask for the grant of a Charter on the Massachusetts model of 1629—'to make them a body corporate with all powers formerly granted to the Earl of Carlisle'.[2] But this counsel of the London interest came a little too late. Clifford's opinion about the relation of a petition to a command was shared by his master; and, far from being given more scope to go their own way, the Barbadians were about to be brought under much firmer control.

If Ministers of the English Administration needed any further reminder of the sins of the planters, they had only to glance at the books of the Royal Company of Adventurers trading into Africa, in which their own personal credit was deeply involved. It was a load of plantation debt that had broken the back of that already crippled Company. A royal order of September 1669, that henceforth Barbadian debtors to the Company should forfeit their lands as well as their goods, had proved insufficient to remedy the damage already done, and the Company foundered.[3] But another, better found and ballasted, to be called the Royal African Company, was already designed; and the Administration had no intention that the history of its predecessor should repeat itself, so far as the sorry record of West-

---

[1] Gentlemen-Planters to the Assembly, CO 31/2, 33-35, 76.
[2] Assembly of Barbados to Sir P. Colleton, &c., 20 Apr. 1671, CO 31/2, 26-31. Other grievances were: abuses and heavy taxes in the Customs, the Acts of Trade, the lack of a Mint, the import duties, the rum tax. By Dec. 1671 they had decided to concentrate on the 4½ per cent. and its 'misuse'; CSPC 1669-74, 674.
[3] 28 Sept. 1669, APCC, i. 872.

India default was concerned. By 1673 it was reckoned in London that the total outstanding debt of the planters amounted to some 1¼ million pounds of sugar. This was no mere commercial deficit; it was a national calamity. It should not recur. So it came about that the new African Company itself became an organ of plantation control.

But plainly the best remedy for Barbadian default was the establishment of a genuinely strong government in the Island.[1] The first step was already taken. Since a new government had been set up in the Leeward Islands, it was now necessary to recast the terms of Willoughby's Commission as Captain-General. His area of authority was now reduced to the Islands of Barbados, with St. Lucia, St. Vincent, Dominica, and 'the rest of the Caribbees to windward of Guadeloupe'.[2] Laws passed by the Assembly in Barbados were now to be in force for two years and no longer, unless confirmed by the King before that time. The Island Government was not to dispose of any offices, 'which now are or have been granted by us or any of our Royall Predecessors'.

The Instructions that were drawn up for Willoughby in April 1672 charged him to ensure that in all votes at least seven of the Council of Barbados should be of one mind. The composition of that Council he must transmit to the Secretary of State as soon as it was constituted—not only the names of its members, but their opinions as well. He might not suspend Councillors until so permitted by the Administration: for arbitrary action by a hot-tempered Governor was as deleterious to

[1] Probably the comments of Lynch and Wheler, both of whom passed through Barbados in the summer of 1671, did not go unnoticed. Lynch remarked dryly of the planters' way of life, 'What they owe in London does not appear here'; Wheler's opinion was that the Assemblymen were now so suspicious of the Crown's intentions that they would never, of their own accord, 'give a shilling to buy a snaffle for their own mouths'; Wheler to Arlington, 8 June 1671, CO 1/26, No. 72. Both admired the political dexterity of Codrington, Deputy-Governor in Willoughby's absence. Codrington, however, 'had nothing but what a Capricious Assembly will give, which is lyttle, unless they are mightily pleased'; Codrington to Willoughby, 15 Jan. 1671, ibid. No. 6.

[2] Commission in CO 29/1, 141-7; Instructions, ibid. 147-52. St. Lucia, Dominica, and St. Vincent were specifically named on Willoughby's request; 17 May 1672, CO 389/5, 109. (Cf. Clifford to Willoughby, 3 July 1672, advising him to get a copy of his new Commission as soon as possible; Egerton MS. 2395, f. 479b.) The Commission to the Governor of the Leeward Islands gave him control of all the islands to leeward of Guadeloupe as far as St. John in the Virgins, which, together with Tortola, had been seized by Jamaican buccaneers in 1664.

good government as was factious opposition by an Assembly. In July he was ordered to take up his post immediately, as the pre-arranged Anglo-French attack on the Dutch was due to take place. Willoughby thus arrived back in Barbados in October 1672, and set about the task of choosing seven like-minded men to insert into his Council. That this, when constituted, included both Sir Peter Colleton and Colonel Sam Barwicke, friends neither to each other nor to himself, indicates the difficulties he encountered.[1]

These four Commissions and Instructions issued between 1670 and 1672 to Lynch, to Wheler and his successor Stapleton, and to Willoughby illustrate the resolve of the new Council of Foreign Plantations to get an adequate grip on colonial administration.[2] When the Council was established in July 1670 it had only ten members, presided over by the Earl of Sandwich.[3] The Lord Keeper, Bridgeman; the Treasury Commissioners, Ashley, Clifford, and Duncomb; and the Secretaries of State, Arlington and Trevor, attended some of the meetings *ex-officio*. In March 1671 the Council was dignified by the addition of grandees such as York, Rupert, Ormond, Buckingham, and Lauderdale.[4] Not all of these were passengers. Ormond was well acquainted with the nature of the trade between Ireland and the plantations. York's interest in colonial matters was well known. Lauderdale often took a surprisingly active part.[5] Clifford, although only present

---

[1] Willoughby to Slingsby, 15 Nov. 1672, CO 389/5, 132; Willoughby to Worsley, 7 Mar. 1673, CO 1/30, No. 11.

[2] CO 389/4 contains these Commissions and Instructions: ff. 17–18 (Lynch); ff. 22–26 (Wheler); f. 40 (Stapleton); and ff. 60–63 (Willoughby). For Wheler's supersession by Stapleton, see Higham, op. cit. 89.

[3] Commission and Instructions, 30 July 1670, MS. Rawl. A. 255, ff. 144–50. The members were Lord Gorges and Lord Allington, two Irish peers; Thomas Grey, son of Lord Grey of Warke; Henry Brouncker, Sir Humphrey Winch, Sir John Finch, Edmund Waller, and Silas Titus. The secretary was Henry Slingsby, who was assisted by Dr. Benjamin Worsley. The President received £700 per annum and the others £500. Sessions were secret, members taking an oath to preserve the secrecy. The Council met twice weekly, at various addresses. It met first on 3 Aug. 1670 at Essex House, Bridgeman's home. Between May 1671 and February 1672 the Earl of Bristol's house in Queen Street was regularly used. In June 1672 Wren drew up plans for a new building to house it; cf. GD 24/4, 216; Andrews, *Committees*, 97 et seq.; Brown, *Shaftesbury*, 146; Root, loc. cit.; Bieber, loc. cit.   [4] 20 Mar. 1671, CO 1/26, No. 43.

[5] Cf. Cal. T.B., 1672–5, 14, 34; CSPC 1669–74, 225, 470, 611; Evelyn, *Diary*, 26 Mar. 1671; Harris, *Sandwich*, ii. 306–7; Brown, *Shaftesbury*, 166 et seq.; CO 389/5, 64–65; CO 31/2, 35–39.

ex-officio, was under royal directions to investigate the neglect of the Acts of Trade prevalent in the Leeward Islands and in the Channel Islands.

Instructions,[1] nineteen in number, charged the Council to examine and report on colonial produce, trade, charters, laws, the actions of officials, the operation of the Acts of Trade, the propagation of the Gospel, and relations with native tribes.[2] It did its best to comply.[3] It harangued Governors on their shortcomings. It summoned merchants to its table—who were, however, left in no doubt that they were there to report rather than to advise. It selected special Commissioners for particular tasks. One Commission was formed to treat with the French about St. Christopher. It set up another to treat with the Dutch about the removal of those English settlers who still remained in Surinam, ceded to Holland by the Peace of Breda. And it planned a third, ostensibly to settle some outstanding boundary disputes in the New England colonies, but in fact to get full information of conditions there, and report 'whether they were of such Power as to be able to resist His Matie and declare for themselves as independent of the Crown'.

For the Plantations Council knew well that New England was the crux of their business. Evelyn's evidence is that the King 'commended this affair most expressly', because of the growing danger that the New England group, led by Massachusetts, might break entirely from their allegiance. Some Council members wanted to send 'a menacing letter', but 'those who better understood the peevish and touchy humour of that Colony were utterly against'[4] making empty gestures of that kind. Sandwich, although he advised caution, agreed that the danger was real. He stressed how great a dependence the West Indies now had on New England for their supplies; if this went on, New England—and not Old—would 'reap the whole benefitt of those colonies'. It was thus essential to 'regulate this people & gett as much hand in their Government as we can'.[5] The best way to break a bundle of sticks was to remove one at a time—

---

[1] Cf. Andrews, *Committees*, 99.

[2] Of whom it may be noted that any who asked protection of the English Government were to be given it.

[3] In all, it met 145 times.

[4] Evelyn, *Diary*, 26 May, 3 Aug. 1671.

[5] Harris, *Sandwich*, ii. 337–41; Beer, op. cit. ii. 253–4.

and the commissioners now appointed would assuredly have settled the business of the Maine boundary to Massachusetts's detriment had not the outbreak of the Dutch war interfered with the whole scheme.[1]

Moreover, Sandwich's death at sea made necessary the issue of a new Commission to the Council of Foreign Plantations over which he had presided. It took a new name, now incorporating in itself the 1668 Council of Trade—thus becoming the 'Council of Trade and Foreign Plantations' as from 27 September 1672.[2] Ashley, who had been created Earl of Shaftesbury in April and was to become Lord Chancellor in November, took Sandwich's place as President.[3]

Sir Thomas Lynch in Jamaica hailed this consolidation of the Council with relief. He hoped, as he said, to find its members his 'guardian angels'[4] and indeed might have found them so in fact had his patron Shaftesbury, its President, remained in Court favour.[5] Lynch had returned to Jamaica as Lieutenant-Governor to the Earl of Carlisle in June 1671. Many tasks faced him there.[6] He found a scattered and demoralized popula-

---

[1] Another organization was set up at this time, of importance in colonial fiscal administration: the Board of Customs, whose Commissioners were subordinate to the Treasury Commissioners. This was a strongly mercantile body. In the period 1671–85 it included Sir Edward Dering, sub-Governor of the Hudson Bay Company; Sir Dudley North, a director of the Royal African and the Levant Companies; Sir Andrew King, sub-Governor of the Royal African Company, related by marriage to Sir James Modyford (cf. Bibliography, Westminster Abbey Muniments, *infra*); Sir Robert Clayton, a member of the Royal African and Drapers' Companies and the Bermuda Company, eventually a director of William III's Bank of England; Sir George Downing; Sir Richard Temple; the Duke of York's secretary, Sir John Werden; and Sir Robert Southwell.

[2] Commission, 16 Sept. 1672, CO 289/4, 70.

[3] Culpeper became Vice-President, Halifax replaced Osborne, Hickman replaced Finch. Thomas Grey was not reappointed. The Council met twice a week, at Lady Villiers's House, in King Street, Whitehall—doubly convenient, therefore, for His Majesty. Worsley succeeded Slingsby as secretary in 1672, and was himself replaced on 14 Oct. 1673—for he would not take the Test—by Shaftesbury's protégé, John Locke. The Commissions of the 1670 and 1672 Councils are much the same; the latter's instructions (47 of them) are more elaborate. The 32 'heads of enquiry' afterwards sent to colonial Governors are modelled on them; cf., for example, 'Inquiries to the Lord Vaughan concerning the Government of Jamaica', 6 Apr. 1676, CO 138/3, 44–49.

[4] Lynch to the Council of Trade and Plantations, 4 Apr. 1673, CO 1/30, No. 19.

[5] Shaftesbury had written almost at once to 'his very affectionate friend and servant' in Jamaica; Shaftesbury to Lynch, 29 Oct. 1672, CSPC 1669–74, 949.

[6] Not the least of which must have been making satisfactory replies to the questions set him by Henry Oldenburg, secretary of the Royal Society, an organization much interested in colonial development. (Slingsby, Povey, Evelyn, Locke, South-

tion.[1] Many of the settlements were decaying for lack of attention; in Port Royal disorders and drunkenness reminded the 'Old Standers' of the wilder days of D'Oyley. There were less white people on the island than there had been in 1664;[2] plantation, accordingly, had made slow progress, although there were now some 9,000 negroes to aid the work. Sir Thomas Modyford's reputation for the diligent encouragement of settlement and plantation in Jamaica stood high (in London);[3] but Lynch found it somewhat inflated, like many other of his predecessor's claims to fame.[4] Modyford had certainly granted 30 acres per head to anyone who gave security to bring out a complement of white servants to Jamaica within two years; but, so long as the contractor covered himself by continuing to pay a like security every two years, the Governor had not cared how, or whether, this obligation was honoured. The result of this policy was that upwards of 100,000 acres had been alienated 'without $\frac{1}{4}d$. rent to the King or a foot planted'.[5] Modyford himself had made a fine plantation in his best Barbados-style; but once that was in a thriving way he had bent all his energies to the promotion of privateering, making that the staple industry of the Island, and its main source of revenue. But now that this activity lay by explicit decree under the Imperial ban, the economic plight

well, Sandwich and Craven were Fellows). The questions included: 'Whether in Jamaica every night it blows off the Island every way at once, so that no ship can anywhere come in by night, nor goe out but early in the morning, before the sea-brise come in?'; 'Whether at the point of Jamaica, wherever you dig 5 or 6 feet, the water that appears does ebb and flow?'; 'Whether in some ground in Jamaica that is full of salt-peter, the tobacco flasheth as it smoaketh?'; 'To observe, whether the shining of fireflies can contract or expand their light as they fly? But especially, whether their light continues some days after they are dead?'; and the more practical inquiry, 'Whether the sugar in Jamaica cures faster in 10 dayes than that at Barbados in 6 months?'; Sloane MS. 3984, f. 194.

[1] 7,768, on 29 Mar. 1673; Edwards, op. cit. i. 301.
[2] Lynch to Williamson, 7 July 1671, CO 1/27, No. 7. Modyford's 'Survey', 23 Sept. 1670, had put the white population at 15,198 (CO 138/1, 61–80); Modyford had, however, confessed in 1671 that he could not say how many people had come to Jamaica since 1664; he suggested dividing the acreage granted (209,020) by 30; CO 1/27, No. 96.
[3] Edward Long has also left it high in history.
[4] For a gloomy picture of Modyford's Jamaica, see the report of John Style to Secretary Morice, 14 Jan. 1669, where he describes the activities of an old soldiers' régime, 'all trained up from boys in rebellion and murder'; CO 1/24, No. 8, and (4 Jan. 1670) CO 1/25, No. 1. Style was nursing several private animosities, and his colours, like those of D'Oyley before him, are too high to be true.
[5] Lynch to Sandwich, 14 Oct. 1671, CO 1/27, No. 40.

of Jamaica was grave indeed.[1] There was no money in the treasury;[2] Lynch reckoned that the revenue amounted to some £1,800 a year, that the expenditure was double that, and that there was very little prospect of improving this adverse balance in his time.[3] The planters were some £50,000 in debt to London merchants because of the sudden blight that had fallen on the cocoa-crop, on which great hopes had been set. Current prices were inflated: the Spanish piece of eight had been raised in value from 4s. 2d. to 5s., while the Spanish doubloon which normally passed at 16s. now stood at 20s.

Lynch found the inhabitants naturally much cast down by their difficulties. Many feared that their plight would soon be worse, for the Island buzzed with rumours that the 4½ per cent. duty that weighed on Barbados and the Leeward Islands was shortly to be imposed upon Jamaica as well.[4] Lynch did his best to reassure them that the King's interest in Jamaica was paternal rather than selfish; 'so far from abandoning of them to be a prey to any particular person' had he not 'settled in England a just and honble. Councell to take care of their interest?'

But he was aware that his arguments failed to carry much conviction. Jamaican opinion was a stubborn plant.[5] He re-

[1] For the history of Jamaica in the 1670's, CO 138/2 is a mine of information: containing Lynch's 'State of Jamaica', 20 Aug. 1671; Cranfield's 'Observations', 14 Dec. 1675; Vaughan's 'Acts, Laws, and Statutes' of 1675; and his 'Present State of Jamaica', 1 Jan. 1676.

[2] The King's revenue in Jamaica was derived from quitrents, fines, forfeitures, and escheats. The land granted by Modyford paid 2s. 6d. per 100 acres; Lynch granted land at ½d. per acre, but this aroused much indignation at home, and his Act was annulled and Modyford's revived; CSPC 1669-74, 1003; 'State of Jamaica', 1 Jan. 1676, CO 138/2, 44-96. Estimates what this revenue should yield varied greatly: Bromfield Corbett ('A Memoriall of what I observ'd during my being in the Island of Jamaica from 10 Jan. 1670/1 to 12 June 1673', Sloane MS. 4020, f. 22) put it at £20,000. The revenue from quit-rents actually amounted to £692. 3s. 5d. in 1665, and, according to Reginald Wilson's accounts, to £877. 16s. 9d. between Oct. 1676 and Apr. 1677; CO 140/3, 611. The Earl of Carlisle and the second Duke of Albemarle, both of whom had hopes of recouping failing fortunes in the Governorship of Jamaica, were to be disagreeably surprised.

[3] Lynch to the Council of Plantations, 4 Apr. 1673, CO 1/30, No. 19.

[4] Edward Long puts their point of view thus: 'They suspected (despite fair words) that His Majesty intended only to set them at work, in order that after they had brought their settlements to any degree of perfection, they might be fleeced at pleasure, and rendered miserable drudges to enrich his privy purse, and gratifie his creatures'; Add. MS. 12408, f. 2.

[5] Lynch to Arlington, 27 June 1671, Add. MS. 11410, f. 371; 7 Sept. 1671: 'People are not willingly steered by such as they think shall be but a small tyme at the helme', ibid., f. 373.

marked how the people 'look upon it as their Magna Carta, that they shall be govern'd in these municipall laws & those of England, & not have anything imposed on them but by their own consents'.[1]

He found, as did Willoughby in Barbados, that the zeal of the English Administration to better colonial defences without itself paying for them played into the Assembly's hands. No principle was so rooted in the West Indies as that of the *quid pro quo*. The first Assembly he summoned, in February 1672, appropriated the royal quit-rents, Virginia-fashion. In May 1673, even while warnings of the imminent appearance in the Caribbean of Evertsen's fleet were resounding in their ears, the members voted not to raise money for fortifications or for any public uses, as they feared the diversion of such moneys more than they did a Dutch descent upon them.[2] Lynch's third Assembly, which he called in 1674 in order to re-enact the laws of 1672, seized its opportunity to make an Act for the suppression of lawyers consequent on its approval that the Revenue Act might continue in force. Faced by these domestic troubles, together with the formidable task of calling in the privateers and patching up some sort of *modus vivendi* with the Governors of the neighbouring Spanish plantations, it is not surprising that Lynch begged, 'for God's sake, frequent Letters & Directions'. But these were never forthcoming. In April 1672 he was still writing voluminous dispatches on the condition and prospects of the Island without receiving a line in reply.[3] This neglect worried Lynch considerably, as he knew that Modyford's influential friends were intriguing against him because of his maladroit handling of the latter's arrest and deportation.[4] Nor did he believe Slingsby's reassurance that it was the outbreak of a new war with the Dutch and the death of Sandwich, the Council's

---

[1] 'The Present State of the Government of Jamaica', 20 Aug. 1671, CO 1/27, No. 22.
[2] A. M. Whitson, *The Constitutional Development of Jamaica, 1660 to 1729* (Manchester, 1929), 52–53; 12–16 May 1673, *Journal of the Assembly of Jamaica* (Kingston, 1811), i. 6.
[3] Cf. Lynch to Williamson, 6 Apr. 1672: 'Never a syllable', CO 1/28, No. 36; 5 July 1672, CO 1/29, No. 6; Add. MS. 11410, f. 560.
[4] Barham's account says that as soon as Modyford obtained a hearing 'he made such a defence' that 'he was justifyed and cleared of all matters laid to his charge'; Add. MS. 12422, ff. 91–92; Lynch to Lyttelton, 5 Mar. 1672, Add. MS. 11410, f. 496.

President, that had caused Jamaica's affairs and Jamaica's Governor to be forgotten.[1]

He hoped the new Council of 1672 would pay him more attention. This it did: but much of the attention proved unwelcome. Worsley wrote him in November of the Council's interest in the laws of Jamaica, 34 of which had just been received.[2] The examination was protracted: of these laws four were disallowed, and only three allowed, by the following June. No pronouncement on the other 27 was made. Perhaps the proceedings were interrupted by the Order-in-Council of April 1673 that all colonial laws should be read at the Board of the Privy Council itself, and that the Council of Trade and Foreign Plantations should prepare, with the assistance of the Law Officers, reasons for the allowance or disallowance of such legislation. Worsley kept Lynch informed of the course of this investigation, and regretted that the Council was 'finding exceptions' to his own body of laws. Lynch sent a polite reminder that the laws of Jamaica were local, and that any assessment of them had to take into account the circumstances they were designed to deal with—for many things that might seem strange or unreasonable in England were necessary for the proper government of Jamaica, a strange, un-English place. No doubt it was the duty of the Council to pronounce whether the colonial laws preserved the King's prerogative and safeguarded his revenues, but of the other detail, surely, they were hardly competent judges.[3]

But the very common sense of this view was unlikely to win him friends among those who were now pursuing 'uniformity' in colonial administration with all the zeal of the converted. Rumours that a grandee was scheduled for the Government of Jamaica were already current in the West Indies, and had drawn from Lynch himself a reminder to Worsley that 'young colonies are made or ruined by their Governors',[4] lest another young man in a hurry like Windsor should be on the way. The

[1] Slingsby to Lynch, 8 Oct. 1672, CO 1/29, No. 35; Lynch to Lyttelton, 5 Mar. 1672, CO 1/28, No. 24. There is evidence, however, that the Plantations Council dealt with Jamaican business in November 1671, in February 1672, twice in April, again in May, and twice in June; Andrews, *Committees*, 140–2.
[2] On 2 Nov.; Worsley to Lynch, CO 389/10, 4, 10.
[3] Lynch to Worsley, 12 Aug. 1673, CO 1/30, No. 58.
[4] Lynch to Worsley, 6 Apr. 1673, ibid. No. 9.

name of a Finch had been mentioned, the Earl of Winchilsea,[1] but the Crown took the more orthodox decision to put Jamaica under the care of the Earl of Carlisle as Governor, for whom Lynch anyway was acting as Lieutenant.[2] By March 1674 Carlisle's Commission as Captain-General was in draft.[3] Carlisle was, however, cold to the idea[4] and passed over his interest to John, Lord Vaughan, while retaining a lien on the property. It was to Vaughan, accordingly, that the Commission was passed on 31 March. And in this Instrument the entire membership of the Council of Jamaica was officially nominated by the Crown.

This was something not entirely new. The first royal nomination to a West-India Council had been that of Richard Povey, as secretary of Jamaica for life, in 1661.[5] The second, made in 1667, concerned a more important person: Sir Tobias Bridge, commander of the forces in Barbados and the Leewards under the authority of William Lord Willoughby as Captain-General. Since no one in Barbados had paid any attention to his nomination, the King ordered Codrington in March 1672 to admit Bridge to the Council forthwith.[6] Codrington took no action. Willoughby himself, once back in Barbados,[7] disposed of Bridge for a time by sending him on an expedition to take Tobago from the Dutch,[8] but in January 1673 he received a sharp note from the King reminding him of his duty to appoint Bridge a

[1] Worsley to Lynch, 9 Dec. 1672, CO 389/10, 13.

[2] Arlington to the Council of Trade and Foreign Plantations, 23 Jan. 1674, CO 1/31, No. 9. Sir Henry Morgan was appointed Deputy-Governor.

[3] 23 Mar. 1674, ibid. Nos. 26, 1–13; CO 138/1, 171–7; Instructions, ibid. 177–85.

[4] He had been appointed Lord-Lieutenant of Durham and Deputy Earl-Marshal of England in 1672.

[5] Commission to R. Povey, 10 Jan. 1661, CO 138/1, 27. He was suspended from his office by Lyttelton because he left the Island without permission. In the interim the place remained in the Governor's disposal. Modyford appointed a nephew; cf. Minutes of the Council of Jamaica, 2–11 Nov. 1664, CO 140/1, 116; Bridges, *Annals*, i. 261. The King ordered Modyford to restore Povey to the place; 30 Mar. 1670, CO 1/25, No. 19; but meanwhile Robert Freeman, a Councillor of Jamaica, had purchased it from Povey; CO 1/27, No. 22.

[6] The King to Codrington, 22 Mar. 1672, CO 389/4, 53.

[7] He arrived back on 17 Oct. 1672. The whole Council, he found, objected to the appointment of Bridge; Willoughby to Arlington, 3 Nov. 1672, CO 1/29, No. 42.

[8] Successfully accomplished by December; cf. Bridge to Willoughby, 21 Dec. 1672, ibid., No. 67. The expedition was certainly Willoughby's own idea, for he could not 'endure to suffer the Dutch to burrow soe near Barbados'; Willoughby to T. Povey, 14 Nov. 1672, Egerton MS. 2395, f. 483.

member of his Council.¹ Thomas Povey also wrote, telling him
of Arlington's displeasure on this same point—a hint that
Willoughby's personal stock was not so high at home as he was
apt to think it. 'I doe in the first place laie it down for a ground',
Povey observed sagely,

that whosoever shal be engaged in such a distant Government as
Your Lordship now is, ought, before hee adventures uppon it, to
secure to himself as many as he can of the principall Ministers neare
the King, and as many of the Principall persons whose Trade or
Busyness relate to that place,²

but Willoughby was soon beyond even the best advice, for he
died that April. It was therefore Sir Peter Colleton, President
of the Council, who finally admitted Bridge as a member.
Storms broke out in the Council and Colleton had an exhausting
time of it; but its bout of self-importance was soon over.³ In
December Sir Jonathan Atkins, an old soldier and former
Governor of Jersey, was selected as Willoughby's successor. It is
his Commission that supplies the precedent for that issued to
Vaughan three months later: for in it the members of the
Council of Barbados were nominated by the Crown.⁴

Atkins spoke his mind on this matter, so vehemently that he
ever after remained suspect as a radical to the English authorities. This deprivation of the Governor's right to appoint his own
circle of advisers he considered a slight on his own integrity and
on that of the office he was to hold. The King could choose a
colonial Council only on advice; if, under this new system, he
debarred himself from taking that of his own sworn Governor,
he would be compelled to rely on the opinions of the Gentlemen-Planters and other self-interested parties in London, whose
views seldom coincided either one with another or with His
Majesty's own best interests in Barbados. How illogical it was,

¹ The King to Willoughby, 7 Jan. 1673, CO 389/4, 77.
² Bridge had been keeping Arlington informed of his troubles; cf. CO 1/29,
Nos. 44, 49; T. Povey to Willoughby, 15 Mar. 1673, Egerton MS. 2395, f. 487.
³ On 27 June 1673; Minutes of the Council of Barbados, CO 31/1, 246;
Colleton to Slingsby, 28 May 1673, CO 1/30, No. 43; John Witham's 'General
View of the affairs of the Island of Barbados', 6 Aug. 1683, CO 1/52, No. 48.
⁴ The draft Commission, the work of the Council of Trade and Plantations, is
dated 19 Dec. 1673; CO 29/1, 153-62. It was officially issued to Atkins on 6 Feb.
1674. Commissions to the appointed Council were sent empowering them to
administer to Atkins the oath for the observance of the Acts of Trade; CO 1/31,
No. 11.

too: for had not Atkins himself been selected for the Governorship because of his experience in military and administrative
affairs, and because a 'planter-Governor' would incline, as
always, too much towards popular government, the curse of too
many colonies? What else, he asked, was to be expected from
the rule of a planter-Council? He foresaw trouble ahead if this
model of colonial government were put through, declaring
himself 'throwne on the rocks by this change', and laden with
fetters before he ever set foot on Barbados.[1]

John Locke remarked that these objections Atkins put forward, 'if a little heated', were not so very wide of the mark.
In the opinion of the Council of Trade and Foreign Plantations, Governors of the Willoughby pattern had been too much
of a law unto themselves, too forceful, too influential, able to
cajole an Administration at home ignorant of colonial conditions into supporting their actions and their demands. The
presence of a nominated Council in the plantations would
ensure that the Governments there would 'immediately depend'
upon the Crown, and not upon a local autocrat, who had so
often in the past taken care that many of his Councillors were
also his debtors, and therefore in his pocket. This new method,
moreover, would align the Government of Barbados to that of
Ireland. 'If I mistake not', Locke concluded, 'they intend to give
His Majesty the same advice in all his Plantations.'[2]

Locke made no mistake. The Council's plan was unfolding.
Scrutiny of the Assembly's laws was a natural corollary to the
nomination of the Governor's Council. The matter was considered at first as one of routine; and it was, indeed, the ill-
wording, rather than any nefarious content, of the laws of
Barbados that first attracted the attention of the Council of
Trade and Foreign Plantations, for the laws were assessed to be
'sometymes faulty in some parts though the maine deserves to bee
establish'd'.[3] Atkins's objections went unheeded. His Instructions, issued to him on 28 February 1674, with an additional
missive in May, were precise.

The Governor must no longer re-enact laws automatically as

[1] Atkins to the Council of Plantations, 1 Dec. 1673, CO 1/30, No. 84.
[2] Locke to Arlington, 6 Jan. 1674, CO 1/31, Nos. 2, 3.
[3] Minutes of Council of Trade and Foreign Plantations, 17 Feb. 1674: a debate
how best His Majesty should confirm colonial laws, adjourned until Shaftesbury
should be present; GD 24/49, 11.

they expired. No law should be re-enacted which the King had not confirmed, except in some great emergency. The Governor was no longer to take refuge in times of difficulty in a declaration of martial law, for henceforth Council and Assembly must give their consent to such a proclamation. The Governor was not to remove judges and justices, or to limit their duration in office. He must not leave places and offices empty, in order to collect the fees attached to them. He was not to dispose of any Patent office. Indeed, although he retained a veto power, Atkins's Instructions told him not what to do in Barbados, but what not to. They provide a telling commentary on the errors of his predecessors. They emphasize less the necessity of firm local government, than of local submission to the metropolitan will. The Governor was left no particle of discretionary power: when three of the nominated Councillors were found to be ineligible—for one was in Bermuda, one was on the bench, and one was in his grave—their places were still filled from on high. Barbados was henceforth to stay in leading-strings. There is no doubt that this solution expressed the contemporary administrative ideal: the organization of a colony at once docile and prosperous, as quiet and as loyal as Surrey. Jamaica was next to be dealt with, and in the same way: the issue of New England, still in debate, might be left to the last.

In November Lynch's Commission as Lieutenant-Governor of Jamaica was revoked.[1] But before Lord Vaughan was formally commissioned in his stead, the King asked the Council of Trade and Plantations to make a close examination of Jamaica's form of government. In particular they were to scrutinize the colonial practice of re-enacting unconfirmed laws.[2] Now, the 'laws of Jamaica' had never lapsed since the days of D'Oyley, Windsor, and Lyttelton. Modyford's Assembly of 1664 had systematized them effectively enough. Lynch's Assembly of March 1674 had just re-passed 46 such laws (and it was to do the same again the following May). But what exactly were these laws of Jamaica based upon? Was it still on 'right reason', as Modyford had stoutly asserted as recently as 1670?[3] This un-

[1] 3 Nov. 1674, CO 389/6, 30–31.
[2] Cf. Coventry to Culpeper (Vice-president), 20 Nov. 1674, CO 1/31, No. 76.
[3] 'The Governor of Jamaicas answers to the Inquiries of His Maties Commissioners', CO 138/1, 96–119.

certainty must be dispersed, forthwith. The Council must re-examine three points already included in the Instructions prepared for Lord Vaughan.[1] It must first make absolutely explicit the clause that forbade the Governor and Council to re-enact former laws. It must strengthen the article obliging the Governor to give an account of all laws enacted. It must consider, further, that clause which appeared with such self-confident regularity in all the Acts of Jamaica that were to hand: that all laws should stand good for two years. Was this not a violation of the royal prerogative of dispensation? The Council reported four days later that indeed it was. The offending clause would be reframed, as follows:

> And the said laws . . . shall continue to be in Force for two Yeares (except in the meantime His Majesties Pleasure shal bee signified to the Contrary) but noe longer, unless confirmed by His Majesty within the two years aforesaid.[2]

The Council further advised that the Governor of Jamaica should not, after 29 September 1675, re-enact any law except on very urgent occasions, but in no case more than once, except with the King's express consent. But just then the process of diligent scrutiny was interrupted by a further, and as it happened the last, administrative change.

On 21 December 1674 the Commission of the Council of Trade and Foreign Plantations was revoked by the King.[3] The simpler explanation for this—that it was costing too much money, some £8,000 a year—is probably the correct one. The removal of Shaftesbury from the Privy Council the previous May may perhaps, as has been argued, have been the death-blow of the Plantations Council, but in that case it was a long time taking effect. Moreover, Shaftesbury had been out of favour since November 1673, when he had been dismissed from his office of Lord Chancellor, yet his attendance at the Plantations Council had continued without any objection by the King. Arlington's fall from favour, too, is unlikely to have had much effect on the organization of colonial and commercial business,

---

[1] Instructions, 18 May 1674, CO 389/4, 92, but they were not issued until 3 Dec.; CO 138/3, 1–27.

[2] Council of Trade and Foreign Plantations to the King, 24 Nov. 1674, CO 138/1, 188–9.

[3] Commission of revocation in CO 391/1, 1. Worsley was ordered to deliver all the books and papers to the Clerk of the Privy Council.

about which he had never been particularly knowledgeable; although it is possible to envisage Danby, the rising star in politics and Arlington's enemy, seeking to undermine all the positions occupied by the latter.[1] Doubtless 'politics' entered into this administrative change, as very few administrative changes at high level are ever made on purely utilitarian grounds, but there is no doubt that the need for economy was an overriding factor.

The books and papers of the Council of Trade and Foreign Plantations were now handed over to the charge of Sir Robert Southwell, the Clerk of the Privy Council. The business the Council had been transacting was to return to its 'accustomed channel', a Committee of the Privy Council itself.[2] An interim Committee[3] to deal with colonial business was set up, until on 12 March 1675 a body of nine Privy Councillors was entrusted with 'the immediate Care and Intendency of those Affaires in regard they had been formerly conversant & acquainted with'. This executive body is generally known as the Lords Committee of Trade.

They quickly set to work. They ordered a collection made of all facts and statistics pertaining to the colonies: in particular the names of officials there, the legal status of the settlements themselves, and how far the various Charters and colonial grants differed.[4] Some of this information eluded search, and Worsley, Slingsby, Duke, Frowde, Locke, and anyone else who had ever had anything to do with colonial business were sharply questioned. Plainly there had been carelessness; where there was laxity in minor matters, there would doubtless be licence

[1] Evelyn notes that when Danby succeeded Clifford as Lord Treasurer in 1673, the Council of Trade and Foreign Plantations 'went in a body to congratulate the new Lord Treasurer, no friend to it, because promoted by my Lord Arlington, whom he hated'; *Diary*, 23 June 1673.

[2] This phrase occurs in the Journal of the Lords Committee of Trade and Plantations, 10 Apr. 1676, CO 138/1, 50. The Duchess of Cleveland struck the fashionable note of economy by demanding from John Locke the sum of £250, the rent for a year and a half's tenancy of Villiers House by the Council of Trade and Foreign Plantations; 22 Dec. 1674, CO 389/4, 120.

[3] On this Williamson, now Secretary of State, did all the work; cf. CO 389/4, 128; CO 391/1, 1, 39.

[4] Journal of the Lords Committee of Trade and Plantations [hereafter JLTP], 24 May 1675, CO 391/1, 24. One query argued ignorance somewhere: '*quaere*, if the Governor of Barbados have the Leeward Islands under him, or that they remain under Colonel Stapleton'; CO 1/34, No. 45.

in great. Thus the Lords Committee from the outset prepared to grapple with, rather than merely supervise, colonial affairs. The Councils of 1670 and 1672 had fashioned a new broom for administration; the Lords Committee now picked it up and swept with it vigorously. They took their duties seriously, themselves more so. No detail should escape their attention. Southwell, whom they employed as their Secretary—and exhausted in that post[1]—reported later that most of the entry-books concerning plantation business were in arrears, some 'even from the beginning', because there had been such 'a constant throng of busyness depending, which filled all hands that were allowed to the service & sometymes more'.[2]

Certainly the fact that, when the Lords Committee wanted to examine all the colonial laws, a general search rather than simple reference to the file was necessary, indicates how far the good intentions of the previous committees and councils to have full knowledge of colonial questions at their fingers' ends had been thwarted by a combination of bad management and bad luck. Much of the work had now to be done over again. From the 47 Instructions to the Council of 1672, material for the *pro-forma* of a questionnaire was extracted,[3] and every colonial Governor was bending his brows over 32 inquiries into his government by the summer of 1676. A circular from the Lords Committee had already warned them all that the latter intended to be their 'very strict inquisitors'[4] for the future; they were now left in no doubt of it.

The Lords Committee had a policy. It was a simple one: to ensure obedience to the authority of the Crown. Had the Crown itself been as strong as its claims, there is no doubt that the 'Old Colonial System' would have been more than a mercantile concept, and that the 'Dominion of New England' would not be the historical curiosity it has become. In the Lords Committee was fashioned a powerful administrative engine; for six years

---

[1] Pressure of work forced Southwell first to ask for an increase in pay, then for release from his duties; Southwell to the King, 24 Apr. 1676, CO 391/1, 111–15. He recommended William Blathwayt as his successor, who was granted a salary of £50 in 1676, an increase of £50 in Nov. 1677, and the right to attend debates in the Privy Council in November 1678; Add. MS. 38861, f. 9.

[2] 31 Mar. 1677, CO 391/2, 8–12.

[3] 10 Apr. 1676, CO 5/723, 21–22.

[4] 6 Apr. 1676, CO 29/2, 45.

the dynamo of monarchy supplied it the power it needed. In those years, 1675 to 1681, English domestic history takes on the attributes of melodrama: heroes and villains change roles, there are cries of plot and counter-plot, Parliament is embattled and good men are crossed in their stars and their courses. The colonial world had its own clashes, some of them as bitter, most of them as highly coloured. In these the West-India settlements played a central part.

V

THE IMPERIAL AUTHORITY AT WORK
1675-85

I

THE Lords Committee of Trade inherited an agenda of unfinished business. Some items were easily cleared up —as, for example, the evacuation of the remaining English settlers from Surinam and their transplantation to Jamaica, an operation ably conducted by Edward Cranfield.[1] Other matters, like the arrears of pay owing to both companies of foot in the Leeward Islands and to Governor Stapleton himself,[2] could be passed over to the Lord Treasurer; for Danby, working hard to prove that simple efficiency in administration might after all be that golden key to prosperity which the Crown had sought so long, was unlikely to shelve this awkward problem further.[3] It was plain, however, that the bulk of the business that confronted the Committee could not be delegated to any-

---

[1] On 1 Sept. 1675: some 250 whites and 981 slaves, 'leaving very few or none unless some Jews'; report of the Lords Committee, 30 May 1676, CO 1/36, No. 75. Bannister had transported the first Surinam contingent, 517 people, in Mar. 1672.

[2] Stapleton was owed £2,100, the companies £4,550. 6s. 8d.; CO 1/34, No. 90.

[3] He did his best with it, indeed. A warrant to pay the whole amount was made out in Feb. 1675, GD 32/43, 66; but the Lords Committee had to press the matter again on Danby's attention in Dec.; CO 153/2, 28–29. He managed to have half the sum available the following month, Jan. 1676; APCC, i. 1052. The Lords Committee were now anxious to establish a fund for the defence of the Leeward Islands (cf. Chapter VI, infra), and Danby called the Farmers of the 4½ per cent. Revenue before him to discuss this project, but the Farmers, then busy calculating their own 'defalcations' on this Revenue, impressed upon him the impracticability of the scheme. Nevertheless, the Lords Committee were able to report to the King in Apr. 1677 that Danby had satisfied all arrears to both Stapleton and the companies; MS. Rawl. A. 295, f. 45.

Danby also looked into Lynch's arrears of pay as Lieutenant-Governor of Jamaica; Lynch was owed his salary (£600) for four years three months. Since a Major-General (Bannister) had suddenly appeared on the Jamaica establishment on 4 Oct. 1674, without any necessity for it, Danby suggested that Vaughan should dock the fees of this office and satisfy Lynch's claims with them; Danby to Vaughan, 4 May 1676, GD 32/43, 148. But Vaughan appointed Modyford's son to the position, when Bannister was murdered in Feb. 1675; CO 389/6, 92.

M

one, and that it would take long in settling.[1] It was a fortunate
circumstance that their Lordships were not hampered by the
necessity to attend Parliament, for that body was not in session
between November 1675 and February 1677.

Their first task, as they saw it, was to impress their importance
on the minds of the colonial Governors. Atkins in Barbados was
now commanded to stop writing breezy letters to his friend Sir
Henry Coventry, the second Secretary of State, and to send
sober dispatches to the Lords Committee of Trade instead. He
must give them at once a full account of the 'state' of Barbados,
together with a 'journal' of all that had occurred since his
arrival there.[2] The Lords Committee then turned to their major
work—that of ensuring obedience in the American colonies to
the Acts of Trade. They asked the Customs Commissioners for
a full report on these Acts. The Commissioners' reply rehearsed
the various bonds that had to be given by shipmasters, and the
Oath 'to doe their utmost that all causes, matters, or things in
this Act conteined be punctually & *bona fide* observed' which
was taken by the Governor—who was liable to removal from
his Government if he broke it.[3] But the Lords Committee now
found, as the Committee of 1668 had found before them, that
nobody had yet administered any such Oath to any Governor,
because nobody had yet been ordered to do so.[4] A *fiat* had gone
forth, but apparently to no one in particular. It seemed that the
regulations about the taking of bonds and certificates were so
much waste paper also, for no copies of either, or of any duplicates of the entry of goods into colonial ports, had ever been
received from any colonial Governor—with the single exception
of the conscientious Calvert who ruled in Maryland—since the
year 1671, the date of the Commissioners' own incorporation.
The whole colonial trade obviously required immediate
organization.

The affairs of New England were thus automatically pro-

[1] Some matters, however, were never settled, as for example the restitution by
the French to the English planters on St. Christopher. Their Lordships had to confess themselves 'quite at a loss to know what to propose more than we have done';
25 Apr. 1678, CSPC 1677–80, 679.

[2] Lords Committee to Atkins, 14 Apr. 1676, CO 29/2, 37–38.

[3] 'Answer of the Commissioners of the Customs about the Acts of Trade &
Navigation', 12 May 1675, CO 324/4, 16–20.

[4] Despite the vote of the House of Commons on 22 Apr. 1671; Stock, *Debates*, i.
397; Lords Committee to Customs Commissioners, 24 May 1675, CO 391/1, 24.

moted from the official subconscious to the forefront of the Administration's mind. It was recalled that the defunct Council of Trade and Plantations of 1672-4 had decided to send Commissioners to Massachusetts, but had not actually done so; the Lords Committee, however, decided to reverse this procedure, and summon agents from that Colony before them. (Which was Mahomet and which the mountain remained to be seen.) Edward Randolph, who bore to New England the royal summons to this effect, reported home that he found there a free commonwealth, to whom monarchy was but a name and the Lords Committee not so much as that. This diagnosis was not new, but repetition could not blunt the point of its implication. It was known that New England traders had already fashioned a triangle out of what the English Government had designed as a bilateral trade. West-India sugar and indigo were being attracted from the channels where in England's view they belonged, to the commercial orbit of New England where they did not. The Lords Committee had an embarrassment of evidence before them of these multifarious activities of New England's merchants and shippers.[1] Certainly in the view of anyone who stood on a Boston quay, the Caribbean must have seemed his best commercial horizon. New England traders were able to sell their own provisions and European manufactures (illegally imported in the first place and therefore custom-free) in the Island colonies at cheaper rates than could England herself. Naturally, Boston, Salem, and Providence skippers and cargoes were made welcome in the ports of the West Indies (and also in Carolina harbours, to the great indignation of the Lords Proprietors).

[1] Cf., for example, a report of the old Plantations Council of 1660; Beer, op. cit. ii. 240; Willoughby to the Privy Council, 16 Dec. 1667: the West-India colonies could not 'in peace prosper or in war subsist' without a close correspondence with New England, CO 1/21, No. 162; Modyford to Albemarle, 20 Feb. 1668, that Jamaica's trade with Barbados normally went *via* New England ports 'because of the constant east winds', CO 1/22, No. 47; Cranfield's 'Observations', 14 Dec. 1675, on New England's shipping at Campeachy for logwood, CO 138/2, 108-21; report of the Captain of *Garland* (4), up from Barbados to victual in New England, Beer, op. cit. ii. 257; petitions of the Royal African Company on New England's 'interloping' on the Guinea Coast, 4 Nov. 1674, 1 Mar. 1676, CSPC 1671-4, 1011, 1065; Atkins to Williamson, 20/30 Apr. 1675, that the Acts of Trade interfered with Barbados' 'natural commerce with New England and Ireland and always would', CO 1/34, No. 57; and letters of Vaughan and Carlisle, 1 Jan. 1676, 20 June 1679.

In the terms of the Acts of 1660 and 1663 there was nothing to prevent an English or a colonial captain from carrying enumerated commodities from one plantation to another without paying a customs duty at either end of the trip and without going to England at all. This permission had been granted to encourage colonial navigation: but, while certainly doing that, it also did more. It encouraged colonial merchants to evade that metropolitan control of their commerce which was the fundamental point of the enumeration policy. For clearly a captain who carried tobacco and sugar to the port of another English colony had less incentive to land the whole of it there than to continue his voyage to the ports of Europe, where he could both get a better price for his cargo and a wider market to shop in.[1]

In 1673 an attempt had been made to deal with this danger.[1] An 'Act for the Encouragement of Trade' decreed that colonial shippers who loaded any of the commodities enumerated in the Act of 1660 must give bond to carry them either to England, Ireland, Berwick-on-Tweed, or to some other colony. In the latter case, they must pay at the port of lading the same duty that they would have had to pay had the goods been imported into England. To collect this duty special officers were appointed by the Commissioners of the Customs in the colonies themselves: collectors, and surveyors (it seems to supervise the collectors). The Act of 1673 thus introduced into the colonies an officer who was not responsible to the local Government at all, but to the Crown in England. This had serious political consequences in New England, where the two forms of authority were by no means synonymous, whatever the law might say on the subject.

Nevertheless, the collectors of the 'Plantation Duty', as the imposts of the Act of 1673 was generally called in the colonies,[2]

---

[1] 'An Act for the prevention of planting tobacco in England and for the regulation of the plantation trade' had passed the Commons in the 1671–2 Session without the knowledge of the Gentlemen-Planters: but finding it in several clauses which made plantation imports into Ireland pay the English duty also, as well as a prohibition of the provision trade to the colonies both from Ireland and New England, they lobbied the Lords with Willoughby's aid and had them removed; cf. Gentlemen-Planters to Assembly of Barbados, 12 June 1672, CO 31/2, 100–1.

[2] The duties imposed were 5s. per 100 on white and brown sugars, 2d. per lb. on indigo, 6d. per cwt. on dyewoods (including logwood), 1d. per lb. on coco-nuts, and 1d. per lb. on tobacco, although this ought to have been 2d. to compare with the English duty; cf. Harper, op. cit. 398. Edwin Stede was appointed Collector

were given no power to interfere with the more serious breaches of the Acts of Trade in general, and mainly because of this the 1673 Act did not 'improve' the regulation of the inter-plantation trade as had been hoped.[1] Accordingly the Lords Committee drew up a Proclamation prohibiting the importation of European goods, which had not been laden in England, into any royal colony. A subsequent Order-in-Council decreed that this should be printed and published in all the colonies.[2] This in its turn was followed by the dispatch of a letter to all Governors, warning them that failure to observe the Acts of Trade would no longer be thought a venial offence, a norm of colonial behaviour; rather would it be taken as an overt defiance of the royal authority, as personified by their Lordships' Committee of Trade.[3] The Acts were not so many exercises in commercial theory, but the laws of the realm. They were therefore advising the King to empower members of his colonial Councils—and they stressed the possessive adjective—to administer an Oath of observance to their Governors,[4] although they admitted that this remedy came a little late. They drew up the form of the Oath itself:

You shal sweare that you will to the best of yr skill and power soe long as you shal continue Governour of this Plantacon well & truly execute & performe[5] all matters & things which by the Statutes made in the 12th & 15th yeares of his now Maties Raigne, you are required (as Governour of this Plantacon) to be sworn to the performance of, so helpe you God.[6]

in Barbados in Apr. 1674. Collectors received a fixed portion of the duties—a fifth in Barbados, Jamaica, Nevis, and St. Christopher; a half in Montserrat, Antigua, and Bermuda. The Gentlemen-Planters of Barbados had protested against the duty, using the interesting argument 'how unpracticable it was to tax those that had no members in their House'; Thornborough (Secretary to the Gentlemen-Planters) to the Assembly, 1 Apr. 1673, CO 31/2, 123–4; *Commons Journals*, ix. 281.

[1] Vaughan reported how the New Englanders were monopolizing the profit of the logwood trade, 'nor will the late Act of Parliament restrain them': Vaughan to Williamson, 20 Sept. 1675, CO 1/35, No. 20.

[2] 24 Nov. 1675, CO 389/3, 23–25.

[3] 4 Apr. 1676, CO 29/2, 44–46.

[4] Cf. Lords Committee to the Attorney-General, 10 Apr. 1676, CO 391/1, 108–9.

[5] The words 'and cause to be executed & performed', with the titles of the Navigation Acts of 1660 and 1663, were inserted into this Oath in Oct. 1677.

[6] The Oath was approved in Council on 28 Apr., and issued 3 May; APCC, i. 878, 880; CO 324/4, 40. But a commission to the colonial Councils to administer this Oath to the Governor was not drawn up until 24 Oct. 1677; APCC, i. 1171.

Individual merchants were meanwhile called before the Committee and questioned about the trade between New England and the West Indies, with further reference to the traffic in logwood from the Honduras coast to France.[1] That some of those so interrogated were 'shy to unfold the mystery'[2] need not be doubted. Edward Randolph, when asked his view, roundly asserted that the inhabitants of New England took no notice at all of the Acts of Trade, for they regularly exported cattle and provisions to Virginia, Maryland, and the West Indies, as well as to Europe;[3] but the comprehensiveness of this list bears better witness to the extent of Randolph's rancour against Massachusetts than to the volume of the illicit trade. But he was the premier colonial 'expert' of the day, and his word carried great weight with the Lords Committee.

This investigation of commerce led the Lords to the inspection of other aspects of colonial life.[4] New England's chief crime was that she had broken into a *champ clos* in the Caribbean; but, even if Massachusetts and her satellites in the north were still beyond official reach, the West-India colonies were not. If the grip on them were tightened, if a vigilant Government could ensure that no willing customers welcomed New England's ships, New England's designs would be thwarted.[5] It was with

[1] For other evidence, cf. CO 391/1, 124-5; Cranfield's report, 30 May 1676, CO 1/36, No. 26; Lynch's report, 7 June 1677, CO 391/2, 117.

[2] 24 Apr. 1676, CO 5/903, 108, 110.

[3] 'Answers of Edward Randolph to several Heads of Inquiry', 12 Oct. 1676, ibid. 114, 116. The resolve to be thorough had already proved its sincerity in an unusual quarter: Captain Sir William Poole, R.N., who brought *St. David* (4) home from Barbados six months late, with a cargo of illicit merchandise aboard, was severely reprimanded and ordered to pay the value of the goods into the Chatham Chest; 15 Dec. 1675, Adm 2/1747, 348*b*. This example, however, did not prevent Captains Billop at Nevis and Heywood at Jamaica from falling foul of the Governors and the Duke of York for the same offence; for Billop's case (who embezzled the cargo seized from an interloper), cf. CO 1/50, No. 28, and Crump, op. cit. 133-4. Heywood indeed broke the back of *Norwich* (4) by overloading her with merchandise (15 Nov. 1682, CO 138/4, 76), and as a result a very strict order was made prohibiting the practice (CO 391/4, 78), but naval corruption of this sort continued as one of the less pleasant features of the West-India scene throughout the eighteenth century.

[4] JLTP, 20 Dec. 1675: 'The laws lately transmitted from Jamaica are to be presented to the Lords, and the Secretary's offices are to be searched for any laws that may be transmitted from the other islands', CO 391/1, 55.

[5] The Lords Committee's attitude to New England itself continued cautious. They say in their report of 6 Feb. 1677: '. . . that altho' New England be in the number of the foreign plantations, yett they have forebore to frame any rules to be

this purpose in mind that the Lords Committee, from the summer of 1676, turned to examine the status of colonial law in Jamaica and Barbados.

The previous May Vaughan had transmitted 45 Acts of the Assembly of Jamaica, expressing himself as pleased with his own skill and sagacity in having passed them through successfully.[1] But these Acts were only re-enactments of the laws that Lynch had passed, and to which exception had already been taken. Now, whether the Lords Committee truly thought that all these loosely assorted by-laws were genuinely pernicious in essence and derogatory in effect to the dignity of the Crown, is not now easy to determine. They certainly did believe, however, that all colonial laws, the good with the bad, were innately dangerous if they were not well founded on the only legal authority of the realm, the power of the Crown. Everyone could see what spirit was now abroad in New England, precisely because insufficient care had been taken on this point.

And indeed, to men on the watch for evidence of colonial presumption, a study of the activities of Lyttelton's Assembly, the first that ever met in Jamaica (between January and March 1664), can only have supplied confirmation of their worst fears. One Act passed in that Session had roundly declared that an Act or Ordinance made solely by Governor and Council was no Act at all. Jamaica, then, it appeared, was a lawless community until the gentlemen of the Assembly condescended to give it a little law. The actions, therefore, of the King's representatives—D'Oyley, Windsor, Lyttelton—were valid only because the Assembly had said they were so! Lyttelton had thrown in his hand, which had improved the situation not at all, since the Council had immediately directed that the secretary, Richard Povey, and any two members of Council had power to act as if the Governor were present.[2] Moreover, the

granted there, inasmuch as they do not yett conforme themselves to the lawes by which other the plantations doe Trade, but take a liberty of Tradeing to all manner of places where they think fitt; so that until His Matie come to a better understanding touching what degree of dependence that Government [Massachusetts] will acknowledge . . .', &c., CO 391/1, 291.

[1] These are in CO 139/4. '[I] do not a little please myself that the Island is like to receive in my government their first fix'd and establish'd laws'; Vaughan to George Legge, Governor of Portsmouth, 23 May 1675, HMC Dartmouth, i. 25–26.

[2] Cf. Whitson, op. cit. 24–27; Minutes of the Council of Jamaica, 22 Mar. 1664, CO 139/1, 23.

Assemblymen had refused to confirm the Revenue Bills that D'Oyley and Lyttelton had drawn up, substituting for these money bills of their own drafting, which contained no mention of the King's name. From this it was but a natural step to the appointment of their own treasurers, who were thus placed in charge of the fiscal administration of the whole Island. Moneys supplied by the votes of the legislature were therefore not entrusted to the executive Government at all; they remained throughout within the purview and consequently the control of the Assemblymen and their appointees.

And although these surprising edicts were repealed in the subsequent Session, this reversal indicated not so much a change of heart in the members of the Assembly as a change of place of the leading factions. The enemies of the authors of the previous legislation naturally repealed that legislation on principle. Sir Thomas Modyford, after a month's trial, came to the understandable conclusion that he could govern Jamaica far better without an Assembly at all. He made the Assemblymen justices of the peace, promoted many to colonelcies in the militia, lent a number of them money, advised them as to their plantations, and so ruled Jamaica with *brio* for seven years.[1] He had explained that he had himself passed Poynings's law in Jamaica, because no one besides himself knew how to frame a law, and because otherwise the colony would not have enjoyed the protection of the 'most perfectly incomparable laws of our own country'.[2] But Modyford's views both of Poynings's law and of English law, as his own actions had subsequently proved, were scarcely those of the Lords Committee of Trade, who now saw as little validity in those other ordinances of Jamaica which for twelve years had remained in a state of illegal petrifaction. Southwell accordingly had to tell Vaughan in July 1676 that few of the 'settled laws' with which his Lordship was so pleased, would be allowed to remain in force.[3]

[1] Cf. Lynch to Bennet, 12 Feb. 1665: Modyford 'would have none to shine in this Hemisphere but himself and his son', CO 1/19, No. 23; and his 'Brief Accompt of the Government of Jamaica since His Maties Restauration', 18 Dec. 1674: 'For that Governor [Modyford] had much more power than his successors, and being well supported in England, and the Collony young and poor, nobody questioned anything'; CO 1/43, No. 172.
[2] Modyford to Bridgeman, 20 Feb. 1668, CO 1/22, No. 46.
[3] Southwell to Vaughan, 28 July 1676, CO 138/3, 88.

Now, in the Commission issued to Lynch in 1671, it was distinctly stated that it lay entirely within the discretion of the Governor and his Council when an Assembly should be convened, and how many members should compose it. But the Government of Jamaica, debarred from recouping its treasury with the funds of freebooting, had found itself unable to dispense with the presence of an Assembly, for, apart from retired privateers and active pirates, the freeholders of the Island were the only men with money.

The very frequency of the sessions of the Assembly (it convened six times between 1672 and 1677) had thus helped to convince its members that their counsel was indispensable to the proper Government of the colony. Moreover, Vaughan had encouraged it to consider itself a miniature replica of the House of Commons, a habit of thought to which it was already too prone.[1] The Speaker, Samuel Long,[2] saw himself—and indeed with some justification—as a tribune of the people, cast in an antique mould. The prolonged argument current in England concerning the privileges of Parliament provided Assemblymen with much welcome ammunition for their own guns, and it was as Englishmen standing up for their rights that they passed once more the Act declaring the laws of England to be in force in the Island.

Vaughan was now echoing Lynch's words: the laws of Jamaica were municipal, 'particularly adapted to the Interest of this Place, soe cannot clearly be understood by those who are Strangers to it'.[3] But the Lords Committee, though certainly strangers to Jamaica, were none to the belief that the King's subjects must obey the King's government. The Executive in England detested the interference of Parliament; accordingly,

[1] In 1670 Modyford had described the conjunction of Council and Assembly as 'an humble Modell of our High Court of Parliament', CO 138/1, 87; and cf. Long, *History*, i. 17. Vaughan went further, describing it as the 'figure' of the House of Commons. He refused to sign Bills in the presence of the Assembly, but had to have them brought to him, 'according to the custom of the Parliament of England', and insisted that Bills must be read three times, and not twice as had previously been the case. In 1677, however, he had to swallow his constitutional pride and sign several Bills in the presence of the Speaker and the whole 'House'; cf. Minutes of the Council of Jamaica, CO 140/3, 613–39, and Minutes of the Assembly of Jamaica, 26 Apr.–15 May 1675, CO 139/1, 143–53.

[2] Once a lieutenant in D'Oyley's regiment. Forebear of the historian Edward Long, who shares most of his views.

[3] Vaughan to Southwell, 28 Jan. 1676, CO 138/3, 31–32.

an Assembly's pretensions to Parliamentary status was unlikely to command official sympathy. 'The rights of Englishmen' was not a cry that could appeal to those who heard in it only a protest against the rights of the Crown. The Lords were now determined to break these usurped powers of the Assembly: to assert both their own authority and that of the royal prerogative they so ostentatiously took on themselves to represent. They therefore set to work to make a constitutional *corpus* of the 'laws of Jamaica'.

The Jamaicans' objection to this interference in what they considered their own business was not based primarily on legal or constitutional grounds at all, but on the less verifiable territory of stout common sense. Jamaica was not a parish in Surrey, and could not be treated as such.[1] Nor could it be governed in the manner of Ireland,[2] for a genuine comparison between the West-India world and the Irish was hard to find. Yet this was a very popular analogy in Whitehall, where politicians recalled the permanent revenue obtained in Ireland in 1662, and the many uses to which the 'Irish establishment' could be put. The power of money smoothed all political paths in Ireland. Why should it not be made to do the same in colonial America, that mine of resources yet untapped? Once it had both a permanent colonial revenue and the precedent that had obtained it firmly in its grasp, the English Government would be well able to deal with the New England colonies and their notions of 'independency'. It was the first step that was hardest to take, but most worth the taking. The Lords Committee thus paid no heed to the Jamaican claim that local legislation should be left to local discretion. They would only take into account the tale of local indiscretion that their investigations had already elicited.

The task of examining the laws of Jamaica took them a year to complete. In the enacting style of colonial laws—'By the Governor, Council, and Gentlemen of the Assembly'—they took exception to this use of the term 'Gentlemen', 'lest those

[1] This was a point of view as old as the English occupation itself. Cf. General Venables's *Narrative*: 'I further moved that my friends should not be made more formidable to me than my enemies, by bounding and streightening me with Comissions and Instructions which, at that distance, could serve but as fetters, contingencies not being possible to be foreseen', in *Interesting Tracts*, 8.

[2] Lords Committee to the King, 16 Nov. 1677, CO 138/3, 45.

. . . which are not Gentlemen might seem to be excluded from their Right of voting in the Grand Assembly'. They complained that Vice-Admiralty cases were too often tried before friendly juries in courts of common pleas. They took particular exception to those Revenue laws that made no mention of the King's name,[1] and ordered that in future revenue laws should be enacted only when the King had given permission; the current phrase 'for the publick use of the Island' must be struck out, and 'to the King's Most Excellent Majesty' be substituted.[2] They puzzled over an Act of Jamaica that appointed the number of Assemblymen. Was the status of an English Member of Parliament established by statutory law in this way? It appeared not. Then there was no reason why a member of the Assembly of Jamaica, who was not even a legislator in his own right, should enjoy such a privilege. But—if he was not a legislator, what then was he? What, anyway, was the role or status of a colonial Assembly? Whose invention was it? D'Oyley had made laws without one—and good laws too, whatever nonsense was talked in Jamaica about them.[3] Here were fundamental matters; but clearly they could not be pronounced upon in a hurry. In the meantime the Committee advised the King that in future he should retain the power to alter or even to revoke the laws of Jamaica once they were passed, 'since a perpetuity in some of them would be inconvenient'.

Yet while these nice points were being weighed in an official balance, there were other, more pressing, inconveniences. Vaughan's position in Jamaica was not strengthened while it became clear to everyone that very soon the Island would have no laws at all: and in fact the laws expired, the two-year limit

[1] JLTP, 28 May 1676, CO 391/1, 121; 6 July 1676, ibid. 156; and cf. Coventry to Vaughan, 31 July 1676: 'His Majesty . . . doth very much wonder how you came to make the Sea, Land, and the Admiralty, Common Pleas: it will make the Council more circumspect in passing your laws, and that very point will be thoroughly considered'; Add. MS. 25120, f. 84; JLTP, 26 Apr. 1677, CO 391/2, 25.

[2] 9 Oct. 1677, CO 138/3, 144. The Governor's title of Excellency was also to be omitted 'in the laws which His Majesty shall enact', 10 Nov. 1677, ibid. 150; and 'where mention is made in the Old Laws of the "publick use", the alteration of style be "for the better support of the Government of this His Majestys Island"'; 20 Nov. 1677, ibid. 161. The Jamaican public holiday (10 May) commemorating the conquest of the Island, was also abolished because of its republican overtones; CO 1/36, No. 70.

[3] JLTP, 20 Sept. 1677, CO 391/2, 118; 6 Nov. 1677, ibid. 145.

having been reached, in April 1677. The Governor waxed increasingly exasperated. He had no instructions and thus had to summon an Assembly—the last thing he wanted to do—in order to re-enact laws to which he knew serious exception was being taken at home.[1] The Assembly when convened presented a Bill of Privileges, the main object of which was to declare the laws of England in force in the Island. Vaughan tried to get some modification of the Bill's terms,[2] but he had ultimately to accept them, including the forthright clause that no one 'should give, grant, or pay any loan, tax, aid, benevolence, or other such like charge but by the Act of Parliament in England naming & relating to this Island or by common consent of the General Assemblys of this Island'.

Naturally, while in these straits, Vaughan was not appeased by being told that the business of Jamaica was being held up at home, as the Lords were greatly fatigued by constantly having to attend Parliament.[3] At the end of April, however, they called in the Treasurer and the Lord Keeper to assist them in sifting the laws,[4] and they canvassed the opinions both of Sir Thomas Lynch and Hender Molesworth—the latter an experienced Jamaican planter, factor for the Royal African Company there and an honest man. It was thereafter decided to present the whole body of Jamaica's laws to the Attorney-General, with a memorandum of their Lordships' many observations thereon, 'for his perusal and opinion how far they are fit to be allowed by His Majesty'.

He was particularly asked to examine that recurrent and perplexing Act of Jamaica declaring the laws of England to be in force there. Was this a necessary Act? How far was it consistent with the King's right of dominion? And what, anyway, did it mean? (In an obscure way, the Lords felt that no colonial enactment held more menace for the future than this, and here

---

[1] Vaughan to Lords Committee, 28 Jan. 1676, CO 138/3, 34. CO 139/5 is a MS. volume of Acts passed by Vaughan in 1677: 8 passed on 9 Apr., 6 on 20 Aug., and 12 on 6 Sept. It is heavily amended and annotated by the Lords Committee.

[2] For example, he inserted a clause, 'that where the laws made in this Island give remedy such lawes in regard of their more easy and speedy releife shall be put in use, & not the lawes of England unless the lawes of England do particularly name or relate to this Island', 2 May 1677, CO 140/3, 572; but the Assembly would have none of this.

[3] Coventry to Vaughan, 16 Apr. 1677, Add. MS. 25120, f. 108.

[4] JLTP, 26 Apr. 1677, CO 391/2, 22–23.

their instinct was sound enough.) Southwell had already told
Vaughan in Jamaica how the authorities looked on this Act.
Jamaicans seemed to see in it their safeguard, but this was
really not so. The retention of such an Act in their laws might
in fact prove to be 'of very evill Consequence' to the security of
the Island. For example, the laws of England did not permit
the establishment of guards and garrisons—but how could
Jamaica survive without a liberal supply of both? The English
Statutes had, moreover, 'taken away the power & authoritye
of the Councell Board'—yet how could a like development be
allowed to take place in Jamaica, where anarchy and the decay
of plantation would be the inevitable result? Surely, all might
fall into confusion in the colony if everything that was law in
England should at the demand of any person there be strictly
put into execution.[1] These were shrewd enough points, but
Jamaicans were not given time to work out all their implications. While the Attorney-General still had the laws of the
colony in his hands, the Lords Committee sent him a request
to draw up a Bill 'like Poynings' Law in Ireland', to govern the
manner of enacting, transmitting and amending these laws 'by
His Majesty here in England'. He was to take care to alter the
style of enactment. The existing preamble 'be it enacted by the
Governor, Council, and representatives of the Commons of this
Island now assembled', must go, and in its place appear the
precise phrase: 'Be it enacted by the King's most excellent
Majesty by and with the consent of the General Assembly.'[2]
Thus was the last gloss placed upon the new text.

The Earl of Carlisle was meanwhile preparing himself at
long last to take over his Commission from Vaughan as Governor
of Jamaica.[3] Carlisle was himself at this time a member of the
Lords Committee, and was thus primed with the official view
of colonial affairs. He was a man of considerable diplomatic
experience,[4] who seemed just the person to put the internal

---

[1] Southwell to Vaughan, 28 July 1676, CO 138/3, 88.

[2] JLTP, 10 Apr. 1677, CO 391/2, 26–28.

[3] Anglesey's *Diary* notes, 20 July 1677: '. . . with the King, who spake to me of
ye Earl of Carlisle's Commission for Jamaica, but I shewing him before Secretary
Williamson that he would be liable to pay 2 Governors he approved my stopping
the Patent'—presumably until Vaughan had quit Jamaica; Add. MS. 18730.
Without waiting for formal leave, Vaughan left Jamaica in Mar. 1678, under the
care of Morgan, and arrived home on 11 May; CO 389/35, 16.

[4] Burnet, op. cit. ii. 277, remarks of him that 'he loved to be popular, and yet to

affairs of Jamaica into proper order, while taking care to ensure her security from external attack. From the first, however, he showed that he had ideas of his own how to govern a colony. He believed that a Governor should be an autocrat. He suggested to the Committee that fines should not be applied to any but the Governor's own use, and that he should retain the power to suspend any member of the Council without first having to obtain the advice and consent of the other members. He went so far as to ask for the restoration of the Governor's former power to appoint his own Council;[1] and although this was refused him, he was accommodated to a certain degree by having the terms of the Council's nomination placed not in his Commission, which was a public instrument, but in his Instructions, which was not. At least this concession, as he remarked himself, would put him in a strong position *vis-à-vis* the principal men of the Island on his first arrival, for they could not be certain to whom office would go, and would accordingly behave themselves in a loyal and co-operative manner.

On Assemblies in general he shared the Modyford view, that they were better when in abeyance. It was his own suggestion that no Assembly should be called in future without the special leave of the King. He had no wish to 'be at the mercy of the rabble every 2 yrs. for what shall defray his expenses', and so be forced to 'little popular tricks to Insinuate by'. In his draft Instructions, therefore, no Assembly in Jamaica was allowed at all, although the Lords later amended this so that one might be summoned in cases of especial emergency; stipulating, however, that Assemblymen when so summoned must take the Oaths of Allegiance and Supremacy.[2]

Carlisle plainly considered that an able Governor armed with full authority would have no need of an Assembly, and thus all faction in the Island, deprived of its wailing-wall, would cease. But how to arrange this? The Lords Committee thought they saw a way. Among the laws Lynch had transmitted in 1673, there was one for raising a public revenue, without any limit of time.[3] If this law was made perpetual, then Carlisle's hope

keep up an interest at Court; and so was apt to go backward and forward in public affairs'.   [1] JLTP, 25 Oct. 1677, CO 391/2, 137-9.

[2] 15 Feb. 1678, APCC, i. 1201-2. This had previously been the duty of Governor and Council only.

[3] Or so they thought; JLTP, 28 Oct. 1677, CO 391/2, 140-2.

might be realized. And how might this be done? Clearly, by reversing the procedure of 'tacking' a money bill to other legislation: in this case those laws that were essential for the good government of Jamaica should be tacked to the desired Revenue Bill, and thus a whole *corpus* of laws could be passed through the Assembly—which thereafter could be dispensed with.[1] After further debate, during which the Lords reported their inability to find anywhere in the Privy Council Registers evidence of any royal confirmation of a plantation law, with the sole exception of the $4\frac{1}{2}$ per cent. duty in Barbados, they decided that this *corpus* should be passed under the Great Seal, and not simply issued on the authority of an Order-in-Council.[2] This done, they issued Carlisle's Commission on 1 March 1678.[3] His Instructions, issued a week later, embodied most of the suggestions he had made.[4]

So it was that, by means of these two instruments alone, and without recourse to any further legislation, the English Administration planned to recast the entire constitution of the Colony of Jamaica. Carlisle carried with him to the Island 40 laws, which were to be enacted together 'as laws originally coming from us', to serve as a 'new model' for Jamaican government. It is not surprising that the Agents for New England in London cast a curious eye on the Earl's Commission;[5] no wonder, too, that when Southwell forwarded a copy of this 'new model' to an interested Ormond in Ireland, he commented dryly that its establishment in Jamaica would give Carlisle 'a little work to do'. But it was necessary work, '. . . for the Assembly there flew high & were in a fair way of treading, in time, the footsteps of New England'.[6]

Nor was the new Governor to be hampered by a lack of funds. He had not only the wherewithal to pay his two companies of troops, but he had discretion to raise moneys in emergency (though by what means was not stated), and enjoyed a salary

[1] This report to the King, which he approved, was signed by Finch, Danby, Worcester, Essex, Craven, Fauconberg, W. Coventry, and Thomas Dolman; 16 Nov. 1677, APCC, i. 1177.

[2] Lords Committee to the King, 15 Feb. 1678, CO 138/3, 182.

[3] Commission in CO 138/3, 198–214; and CO 389/6, 247–54. Carlisle took the Oath as Governor on 22 Mar.

[4] Instructions in CO 138/3, 216–51, dated 30 Mar.

[5] JLTP, 28 Mar. 1678, CO 391/2, 232.

[6] Southwell to Ormond, 13 Nov. 1677, HMC Ormond, iv. 386.

of £2,000 a year, with the perquisite of a third of all fines, as he had suggested. The appearance of the local administration was further improved by the replacement of Sir Henry Morgan by Sir Francis Watson, and a new Major-General was put in charge of the forces. On 18 July 1678, resplendent in all these trappings of power, the Earl of Carlisle arrived to govern Jamaica after the Lords Committee's fashion.

He met the Assembly for the first time on 2 September,[1] and in his opening address referred to Jamaica as His Majesty's 'darling plantation'. He then presented His Majesty's laws for the fortunate inhabitants. The Assembly's reaction was immediate.[2] On the 13th a committee of Assemblymen presented the House's formal objections to the laws. The Revenue Bill ought not to pass; no money had ever been raised in Jamaica by the order of Governor and Council alone, save in General D'Oyley's day—when anyway the Council (being an elective body) had performed the legislative functions of an Assembly. To saddle a young and growing colony, whose circumstances were in constant flux, with a perpetual law of any sort was in itself a foolish thing to do. And what, pray, were those 'ordinary contingencies' for the support of the Government so obliquely referred to in the Bill? Why not name them?[3] Carlisle's answer to this particular objection was curiously honest. He said that since the revenue that might be raised under the Bill was anyway likely to fall short of the amount required for the maintenance of the Government of the Island, the Jamaicans need have no fear that it would be diverted—the implication being that had a surplus been obtainable, diversion would assuredly have been its fate. But in truth the members of the Assembly were not really interested in the Governor's replies to their questions. They were out to obstruct. Continuing their attack on the laws one by one, by 1 October they had voted out 36 of the 40 Bills. Three days later they addressed Carlisle formally that this 'method & manner of passing laws . . . is absolutely impracticable. . . . Nor can we believe that His Majesty would

---

[1] *Journal of the Assembly of Jamaica*, 2–30 Sept. 1678, CO 139/1, 195–206.
[2] So is that of all Jamaican historians. Even the mild Bridges is infected by his mentor, Long, to describe the system as 'iron fetters on a helpless people'; *Annals*, i. 285. Long himself speaks of 'the badge of slavery manufactured for them by the Lords of Trade'; *History*, i. 199.
[3] *Journal of the Assembly of Jamaica*, 13, 25 Sept. 1678.

have made this alteration, had he been truly informed of his own interests'. Surely the Governor himself, so wise, so experienced in public affairs, could see plainly enough by now what were the true conditions and necessities of Jamaica, 'which at a great distance is impossible to be known, being always distinguished with the false colours of interest and design'? Carlisle's comment on this occasion was reserved: 'You are very dogmatical in your opinions', he told them. To Coventry he reported that 'popular discourses prevail here as in England',[1] and on 11 October he dissolved the Assembly, having been able to settle the Revenue for one year only.

His dispatches home to the Lords Committee were, however, less reserved. As early as July 1678 he saw the sense in the Council of Jamaica's objection to this clause in the Militia Bill: 'but that in all things [the Governor] may upon all occasions & contingencies act as Captain-General and Governor-in-Chief according to and in pursuance of all the powers & authorities given unto him by His Majesty's Commission.' This might be construed (and was) to give to the Governor a blanket power over local life and property, as well as authority to execute all further Instructions that might be sent him in his military capacity as Captain-General, without reference to the laws of the Colony.[2] Herein a sinister intention was read by the Assembly where in fact there was none, and Carlisle pointed out to his peers that this matter might very easily have been adjusted and these fears lulled if such adjustment had been legally possible; but since the Governor was bound to the observation of every detail in the laws and was debarred from using his own discretion and common sense, the fears remained to poison further (if that were possible) all chance of good relations between the Government and the people of the Island. Certainly Carlisle's heart was no longer in the business: 'they will want', he urged in November 1678, 'temporary laws till the Colony bee better grown.'[3]

[1] Carlisle to Coventry, 11 Sept. 1678, CO 138/3, 250.
[2] Cf. the 'Objections of Jamaica', 9 Oct. 1679, CO 1/43, No. 134; and the 'Address of the Assembly to Governor Lord Carlisle': 'In the Militia Bill power is given to the Governor which is not given to the King of England over the militia'; 23 Nov. 1679, ibid. 157.
[3] Carlisle to the Lords Committee, 18 July 1678, CO 138/3, 245. And he adds a curious remark on 24 Oct.: 'I have met with the difficultys here I foresaw, but

But his words were now falling on deaf ears. The King had been long at Windsor; had even failed to appear at Newmarket; had done no business. Plantation affairs had to await his return. But just as he did so, distraction came. All politicians now paused to watch, in painful fascination, the unravelling of that conspiracy against the executive authority in England which was so conveniently defined as the Popish Plot. Coventry apologized to all the colonial Governors in November that their affairs should be so neglected by their Lordships, but 'You may easily imagine a tree so rooted as my Lord Treasurer could not be rooted up without shaking the ground round about him.'[1]

So, while the ground in Whitehall seamed and split, Carlisle was left to preside over uneasy conditions of stalemate in Jamaica.]

Meanwhile, Governor Sir Jonathan Atkins in Barbados had been trying, with but scant success, to comply with the stream of requests for information that poured from his 'strict inquisitors', the Lords Committee. They expected to hear from him 'by every single ship'.[2] When, after much prodding,[3] he did send the Lords a manuscript book of the 22 laws that had been passed in Barbados since his arrival in 1674, it was only to be told that he was still not alive to what was required of him. The Lords wished to see not his laws alone, but the laws that had been re-enacted by the Assembly—all laws, in fact, that were either now or had ever been in force in Barbados. Southwell impressed on Atkins that the Lords were truly in earnest about this, and urged the Governor for his own sake to make haste to comply.[4] Alas, when Atkins obeyed at last, the Committee had no time to consider the laws—for they were all 'from His Majesty to the constable' engrossed in the Plot.

But it was not his sloth in this alone that had set Atkins's stock low at home. It seemed he had become more Barbadian

could neither avoid nor prevent in England', CO 138/3, 256; 15 Nov. 1678, ibid. 273–4.

[1] Coventry to Carlisle, 16 Nov. 1678, Add. MS. 25120, ff. 132–8.

[2] Lords Committee to Atkins, 21 Dec. 1676, CO 29/2, 76.

[3] On 10/20 Nov. 1678 (Atkins, trained to official life in Jersey, always used the double date) he wrote to the Lords Committee that their letter of 14 Apr. 1676 had not reached him until July 1678 'and 'tis often so here'—but this seems to be an exaggeration; CO 1/42, No. 143.

√   [4] Southwell to Atkins, 27 Nov. 1677, CO 29/2, 192–3.

in his views than the Islanders themselves.[1] He wrote argumentatively, not as to superiors, but as to equals, and often in cheerful denigration of their opinions. And one of his major complaints, that an increasing number of local offices was being removed from the Governor's power of appointment, increased the Lords' irritation to wrath. Their tone of righteous indignation was perhaps the louder because they knew that, in this particular matter, they stood on dubious ground.

This was, of course, a long-standing colonial grievance. In January 1661 one of Walrond's first acts as President of the Council in Barbados, once Colonel Modyford was out of his way, had been to suspend the holding of all Patent offices in the Island until the King's pleasure concerning them should be known.[2] In March, while the debate on the future of the Carlisle Patent to the Province of 'Carliola' was at its height in England, the President wrote home anxiously that, whatever happened to that great office, he trusted that the King would not 'interest himself in each little office here', but leave their disposal to the Governor, 'as used to be the custom'.[3] It was a trust that was misplaced. Appointment to colonial office was too cheap and convenient a solution to Charles's problem, how best to reward zeal in his service without charge to himself, for him to discard it. An order by the Council of Plantations to register the issue of all such colonial Patents[4] indicated that there would be many. Such appointments at this time were normally made directly by Commissions under the Great Seal, or under the sign manual and signet. The Governor's Instructions forbade him to interfere with these Patent officers in the enjoyment of their positions—'a direct infringement upon the discretionary power of appointment lodged in the Governor by his own Commission'.[5]

This royal habit probably did less harm when used on a large, generous scale, the scale of the Carolina and Pennsylvania grants: one John Collins was presented thus with the island of

---

[1] Cf. John Witham (Deputy-Governor) to Jenkins (Secretary of State), 8 Aug. 1683: 'The dignity of the Government was much impaired by Sir Jonathan Atkins, who was ever afraid of offending the Assembly'; CO 1/52, No. 50.

[2] Minutes of the Council of Barbados, 2 Jan. 1661, CO 31/1, 39.

[3] Walrond to Nicholas, 29 Mar. 1661, CO 1/15, No. 36.

[4] On 4 Feb. 1661, CO 1/14, No. 59, p. 14.

[5] L. W. Labaree, *Royal Government in America* (New Haven, 1933), 102.

Barbuda in July, and Francis Lord Willoughby with St. Lucia in November 1663, Albemarle with the Bahamas in 1670. But Governors found the practice very irksome when it was used not to benefit themselves, but to promote those who should have been their own subordinates.[1] Lord Windsor's Instructions contained an assurance that no one should hold more than one office at a time, or hold any by deputy; but even before he left for Jamaica he was constrained to obstruct the issue of a Patent to John Mann as Surveyor-General of the Island, as well as that of Lynch to the Provost-Marshalship. And Francis Lord Willoughby took an independent stand indeed; he jailed and deported Sir Robert Harley, who held the King's Patent for the office of Keeper of the Seal in Barbados and the Leeward Islands.[2]

It was not only the Governors who objected to such patentees. The colonists themselves naturally resented valuable offices going to 'foreigners', often of a marked incompetence. The protracted dispute of which Francis Cradock was the centre provides a case in point. In August 1660 he was granted a Patent under the Great Seal to the Provost-Marshalship of Barbados for life.[3] The following May the first of many petitions on the subject was presented by the Barbadians. The Provost-Marshal was also custodian of the records of all grants and conveyances of land; the planters, already fearful of official interference with their tenure, preferred to have these controversial deeds under the care of a person of their own nomination, accountable to themselves alone. Their preference went unheeded; but the Barbadians naturally continued to dwell on it.[4] The Provost-Marshal, they pointed out in June 1664, 'is in the nature of a sheriff,[5] and, according to the fashion of sheriffs, 'ought not . . .

---

[1] Cf. Willoughby's 'prayer' to the King, 4 Nov. 1663, 'not to make any grants interfering with his'; CSPC 1661-8, 578.

[2] The Patent is dated 5 June 1663. The appointment was made in Barbados on 25 Aug.; HMC Portland, iii. 273, 277.

[3] 2 Aug. 1660, CSPC 1574-1660, 33, p. 487.

[4] President, Council, and Assembly of Barbados to the King, 27 May 1661, CO 1/15, No. 58. For the further representations of William Willoughby (his brother's agent) on the matter, cf. 22 June 1664, APCC, i. 624.

[5] This was also the opinion of Sir Thomas Modyford, who may indeed have first driven it into the heads of the Barbadians. One of his first requests as Governor of Jamaica was for the appointment of a Sheriff, as a Provost-Marshal was 'an officer only fit for an Army'. Lynch held the Patent: Modyford hoped it would be

to continue in office beyond one year'.[1] The legal aspect of this
argument attracted some official attention, and the Attorney-
General was directed to examine the nature of a Provost-
Marshal. It was found to be a military office, with no sanction
to exercise power in civil law.[2] Meanwhile, however, Cradock
—who had never yet enjoyed the fees and perquisites of his
office[3]—had taken his grievance to the Privy Council. The
latter looked into the matter in February 1665, again in June,
and once more in July 1666, without coming to any decision on
it.[4] On 18 January 1667, however, they upheld Cradock's
Patent as Provost-Marshal and his rights thereunder, but decreed that the duties of sheriff should be detached from the
office and put in the charge of a properly constituted sheriff; the
latter officer should be appointed by the Governor, and must
not hold the post more than once in five years.[5] This must have
seemed to the Administration an equitable and therefore a
satisfactory solution of the question. It had not yet dawned on
the administrators that it was not just this individual case, but
the general principle of the Patent Office itself that was taken
such exception to in Barbados. On some, indeed, it never
dawned; the Duke of York, the last man to catch a nuance,
continually asked colonial Governors to 'serve' his interests by
appointing some particular person to office—for the Lord High
Admiral was not to be deflected from the exercise of patronage
by Barbadians or by anyone else.[6]

cancelled and Lynch given one as Sheriff in its place; Modyford to Sir J. Modyford, 21 July 1664, CO 1/18, No. 94. Lynch left Jamaica in 1665, but his deputy
retained the Provost-Marshal's office; Modyford to Arlington, 16 Nov. 1665,
CO 1/19, No. 127. And no change was made during this period; in 1683 Provost-
Marshal and Sheriff were still one office in Jamaica; CO 138/4, 212–28.

[1] 'Reasons of the Council of Barbados against the Patent', 22 June 1664,
CO 1/18, Nos. 76–78.
[2] Report of the Attorney-General, 26 June 1665, CSPC 1661–8, 759, ii.
[3] The King had ordered that Willoughby should restore Cradock to the office
when he arrived at Barbados (Mar. 1662, CO 1/16, No. 38), but Willoughby never
did so.
[4] Cf. 24 Feb. 1665, APCC, i. 648; 16 June 1665, ibid. 660; 6 July 1666, ibid. 683.
[5] Order-in-Council, 18 Jan. 1667, ibid. 696.
[6] Cf. York to Willoughby, 23 Mar. 1668, to instal 'my servant', Richard Morley,
as Secretary to Barbados; Adm 2/1745. He also wrote to Vaughan on 19 Feb.
1675 pressing the claims of Sir John Griffith as agent for Jamaica in London, with
the pointed remark that he would look upon Vaughan's compliance therein 'as a
remarke of your particular respects towards me'; Adm 2/1746. He commanded
both Vaughan and Atkins to give all aid to Cranfield, going to Surinam; and he

Cradock died in 1667 before he could enjoy his office, which then passed by Patent to a Groom of the Bedchamber,[1] a certain John Hamilton who never set foot in Barbados nor had any intention of doing so, to the relief of the inhabitants. In July 1670, however, the Patent was transferred to Edwin Stede. This shocked the Barbadians. Stede was unpopular in the Island principally because he was factor to the Royal Company there, and was therefore, from the planters' point of view, an official debt-collector. He petitioned the King, who wrote at once to Willoughby that this obstruction of a royal patent constituted 'an entrenchment upon our royal authority';[2] and accordingly it was stated in Willoughby's new Commission that no place in Barbados should be granted by the Governor without the King's knowledge and consent. On his arrival back in Barbados, Willoughby installed Stede in the office;[3] but after the Governor's death the judges fell to wrangling about the legality of the Patent. One of them, Humphrey Walrond junior, went so far as to declare that the Patent was in the power of the Government of Barbados, in accordance with a law passed there before the Restoration—one indeed that had never been confirmed, but to be sure had never been disallowed either. Stede challenged him to put this opinion on record, and when Walrond would not, Stede warned him that he would have to report it to the authorities at home. Walrond only retorted that he had no doubt his 'Interest in the Court of England' was greater than Stede's.[4] If this was a fair sample of the behaviour of Barbadian judges, it is not surprising that the Council of Trade and Plantations became very eager to inspect those unconfirmed laws of the Island.

The Instructions issued to Atkins in December 1673 included an order neither to obstruct nor to permit obstruction of those

recommended Brigadier Thomas Hill of the Guards as Deputy Governor of St. Christopher; York to Stapleton, 8 Mar. 1680, 25 Aug. 1682, Adm 2/1746.

[1] 21 Aug. 1667, CSPC 1661-8, 1556. William Lord Willoughby protested that 'that place is by an Act of this country established in the Governor's disposal, and likewise in his Patent from His Majesty'; Willoughby to Arlington, 26 Nov. 1667, CO 1/21, No. 149.

[2] The King to Willoughby, 27 Mar. 1671, CO 324/2, 27-28.

[3] On 17 Sept. 1672, and made him Secretary on 22 Oct.; CO 31/1, 198. In May 1679 Stede was appointed a Councillor by royal command; CSPC 1677-80, 889, 989.

[4] 'The State of the Case of Edwin Stede, Esq., Provost-Marshal of Barbados', 24 Nov. 1673, CO 389/5, 70-71.

who held office by virtue of His Majesty's Great Seal. Before
Atkins's arrival, Sir Peter Colleton and the Council of Barbados
warned the Assembly there that there was a new broom sweep-
ing, and that the King would take very ill their continued protestations against the granting of the places of Secretary,
Provost-Marshal, and the clerks under the Great Seal.[1] It was
wise advice, for the decade was to see a marked increase in the
number of offices so granted, in Jamaica as well as in Barbados.
Whether Sir Thomas Modyford's statement that Clarendon had
promised him that no grants to office would pass under the Seal
until the Governor had given his opinion was true,[2] or not, no
longer mattered. Clarendon was gone and Modyford was no
longer Governor. (Both gone indeed, but not forgotten: the
latter's son Charles was granted the office of Surveyor-General
in Jamaica in April 1675; the former's son Rochester was
granted all duties paid on logwood imported in September
1676.[3]) In November 1675, January 1676, and February 1677
other royal appointees filled the posts of Secretary in Jamaica,
Clerk of the Markets and Fairs in Barbados, and Clerk of the
Supreme Court in Jamaica.[4]

Thomas Martyn and Leonard Compeare, merchants of London who in April 1674 were appointed Receivers-General of
the Revenue in Jamaica, met there the treatment Stede had
received in Barbados. Martyn, arriving in Jamaica in February
1676, found himself debarred from his proper fees and perquisites, and a local Collector already appointed, with Lord
Vaughan's consent. Martyn's very presence seemed to the
Assembly as an insult, for money raised in the Island had been
collected by locally appointed officials for some ten years past.
His personality and behaviour were not endearing.[5] Having
attempted to bribe Vaughan to admit him to office, he went
on to commit a breach of 'privilege' of the Assembly by filing
a bill in Chancery against the Speaker and another member.[6]

---

[1] Minutes of the Council of Barbados, 8 Apr. 1674. Colleton remarked (what
may well be true) that William Lord Willoughby had done his best to get His
Majesty to repeal these Patents, but that the King in 'Open Councell' had declared
that he would have his Patents obeyed; CO 31/1, 265–8.

[2] Cf. Modyford to Bridgeman, 16 Mar. 1668, CO 1/22, No. 54.

[3] 8 Apr. 1675, CO 324/2, 64; 13 Sept. 1676, T 11/8, 273.

[4] T 11/8, passim.   [5] Cf. Whitson, op. cit. 65–67.

[6] Minutes of the Council of Jamaica, 19 May 1677, CO 139/1, 163–74.

For this he was promptly clapped in gaol. The fifth count against him struck the sonorous note now inevitable in the *pronunciamientos* of the Assembly of Jamaica: the luckless Martyn had betrayed the rights and privileges of 'the Commons of this Island . . . publicly asserting that the Governor, Councell, & Assembly could not raise any money here to the publick uses of the Island but what he ought & must collect by vertue of his Patent'[1]—a charge that was naturally construed by the Lords Committee as yet another impudent attack on the royal authority.[2] Vaughan was censured for countenancing this piece of defiance; nor did his later obstruction of a Patent as Clerk of the Supreme Court (issued to a gentleman who had already appointed three deputies to the office) improve his standing.

The reoriented Privy Council of 1679 was in its early days an assertive body, and its members perhaps saw in pluralism too sharp a weapon to leave unsheathed in the King's hands. At any rate they tried to prevail upon Charles to drop it, urging him to pronounce that in future his severe displeasure would be visited upon any colonial patentee who was also an absentee.[3] They referred to 'abuses that have recently crept into the plantations in respect of offices'. Formerly the powers claimed by Governors had been so absolute that they had challenged the validity of the appointments made by the King under the Great Seal. These days were thankfully over; but now, it appeared to their vigilant Lordships, there had been 'a rush into the other extream'. Governors had been deprived of their necessary authority, for offices were being filled by the King 'through private solicitation of persons in no way connected with the plantations, without the knowledge or approbation of the Governors'. Coventry had previously recommended that an inspection should be made of all colonial offices, so that they might then be classified in two groups: those that 'may fitly be filled' by the King, and those that should be left in the Governor's disposal.[4]

The new Lords Committee implemented this suggestion.

---

[1] *Journal of the Assembly*, i. 17, 25 May 1677.

[2] The King ordered in Council that one of Carlisle's first actions when he arrived in Jamaica must be to set Martyn at liberty; 22 Dec. 1677, CO 1/41, No. 136.

[3] Cf. their objection to the Patent of John Byndloss, 12 Dec. 1679, CO 324/4, 71–73.   [4] JLTP, 13 Nov. 1679, CO 391/3, 99–100.

They instructed Carlisle in Jamaica, and the two other West-
India Governors, to transmit an account of each of the public
offices and their authority, and state whether, in their opinion, a
particular post should be filled by the King or by the Governor.[1]
But in this period of political confusion the King's promises were
more hollow than ever. Royal generosity was surely a Prerogative matter. It was not fitting that certain Lords of his Council
—or for that matter colonial Governors, his own subordinate
commissioned officers—should decide when and in which
spheres it must operate. Accordingly, the Countess of Bristol
(who had the good fortune to be the mother-in-law of Secretary
of State Sunderland) was allotted by Patent the proceeds from
the sale of illicit cargoes of negroes in Barbados.[2] Sir Henry
Morgan's brother was found a post as Clerk of the Crown in
Jamaica in February 1680.[3]

The Lords Committee of Trade, justifiably irked, agreed to
move the King to pass no more colonial grants without first
notifying them.[4] In October they recommended, with success,
that a clause should be inserted in Sir Richard Dutton's Commission as Governor of Barbados voiding all patents of office,
excepting those of the Secretary and Provost-Marshal, if the
holder did not reside in the Island, at the same time declaring
that no further Patents would be granted under the Great Seal.[5]
An Order-in-Council to this effect was in fact issued. Nevertheless, a royal warrant countersigned by Secretary Conway instructed Dutton on 11 March 1681 to admit certain persons to
certain offices. On 20 April 1682 the Lords of Trade repeated
their previous recommendation when they found that a new
Patent for an office in Barbados was being issued;[6] but the tone
of this remonstrance was gentle, and plainly lacked confidence
that any attention would be paid to it. And it was, of course, of

---

[1] Lords Committee to Carlisle, 16 Jan. 1680, CO 138/3, 353.
[2] 15 May 1679, CO 389/9, 9. John Witham, appointed by command to the
Council of Barbados (15 June 1677, CO 389/6, 208), was the Countess's agent
(CO 324/2, 159). Despite the King's express command (19 May 1679, CO 29/2,
262–3), Atkins obstructed the Patent; cf. Atkins to Southwell, 22 Dec. 1679,
CO 389/9, 19. The Countess's proceeds from 1683 to 1687 amounted to some
£2,500; Beer, op. cit. i. 171.   [3] 7 Feb. 1680, CO 324/2, 163.
[4] JLTP, 17 Aug. 1680, CO 391/3, 191.
[5] Lords Committee to the King, 22 Oct. 1680, CO 29/3, 24–25.
[6] Conway to Dutton, 11 Mar. 1681, CO 29/3, 151; Lords Committee to the
King, 20 Apr. 1682, CO 391/4, 16–17.

no effect. Colonial patronage was too tough a plant to be felled by the blunt axe of seventeenth-century administrative zeal;[1] it was to grow unchecked to its full height in the peaceful garden of the eighteenth century.

What had principally angered Governor Sir Jonathan Atkins in the first place was the appointment by Patent of the 'naval office' in Barbados to Abraham Langford[2]—the more so as Vaughan in Jamaica had already appointed his own man to the same office.[3] Coventry tried to allay Atkins's declared fear that all offices in Barbados were passing from the Governor's control to the King's; but the Secretary left him in no doubt that, if it came to a dispute on the matter between Barbados and the Crown, it would not be Barbados that won.[4] For the King was determined to be 'a little better acquainted with those that bear offices in his Plantacons than of late he hath been, for till some later Orders of the Council, His Majesty hardly knew the Laws or the Men by which his Plantacons were Governed. The Governor was the only person known to him'. But now, however, 'His Majesty was resolved . . . to let them know, they are not to Govern themselves, but be Governed by him'. The reason for this was that 'some late Stubborn Carriage in the Plantacons will Occasion a stricter Enquirie into their Comportments than hath hitherto been made'.

Accordingly Coventry gave to Atkins 'the advice he would his brother' to co-operate with and not to obstruct the intentions of the Administration.[5] After all, no Lord-Lieutenant of

---

[1] An interesting grant, showing the King's independent view of the matter, is that to Nell Gwyn of the revenue of the logwood duties for 21 years from 29 Sept. 1683; Beer, op. cit. i. 82.

[2] Patent, 8 May 1676, CO 29/2, 193–7. He was also appointed Register of the Admiralty; cf. York to Atkins, 24 Sept. 1679, Adm 2/1746.

[3] Reginald Wilson, on 26 June 1676, CO 1/37, No. 12. Wilson was dismissed by Carlisle, but in 1681 successfully applied for a Patent under the Great Seal; CO 1/47, No. 53.

[4] Coventry to Atkins, 28 Nov. 1676: '. . . Obedience to HMs Great Seale . . . will not be controul'd by any seal in the Barbadoes. . . . I hope [the Assembly] are not so insolent as to declare to the King who are fit or not fit to serve him till his opinion be first known. In conclusion, HM is resolved to continue his Great Seale as far as by law he can, and those of his learned Councell tell me that is far enough. . . . Do not believe the Assembly hath any authority to balance that of a Great Seale'; Add. MS. 25120, f. 96.

[5] Atkins had thus to admit Langford to the Naval Office, but kept in his own hands the perquisite of warrants of arrest. This caused another agitated correspondence.

Ireland had ever protested thus against Patents issued under the Great Seal, and surely Ireland might 'pretend a little before Barbados'?[1] When, later, Atkins complained that a Patent as Clerk of Markets and Fairs in Barbados had gone to an aged person incapable of attending to the duties of this post, Coventry could only ruefully apologize and repeat his theme, 'All I can say is that His Majesty must be obeyed'. Atkins thereupon declared that he could have no confidence in the earlier assurances he had been given, that royal grants of office in the Island would be neither frequent nor extravagant.[2] The aspersion thus cast on the integrity of his superiors by the Governor of Barbados did not enhance the reputation of that officer in Whitehall.

Sir Jonathan was, however, never able to grasp that honesty in a colonial Governor had its political limitations, or that a close identification with the interests of those whom he governed was liable to be misconstrued. Perhaps it was the constant assumption by Atkins that they did not know what they were about that galled the Lords Committee most deeply, for the Governor continued to exhort them to better things in an atmosphere that grew increasingly chilly. 'One thing', he adjured them, 'you may admitt as a Maxim—that whensoever you intend to plant a new Collony, you must make their Port a free Port for all people to trade with them that will Come.'[3] The Acts of Trade had ignored this Maxim: it followed that they would in time ruin all the King's plantations. It is thus not odd that Atkins found it hard, as he remarked himself, to make their Lordships 'apprehend the reality of things here meet'.[4] They were not prepared to sit at their subordinate's feet while he dispensed Maxims, and a very stiff letter from the King was the Governor's reward.[5]

But true to their zeal for investigation, the Committee looked again at these same Acts of Trade on which Atkins held such startling views; but as the man they called in to advise them was one of the commercial system's authors, Sir George Downing, they were unlikely to receive an impartial account of

[1] Coventry to Atkins, 21 Nov. 1677, Add. MS. 25120, f. 120.
[2] Atkins to the Lords Committee, 3/13 Feb. 1676, CO 29/2, 47–57.
[3] Atkins to Lords Committee, 4/14 July 1676, CO 1/37, No. 22.
[4] Atkins to Lords Committee, 3/13 May 1677, ibid. 177.
[5] The Lords Committee drafted this on 10 Nov. 1676, and it was sent to Atkins by the King on 9 Dec.; CO 268/1, 51–53, 60–63.

its usefulness—nor did they. A second opinion, taken from Sir Peter Colleton, was less dogmatic: he suggested (cautiously) that some of the customs restrictions might properly be relaxed, and went on to draw an erudite analogy with the way they managed sugar-duties in Portugal. The Committee's report,[1] however, backed Downing's opinions, indeed with such emphasis that the Assembly of Barbados made no further attempt to block the operation of the Acts. Were subjects to petition against the laws they lived under, there, in the Committee's view, was an end of all good government. It is worth recalling that this solemn pronouncement was made at a time when the English Parliament was so riddled with suspicion of the Executive's intentions that the latter did not dare transact any business there; there is no doubt that the Lords had the conduct of the Commons in mind when they wrote these words. They stressed that the Assembly of Barbados would never have gone so far as to petition on this matter had they not been encouraged by Atkins. The offending Speaker, who was also Chief Justice, was removed by the King's order; but the Governor's was the more heinous sin.[2] Exasperated by these and other 'extravagances', the Committee tended more and more to by-pass Atkins in their pursuit of information on Barbadian conditions. When he protested, they reminded him that the King was at liberty to consult whom he pleased on his affairs, and if they had had to apply to outside sources for news of Barbados, that was only because they were always 'so imperfectly instructed' by Sir Jonathan himself.[3]

The onset of the Popish Plot provided Atkins with a respite from the displeasure of the Lords Committee. This must have come as a great relief—although he could not forbear, in the public interest, from an acid comment or two on their Lordships' neglect of their proper function—but it was not of long duration. Although the King had to endure an invasion of his Privy Council by the leaders of the Opposition, the Exclusionists,

[1] JLTP, 2-7 Nov. 1676, CO 391/1, 240-2.
[2] The King to Atkins, 18 May 1677, CO 389/4, 153. On 13 Dec. the irrepressible Assembly petitioned about Speaker Sharpe's removal; CO 31/2, 282-8. In 'A relation of some actions of Judge Sharpe' (in Colleton's handwriting) he is stated to have said that 'he had as good blood in his veins as any Charles Stuart, and other objections of a most blasphemous nature'; CO 1/40, No. 98.
[3] Atkins to Lords Committee, 6/16 Sept. 1677, CO 324/4, 187-8; Lords Committee to Atkins, 19 Jan. 1678, CO 391/2, 205-6.

there was no immediate change in the method of directing plantation affairs. Shaftesbury, having inserted himself as Lord President of the Council, returned to the Lords Committee of Trade, while York was obliged to retire both from that and from the kingdom. The Committee now had 22 members,[1] but of these 12 had served before. On 1 May this body informed Atkins of their constitution 'under the same regulation as formerly'.[2]

In July they resumed their inquisitorial tactics. Why had no answers to many of the 32 heads of inquiry yet been returned from the Governor of Barbados? News of the Island still came to them obliquely: the Farmers of the 4½ per cent. had petitioned them in complaint of two Acts of Barbados, passed respectively in November 1675 and in January 1679, whereby the Assembly there had decreed that the Farmers should restore the duty paid them if the goods exported were lost or captured at sea.[3] Yet these laws had not been among those that Atkins had, at long last, transmitted.[4] They were anyway disallowed—but Atkins's iniquity in concealing these laws was worse than the laws themselves.[5] He must in future transmit all Acts within three months of their passing in the Assembly. Upon default he would be recalled.[6]

Atkins now sought to give the Committee the solid information they sought, but his efforts came too late. His answers to

[1] JLTP, 22 Apr. 1679, lists them: Finch (Chancellor), Shaftesbury (Lord President), Lauderdale, Ormond, Winchester, Worcester, Arlington (Lord Chamberlain), Bridgewater, Sunderland (Secretary of State), Essex (First Lord of the Treasury), Bath, Fauconberg, Halifax, Henry Compton Bishop of London, Holles, Russell, Cavendish, Henry Coventry (Secretary of State), J. Ernle (Chancellor of the Exchequer), E. Seymour, H. Powle, W. Temple. Robartes was added on 27 June; CO 391/3, 1-2: Lawrence Hyde on 26 Nov., and Leoline Jenkins on 14 Feb. 1680. Cf. also Turner, *The Privy Council*, ii. 1 et seq.

[2] Lords Committee to Atkins, 1 May 1679, CO 391/3, 10-11.

[3] Petition of Strode and the Farmers, 18 June 1679, CO 1/43, No. 73.

[4] JLTP, 26 June 1679, CO 391/3, 30-37.

[5] Cf. the King to Atkins, 24 July 1679, 'not to intermeadle with our Revenue so that any part of it may bee there be lessened or interrupted without first receiving our especial commands', CO 29/2, 275.

[6] Lords Committee (i.e. Shaftesbury, Anglesey, Bridgewater, Bath, Ernle) to Atkins, 26 July 1679, ibid. 277-83. Coventry wrote the previous day: 'You will with this packet receive a letter from His Majesty countersigned by me, which I fear will not be very pleasing unto you, but I assure you the letter was not of my drawing, but drawn by a Clerk of the Councell in pursuance of a report made to His Majesty from the Committee of Plantations and by the Councell presented to His Majesty for signature . . .'; Coventry to Atkins, 25 July 1679, Add. MS. 25120, f. 143.

the Committee's questions of the previous July were regarded as suspect before they were even read, and as untrue immediately afterwards. The Committee called in Drax and Colleton, and asked the Commissioners of Customs to submit figures of the ships laden with enumerated commodities which had cleared from Barbados between April 1678 and October 1679, as they did not consider the account that Atkins had given them reliable. Colleton also cast doubt on the Governor's account of the laws —he himself knew of no laws passed since October 1678—and on the statistics concerning the numbers of inhabitants, and the volume of shipping.[1] The Lords Committee (on this occasion Anglesey, Clarendon, Radnor,[2] Sunderland, Worcester, and the Secretary of State, Sir Leoline Jenkins) took these criticisms as fact and wrote a letter to Atkins filled with more than the normal number of asperities;[3] and it was on 31 July that Sunderland apprised them of the King's definite intention to recall Atkins and to appoint Sir Richard Dutton in his place. They were forthwith to draft the necessary Instruments of Government.[4]

The scrutiny of the laws of Barbados therefore continued. On this matter, however, they found the Gentlemen-Planters less malleable than usual. The merchants held that the laws promulgated by the first Earl of Carlisle in Barbados were still in force, unless they had been directly repealed. That Earl had been as a prince palatine in 'Carliola', and his word had assuredly been law. Even those laws enacted by his successor, Francis Lord Willoughby, must be held as good, since no royal objection or exception to them had ever been made till now.[5] This stout opinion gave the Lords Committee, already dismayed by the legal impasse which faced them in the affairs of Jamaica, considerable pause. In a last effort, they directed their secretary, William Blathwayt, to find the answers to four vital questions. Were laws in Barbados perpetual, without the royal

[1] JLTP, 10 June 1680, CO 391/3, 169–72. There was, in fact, a good deal of inaccurate information in it; 14 June 1680, ibid. 173–7.
[2] Radnor was appointed Lord President *vice* Shaftesbury on 24 Oct. 1679; CO 391/3, 81.
[3] Lords Committee to Atkins, 6 July 1680, CO 29/3, 7–9.
[4] Ibid. 10.
[5] They did, however, agree with the Committee that all laws passed since the death of the elder Willoughby were governed by the two-year limit unless they had been confirmed by the King; JLTP, 4 July 1680, CO 391/3, 46–51.

confirmation? Might the combination of Governor, Council, and Assembly repeal a law confirmed by the King? Could Barbadian laws transmitted to England be partially amended there, or must they either be accepted or rejected outright? Lastly, had the King power to dissent to any law of the Island, of whatever standing, which he had not confirmed, and was such a law immediately void thereafter?[1]

These questions have considerable significance, as they indicate the grooves in which the official mind was working. The answers have not been recorded—and this, too, provides a good illustration of seventeenth-century administrative practice; for it is not to be doubted that Blathwayt asked the opinion of the Crown Law Officers, nor that the Officers gave one. The opinion given cannot have suited the Lords Committee's book— or else it would appear there. Yet on it the political future both of Barbados and Jamaica (and with them the other American colonies) depended.

The Administration had returned to the consideration of Jamaica's affairs in the spring of 1679. These were in no better case than they had been the previous autumn. But although the new Lords Committee adhered to the resolution to make no alteration in the 'new model' for the colony, they could not agree whether to put an ultimatum to Jamaica that the King would govern according to the Commission issued to D'Oyley unless the Island fell in with the royal wishes; and so they compromised by allowing Carlisle in the meantime to continue Vaughan's laws in force by Proclamation.[2] They resumed the whole problem of the laws and government of Jamaica in a report which was submitted to the King on 28 May, but unsigned, as it seems there was still some measure of disagreement. The objections made by the Assembly of the Island to the Militia Bill and to the perpetual Revenue Bill had been again reviewed, and seemed as unpalatable as ever. The Jamaicans continued to insist, despite all assurances to the contrary, that if their revenue were organized under the system now envisaged, it would be liable to diversion. Another of their more insulting accusations was that there were 'fundamental errors' in the *corpus* of laws that Carlisle had presented to them. They reiterated their

[1] JLTP, 10 July 1680, ibid. 81.
[2] 4 Apr. 1679, APCC, i. 1257.

complaint that their rightful 'deliberative power' was being removed from them. They insisted that the laws were too inflexible to be of any service to the community, since 'the nature of all Collonies is changeable'. This new model of government was, in fact, only a façade for the institution of an absolute government. The King, in giving his consent to it, had been misled by his advisers—the same charge that other 'Americans' were one day to level against King George III.

But this was to call a spade a spade: and the Lords Committee was greatly shocked. No one of these radical views could be upheld for a moment. This suspicion of the colonists that a perpetual revenue might be 'diverted' was unworthy; did it not expressly say in Carlisle's laws that the Revenue was to be devoted to the 'better support of the Government'? Did subjects not trust the King's own word? Furthermore, for Jamaicans to assert that there were errors, and fundamental errors at that, in laws so painstakingly drawn up by the best legal talents in England was a gratuitous impertinence. And did not the King's gracious permission that an Assembly might still be called from time to time give sufficient proof that he and his advisers were well aware of the 'changeable' nature of colonies? As for the deliberative power that Jamaicans professed to see slipping from their grasp—in truth it was not that they feared to lose, but the executive power, to which they had no right at all, having filched it unlawfully from the King's prerogative. It was indeed because they had so openly done so in Vaughan's time that their vigilant Lordships, as His Majesty's trusted Councillors, had advised the King to 'take the reins of Government' into his own hands. And what insolence it was for the Assembly to describe the Governor as an officer wielding absolute power when he was but the instrument of the King and the Privy Council!

The Committee thus officially refused to face the real issue, that it was the royal government itself that was challenged, but their awareness of it made their resentment very deep. They ended their dispatch in a high tone. 'Lastly and in the general', ran their pronouncement,

We humbly conceive that it would be a great satisfaction to your subjects there inhabiting, and an invitation to strangers when they shall know what laws they are to be governed by, and a great ease to the planters not to be continually obliged to attend the Assemblies to re-enact old laws which His Majesty has now thought fit in a proper form to ascertain and establish: whereas the late power of making temporary laws could be understood to be of no longer continuance than until such wholesome laws, founded upon so many years' experience, should be agreed on by the people and finally enacted by Your Majesty in such manner as hath been practised in other of Your Majesty's dominions, to which your English subjects have transplanted themselves. For, as they cannot pretend to farther privileges than have been granted to them either by Charter or some solemn Act under your Great Seal; so having, from the first beginning of that plantation, been governed by such Instructions as were given by Your Majesty unto your Governor—according to the power Your Majesty originally had over them, and which you have by no one authentic Act ever yet parted with;

and having never had any other right to Assemblies than from the permission of the Governors, and that only temporary and for probation, it is to be wondered how they should presume to provoke Your Majesty by pretending a right to that which hath been allowed them merely out of favour, and so discourage Your Majesty from future favours of that kind: when *what Your Majesty ordered for a temporary experiment*, to see what form would best suit with the safety and interest of the Island, *shall be construed to be a total resignation of the power inherent in Your Majesty and a devolution of it to themselves and their wills*, without which neither law nor government, the essential incidents of their subsistence and wellbeing, may take place among them.

There should be no truckling to these persons, for what was decided in this case of Jamaica would provide 'the measure of respect and obedience to your royal commands' in other colonies.[1] Carlisle must present the laws again, to a new Assembly. If they were again refused, he should be given those extraordinary powers that D'Oyley enjoyed. In the meantime the Lords Committee awaited news from the Governor.

Every dispatch from Carlisle, however, brought them a sharp disappointment. Carlisle, after working 'harder at this business than at anything before in my life', had been greatly irritated by the apparent lack of notice that his efforts had attracted; he was now entirely of the Jamaicans' point of view.[2] He talked

---

[1] Report of Lords Committee to the King, 24 May 1679, APCC, i. 1274.
[2] Carlisle to Williamson, 24 Oct. 1678, CO 1/42, No. 137. Cf. also his letter to Coventry, 18 Feb. 1679, complaining that since his arrival in Jamaica he had only

now in his dispatches of the *grievances* of the Island.[1] In August he called an Assembly without instruction to do so, and told the members he was going to send his Lieutenant-Governor, Sir Francis Watson, home to England to negotiate 'for us' a return to the previous method of legislation. If Watson was unsuccessful in this, then he himself would go the following spring and try his own skill.[2] Greatly heartened by this, the Assembly agreed in October to pass another Revenue Act, to be valid six months. Carlisle was plain with their Lordships: he told them flatly that in his judgement the Assembly would never be induced to accept the 'new model'. Jamaicans would never consent 'to make chains for their posterities'.[3]

This defection of a favourite son naturally alarmed the Lords Committee. They could not browbeat Carlisle as they did Atkins; but they made it clear to him that the sin in so great a man was itself so much the greater. And in other matters Carlisle had shown himself irresponsible. He, too, had not troubled to answer the 32 'Heads of Enquiry', though these had been twice sent him,[4] together with a copy of the answers Sir Thomas Modyford had returned, to serve him as a guide.[5] The Lords grew very testy, and by January 1680 were demanding of Carlisle 'a categorical answer' to their questions, but again this had no result.[6]

Indeed the Lords, goaded by Atkins and despised, as it appeared, by Carlisle, had much to complain of. They therefore determined, since Governors were proving themselves such unwilling instruments, to improve their communications with the colonies in other ways. Not only must Governors now submit quarterly reports to them 'besides the present obligation', but a correspondence was to be instituted between the Secretary of each colony and the Clerk of the Privy Council who attended the Lords Committee. In addition to this, the Clerk of the colonial

had two official letters from England; CO 138/3, 288. Coventry answered him with the excuse of the Plot, 2 June 1679, CO 389/6, 298.

[1] Carlisle to Lords Committee, 20 June 1679, CO 1/43, No. 76.

[2] 20 Aug. 1679, CO 139/1, 216.

[3] Carlisle to Coventry, 15 Sept. 1679, CO 138/3, 331. Edward Long borrows this phrase, but attributes it to his forebear Samuel.

[4] 25 Mar. 1678, 31 May 1679; CO 138/3, 196, 316. Carlisle brusquely referred them to 'a book called the State of Jamaica lying in the Plantation Office'.

[5] JLTP, 22 Dec. 1679, CO 391/3, 111–12.

[6] Lords Committee to Carlisle, 14 Jan. 1680, CO 138/3, 348.

Assembly was to forward to them copies of all laws that had
passed during the Session, so that a Governor's word on this
might be checked—or, as the Committee preferred to express
it, so that 'a more generall and united application of the
Endeavors & Services of all such as are interested in the discharge of publick affairs'[1] should be at the Administration's
disposal. These new Instructions must be obeyed; it was the
failure to obey instructions that had in some colonies 'had no
better effects than a Rebellion', and in others had 'occasioned
such mischeifs & abuses as are not easily to be remov'd'.[1] The
necessary orders were therefore sent out to all colonies in
January 1680[2]—and the various officials in the various Leeward Islands duly received a sharp reprimand the following
year for having paid no attention.[3]

The closing months of 1679, however, saw the growth of an
inclination in the Lords Committee to examine Jamaican
affairs on their merits.[4] They listened to Sir Francis Watson;
they asked the Law Officers whether that clause in the Militia
Bill,[5] which caused the colonists such alarm, was really open to
a sinister interpretation, and then asked them to amend it; and
they desired both Lynch and Vaughan to set down in writing
what they knew of the Government of Jamaica since the
Restoration.[6] Lynch's report gave them much to think about.
The Assembly had stated that it had never passed a Revenue
Act without limitation of time, and that Lynch's Act had been
of two years' duration only: the Lords had asserted the contrary. Lynch now pointed out that it was because the King had

[1] JLTP, 13 Nov. 1679, CO 391/3, 89-100, 357.
[2] Lords Committee to colonial Governors, circular, 14 Jan. 1680, CO 138/3, 353-5.
[3] Lords Committee to the secretary of the Leeward Islands, 12 Mar. 1681, CO 153/2, 458. The Council of Nevis pointed out sensibly in July 1682 that they had often nothing worth writing home about; CO 153/3, 53-54. Ironically enough, when the Councils of St. Christopher, Nevis, Antigua, and Montserrat wrote home one after the other in Feb. 1684, to urge that Stapleton should be continued as Governor despite his wish to retire (CO 1/54, Nos. 22, 31, 34-36), it was but to receive a cold retort from the Lords that they were presuming to advise on a matter on which they had no competence; JLTP, 7 May 1684, CO 391/4, 286-90.
[4] Cf. CSPC 1677-80, Nos. 1140-1, 1182, 1240.
[5] Which the Lords Committee had stoutly upheld in February; APCC, i. 1247.
[6] 22 Dec. 1679, CO 1/43, No. 176. Vaughan refused the task. He 'would not presume to decide such high matters as the rights that Englishmen may lawfully claim in places acquired by conquest'; ibid. No. 175.

neither confirmed nor disallowed that particular Act, that the Assembly had gone on to renew it every two years since. Lord Vaughan, for reasons doubtless best known to himself, had not forwarded that 'law of Jamaica' among those that he had transmitted in 1675. At the end of the following two years he had rejected the Revenue Bill anyway, and so there was none. But there was no 'perpetual Revenue' Act in Jamaica, and the Lords Committee could not invent one. Nor, in Lynch's view, would the Assembly ever allow one to pass, for 'the Irish system (they say) was desired by the English to support them against the Irish, but in Jamaica they are all English'[1]—so, accordingly, any form of coercive government was out of place. One trusts that Lynch made this point with a straight face in their Lordships' presence. He made a better point when he remarked that even although their Lordships' plan to dispense with the Assembly in Jamaica might ultimately succeed, the planters would contest every executive action in the Courts of the Island, where they would assuredly never fail to command the loyal support of judge and jury. It was perhaps possible for the English Government to subvert the constitution of Jamaica; but it was certainly not possible for it to subvert the fundamental principles of English law. The Lords Committee, whose own respect for the letter of that law verged on the pedantic, began to waver.

In January 1680 they interviewed a number of merchants, who stressed the anxieties of Jamaica and the gloom that prevailed there while this unnecessary constitutional uncertainty continued. In March the secretary, William Blathwayt, put to the Crown Law Officers further questions from the Lords Committee, the content of which gave evidence of a deal of fundamental thinking. Had the King's subjects in Jamaica a *right* to be governed by the 'laws of England'[2] as Englishmen, 'or [either] by virtue of the King's Proclamation, or otherwise'? And, if they had such a right, was it a natural right, inborn in all Englishmen?—or, in this case of Jamaica, did it issue only from that Proclamation Lord Windsor had made to the settlers

---

[1] Lynch to the Lords Committee, 18 Dec. 1679, CO 1/43, No. 172.

[2] The phrase was now a shuttlecock between the two parties. Cf. JLTP, 5 Mar. 1680: 'To the seventh objection [of the Assembly] it is replied that nothing has been done to take away their enjoyment of all the privileges of English Subjects since they are governed by the Laws & Statutes of England'; CO 391/3, 255-6.

in the year 1662?[1] Furthermore, if subjects in Jamaica laid claim to the 'laws of England', must they not also logically submit to the imposition of such statutory duties as Tunnage and Poundage? Or was this Statute applicable to England alone, and not elsewhere?[2]

The replies of the Law Officers to these queries, given over a month later, were evasive. They made the point that the phrase 'the laws of England' was indefinite in meaning—in this agreeing with a thoughtful excursus of Sir Jonathan Atkins, who had observed that even the laws of England were 'temporary and in the hands of Parliament'. Jamaica was governed by laws enacted there by the King's authority—so much was certain; but they confessed their uncertainty on the other issues raised. They could not even agree on the interpretation of the word 'dominion' in the Statute of Tunnage and Poundage. (It did not apply, for instance, to the Channel Islands.)[3] But to the Lords Committee it seemed that this was too useful a weapon to let rust while lawyers argued—and so they warned the Jamaicans that if they continued to stick out for the 'laws of England', they might very well be saddled with Tunnage and Poundage, which was indisputably one of them.[4]

Carlisle, true to his promise to the Assembly, had by now returned to England.[5] He came partly to fight the colonists' battle, partly to clear himself of charges brought against him by Long, and partly to shrug himself free from the whole business, of which he was by now heartily tired; for he had been considerably stung by an acid letter sent him by the Lords Committee in January, detailing his shortcomings at length. In obedience to a directive of 5 March 1680,[6] he brought Long and Beeston with him as State prisoners. These two, however (as the

[1] It seems that the Lords had not heard of this Proclamation until Lynch mentioned its existence.
[2] Blathwayt to the Crown Law Officers, 11 Mar. 1680, CO 138/3, 376–7.
[3] Edwards, op. cit. iii. 352–3.
[4] JLTP, 27 Apr. 1680, CO 391/3, 164–5, 167.
[5] Watson, on returning to Jamaica in Mar. 1680, had given Carlisle the King's verbal leave to return, of which the Lords Committee had not heard. An Order-in-Council was therefore issued on 8 Nov., forbidding any colonial Governor 'uppon any Pretence whatsoever' to come home without leave; CO 324/4, 82–83. This was reissued on 3 Nov. 1681, and sent to Lynch in Jamaica on 21 Sept. 1682, CO 138/4, 74. It was because of his violation of the order that Culpeper was dismissed from his Governorship of Virginia.
[6] Edwards, op. cit. iii. 347–8.

Privy Council was soon to find), were men of tenacity and sub-
stance, who could not be treated as mere malcontents and
rabble-rousers.

The Jamaican crisis had now reached deadlock.[1] Twice the
Assembly had been ordered to pass the *corpus* of laws, and twice
it had refused to comply. The focus of the debate now moved
from the *corpus* as a whole to the Revenue Bill in particular, for
both sides recognized this measure as the key to the matter.
Carlisle showed the Committee that the Revenue Acts passed
by D'Oyley and by Lyttelton were so loosely phrased that they
could bear any number of conflicting interpretations. The
Lords then brought Long before them and asked him why the
Jamaicans should so stubbornly object to the institution of a
perpetual Revenue Act—and the fact that they asked for a local
opinion at all vividly illustrates their change of temper and attitude; for to do so was to admit the validity of Jamaica's argument that her distance from England made the imposition of
autocratic government impracticable.[2] Long's reply was round
enough. The people of Jamaica had no other way of making
their grievances known to the Crown than by keeping the
Governor dependent on the Assembly. They knew that, once
such an Act was passed, the Governor would have no further
need of an Assembly. They would therefore continue to resist
the measure. Here was common sense of a high order; and,
faced squarely with the issue, the Lords took refuge for the last
time among lawyers.[3] They summoned the Chief Justice, North,
to their board, to answer two fundamental questions. Had the
King—by Windsor's Proclamation of 1662, or by any Statute
of England or Act of Jamaica—divested himself of his powers
in that colony?[4] (In other words, was the grant of English law
and the power to legislate to Jamaica revocable by the Crown?)[5]
Secondly, were the Revenue Acts passed by D'Oyley and
Lyttelton still in force?

[1] Cf. Whitson, op. cit. 102.

[2] Cf. L. M. Penson, *The Colonial Agents of the British West Indies* (London, 1924),
73: 'A short period of personal contact had done what long correspondence could
not do.'

[3] There was a debate in the Privy Council on Jamaica on 23 June 1680. CO
138/3, 382.   [4] JLTP, 14 Oct. 1680, CO 391/3, 214–16.

[5] This, of course, was the point at issue in *Campbell* v. *Hall* (1774), decided in the
Crown's disfavour by Mansfield; cf. A. B. Keith, *Constitutional History of the First
British Empire* (Oxford, 1930), 14–17.

North's answers to these questions are not recorded. From this it may be deduced that the answer to the first was Yes and to the second was No. In the Lords Committee's Journal appears their own opinion in regard to the second question, that Windsor's Proclamation referred only to the settlement of property in Jamaica and not to the settlement of Government.[1] Had North agreed with this the Journal would certainly say so. But Long had no difficulty in demolishing this curious contention without legal assistance. He pointed out, what was quite true, that Sir Thomas Modyford had voided all Lyttelton's Acts and that no one in England had gainsaid his action. Moreover, Windsor's Instructions had empowered him to make laws for two years only, unless confirmed by the King. The King had not confirmed them before Modyford's assumption of the Government. Because of royal negligence, should Jamaica have gone lawless, like a drifting ship? And even if the actions of D'Oyley and Lyttelton were still held to be valid, they would not serve their Lordships' turn, for it was a plain fact that neither of these Governors had had any power to make laws without the aid and consent of their Councils. From this it followed that the inhabitants of Jamaica, 'as Englishmen, ought not to be bound by any laws to which they had not given their consent'.[2]

The voice of Jamaica was thus the first to enunciate before the metropolitan Government this famous doctrine of the American Revolution; and it was while Long's words were sounding in their ears that the Lords decided to abandon the contest with Jamaica. He and Beeston were sent to attend North, and the official admission of defeat can be seen in the words of their instructions. They were to explain to the Chief Justice what terms would induce the Jamaicans 'to settle the Revenue for the support of the Government, and to the end matters may be brought to an accommodation'. On 27 October North reported back to the Privy Council that Long and his friends offered to grant a perpetual Act to pay the Governor's salary, together with a Revenue Act of seven years' duration, in return for the continuance of the Island's former constitution. The Council left it to the Lords Committee to get the matter settled

---

[1] JLTP, 20 Oct. 1680, CO 391/3, 219.
[2] Blathwayt to North, reporting Long's words, 20 Oct. 1680, CO 1/46, No. 23.

on this basis and meanwhile wrote to Morgan in Jamaica telling him to call an Assembly and to pass another temporary Revenue Bill. From the imperial point of view, the matter was closed.[1]

The Lords Committee was left to the task of saving face. In this contest they had throughout taken their stand on law—and they had now found that law would not support them. Fortunately, the circumstance that a new Commission was then being drafted for a new Governor of Barbados gave them the chance to retire without loss of dignity from the impasse into which they had strode with such confidence. The sacrifice of Sir Jonathan Atkins preserved their prestige. The Commission for his successor, Sir Richard Dutton,[2] was not an authoritarian document; and if the Jamaicans would consent to align themselves with this pattern for Barbados, it need not appear that the second thoughts of the Administration had been forced on it by the pressure of political circumstance.

In Dutton's Commission the members of the Council in Barbados were no longer directly nominated by the King. The Governor was to transmit for the royal approval the names of the 12 men whom he considered most fitted for this position, together with those of the two whom he thought most suitable to succeed him in the case of his absence or death. All members of the Council should take the Test.[3] All the present laws were to continue in force in Barbados until disallowed or otherwise excepted to by the King—there was an implication here that a number of them would certainly meet that fate shortly. If the Governor did not forward copies of all laws passed in the colony to England, as instructed, he would in future forfeit a year's salary; that this would be the more keenly felt, the salary itself was advanced to £1,200 a year. The Governor must take a new Oath, that he would in fact obey the terms of his Commission and Instructions. The Secretary of the colony, and the Clerk of the Assembly, would forfeit their positions if they, too, did not strictly comply with the orders they had received to send home to the Lords Committee the required information on the conditions of the Island. Mention of the King's name must occur in any Bill

[1] Cf. Edwards, op. cit. iii. 360-3.

[2] Lately Lieutenant of the Duke of York's troop of Horse Guards; HMC Ormond, v. 330.

[3] An addition to the Instructions, made on 18 Sept. 1680; CO 391/3, 198.

promoted to raise money, and the word 'representative', capable of so many diverse and dubious interpretations, should not appear anywhere in the language of the laws. All returns of revenue must be transmitted to the Treasury in England, although the Assembly might be permitted to examine the accounts. The laws were not to declare any duration to their own validity, unless they were designed to deal with some specific local issue. The better that a watchful eye might be kept on the development of the colony, an Attorney-General would be appointed to reside on the Island.[1] This was the full Commission that was issued to Sir Richard Dutton on 22 October 1680.[2] Six days later the Lords Committee forwarded it to the King in Council as suitable also for the constitution of Jamaica.

Carlisle was next authorized by the Lords Committee to tell the Assembly in Jamaica that in future Assemblies should be summoned there 'after the manner and form now in practice'.[3] Such Assemblies would, as heretofore, have the power to make laws with the advice and consent of the Governor and Council. The enacting style of these should state the fact simply: 'By Governor, Council, and Assembly.' The laws that they made were to agree 'as far as may be' with the laws of England. All were to be sent home for the King's confirmation within three months of their passing. The King reserved the right of disallowance, and the Governor retained the power of veto.

Two sets of Instructions[4] (the one to be made public, the other to be kept for his private use) were handed to Carlisle in London in November. The first set told him to announce the above gracious decisions officially to his Assembly when next he convened it. While its members still felt grateful, he must get their consent to a perpetual Revenue Bill, assuring them that the proceeds both from this and from the royal quitrents would always be devoted to the public service of the Island. The private Instructions told him that, if he could not obtain this

[1] JLTP, 6 Aug. 1680, CO 391/3, 183. Francis Lord Willoughby had asked for such an officer on 29 June 1664 in a letter to Arlington; CO 1/18, No. 81. In Jamaica, Modyford had appointed an 'Advocate-General' on 1 Jan. 1667, CO 140/1, 155-66.

[2] Commission in CO 29/3, 25-37. Instructions, ibid. 37-53; Vice-Admiral's Commission, 25 Nov. 1680, ibid. 102-3.

[3] 'Powers given to the Earl of Carlisle for legislation in Jamaica', 3 Nov. 1680, CO 138/3, 444-7.

[4] CO 1/46, No. 31; CSPC 1677-80, 1571-2.

> Revenue in perpetuity, he must try to get a Bill through that would hold good for as long a period as possible—anyway for not less than seven years. Clearly he would have to do some bargaining; he might, for example, withhold consent to those Acts that improved the judicial system, until the Revenue was safely passed. Thereafter, there was no reason why Carlisle should call another Assembly until the Act had expired—for the Lords Committee saw no reason to change their opinion that too much latitude in summoning Assemblies had been given to Governors in the past. Carlisle was permitted to 'insinuate' the gist of these private directions to selected Assemblymen of influence, the better to assist him in his task. In all other respects the terms of the Commission and Instructions that had been issued to him on 1 March 1678 were to hold good.

The Lords Committee, however, felt that a new Governor in Jamaica would have a better chance of carrying out these directions than the Earl of Carlisle, who was now a figure of controversy, with devoted adherents and bitter enemies both in Port Royal and in Whitehall.[1] Carlisle himself had had more than enough of the constitutional problems of Jamaica, and was quite willing to relinquish the post to Sir Thomas Lynch, who was thus for the second time called to that service.[2] In the meantime Carlisle's private and public Instructions were forwarded to Morgan.

> The Committee's first intention was that Lynch should again go to Jamaica as Lieutenant-Governor, Carlisle's rights as Governor being thus preserved;[3] but it was decided later that, in order to strengthen Lynch's authority in the Island, Carlisle might be omitted altogether from their considerations, and so Lynch was styled Captain-General and Commander-in-Chief in his stead.[4] His Commission was issued on 6 August 1681.[5] At the same time the Commissions of Sir Henry Morgan—the Lieutenant-General in Jamaica, who had been holding the fort

[1] There was a hearing in Council of complaints against Carlisle on 19 Jan. 1681; APCC, ii. 22.

[2] To the consternation, it appears, of Sir Henry Morgan and Receiver-General Thomas Martyn, both for excellent reasons; Sloane MS. 2724, f. 225.

[3] Cf. draft Commission, CO 391/3, 261–2.

[4] Ibid. 271. Long says that Carlisle declined to go again to Jamaica.

[5] Blathwayt wrote to Sir John Werden, York's secretary, asking for a Commission of Vice-Admiralty for Lynch, 15 July 1681, CO 138/3, 483; Lynch's Commission to be Captain-General and Vice-Admiral is in CO 138/4, 1–18.

manfully ever since Carlisle's departure from the Island—and
of Sir Francis Watson were revoked. This was done partly to
economize on the 'establishment', and partly because both
Morgan and Watson, for different reasons, were distrusted by
the Lords of Trade. One notable concession was given to Lynch.
He might still appoint, and suspend, his own Councillors. He
was also to inspect all Patent offices, and in regard to those held
by absentees, he might consider 'of a law like unto that in
Ireland' for the removal of the inconveniences that arose
thereby.[1] Otherwise his Instructions[2] followed those given to
Carlisle. The Governor's first task was still to secure the passage
of a long-term Revenue Act,[3] and until that was safely accomplished he must deny the passage of any other legislation by the
use of his veto, with the exception of two immediately necessary
measures—an Act for naturalization, and one for the better
suppression of pirates and privateers.

II

In this concentration on obtaining an assured colonial
revenue, the Lords Committee showed a new-found wisdom.
They had learned two things from their contest with the
Assembly of Jamaica; first, that a watertight legal case was
essential if any successful onslaught was to be made against a
colonial constitution; and, secondly, that if the necessities of
Government on which the Assembly traded could be removed,
so by the same operation would be the latter's own sting. With
an assured revenue, a Governor might dispense with an Assembly. Vaughan, Atkins, Carlisle—all had trodden, for one
reason or another, the path that their Assemblies had laid down
for them. But were perpetual Revenue Acts established in each
royal colony, no Governor would be either tempted or forced to
walk that way.[4]

It was therefore as a first step to this end that William

---

[1] Order-in-Council; 28 July 1681, ibid. 40.

[2] Lynch's Instructions, 8 Sept. 1681, ibid. 17–39.

[3] The King declared on 19 Oct. 1681 that all laws passed by Morgan would be
made null and void unless a Revenue Bill were passed with them; CO 389/8, 90.

[4] The Assembly's habit of giving 'presents' to the Governor had accordingly to
be curbed. Dutton, after touting assiduously, received one of £1,500: he was
instructed to return it; 15 Dec. 1682, CO 29/3, 150–1. A general Instruction on
this was sent to all colonial Governors on 15 Dec. 1684; CO 324/4, 91.

Blathwayt, secretary to the Lords Committee, was granted a
Patent on 19 May 1680,

for erecting and establishing an office of general inspection, examination and audit of all and singular accounts of all moneys arising or
accruing or which shall arise or accrue to the King from any of his
foreign Dominions, Colonies, and Plantations in America.[1]

For the moment these terms of reference applied only to the four
royal colonies there: Jamaica, Barbados, the Leeward Islands,
and Virginia. While the case of Jamaica's revenue was still unsettled, the Lords hoped that this new appointment would
dispel the Island's fears that its revenues were, if not misapplied,
at least carelessly manipulated at home: the Treasury Commissioners stressed their desire that Jamaica 'may not, for the
future, have the least colour to complain'.[2] But, of course, the
appointment of yet another official whose salary had to be
found from colonial revenue was unlikely to be hailed as a
blessing by the colonists themselves.

Blathwayt, setting to work, found at once an accumulation of
arrears in the $4\frac{1}{2}$ per cent. revenue: the last three years of the
1670-7 Farm in Barbados, the entire seven years of the Leeward Islands' Farm, and the three years of the new Farm established there in 1677.[3] When he reported this to the Treasury
Commissioners, they ordered the Farmers to bring these accounts in for audit immediately.[4] Jamaica's accounts were in
no better case: none at all were to hand for the whole period of
Vaughan's Government. What the royal revenue from rents,
prizes, fines, forfeitures, and duties had been in that time was
therefore a mystery. Perhaps it was a mystery that concealed
a reality of riches? Here anyway was another spur to the overhaul of the system of colonial audit.[5]

---

[1] Patent in Cal. T.B., 1679-80, vi. 544-5; T 64/88, 1. Accounts were to be
retroactive to 1672.

[2] Lords of the Treasury to Carlisle, 30 June 1680, T 64/88, 15-17.

[3] For the returns from the $4\frac{1}{2}$ per cent. duty, cf. Appendix, *infra*.

[4] 16 June 1680, T 64/88, 12. Blathwayt's discovery was on a par with Dutton's in
Barbados, that since the year 1666 no ships had entered bonds there that they would
not unlade their enumerated commodities save in England or in the other colonies;
some £200,000 worth of goods were therefore uncertified; Dutton to the King, 7 Sept.
1681, CO 1/47, No. 58. The Lords Committee made it a standing rule in future
that shipmasters should enter their lading with the King's collector as well as with
the naval officer, but complaints still came in of 'ships which frequently come from
the plantations with sham and unintelligible certificates'; HMC Ormond, vii. 243.

[5] On 24 Aug. 1683, in the Commission for Howard as Governor of Virginia, a

Meanwhile the Lords Committee recommended that in future the Receiver of the Island should send home a return of his accounts every six months, so that Blathwayt might allow or disallow it.[1] But Vaughan's Receiver, Thomas Martyn, had spent his time of office in jail, and even when released he was unable to sort out the fiscal chaos.[2] Accordingly, Blathwayt appointed Reginald Wilson, the naval officer in Jamaica, as his own deputy there.[3] He then turned to consider the fiscal affairs of the Leeward Islands. Here again all was guesswork, and one guess estimated that the Islanders owed the King some £20,000. The Lords Committee had previously reported adversely on the existing system of farming the Revenue there. The Governor, they suggested, should be authorized to levy the $4\frac{1}{2}$ per cent. duty himself, and the proceeds should be applied to the construction of a substantial fort in each Island. This would be at once a cheap and popular method of defending these very vulnerable colonies.[4] It was a good scheme, and the Commissioners of the Treasury began to negotiate along these lines with the Farmers, who were agreeable to the idea provided the Exchequer saw to it that they did not lose by the arrangement. But as soon as Colonel Strode's accounts were in Blathwayt's hands, it was plain that the Farmers and the Exchequer were unlikely ever to agree whose was the profit and whose the loss. Strode and his partners claimed a large amount for 'defalcations' —so much for short entries, so much for the three-year period that St. Christopher had been granted immunity from the duty. A Treasury Committee inspected the first claim, the Commissioners of Customs sifted the accounts of St. Christopher to verify the second. Blathwayt himself reckoned that Strode's rebate properly amounted to some £300 only. Sir Charles Wheler then

clause was inserted ordering him to take an account of public moneys, and to report as to his predecessor's management of the same. A memorandum noted that this should be a standing Instruction in future to all incoming Governors; CO 324/4, 187-91.

[1] Lords Committee to the King, 22 Oct. 1679, CO 153/2, 392-9.

[2] Lynch described him as 'the most unpracticable fellow I ever met with'. On Martyn's death in 1684 he ordered the Attorney-General to bring a *scire facias* against the Patent; cf. Lynch to the Lords Committee, 24 Aug. 1682, CSPC 1681-5, 668; CO 140/4, 43-45, 50-51.

[3] T 64/88, 71-74. Cf. also 'Governor of Jamaica's Instruction to Reginald Wilson', 1687, in MS. Rawl A. 171, f. 199.

[4] Cf. JLTP, 1 Oct. 1679, CO 391/3, 70-72; and their report of 22 Oct., in CO 1/53, No. 146.

interpolated a claim for over £2,000, owed him for arms and
ammunition supplied.[1] This confusion caused the Lords of the
Treasury to order the Farmers to allow their account-books both
in England, and in Barbados and the Leeward Islands, to be
inspected, and copies made of them by Blathwayt in England,
by the Secretary and the Provost-Marshal in Barbados, and by
Sir William Stapleton in the Leewards.[2] Stede in Barbados
found the Farmers' agents obstructive,[3] but they eventually
acquiesced. Stede himself was appointed official Receiver by
Blathwayt in December 1682.

But farming the 4½ per cent. revenue was plainly not an
efficient way of securing a colonial revenue, and when the 1677
Farm expired in 1684 it was not renewed. A paper setting out

Proposalls humbly offered for the more regular controle of His
Maties duty of 4 and ½ per cent. in Barbados and the Leeward
Islands, to prevent the inconveniencys attending the farming
thereof, in non-payment of rent, defaulcations, & other fraudulent
pretences[4]

explains the motives of the Administration. The Proposals suggested that this branch of the Revenue should be committed to
the management of a Commissioner or Commissioners resident
in London, under the supervision of the Treasury. Such Commissioners should receive and dispose of all the colonial produce
imported into England from these colonies. They should have
power to appoint the necessary officers to collect the revenue
there. Three reasons were argued against granting a renewal of
the Farm. The Islanders would more readily pay the duty to
royal Commissioners than to Farmers, whose constant 'defalcations' lost the Island money that should have gone toward the
cost of defence; royal officials would be treated with more
respect than any local person Farmers would appoint; and
thirdly, it was highly doubtful whether the Farm would find any
takers, it was such an uncertain and profitless business. These
were convincing arguments: and on 2 September 1684 the
Customs Commissioners were instructed to take over the management of the 4½ per cent. revenue in Barbados and the Lee-

[1] 6 Nov. 1680, T 64/88, 68, 83.
[2] 28 Oct. 1680, ibid. 54.
[3] Stede to Treasury Lords, 1 Feb. 1681, ibid. 76.
[4] Add. MS. 28089, f. 43.

ward Islands, and to appoint Stede and Gascoigne to be the chief Commissioners there.[1] Thus the $4\frac{1}{2}$ per cent. duty was confirmed as the perpetual Revenue in the richest colonies of the Caribbean.[2]

The affairs of Jamaica, after an unpromising start, also ended happily. After wrangling with the Assembly for six months, Sir Henry Morgan managed to get from it in November 1681 a Revenue Act valid for seven years. His racy dispatches made a great deal of the battle he had waged, painting a vivid picture of the triumph of a devoted servant of the Crown over a set of very slippery customers.[3] But this was a somewhat biased view: for along with the Revenue Act the Assembly had passed their well-thumbed Bill declaring the laws of England in force in Jamaica; and with that Act, they had passed *en bloc* all the other measures they thought fitting for the security of themselves and their property. The idea of a *corpus* of laws, it now appeared,

---

[1] Gascoigne was Stede's fellow-factor in the Royal African Company's employ.

[2] The question of scrapping the duty as well as the Farm had already been raised. Willoughby had been empowered to look for a substitute revenue in 1672; CO 389/4, 57–58. So was Dutton in 1680; Lords Committee to the King, 22 Oct. 1679, CO 1/43, No. 146, and JLTP, 12 Oct. 1680, CO 391/3, 212–13. Colleton and Drax, encouraged by Shaftesbury, made an offer in July 1679 to buy the Farm outright; JLTP, 4 July 1679, ibid. 50. The Assembly of Barbados was eager to support this scheme; Journal, 22 Oct. 1679, CSPC 1677–80, 1157. Blathwayt advised against it, however, and henceforth it was the demerits of the Farmers, and not of the duty, that attracted official attention; Blathwayt to Lords of the Treasury, 6 Oct. 1680, T 64/88, 44–45. Barbados, however, continued to think up alternatives: the Council suggested in July 1681 that the King should be offered a revenue of £5,000 a year for 31 years for the annulment of the Farm and the duty—or £6,000, if the Leewards' Farm was included. The sum could be raised by a duty on wines and liquors; Minutes of the Council of Barbados, 8 June, 20 July 1681, CO 31/1, 407, 419–20. The Assembly, however, scotched this notion in October, believing that anyway monarchy 'was on its last legs in England'; Dutton to Jenkins, 14 June 1681, CO 29/3, 72–75. Three years later, however, they had second thoughts, and put in a bid to farm the revenue themselves at a rent of £6,000 for 11 years—raising the sum by taxing all estates of 10 acres and upwards 21*d*. They passed an Act to this effect on 19 Mar. 1685, but on the advice of the Customs Commissioners it was disallowed. $4\frac{1}{2}$ per cent. anyway brought in more than £6,000; Edwards, op. cit. i. 539–40. Worse was to come Barbados' way: for King James II, as eager to dispense with Parliamentary supplies as his brother, imposed further duties of 2*s*. 4*d*. per 100 muscovado, and 5*s*. on 'whites' (1 Jac. II, c. 4; cf. HMC Egmont ii. 155)—thus, in Edward Lyttelton's words, holding Barbadian 'Noses to the Grind Stone' until 1693; *Groans of the Plantations*, 9.

[3] Morgan to Lords Committee, 18 May 1681, CO 1/46, No. 145; 6 Nov. 1681, CO 1/47, No. 63. The Council of Jamaica dissociated itself from the headstrong actions of the Assembly in a letter to the Lords Committee, 17 Jan. 1682, CO 138/4, 56–61.

had been too much popularized in Jamaica. The Assembly declared that their Acts were to 'remain and continue in force and virtue according to the respective tenours . . . without any change, alteration, or diminution in point of time or otherwise'. The King must confirm them—for, if he did not, the Revenue Act itself would fall. All money raised in the Island should be applied to the support of the Government. The Receiver-General should report once a year to the Assembly with the accounts: this meant that the Assembly must therefore convene at least once a year. A change was made in the controversial clause of the Militia Bill, to the effect that no Governor under its powers could force any inhabitant to service, or do anything contrary to the laws of England. 'God forgive 'em', remarked Morgan tolerantly of the recalcitrants who had been thus hard at work, 'I doe'; and although he was aware that some of this might come amiss with the authorities at home, he continued to urge the Lords Committee to take care how they amended these laws, for if they were rejected, it would be hard to get any Revenue Act of any sort whatever from the Assembly again.[1]

Sir Thomas Lynch arrived as Governor and Captain-General on 15 May 1682. Jamaica was in different case from what it had been on his arrival as Lieutenant-Governor 11 years before. Now there were 50,000 slaves on the Island, indicative of the great progress made in planting. He reckoned that 108,700 acres were cultivated, 209,920 patented.[2] Trade was brisk and money plentiful. But one thing that had not changed at all was the irrepressible buoyancy of the Assembly.[3] Lynch was still uncertain what the Lords Committee would do about that body's legislative activities, but of course he knew that the Administration would never consent to pass a body of laws 'so tacked'.[4] In a speech to the members of the Assembly[5] he insisted that this was the favourable moment to put their affairs in order, and to improve the hostile, suspicious relations that

[1] Morgan to Lords Committee, 9 Apr. 1681, CO 138/3, 481. Morgan to Jenkins, 8 Mar. 1682, CO 1/48, No. 37.

[2] Lynch's 'Description of Jamaica', 20 Sept. 1683, CO 138/4, 212-38.

[3] Its membership, 18 in 1671, was now 32.

[4] Lynch to Jenkins, 20 June 1682, CO 1/48, No. 110; Lynch to Lords Committee, 29 Aug. 1682, CO 138/4, 78-91.

[5] In case anyone thought of making a familiar point, he assured the Assembly that it was lawfully convened, being that which had originally been summoned by the King's writ to Carlisle.

had existed between Jamaica and the home Government for so
long. Surely the recent appointment of a colonial Auditor-
General had allayed their fears that the revenue they raised
would be diverted? The Assembly listened to this, and decided
to pass a new Revenue Act. It was again valid for seven years,
but it made no provision for an annual Session and omitted the
other 'distressful and offensive clauses'.[1] In relief Lynch sent this
home, and waited anxiously for news.

Morgan's laws had been received in England in June, but the
Lords Committee did not begin to examine them until October.
When they did so they were greatly shocked. They had thought
themselves to have retired gracefully, and on the whole un-
obtrusively, from the contest with the Assembly of Jamaica.
From the content and language of Morgan's laws, however, it
was clear that the Assembly thought that it had driven the
Lords Committee, and with them the authority of the Crown,
stricken from the field. These laws set out the planters' own
terms for the Government of Jamaica, and a bland confidence
that their acceptance was a foregone conclusion pervaded them
all. For a time it seemed likely that the Lords Committee would
descend in wrath upon them, and there were again dark threats
of imposing Tunnage and Poundage to obtain the desired
Revenue.[2] They insisted that the tacked laws would not be
allowed until the Assembly had presented a proper Revenue
Act. Blathwayt was sent to consult North, C.J., once more, and
the whole dispute would assuredly have flared up again had not
Lynch's dexterity prevented it. When his letter announcing the
passage of a new Revenue Act was received in January 1683,
the Lords declared themselves 'much satisfied with this'.[3] In
February they confirmed this Act for seven years, together with
the majority of the other Acts that Morgan had transmitted.[4]

[1] 20 Sept. 1682, CSPC 1681-5, 699, 711; Lynch to Lords Committee, 29 Sept.
1682, CO 138/4, 92-96.
[2] Cf. JLTP, 8 Nov. 1682, CO 391/4, 74-75.
[3] JLTP, 11 Nov. 1682, ibid. 77; Blathwayt to North, 18 Dec. 1682, CO 138/4,
77-78; JLTP, 12 Jan. 1683, CO 391/4, 97-100.
[4] Lords Committee (i.e. North, Halifax, Albemarle, Arlington, Ailesbury, Bath,
Chesterfield, Clarendon, Conway, Ernle, and Jenkins) to Lynch, 17 Feb. 1683,
at the same time asking him to send over the names of 12 men whom he thought
most suitable for appointment to the Council of Jamaica, 'that His Matie may in
future appoint noe person whose character he does not know'; CO 138/4, 127-35;
and the King to Lynch, 23 Feb. 1683, ibid. 135-7. On the same day he disallowed

Nevertheless, the Lords still had their hearts set on getting a perpetual Revenue Act out of Jamaica, and they pressed Lynch to do all he could to this end. Lynch again applied himself to the Assembly, adjuring them that 'Princes cannot be bound, they must therefore be trusted'.[1] This must have appeared a flimsy argument to the Assemblymen; but they trusted Lynch more than they did the King. Again they hearkened to his words of advice, and on 18 October passed yet another Revenue Act, this time to be valid for 21 years. The Administration accepted this bird in the hand, very sensibly; and as a result those laws of Jamaica that had been previously confirmed for seven years were now confirmed for 21 years as from November 1683.[2]

While the last five years of the reign saw this improvement in the administrations in the West Indies, they saw also a diminution in the self-importance of the Lords Committee of Trade.[3] They did not meet as frequently, nor did they now do so in the same high confidence. Their function was of course still necessary, and the Committee system survived the upheaval in the Privy Council in 1679. A glance at the background of English politics is necessary to explain the situation. When the Council was reorganized on 22 April four new Committees were established: for Tangier, for Ireland, and for 'Intelligence', as well as that for the business of trade and plantations. But their members were soon made aware that they were not in reality at the heart of affairs. Few persons were. The King, forced to dismiss Danby and hemmed in rather than advised by a ring of 33 Privy Councillors—at their head the 'Country party' leaders and Exclusionists—henceforth shared few confidences. The Council naturally suffered in prestige from this neglect, and the King, skilled in playing off the weakness of one man against the ambition of another, presided affably over a structure of government that he knew must disintegrate before long.[4] The triumph

the Act of Jamaica that declared the laws of England to be in force there; CO 138/4, 126-7.

[1] Lords Committee to Lynch, 14 Feb. 1683, ibid. 119-24; *Journal of the Assembly of Jamaica*, 5 Sept. 1683, CO 140/2.

[2] The Acts so confirmed are listed in CO 139/7, 249-81.

[3] Fortescue, in his Introduction to the Calendar of State Papers, Colonial, 1681-5, puts this down to 'apathy, slackness, and procrastination' and states that everything was paralysed by the indolence of the King. I do not agree with this.

[4] Sunderland replaced Williamson as Secretary on 10 Feb. 1679. Shaftesbury

of Court over Country at Oxford, over the municipality of
London, and over the Rye House conspiracy, all served to
prove to aspiring politicians that there was but one road for
them to take. The public offices now filled with second-genera-
tion Royalists who were not Cavaliers at all, and the new 'Committee of Intelligence' was more secretive in its doings, and
certainly more close-knit, than the old so-called 'Cabal'.

In these circumstances the other Committees, including that
of Trade and Plantations, had to deflate their previous pretensions. On fiscal matters the Lords of Trade had now to defer to
the expertise of a man who had been their own servant, and to
admit the superior qualifications of those Lords who were Commissioners of the Treasury. They could do very little without
the King's presence; and, as the King preferred to lend his
presence to other society, it turned out that they did very little
at all. The Secretary of State, as servant of the King, now re-
asserted his importance, in foreign and colonial as in domestic
affairs.[1] In 1675 Sir Jonathan Atkins in Barbados had been told
not to communicate with the Secretary of State but with the
Lords Committee of Trade, and as late as 1679 Secretary
Coventry had told him that even a royal letter countersigned
by himself was not necessarily of his drafting; but now in 1681
Lynch in Jamaica was instructed that his first responsibility in
office was to communicate with the Secretary, 'in whose Department you are'.[2] Lynch's own remark in 1683 that he had
not had a line from Sunderland, Halifax, or Clarendon,[3] is

was replaced by Robartes, now Earl of Radnor, as President of the Council.
Lawrence Hyde replaced Essex in Council, and was created Earl of Rochester in
November 1681—a signal to the hesitant. Prince Rupert, Holles, and Lauderdale
all died in 1680. Coventry was displaced from the second Secretaryship in April
1680 by Sir Leoline Jenkins—'a great asserter of the divine right of monarchy',
says Burnet (op. cit. ii. 257)—and Halifax replaced Anglesey as Lord Privy Seal
on 8 Aug. 1682. 'The Lord be praised', wrote Anglesey, 'I am now delivred from
Court snares'; Diary, Add. MS. 18730.

[1] At a meeting of the Council in Oct. 1682, when the King was absent, a matter
of selling guns to France succeeded that of sending guns to Maryland. In the
debate, Jenkins 'took the liberty to assert that it was the Duty of the Secrys soe to
manage those Corresponies that his Maty should direct, that he should have a
constant and punctual account of it; but that they were not at liberty to carry any
part of their Intelligences to the Council, unless His Maty directed it specially soe
to be done'. His colleague Conway admitted that this 'was constant to the practice of later years'; Turner, op. cit. ii. 78–79.

[2] Additional Instruction to Lynch, 28 Sept. 1681, CO 138/4, 46.

[3] Lynch to Blathwayt, 22 Feb. 1683, ibid. 147.

further indication that it was now the individual grandee, and not a corporate body of peers, with whom a colonial Governor now expected to deal. It was Sunderland alone who signed the royal letter to Stapleton, ordering him to hasten the naval officer's accounts of the Leeward Islands to the Lords Committee of Trade;[1] Jenkins who warned the Governors in the West Indies that they were expected to lend their full support to the factors of the Royal African Company.[2] The Lords Committee had to ask Sunderland to ask the King to send frigates to the Caribbean to combat the growing menace of piracy there, where previously they would have made this recommendation direct.[3] When Lynch died in August 1684, his successor, Hender Molesworth, was instructed to transmit the names of his Council to the Secretary, as well as to their Lordships. The Lords Committee of Trade still had their uses, indeed—but as subordinate functionaries.

Moreover, their province was now constantly invaded by the Privy Council itself, which resuscitated an interest in colonial affairs that had lain dormant since the years 1664-7. The great question of Massachusetts and the revocation of its Charter was of course a matter for the King-in-Council, for it had too much political significance either to be initiated, or dealt with, by a Committee alone. The grant of great territories in America to William Penn in 1681; the creation of a new royal colony in New Hampshire in 1682—another stick detached from the New England bundle; the evacuation of Tangier ('to save charge, that the Court might last out the longer without a Parliament')[4] in 1683; the permission to Stapleton to summon a General Assembly of the freeholders and planters of all the Leeward Islands;[5] and the reservation to the Crown in his successor's Commission of all appointments of Deputy-Governors and Councillors in the Islands,[6] were all debated and decided in the Privy Council. The day of the colonial 'expert'—the merchants who were so, and the politicians who had made themselves so— was now going. A process of centralization, in colonial as in all

[1] 11 Nov. 1681, CO 153/2, 461.
[2] 22 Mar. 1682, CO 1/48, No. 46.
[3] 21 Sept. 1680, CO 391/3.
[4] Burnet, op. cit. ii. 438.
[5] The King to Stapleton, 7 May 1683, CO 389/8, 210-12.
[6] Commission to Sir Nathaniel Johnson, 12 Dec. 1686, CSPC 1685-88, 858.

other affairs of the realm, had begun; a process that was to
reach its climax in the construction of a royal 'Dominion' in
America and in King James's appointment (in 1688) of a Committee of the whole Council for the business of Trade and
Foreign Plantations.

VI

THE DEFENCE OF THE WEST INDIES

THE domestic battle for the constitution of Jamaica was fought out against a background of international tension. In 1671 the graveyard of the enmity between Englishman and Spaniard in the West Indies was still strewn with bones of contention. The English indeed made a genuine effort to eradicate privateering: a Proclamation issued by Lieutenant-Governor Sir Thomas Lynch in August promised pardon not only to those who had accompanied Morgan to Panama, but to all those who had followed 'the Course' since 1660. If they came in, the privateers would be granted 35 acres in which to plant, and thus would earn the King's warm commendation (which would be the warmer if they surrendered to his officers the outstanding tenths and fifteenths that were owing to him).[1] But an allotment of 35 acres of uncleared land did not attract the men of the sea, most of whom had previous experience of small-holding in the islands, and of the fate that met it in a sugar-economy. Jamaica's debt stood at £50,000, her cocoa was recently blighted, her tobacco was struggling and sparse. Although sugar-planting was beginning to thrive, negro labour was still scarce and expensive, and seemed likely to remain so. The immediate outlook was, if not barren, at least bleak. As in Windsor's day, hard work in a hot sun had no glamour for men who enjoyed the freedom of the seas, and the number of rovers increased, 'like weeds or Hydras'.[2]

There was, however, one other occupation where the certainty of a quick profit repaid the effort it required. This was the cutting of logwood. Ships from Jamaica had been going to the shores of the Bay of Campeachy in Yucatan to cut this and other

---

[1] Minutes of the Council of Jamaica, 12 Aug. 1671, CO 140/1, 223–5; cf. Instructions to Lynch, 31 Dec. 1670 (issued 31 Jan. 1671), CO 138/1, 88–95. Lynch was, however, cautioned not to press this point too far, lest it discouraged the rovers from coming in at all.

[2] Lynch to Williamson, 13 Jan. 1672, CO 1/28, No. 3. In a list of the 'King of England's Territories in America' (c. 1675) it is said that there were about 4,000 privateers in Jamaica, but this is an exaggeration; Sloane MS. 3861, ff. 62–67.

woods since 1662. Logwood was a commodity that commanded an eager European market, one moreover which had never yet been properly exploited, for Sandwich reported from Madrid in 1668 that the Spaniards imported only some 500 tons of 'Campeachy wood' annually. Logwood-cutting had an attraction of its own. The cutters lived a rough existence not unlike that of the cow-killers, the original *boucaniers* of Hispaniola; it was a free life, well suited both to their privateering organization (a ship's crew cut what a ship could carry) and to their independence of spirit. Moreover, it served to keep the more formidable types, men who would have made not planters but nuisances of themselves in Jamaica, at a good arm's length from the Island. Before his removal from the Governorship, Modyford had advised Arlington of the growing popularity of logwooding as an occupation, and had stressed its convenience as a means of profitable employment for the privateers when, as he foresaw, their use at sea was disowned by the English Administration. He insisted that these people would never make planters.[1] He asked the views of the Administration on the subject, but he received only a cautious reply from Arlington that did not commit either the Secretary personally or the English Government officially one way or the other.

In the autumn of 1670 there were a dozen ships at Campeachy, at Cape Gracia Dios in Darien, on the Moskito Coast of Honduras, and in other 'deserted places' (where the Spaniards had no possible case to accuse them of trespass, as there were no Spaniards there), even while the more venturesome privateers were equipping themselves to accompany Morgan to Panama. And although the loot of that expedition dazzled the eye, those who had opted to do some honest work did not lose so greatly thereby, for logwood cargoes were just then fetching from £25 to £35 a ton. Some 2,000 tons were cut in the single year 1671.[2]

Lynch's first letters home—to Sandwich, to Arlington, to

---

[1] Modyford to Arlington, 18 Dec. 1670, CO 1/25, No. 103.
[2] Modyford to the Lords of the Privy Council, 28 Sept. 1670, CO 140/3, 38-39; Modyford to Arlington, 31 Oct. 1670, CO 1/25, No. 59; (Long says that England had to pay from £100 to £130 per ton for foreign logwood); Lynch to Slingsby, 5 Nov. 1672, CO 1/29, No. 43. Modyford reckoned in March 1671 that 32 ships of Jamaica plied a regular logwood trade; cf. CSPC 1669–74, 704, iv. Lynch by proclamation organized these into squadrons of four with a Commander; ibid. 945, ii.

Williamson—all asked as his predecessor had done for explicit instruction about this trade. Was the cutting of logwood by Englishmen on Spanish territory a legal employment? Was it contrary to the terms of the Treaty of Madrid? The Spanish Governor of Campeachy was already complaining of trespass on his coasts, not merely by ships from Jamaica but by many from New York and New England as well.[1] Lynch felt it well to walk warily. Spanish hostility was no great threat to the physical security of Jamaica itself, but it could easily throttle the Island's trade if it was provoked. Jamaica needed peace to recoup from a decade of troubles—peace and new efforts at settlement, for 2,000 of her original settlers were scattered. No doubt logwooding was a 'hugely advantageous' trade, no doubt too that it supplied a ready-made answer to the problem how to occupy a privateer who was now officially debarred from his old manner of making a living; but Lynch feared that its very popularity was likely to thwart those other hopes that the English Administration had in mind when it signed the Treaty, of 'stealing into a little commerce' with the Spaniards in America.[2] (These hopes were doomed to disappointment from the start; Lynch had already sent three times to Carthagena and seen his ships come back 'without so much as an imeralde'.)

Arlington once more sent an ambiguous answer—'not to choque with Spain for small things'[3]—but as he did not directly order the prohibition of logwood-cutting, the Council of Jamaica advised its continuance in March 1672. The same month Arlington asked Godolphin at Madrid to sound the Court there on this issue. Godolphin replied in May that Spain, who claimed the very seas of America as her private property, was not likely to throw open to the riff-raff of the Indies lands to which she had actually a valid title, whether these were inhabited or not. Certainly she would never permit them to become inhabited by such. Nevertheless, since the doctrine of effective occupation had a long English tradition behind it, Godolphin advised that

[1] Lynch to Arlington, 17 Dec. 1671, CO 1/27, No. 58.
[2] Cf. his letter of 28 Apr. 1673 to the Council of Trade and Foreign Plantations, advising bringing Campeachy firmly under the King's Government, which should enumerate logwood and have it all sent to England; CO 1/30, No. 29.
[3] Cf. Lynch to the Council of Plantations, 10 Mar. 1672—'which I take to be a tacit prohibition'; CO 1/28, No. 27; Minutes of the Council of Jamaica, 20 Mar. 1672, CO 140/1, 289.

England should connive at, while not directly authorizing, the cutting of logwood on these coasts.[1] In July the Council of Plantations advised the King to this effect, and in October Worsley sent Lynch the Council's opinion that logwooding was permissible so long as it took place in 'desolate & uninhabited places'.[2]

Beef Island and Triste in the Bay of Campeachy therefore continued to ring with the blows of Jamaican and New England axes; it was estimated that there were 900 men there in the spring of 1672.[3] Spain in righteous indignation began to retaliate. She captured at sea any English ship she could master. She hired buccaneers to act as her police, the English Captains Yellowes and Fitzgerald being two of the more notorious.[4] Lynch exclaimed angrily that by this kind of action in peacetime Jamaica had lost more than in the seven years of Modyford's war.[5] Spain's case was, however, a good one. The Treaty of Madrid had allowed the English freedom of navigation in the Indies, but had said nothing about freedom of trade. Logwood in an English ship was therefore contraband, and Englishmen cutting it on a Spanish shore were thieves. The Queen Regent issued a *cedula* on 22 June 1672, 'that such as shou'd make invasion or trade without license in the ports of the Indies should be proceeded against as pirates', and as a result Lynch reported in July 1673 that 40 English ships had been lost during the year.[6] England's answering case was, as usual, based on ingenious legal technicality. No 'invasion' of Spanish territory had taken place. The English logwood-cutters had been visiting these coasts since 1664. Their settlements were therefore covered by the clause in the Treaty of Madrid which stated that the King of England might 'hold and keep all those lands in any part of America' which were, at the time of signature, actually in English hands.

The official air between London and Madrid was thus soon

[1] Godolphin to Arlington, 10/20 May 1672, CO 1/28, No. 53.
[2] 8 Oct. 1672, CO 1/29, No. 35; CO 389/10 (Journal of the 1672–4 Council, 34 pp. only), 1.
[3] Richard Browne to Williamson, 28 Sept. 1672, CO 1/29, No. 33.
[4] It was these men's activities that induced the Administration to issue a Proclamation recalling English subjects from the service of 'a foreign prince'; cf. 11 Mar. 1674, APCC, i. 984.
[5] Lynch to Slingsby, 9 Oct. 1672, CO 1/29, No. 37.
[6] Lynch to Worsley, 8 July 1673, CO 389/5, 173–6.

curdled with charge and countercharge. In March 1673 Arlington sent a warning to Jamaica that the Spaniards in their wrath
were planning to conjoin with the Dutch to invade the Island.[1]
By February 1674 the lengthening list of English captains' petitions against incessant Spanish attack induced the Council of
Trade and Foreign Plantations to move the King to ask reparation of the Court of Spain—and, failing Spanish compliance, to
assert his right to issue letters of reprisal to the aggrieved captains.[2] Godolphin, although doing his best to prove to Penaranda
'how much better founded our complaints are than theirs'[3]
made little impression, for those members of the Council of the
Indies who had been reluctant to agree to the negotiation of any
American Treaty with England in the first place were now in
the ascendancy at the Spanish Court.[4]

But the Spanish envoy in London, the Marquis del Fresno,
made better headway there: more, indeed, than he intended.
He inveighed against Lynch for having countenanced the continuance of privateering in Jamaica in defiance of his express
instructions.[5] It was a false accusation; but doubtless to the
Spanish mind logwooding carried out by privateers was no
different from the normal forms of freebooting in which Jamaica
under Modyford had indulged. At any rate, the English Administration, unwilling to have a policy of connivance once
more exposed to the daylight, consented to meet del Fresno's
objections, and so sacrificed 'the only man who has resolutely
obeyed His Majesty in these Indies'.[6] The 46th Instruction

[1] Arlington to Lynch, 4 Mar. 1673, CO 140/3, 339.
[2] Order in Council, 11 Mar. 1674, CO 1/31, No. 12.
[3] Godolphin to Arlington, 19/29 Nov. 1673, SP 94/62, 294a-5.
[4] He instances how the Council of the Indies sent 40 English seamen, captured
in the Panama expedition, to the galleys and mines, despite their pardon by the
Queen. Cf. his letters to Arlington, 27 Dec./6 Jan. 1672, SP 94/59, 101; 20/30 Aug.
1673, SP 94/62, 103; 25 Apr. 1674, 15 Aug. 1674; Bebington, op. cit. 199, 225.
[5] Cf. del Fresno to Arlington, 11/21 Jan. 1674, SP 94/63, 9-9a.
[6] Lynch's own description of himself; Lynch to Williamson, 12 Aug. 1673,
CO 1/30, No. 57. The Venetian envoy reported that del Fresno himself was much
disturbed at Lynch's removal, particularly as there were rumours current in
London that Modyford was to replace him; VE, 3 Aug. 1674, Cal. S.P. Ven.,
1673-5, 369. del Fresno himself had reported to his Court that he found Charles
inclined to send Morgan to Jamaica; 22 Feb. 1674, SP 94/63, 42. Barham's account
is as follows: 'Notwithstanding all the endeavours of Sir Thomas Lynch could not
suppress the privateering, but went on so vigorously that complaint was made of
it in England; therefore in Mar. 1675 John Lord Vaughan was sent Governor of
Jamaica with orders from the King and Council for Sir Thomas Lynch to appeare

issued to Lynch's successor, Lord Vaughan, bade him, in case of any injuries done by Spaniards to Englishmen of Jamaica, to report these at once—but not to allow reparation to be sought in any other way than was set down in the Treaty of Madrid. The question of logwooding was again left open; Vaughan was neither to forbid nor abet it. In fact the English Administration was in one of its normal dilemmas: it could hardly declare openly its right to cut logwood on Spanish territory, but, on the other hand, 'a total abandoning of it was as uncounsulable'.[1] Cutters, however, were to understand clearly that if they continue to cut wood, they did so entirely at their own risk. The additional Instruction sent to Vaughan in December 1674, allowing him to issue commissions of reprisal if absolutely necessary,[2] is a sign not so much of a firmer policy as of further vacillation.

The return to Jamaica of that redoubtable team, Sir Thomas Modyford and Sir Henry Morgan, in the train of Lord Vaughan, and the subsequent promotion of both to office, greatly alarmed the Spaniards.[3] Morgan used his position as Lieutenant-Governor,[4] Judge of the Vice-Admiralty Court, and member of the Council, to further the interests of the Jamaican privateers. He could not openly issue them letters of marque in the old style, but he could, and did, recommend the soundest of them

at Court and answear to such articles as were presented against him by the Spanish Ambassador for maintaining Pyrats in those parts'; Add. MS. 12422, f. 93. But this was ostentation, for del Fresno's benefit; the King later sent an instruction to Vaughan not to molest Lynch in any way. Long calls it flatly 'a sham recall', *History*, i. 302.]

[1] Cf. Coventry to Vaughan, 31 Dec. 1674: 'As to the cutting of logwood . . . there are so many arguments pro and con, that though often agitated in Councel here, it hath not yet been thought fit to come to a resolution upon it—but as to the carrying of it when bought elsewhere, it is undisputable by our Treaty that English shipps may carry any goods which are not Counterband (amongst which logwood is not) . . . without any contradiction from the Spaniard'; Add. MS. 25120, f. 43; 23 July 1675, ibid., f. 47.

[2] Coventry to Vaughan, 31 Dec. 1674: 'but that your Lpp must look on as the latest Remedy'; ibid., f. 43.

[3] Lynch to Williamson, 20 Nov. 1674, CO 1/31, No. 77; Beckford to Williamson, 17 May 1675, that the Queen of Spain had ordered the Governor of St. Jago de Cuba to advise her immediately Modyford and Morgan returned to the Indies; CO 1/34, No. 79.

[4] Morgan (as Lieutenant-Governor) in fact arrived in Jamaica before Vaughan did, a sore point with the latter. It was therefore to Morgan that Lynch demitted the Government; cf. Minutes of the Council of Jamaica, 7 Mar. 1675, CO 140/3, 386-8. Sir Thomas Modyford was appointed Chief Justice in April.

to his old acquaintance d'Ogeron on Hispaniola, and thus a continuous stream of English privateers went to strengthen the growing power of the French buccaneers both there and on Tortuga. Morgan took a 'commission' for this service from the French, and the King of England lost to the King of France those tenths and fifteenths that would otherwise have accrued from the 'purchase' his subjects made at sea. It was for this that King Charles expressed his 'very bitter resentment', and declared his intention to make 'a Plantacon of Jamaica, and not a Christian Algiers'.[1]

But the force of this resolve was not constant. Although the King had ordered Vaughan in August 1675 to deal drastically with any who sought to pay off old scores against Spain under a French commission, he nevertheless instructed Coventry in December to take a high tone with the new Spanish envoy de Ronquillo, to the effect that Spain would only have herself to thank if the Caribbean boiled once more. Spain cannot have been surprised; the Court of Madrid had long since taken Charles's measure—'They will sooner trust ye Devill of Hell (this is their very expression)', wrote Godolphin apologetically, 'than the King of England.'[2] Godolphin hoped that the relations of the two Powers would improve when the King of Spain came of age and took affairs in hand (October 1675), but in fact the shifts of political fortune, whether in Madrid or in London, could have little effect in the Caribbean. Spanish Governors there were now answering all Vaughan's protests with open contempt: asserting, in the selfsame language that John Hawkins had heard from their forebears in office, that they looked on every Englishman in those seas as an enemy, and on all ships that had aboard anything of the growth of the Indies as good prize.[3] It says much for the pertinacious zeal of the Lords Committee of Trade that they made as patient a scrutiny of this high claim as they did of everything else;[4] but even so, they came at

[1] Coventry to Vaughan, 8 June 1676, Add. MS. 25120, f. 47.
[2] Godolphin to Coventry, 1 Oct. 1677, SP 94/64, 182.
[3] Cf. 'Report touching Injuries done the English by the Spanyards in the West Indies', 11 July 1677: '. . . And when [the master of the *Swiftsure*] shewed him his passe from my Lord Vaughan, the Spanish Captain said hee car'd not for it, having a Comission from His Catholick Majesty and the Governour of the Havanna to take all the English they met on the Coast . . . although it were sugars from Jamaica, that Iland belonging to his King', CO 389/11, 346–56.
[4] Dr. Leoline Jenkins (Judge of the Admiralty, later to be Secretary of State)

last to the conclusion that logwood was indeed not 'counterband', and instructed the Secretary to 'expostulate' very strongly with de Ronquillo.[1]

Vaughan, like Lynch before him, had in duty bound issued a Proclamation calling in all privateers,[2] and a second forbidding Englishmen from taking commissions-of-war from 'forrain Princes or states as are enimies to the Catholique King'.[3] But neither of these measures was popular in Jamaica. Opinion there had again veered round to the view that privateering was, as in Modyford's time, a 'necessary guard', and the planters were dismayed that it should be so strictly prohibited while the Spaniards preyed upon their commerce at will. To be sure, the presence of the buccaneers on Tortuga and Hispaniola, with their tradition of bitter hostility to Spain, was some comfort; but no Englishman in the Indies trusted the ultimate intentions of the French and these, their motley auxiliaries. Indignation that their Island was forced to depend on these unpredictable persons as a shield for defence roused Jamaicans to anger. The English Government would apparently do nothing to protect the King's subjects, who were abandoned to Spanish malevolence in the Indies, whose trade was spoiled and whose sailors pent in dungeons in Havana and other Spanish strongholds.[4] The Assembly of Jamaica saw in the home Government's interest in their laws only a pettifogging interference rather than any genuine concern for the Island's welfare, which would have been better expressed by the dispatch of a fleet of frigates. The legalist attitudes struck by the Lords of Trade were ill-timed to

had cautiously warned the Lords Committee on 8 Oct. 1675 that 'some clarification' of the Treaty of Madrid appeared to be required, as Spain was making unilateral decisions on what was and was not prize in the American seas without due notification to the other contracting party; cf. Chalmers, *Opinions*, ii. 323–8.

[1] Order-in-Council, 11 July 1677, CO 1/41, No. 8. Executing it, it seems that Coventry told de Ronquillo that 'His Majesty had 400,000 [!] subjects in the West Indies who might eventually make any to repent that should unjustly provoke his Majesty or despoil his subjects'; Cf. Southwell to Ormond, 1 Sept. 1677, HMC Ormond, iv. 375.

[2] Vaughan also supported Lynch's opinion that the annexation of Campeachy to the Government of Jamaica would best solve the logwood dispute; Vaughan to Williamson, 20 Sept. 1675, CO 1/35, No. 20.

[3] Issued on 15 Dec. 1675 (CO 138/3, 41), following a royal Instruction of 23 Aug. (CO 389/6, 69–70).

[4] Beckford to Williamson, 6 Dec. 1675, CO 1/35, No. 55; Vaughan to Coventry, 4 Jan. 1677, CO 1/39, No. 1; 28 Jan. 1677, ibid., No. 28: 'Worse used than they would be if they were in Argiers', 11 July 1677, APCC, i. 1152.

the point of folly. This feeling in the Island goes far to explain the dogged refusal of the Assembly to compromise throughout the protracted constitutional struggle. The colonists could not forget that the privateers of Jamaica had taken the measure of Spanish America before, and might as easily do it again; for, as Peter Beckford the secretary put it, it was obvious that the Spaniard had more to look after in the Indies than he could keep.

Vaughan himself did not employ Lynch's language about weeds or hydras when he referred to privateering. He remarked only that 'these Indies are so vast & rich & this kind of Rapine so sweet that it is 1 of the hardest things in the world to draw those from it that have used it so long',[1] and added later that the appointment of the Governor's Council over the Governor's head did not make this task (or indeed any task) the simpler,[2] since its members were mainly 'old Standers & Officers of Cromwell's Army'. In consequence, 'let His Matie send what Orders he will about Privateering, there are almost none to execute them but who are in one way or the other interested'. Such comments did not help to commend the Governor to his superiors, who were always nettled by diagnoses that conflicted with their own.

Moreover, they were by no means convinced that Vaughan himself was not one of those who were 'in one way or the other, interested'. When Morgan's trafficking with the French became too obvious to be concealed, Vaughan dismissed him from his commands, and turned both him and his brother-in-law Robert Byndloss out of the Council.[3] This in official eyes was improper conduct; a colonial Governor was no longer permitted to carry so high a hand. Coventry sent Vaughan a stiff letter stressing the King's displeasure that a man in whom he placed full confidence should have been so dispensed with on the Governor's own responsibility.[4] Caught between these fires, Vaughan ap-

---

[1] Vaughan to the Lords Committee, 4 Apr. 1676, CO 1/36, No. 40.
[2] Cf. Vaughan to Coventry, 28 May 1677, CO 1/40, No. 93.
[3] Cf. Vaughan to Williamson, 2 May 1676, CO 1/36, No. 58.
[4] Cf. Coventry to Vaughan, 30 July 1675, Add. MS. 25120, f. 51. Vaughan had appointed Morgan to the Council in Mar. 1675, at the same time making Charles Modyford Major-General *vice* Bannister, deceased. The King objected on four counts to the latter appointment: the Major-Generalship was a redundant office when there was both a Governor (Captain-General) and a Lieutenant-Governor (Lieutenant-General) in the Island; Modyford anyway was not a soldier; he was an absentee, living in London; and he was the son of Sir Thomas. 'It is not

pears to have abandoned hope of accommodating anyone save himself, and—with Sir Thomas Modyford's sure hand at his elbow to guide his novice's steps[1]—to have introduced himself to the West-India industry of illicit trading.[2] It is therefore not surprising that the Lords Committee of Trade, as they read an accumulation of reports that the Governor of Jamaica was so misconducting himself, that the Lieutenant-Governor and some Councillors were trafficking in French commissions to pirates, and that the Assembly were doing their utmost to institute a biennial control over the laws of the Island as if that were their right and not the Crown's, only became more determined to overhaul the entire system of government in Jamaica.

Spain could not have taken so strong a line against the English at sea between 1672 and 1678 had not all three of her encroaching neighbours in the Caribbean—English, French, and Dutch —been so greatly preoccupied with their own motives and manœuvres.[3] On 17 March 1672 England and France in alliance declared war against the United Provinces. In this contest Spain naturally ranged herself with the Dutch,[4] for the

unknown to you', wrote Coventry, 'with what difficulty it was obtained of His Majesty to admitt Sir Thomas Modyford to his presence, and give permission to his going with you [to Jamaica]: if you manage not your kindness to that family with great discretion you will be far from doing them or yourself a kindness. . . . Be the merits of that family what it will and your kindness to them what it can, this is a much readyer way to offend the King than advance them, and possibly create such a jealousy as may lessen that very good esteem the King hath of you. The King doth not intend the Island shall be solely in the power of any one family or party, and the King expecteth from your Lpp. that you should balance the parties and factions, and not be of any.' The King's order was that Morgan should be readmitted to the Council, and to office. If he was proved unworthy of these honours, steps would be taken against him, 'but in the meantime His Majesty will not endure that a Lieutenant-Generall by His Commission shall be left out of all power military and civill, and others put in who never were approved by him'.

[1] Sir Thomas Modyford, already Chief Justice of Jamaica, was appointed to the Council in Apr. 1677; cf. Minutes of the Council of Jamaica, 4 Apr. 1677, CO 140/3, 552.

[2] So says Mr. [Ralph] Nevil in a letter to the Earl of Carlisle, printed in *Interesting Tracts relating to the Island of Jamaica*, 105–17—but Nevil on his own showing was a warm admirer of both Morgan and Byndloss, Vaughan's enemies.

[3] Cf. Newton, *The European Nations*, c. 20.

[4] Cf. Godolphin to Arlington, 19/29 Nov. 1673: 'I have now certaine intelligence of [Evertsen's] squadrons being lately at Porto Rico bound for Carthagena to take in some Spanish souldiers there on the designe of attaquing Jamaica, which this people would be glad to recover by the Dutch hands, but I hope all our Western Collonies are forewarned to stand upon their guard, particularly Sir Thomas Linch'; SP 94/62, 298a–9.

Court of Madrid knew how far-reaching were Louis XIV's plans for all the Netherlands, Dutch or Spanish. At the outset Spain feared that some Anglo-French compact would be made to divide Spanish property and possessions in the Indies. Louis had agreed in advance to any gains that the English might make from the Dutch, and his approval of the seizure of St. Eustatius in 1672[1] by Governor Stapleton and the militia of Nevis showed that this was no mere gesture. Would the blessing of France also be given to England, should the latter mount a similar campaign of aggression against the Spanish mainland territories in America?[2] Here Spain plainly saw the sword of Damocles; but, luckily for her, the policy adhered to by the Governments of England and France in Europe and that pursued by Englishmen and Frenchmen 'beyond the Line' were still two very different things.

The Anglo-French bitterness and rivalry in the West Indies had in no way subsided since 1666. English memories of the loss of St. Christopher and the ruin of Nevis and Antigua were still green: 'Twenty years of peace', as Christopher Jeaffreson wrote, 'will hardly resettle the devastation of one year's war.'[3] It was Lynch's opinion that although you did them all the civilities imaginable, relations with the French could never improve while the buccaneers of Tortuga and Hispaniola continued to take their toll of English shipping;[4] while Wheler reported from the Leeward Islands that it was 'a miracle that the French and English do not every day draw their swords'.[5] Moreover, by the 1670's English commercial competition was at last (if slowly still) beating out the Dutch;[6] the captors of St. Eustatius found it glutted with unsold goods. Thus it was very hard for the planters to watch a new potential rival growing up in

[1] It was restored to the Dutch in 1682; CSPC 1681–5, 460.

[2] The Venetian envoy in France had noted on 17 Sept. 1670 how 'the Government here has almost made up its mind to yield to the strong representations made to the King by Buckingham to induce His Majesty to renounce and abandon entirely the trade of the West Indies, which so far has proved of no advantage of this Crown and which inflicts sensible injury on the affaires of the British King'; Cal. S.P. Ven., 1669–71, 317.

[3] J. C. Jeaffreson, *A Young Squire of the Seventeenth Century* (London, 1878), i. 215. St. Christopher indeed never recovered, and henceforth suffered a constant drain of its population.   [4] Lynch to Sandwich, 14 Oct. 1671, CO 1/27, No. 40.

[5] Wheler to the Council of Plantations, 6 Mar. 1672, CO 1/28, No. 25.

[6] Shaftesbury's rhetoric concerning the destruction of 'Carthage' struck his contemporaries (as it has done his posterity) as windy for this very reason.

Hispaniola just when the measure of an old enemy had been taken. The secession of England from the war in Europe, the separate peace she made with the Dutch at Westminster in February 1674, the dissolution of the French West-India Company in December, and the subsequent strengthening of French royal administration in the West Indies, made any Anglo-French co-operation in the Caribbean seem even less likely. The English watched hopefully the attack of de Ruyter's fleet on Martinique in July 1674, and were disappointed when it was beaten off.

When Admiral d'Estrées began his series of 'American Promenades' in the autumn of 1676, every English and every Spanish eye watched his progress in painful fascination. Barbados and the Leeward Islands looked hastily to their defences, and Sir Jonathan Atkins could not forbear yet another sharp dig at official incompetence—'never a frigate',[1] yet 12 French sail-of-the-line in the vicinity. d'Estrées attacked Tobago in March 1677, retired overseas to capture Goree on the Gambia, and was back by November, this time to capture Tobago.[2] Vaughan in Jamaica feared a French occupation of all Hispaniola, and what the consequences of that to Jamaica might be, 'anyone may imagine'.[3] But the immediate problems of the English Administration were sufficient; to imagine the evils of tomorrow would unseat its collective reason. Worsley had been uttering prescient warnings since 1668[4]—that if the French King should not only protect, but place himself at the head of the buccaneers in the Indies, the English could not promise themselves a day's security at Jamaica. Before long 'it would be as great an affair of state to balance power in the West Indies as it is now amongst Princes in Christendom'.[5] The day that Spanish power in America fell before that of France, the English

[1] Atkins to Lords Committee, 6/16 Dec. 1676, recounting the meeting of a Dutch squadron, 'who have rowed up and down these seas these last 6 months', with d'Estrées' 12 sail; CO 29/2, 148-9. d'Estrées paid a courtesy call at Barbados.
[2] Godolphin reported from Madrid the anxiety there that d'Estrées would proceed to Carthagena or Santo Domingo. 7 Apr. 1678; Bebington, op. cit. i. 375.
[3] Vaughan to Lords Committee, 28 Jan. 1676, CO 138/3, 36-38.
[4] Worsley to Ashley, 24 Feb. 1669, GD 24/49, 4. Cf. 'Dr. Worsley's discourse of the privateers of Jamaica', Dec. 1668, Add. MS. 11410, f. 623; and MS. Rawl. A. 478, f. 53.
[5] Worsley to Lynch, 30 Nov. 1672, CO 1/29, No. 51; Worsley to Willoughby, 17 Dec. 1672, ibid., No. 66.

doom was sealed. But it was no comfort to the English Administration which he served to reflect that the doctor might very well be right. It was not the master of its own fate. It was most certainly not the captain of the soul of Louis XIV.

> The local problem in the West Indies was considerably eased in the spring of 1678 when d'Estrées, after a rendezvous with 1,000 buccaneers at St. Christopher as the start of an expedition against Curaçao, ran his fleet on to the rocks at Avès. Carlisle was able to end martial law in Jamaica; Stapleton promptly took his opportunity to make a treaty with the French Governor on the neutrality of St. Christopher.[1] The buccaneers under de Grammont were now left in command of the seas, and they were more the problem of Spain than of England. In May Charles made another private bargain with Louis: in August a treaty of European peace was negotiated at Nijmegen; and thus the French account with the United Provinces was, for the moment at least, squared. This treaty, however, made no reference to the West Indies—a most significant omission in the eyes of both England and Spain.

In the spring of 1679, while Europe was still at peace, d'Estrées and a great fleet again returned to the Caribbean. No one knew precisely why.[2] It soon became clear, however, that he was there to make an inventory of the Spanish Indies for his master. He cruised about the islands, paying courtesy calls on Stapleton at Nevis and on Carlisle in Jamaica, to whom he murmured that it was indeed an admirable Island but that the French would have a better in Cuba.[3] He showed less courtesy to Spanish officials and Governors while his agents carried out surveys of Spanish fortifications and defences. He sent de Grammont and his men to probe likely weak spots in the Spanish ring, such as at La Guayra, while to the official Spanish protests he disclaimed all knowledge of any such action. It seemed plain both to the anxious English and the frightened Spaniards that one day when his master decreed d'Estrées would stop trailing his coat, and go into action.

[1] 9/19 May 1678. Treaty in Davenport, op. cit. ii. 256–60; CO 1/42, No. 98. Stapleton received an authorizing Commission in July; CSPC 1677–80, 745.

[2] Coventry had warned Atkins back in Oct. 1678 that the Fleet was coming: 'I know no design they can have in those parts but upon us, tho' at present we are upon good terms'; Add. MS. 25120, f. 129.

[3] Carlisle to Coventry, 10 July 1679, CO 138/3, 304.

The buccaneers, pleased by their new status as the friends and agents of a great European Power, had increased the scope of their activities accordingly. In October 1678 they descended on Campeachy itself, dispersing the settlement and taking the ships that rode in the Bay. Carlisle reported that some 1,200 men, many of them English but all with French commissions, were involved in this exploit. In January 1679 he asked for further guidance.[1] Like Lynch and Vaughan before him, he urged that Campeachy needed some form of government, were it only for self-defence and to prevent its becoming another buccaneers' base like Tortuga.[2] But before such a government could be instituted, the legal rights to the territory had to be clearly defined, and this of course involved the greater question of relations with Spain as a whole. Carlisle added his weight to the opinion that it was France and not Spain that was the principal foe of England in the West Indies, and that all the brutalities of Spanish sea-captains against English shipping, however infuriating these were, did not constitute so grave a threat to the English in the West Indies as would a French capture of Havana, the 'key' to the Caribbean world.[3] This was a line of argument that already carried weight at home with those who distrusted the little that was known of the King's policy towards France—and their name was legion, as Oates had illustrated.

One thoughtful memorandum, dated April 1678,[4] which had come to the notice of the Lords Committee, considered that the best solution to the problem of defence in the West Indies would be a conjunction of the English with the Spanish power to expel the French from those seas. Sixteen sail-of-the-line and three regiments of troops—England finding the ships, Spain the soldiers—would surely be a force sufficient to reduce Martinique, the focal point of French prosperity in the Indies, as well as the buccaneer strongholds in Tortuga and Hispaniola. Such a policy of aggression had the considerable merit of being both

[1] Carlisle to Coventry, 24 Oct. 1678, ibid. 283; 26 Jan. 1679, ibid. 286.
[2] He suggested setting up a Governor at Triste; 28 May 1679, APCC, i. 1275.
[3] Carlisle to Coventry, 10 July 1679, CO 138/3, 329.
[4] 'Considerations about the present affaires of the West Indyes', 7 Apr. 1678. It was to England's interest that the Spaniards 'should keep the colonies they have, for they are few, lazy, rich and disingenious & need our ships, trade, and mtures., of which we may make great advantage as the Dutch have, who have gott infinitely more by serving and corresponding fairely with them than ever they did by their warr & privateers, although they had great success'; Egerton MS. 2395, f. 575.

quick and cheap; it would cost only half the sum that would be
required to build up and maintain a defensive strategy in the
Caribbean over a long period of time. Now was plainly the time
to set about it, for in ten years the French would have out-
stripped their rivals both in population and in produce. What
could England lose by such a Spanish alliance? The old argument of the European traders was repeated: 'It's the interest of
England to have no more colonies; more Plantations would too
much draine the Kingdome & disperse the Kings Subjects.' All
that was necessary was to convince the Spaniards that this
indeed was the true policy of England, 'that they may not
scruple our seeing their Ports for fear we should take them hereafter'.¹ There was much sense in this; and in March 1679 the
King ordered Carlisle to discourage the further cutting of logwood in the Bay of Campeachy until some amicable arrangement on the business should be made 'in the next Treaty', while
the Lords Committee forwarded a belated opinion that the
island of Triste was indubitably a Spanish possession.²

This new approach to Spain was, however, always a *pis-aller*,
half-heartedly pursued; it came about principally because the
Court of Madrid had offered King Charles a handsome subsidy
for his alliance, and Charles, whose French supplies were then
cut off, could not afford to ignore it. Godolphin's successor as
envoy to Madrid, Sir Henry Goodricke, was instructed on

¹ Cf. an unsigned letter, 3 June 1678, Madrid, in SP 94/65, 40A: 'It is most
certaine he [Louis] will take what place soever he attempts, soe disheartened &
ill-provided they [the Spaniards] are in the Indies; as for your [i.e. England]
engageing in a warr for this nation [Spain]'s interest you will find yourselves much
mistaken, for you must not depend upon any Army of theirs, or in any fleet, or
money offered; tho' they would make you all the promises imagineable.
  'If you engage in a warr, be sure to gett either of two condicons of them: which
is, such great conveniences in the trade of the West Indies that you may be able
to support the war out of it, & ruine the French in the great interest they have in
that trade. . . .
  'If you are so far engaged as that you must declare a war, in my opinion its convenient you make this proposition to Spayne, and if they deney you, you have the
satisfaction to know surely their kindness towards you, and to take your measures
with them. . . . The King making these propositions to Spaine, & they deneying
him, as i believe they will, so little faith they have in him, for they are both stupid,
ignorant, and misinformed; then the King will have that satisfaction in mind, and
before God and the world that noe man can blame him for any action he does
afterward in order to his own security & interest.'
² The King to Carlisle, 29 Mar. 1679, CO 324/2, 146; JLTP, 22 May 1679,
CO 391/3, 11-16; and 28 May 1679, CO 138/3, 309.

2 June 1679 to find out on what terms Spain would allow the English to trade to Campeachy, but the whole matter then became entangled in the meshes of European diplomacy, and no more was heard of it for a time. Carlisle as instructed issued a Proclamation forbidding the cutting of logwood, but remarked morosely that the Spaniards seized English ships for cocoa anyway.[1] In April 1680 the Spaniards raided and dispersed the English logwood camp at Triste,[2] which of course had continued to operate despite the diplomatic approaches in Europe and the Proclamation in Jamaica, and then went on to capture New Providence in the Bahamas even as the Englishmen Sharp and Sawkins were plundering Santa Marta on the Main.[3] But the Council of Jamaica (taking advantage of its new orders to unburden itself frequently to the Lords Committee) wrote a bitter letter pointing out that there was one essential difference between the depredations that were committed by Englishmen and by Spaniards in the West Indies: Spain's agents were 'encourag'd and own'd by Authoritye, and What our Privateers doe' was not.[4] Carlisle supported this point. It could not be disputed that Spanish property had suffered and was suffering considerably from the actions of English outlaws, but the injuries inflicted on Jamaican goods and shipping were instigated by Spanish officials. But Carlisle could not be allowed to have it both ways; either it was the French, or the Spaniards, who constituted the most serious menace to English security in the West Indies. The Administration was now convinced that the French threat was the greater. The manœuvres of d'Estrées were scanned as anxiously in London as in Bridgetown and Port Royal. Spanish hostility was certainly a serious irritant, but French hostility could bring about disaster.

Thus in May 1680 Sunderland was again urging the conclusion of a new Treaty with Spain. He argued that this would be a popular move, one bound to please the Parliament that must soon be summoned, whose members would sooner have allied with Barbary pirates than with His Most Christian Majesty of France. Sunderland proposed to make a defensive alliance with

[1] Carlisle to Coventry, 13 Aug. 1679, CO 138/3, 324.
[2] Cf. the Treaty 'given in the island of Terminos, 1680' between the English on Beef Island and the Spaniards at Triste; APCC, ii. 121.
[3] Cf. Edwards, op. cit. i. 184, note (d).
[4] Council of Jamaica to Lords Committee, 20 May 1680, CO 138/3, 409-10.

Spain, to operate in any part of the world. In return for a monopoly of the logwood trade, England should aid Spain against the
menace of France in the Indies. But Sunderland did not get his
monopoly; indeed, the Spaniards in America, their *guarda-
costas* now in action, were pursuing the English in the Caribbean
the more vindictively because of the insults they themselves had
suffered at French hands. The Court of Spain, concentrating as
usual on the security of the Netherlands, made the necessary
promises, and on 9/19 August 1680 a Treaty was signed at
Windsor.[1] In this way Spain sought to reinsure herself against
French attack—but, as it happened, it was not France but
Spain herself, infuriated beyond reason and caution by the
buccaneers' attack on Vera Cruz, who declared war (December
1683). England did not stir to implement the Windsor Treaty,
and the hostilities were over within six months, when a truce
was arranged at Ratisbon.[2] France was still master of the situation, in Europe and the Indies.

In Jamaica this was not so obvious. Why should wariness of
France necessitate truckling to Spain? Morgan rumbled in fury
about the 'Un-Christianlike' conduct of the Spaniards—'who, at
the King's pleasure, might be so easily humbled'.[3] Both the
Madrid Treaty of 1670 and the Windsor Treaty of 1680 showed
that the English Administration had not lost hope of establishing a trade with the Spanish colonies in America—but to continue to look for such an outcome in face of all the evidence of
the mutual hatred between the two nations there was surely
plain foolishness. 'Why they should have credit at Whitehall &
we want it', expostulated Morgan to Sunderland, 'I leave to
Your Lordship.'[4]

Sunderland could indeed have told him why the urbanity of
d'Estrées was more to be feared than all the rage of Spain, but
it was never the habit of a Secretary of State to explain colonial
policy to the men on the spot who were relied upon to carry it
out. Lynch, on his reappointment to the Governorship of
Jamaica, got as little official assistance. Before he set out he put

[1] Treaty in Davenport, op. cit. ii. 266–74. Charles continued to negotiate with
Louis, both personally in 1681 and through Preston's mission in 1682; cf. Preston
to Jenkins, 10/20 Sept. 1682, HMC Rep. vii (F. Graham), 336*b*.

[2] July 1684; Davenport, op. cit. ii. 286–92.

[3] Morgan to Lords Committee, 15 Sept. 1679, CO 138/3, 337.

[4] Morgan to Sunderland, 1 Feb. 1681, CO 1/46, No. 94.

some searching questions to Secretary Jenkins, who knew his law and custom of the sea as none other. Were the French buccaneers recognized by, and therefore agents of, the French monarchy, or were they not? If they were not, was he, Lynch, to treat them as pirates? And if they were, what should he do?[1] But inquiries so sharp might shear the diplomatic net; accordingly, no answers were returned him. M. Barrillon in London was desolated to hear that lawlessness was rife in the Caribbean, but he had no official cognizance that Frenchmen were in any way involved, and so had no satisfaction to give Lynch.[2]

In thus trying to assess the extent of the power of France in the West Indies rather than that of the pirates, Lynch showed his usual acumen—for the high self-confidence of the latter was only a measure of the strength of the former. The sea-roving fraternity *by itself* was unable seriously to injure English commerce in the Caribbean; in the long run, the competition of the settled French Antilles and the Dutch islands constituted a far graver menace. Yet, even although he knew that it was to England's interest to maintain the Spanish power in America for as long as was possible, Lynch found, as had Vaughan and Carlisle before him, that it was very difficult—when actually in Jamaica and responsible for the Island's safety—to keep calm in face of Spanish affronts of such magnitude as daily afflicted Jamaican shipping and trade. It was now not logwood alone that the Spaniards seized as prize, but cocoa, sugar, indigo, ginger, any *frutas dessas Indias,* 'as if a century had not passed!'[3] He reckoned that since 1672 Jamaica's commerce had suffered a loss of some £25,000 at Spanish hands. Three hundred of her logwood-cutters were held prisoner, in Yucatan and elsewhere.

[1] Lynch to Jenkins (from Plymouth), 1 Nov. 1681, CO 1/47, No. 84.

[2] Cf. JLTP, 14 Feb. 1682: 'Mr. Secretary Jenkins informs the Committee that, having discourse with the French Ambassador touching this matter, hee had understood from him that the usual terms of the Commissions given to the French men-of-war sailing to these parts run thus: "*Courir sus au gens sans aveu.*" Whereupon Their Lpps. agree to move His Majesty in Councell that a Memoriall be given to the French Ambassador here, & another to my Lord Preston [envoy] to the French Court that . . . the power of the Commissions to these privateers [be] limited, and that in case the French Governor shall continue to grant commissions of this nature he be ordered to distinguish between the English & the Spaniards. Their Lpps. will offer that Sir Thomas Lynch may have directions to seize such vessels'; CO 391/4, 121–2—but it does not appear that Lynch was ever so directed.

[3] Lynch to Lords Committee, 12 Sept. 1683, CO 1/52, No. 95; Lynch to Jenkins, 26 July 1683, ibid., No. 35.

To stop this drain on English strength Lynch continued Carlisle's prohibition of further trading to Campeachy, although this, of course, did not prevent privateers from continuing to visit there, nor their reoccupation of Triste itself in April 1682.[1] The Spanish *guarda-costas* were now policing the seas regularly, and their idea of police-work was rough and ready. In July 1683 Lynch sent a sharp letter to the Governor of Havana, telling him that in future he would take it as a violation of the peace and a tacit declaration of war were any further honest traders seized, tortured, or murdered, if any more official dispatches were intercepted, or if any other ships carrying the produce of the Indies were illegally made prize. A stinging reminder to the Governor of Carthagena that the pirates of whom he complained would never have had such success had Spanish valour been as forward in dealing with them as it had been in harassing the peaceful commerce of the Caribbean,[2] may have relieved Lynch's feelings, but can have done little other good.

The threat of war was of course an empty one, since the Governor by his Instructions was prohibited from levying war without the King's consent;[3] the shadow of Sir Thomas Modyford's indiscretions stretched for long over the West-India world. Lynch therefore characteristically turned from railing at what he could not prevent to dealing with what he could, and squared to the issue of piracy. He said himself that his main business henceforward was to be the historian of piratical deeds. He found the Indies now 'full of desperate rogues'.[4] The breakdown of any pretence of cordial relations with Spain, together with the cynical league of d'Estrées's royal Fleet with every rover who chose to hunt as jackal to the lion, and the dispersion of those English privateers who had taken to logwooding, had led to a proliferation on the seas of the brood of Ishmael, neither privateer from Jamaica nor buccaneer from Tortuga, but pirate—pirate from St. Thomas, Tortola, the Bahama cays, the Carolina coast—whose ships rode in the lee of the trade-routes,

---

[1] Long, *History*, i. 341.

[2] Lynch to the Governor of Carthagena, 9/19 Apr. 1684, CO 1/54, No. 72.

[3] Lynch's 61st Instruction, a discretionary clause, 'provided always . . . that you doe not, by color of any power or authority hereby given you, commence or declare warr without our knowledge and particular commands therein'; 8 Sept. 1681, CO 138/4, 39.

[4] Lynch to Jenkins, 6 Nov. 1682, CO 138/4, 112.

and to whom all encounters signified profit and prize. An English pirate had no scruples in molesting an English ship.[1] A French *flibustier* would often fly the English flag at his mast-head out of devilment (as the story of *La Trompeuse* shows)[2] knowing well how eager the Spaniard was to believe that every sea-rover was an Englishman. French buccaneers made small distinction between English and Spanish ships when they were on the hunt for casual prize, although a Spanish crew was likely to suffer the worse at their hands. Stapleton protested to Coventry in 1680 how it fretted him 'to nothing but Skin & Bones to see such iniquities put on the King's Flag by even the French merchantmen'[3] in the Leeward Islands; but sometimes English and French rovers could combine for mutual benefit, most notably in the fierce raid carried out by de Grammont and van Horn on Vera Cruz in 1683.[4] Lynch's vigorous measures against the pirate fraternity included the building of a 50-oar, 60-man galley, together with a large number of shallow-draught sloops. The use of this home-made fleet considerably improved conditions in the immediate neighbourhood of Jamaica. He was able to write in 1683 that 'we doe not hear of a Pyrat from the East of Porto Rico to the Gulph . . . a canoa of ours may pass anywhere and all the French privateers treat our vessels with greater respect than ever'.[5]

Although the Lords Committee commended Lynch's action and its successful outcome, an aspect of it struck them that had not troubled the Jamaicans. Blathwayt sent an inquiry to the Attorney-General, whether the Vice-Admiralty Court in Jamaica had in fact power to grant commissions, and to fit out ships in this way to pursue pirates? For what sort of outlaw was a pirate, after all? He was plainly an exception to a rule, but to what rule?

It was a nice point that had long occupied the legal minds in the Administration. Back in 1673 the King had ordered Lynch,

---

[1] The Council of Jamaica reported on 20 May 1680 that the pirates had one 28-gun ship, one 24-gun ship, one 12-gun ship, and one 8-gun ship, besides sloops and barques 'all extraordinarily well manned, & much better armed than any of our European shipping'; CO 1/44, No. 62.

[2] Cf. CSPC 1681–5, 1343.

[3] Stapleton to Coventry, 10 July 1680, CO 1/45, No. 44.

[4] See the account in SP 94/69, 308.

[5] Lynch to Blathwayt, 16 July 1683, CO 138/4, 155.

then Lieutenant-Governor in Jamaica, to ensure that pirates and all offenders at sea (including illicit traders) were tried by Vice-Admiralty procedure in future; cases involving them were not to be heard in the Courts of Common Pleas, where only too often their friends on Bench, jury, and in the witness-box saw to it that acquittal came their way.[1] Vaughan and Morgan hanged a lot of them, but the Lords Committee were dubious about the propriety of allowing one subject of the Crown to hang another without express authorization; so Vaughan was instructed to try pirates in future according to the Statute of Oyer and Terminer of 28 Henry VIII.[2] At the same time they recommended that every Governor should take to his post a dormant Commission of Oyer and Terminer, for use when necessary.[3]

The marked increase in the pirate population of the Caribbean, however, convinced them that a Governor needed more extensive powers. The answer to Blathwayt's question was no; but in May 1684 the Lords Committee recommended that in future a Governor should have power to pursue pirates at sea as Lynch had done.[4] The Commission drawn up in December for Lynch's intended successor as Governor of Jamaica, the Earl of Carlisle's brother, Sir Philip Howard, therefore included the necessary authority.

The Law Officers—who, together with Samuel Pepys and York's 'Advocate', Sir John Werden, conducted the investigation of this business—took the occasion to try and resolve another colonial anomaly. The issue of the pirates broadened to an examination of the powers-at-sea in general held by the colonial Governors. Disputes between the local Governments in the West Indies and officers of the Royal Navy (who, earliest of all Englishmen, developed the famous superior attitude to-

---

[1] D'Oyley had sent at least three pirates home to the Marshal of the Admiralty (Adm 2/1732, 104a), but on 6 Feb. 1665 Modyford, who knew his law, tried and condemned 14 pirates 'under the Statute of Henry VIII', although afterwards reprieving them; Modyford to Arlington, 20 Feb. 1665, CO 1/19, No. 27.

[2] Cf. Orders-in-Council of 21 July, 28 July 1676, APCC, i. 1089, 1091.

[3] JLTP, 13 July 1676, CO 391/1, 168. A standing Commission of Oyer and Terminer was approved on 5 Dec. 1677, and one of the laws in Carlisle's corpus authorized him to prosecute pirates as though they were offenders on land, by virtue of the terms of the Statute of Henry VIII; cf. APCC, i. 1181, and 'Acts prepared by Their Lordships for Jamaica, approved by His Majesty', 15 Feb. 1678, PC 5/1, 53.

[4] 21 May 1684, CO 324/4, 107.

wards 'colonials')[1] had long been a feature of colonial life. The Duke of York, although well aware how 'refractory and disobedient' many of his captains were, early insisted that the Governor should send all the details of a dispute to the Admiralty, but must take no action against the officer himself.[2] As William Coventry commented in 1662 to Walrond, who was then closely engaged with Captain Whiting of the *Diamond*, this order was given not for indulgence to the officer 'but for security to the King's service, which cannot but be delayed at least when a Commander is imprisoned'.[3]

There the matter rested until Lynch held a court-martial on Captain Heywood of the *Norwich*, whose ship had foundered as a result of being overloaded with merchandise. There was a great to-do about *ultra vires* and *a priori* evidence, and Lynch wrote a number of exasperated dispatches on the subject: 'If you take away power to call Courts-martials & command all criminals to bee sent to you with scrolls & affidavits, I suppose you intend to extinguish the Duke's maritim power'—the fact that he put in this dig at his superiors, most untypically, is evidence of his failing patience—'for I shall not hereafter dare to give my commissions nor will any of these inhabitants ever serve, for they think it as hard to be sent to England as those there would to bee sent hither'. In regard to the *Norwich*, he insisted that he had used the same method 'that has been practised here by all the Generals these 27 years & must bee soe still, or this Government will bee reduced to confusion'.

The case of Captain Churchill of the naval sloop *Falcon* roused the Governor again. (Churchill, who was drunk, ducked the mate of a merchant-ship in the harbour, and the man afterwards died of fever.) Lynch exclaimed:

Your Lpps. may be pleased to consider
It's denying them right to send them with affidavits into another world.
It was never heard that it was possible to command seamen or soldiers without a power to punish.

[1] Cf. Fortescue's comment in the Introduction to CSPC 1681–5: 'Even now [1899] the Admiral on a colonial station is reckoned by the colonists as a far greater man than any Governor' (p. xxxvi). This is still true at least of present-day Malta, Gibraltar, and Hong Kong.
[2] York to Windsor, 29 Apr. 1662, Adm 2/1732, 178.
[3] W. Coventry to Walrond, Apr. 1662, Adm 2/1745.

If the Duke be Lord High Admiral here, hee [Lynch] has the same power the Lords Admirals have in England.[1]

These remarks were doubtless weighed by the authorities, but all had to be done by rule, and Blathwayt inquired of the Attorney-General in December 1683[2] whether the colonial vice-admirals had indeed powers to punish disobedience and disorders at sea on the King's ships. The answer was, again, no. Lynch's court-martial on Heywood therefore could not be upheld, and all Governors were notified that they had no such powers: they must send home for trial any culpable officers and men, after they had collected the necessary depositions.[3] Howard's Commission allowed him to grant to a naval officer a commission to hold a court-martial, but no more.[4] Thus the Admiralty did its part in the current policy of administering colonies firmly from Whitehall.

The permission to Lynch to pursue the pirates at sea with what forces he could muster, together with that to Stapleton to mount his own campaign against the Carib Indians of Dominica, indicates that the Administration was compelled to leave the policing of the Caribbean to the enterprise of the colonists themselves. In fact England had no organized answer to the baleful presence of the *guarda-costa*. Although Jamaica had so often been defined as 'His Majesty's frontier dominion' in America, the defence of that frontier was never co-ordinated by His Majesty's Government.[5] To obtain such a co-ordination would have cost England more than she could afford, and it was a keen realization of this that induced the Crown from the 1670's to seek a permanent colonial revenue. (The English Administration was to make the effort again a century later, and for precisely the same reasons.) It was not only that England's financial resources were few: so, too, were her defence

[1] Lynch to Lords Committee, 12 Sept. 1683, CO 138/4, 161–3, 177.

[2] 20 Dec. 1683, ibid. 223–4.

[3] 4 Mar. 1684, ibid. 235.

[4] CSPC 1681–5, 1065; Crump, op. cit. 115: 'The problem of how to deal with officers and men of the Royal Navy, who committed offences on shore, was left unsettled. Molesworth, even in 1689, was still unable to obtain any answer to inquiries on this point.'

[5] Non-co-ordination was not, however, peculiar to the English colonial system, as may be gathered from Lynch's letter to Arlington of 27 June 1671, commenting that Santo Domingo 'must hold very little correspondence with the Main, for they knew nothing of the businesse of Panama'; Add. MS. 11410, f. 372.

forces. The Crown was allowed its 'guards and garrisons', but no more than these, lest Cromwell's power revived anew; and the Navy at the Restoration was as small as its debt was large:[1] it could muster only 129 ships all told. By 1675, after two fierce struggles with the formidable sea-power of the Dutch, that number had been reduced to 100.[2] England, therefore, never had any ships to spare for colonial defence. 'This Island if rightly supplied with men and ships', declared William Lord Willoughby of Barbados, 'may give Checkmate to Don, Hanns, or Mons[r], when my Master pleaseth.'[3] 'Your Lordshipps will know', remarked the Councillors of Antigua in 1680, 'that good and well equipped frigates are the brazen walls of Islands.'[4]

Indeed they did: but knowledge in this case was not power. In times of emergency colonial Governors had to rely on what weapons they could find or fashion: on the privateers, as in Jamaica, or on the impressment of merchant ships, as in Barbados and the Leeward Islands. Such improvisations often raised more problems than they solved, by setting litigation on foot and colonists' tempers on edge. Thus, although the King might warn his colonial subjects that distance of place entailed no diminution in the strength of his justice and power, there is no doubt that they would have been more eager to respect both these attributes had they more frequently seen visible symbols of Majesty, in the shape of ships-of-the-line, riding in their harbours.[5] The King indeed circularized the plantations on the outbreak of the Dutch War in 1672, and assured the Governors and all his loyal subjects that 'we shall not be wanting on our part on all occasions to help and succor them to the utmost of our power'[6]—but what was this assurance worth, when the utmost of his power was only the dispatch of a fourth-rate frigate,

[1] Some £1,300,000; Tedder, op. cit. 46.

[2]

Rate	1	2	3	4	5	6	
In 1660 . .	4	11	15	40	37	22	MS. Rawl.
In 1675 . .	8	9	22	37	16	8	A. 197.

[3] Willoughby to the King, 16 Sept. 1667, Stowe MS. 755, f. 19.
[4] Council of Antigua to the Lords Committee, July 1680, CSPC 1677–80, 1441–2.
[5] Beer, op. cit. i. 108, observes that in inaugurating its commercial system, the Restoration Administration had assumed a burden of imperial defence, 'in return for which it was considered justifiable to restrict and mould the economic life of the colonies'. An undefended colony thus saw no reason to conform to this mould.
[6] The King to Governors, 2–6 Apr. 1672, CO 389/4, 55–56.

or two at the most? Although there were often rumours current in the West Indies that a great fleet was coming to do great things there—in October 1670 Prince Rupert was confidently expected, with 25 men-of-war and 5,000 soldiers[1]—in all Charles II's reign only one fleet ever came: that of Sir John Harman to the Leeward Islands in 1667,[2] where it did such good work[3] that the gap left by its withdrawal only seemed the greater. For the expense of maintaining it in being was too heavy; as it was, both William Lord Willoughby and Harman himself had 'to pawn their shirts' to pay the seamen.[4]

West-India Governors repeatedly asked for the protection of the King's ships. In 1662 Lord Windsor was appointed Commander-in-chief of all the King's ships in Jamaica,[5] but this style and title had little reference to fact, for of the four frigates with which he set out to his Government he was allowed to retain only two.[6] In 1663 Francis Lord Willoughby requested two frigates for Barbados—'in case the Spaniards should Trade with the Iland itt would be a greate Incouragement to them to see a mann-of-war riding in the Road for their Protection,' to which the King agreed, 'if the exigency of affairs will permit'.[7] The exigency did not permit, although there were three French frigates regularly at Martinique from 1664. Lacking the necessary cruiser, Willoughby settled a thousand people on the island of St. Lucia in lieu, the better to keep watch from this base on the French proceedings.[8] At Jamaica Sir Charles Lyttelton stressed that only the King's frigates could control the

---

[1] Richard Browne to Arlington, 12 Oct. 1670, CO 1/25, No. 76.

[2] One 3rd-rate, ten 4th-rate, one 5th-rate, and four 6th-rate frigates. Cf. orders of 5 Oct. 1667, Adm 2/1745.

[3] For example, the resettlement of Antigua and Montserrat, the attack on the French at Martinique, the capture of Surinam and Cayenne.

[4] W. Lord Willoughby to Arlington, 2 Dec. 1667, CO 1/21, No. 154.

[5] Similar Commissions were issued to Atkins and Vaughan in Aug. and Nov. 1674; Adm 2/1755, 33.

[6] Orders of 16 Apr. 1662, Adm 2/1725. *Centurion* went to Cuba with Myngs; *Griffin* Windsor sent out privateering under Captain Swart, who, returning to Jamaica two years later, was highly indignant when Sir Thomas Modyford commandeered his ship for the King's service. Cf. Swart to Windsor, 26 June 1664, CSPC 1661–8, 763.

[7] F. Lord Willoughby to the King, 10 Sept. 1663, CO 1/17, No. 78; the King to Willoughby, 11 Jan. 1664, CO 1/18, No. 1.

[8] F. Lord Willoughby to Arlington, 25 Aug. 1664, ibid. No. 97; to the King, 16 Oct. 1664, Bodl., MS. Clarendon 82, f. 132.

privateers.[1] Modyford repeatedly made the same point. He asked for frigates twice in 1664,[2] and again in the next two years; for without them it was plain that the buccaneers of Tortuga had to be 'tempored' with.[3]

The impact of war on the colonies in the Caribbean made the necessity of some standing naval guard there plain to all the colonists. William Lord Willoughby would have felt quite at ease in Barbados had he only had '3 or 4 nimble 5th-rate ffriggats'.[4] One of Joseph Williamson's odd correspondents, a privateer surgeon named Browne, wrote expansively that 15 or 20 3rd-, 4th-, and 5th-rate ships would overrun all the West Indies very speedily, and thus add 'a splendid diamond to his sacred Majesty's Crown'.[5] This was pipe-dreaming; Governors would have been more pleased had they been only allowed to retain the frigates that brought them to their Islands. Sir Thomas Lynch took two to Jamaica in 1671, *Welcome* with himself on board and *Assistance* to take Sir Thomas Modyford home prisoner.[6] But there was no ship at Jamaica between July 1672 and August 1673, although England was again at war with the Dutch. Then two frigates arrived, causing 'huge rejoicing'.[7] Pressure had been brought to bear by the Council of Trade and Foreign Plantations, who feared a Dutch invasion of Jamaica; and they had also seen to it that Willoughby's plea for two frigates for Barbados was at last met.[8]

---

[1] Report of Sir C. Lyttelton, Oct. 1664, CO 1/18, No. 111.

[2] Modyford to Sir J. Modyford, 21 July 1664, ibid. No. 95.

[3] Not until 1668, when it was clear that the privateers of Jamaica were getting out of hand, was York directed to send a 5th-rate there, 'to suppress the insolence of privateers uppon that Coast'; 17 Feb. 1668, APCC, i. 751; Adm 2/1745; Albemarle to York, 12 Mar. 1668, CO 1/22, No. 51. The ship sent was the *Oxford*, which Modyford commandeered and sent a-privateering under Morgan in a design on Carthagena.

[4] W. Lord Willoughby to the King, 3 June 1667, CO 1/21, No. 54.

[5] Browne to Williamson, 7 Aug. 1670, CO 1/25, No. 51.

[6] Modyford was actually sent home in a merchant-ship. Lynch retained the *Assistance* until July 1672, parting from it most reluctantly; Lynch to the King, 6 July 1672, CO 1/29, No. 7.

[7] Lynch to Worsley, 12 Aug. 1673, CO 1/30, No. 58.

[8] Willoughby's memorandum, 8 Apr. 1672, CO 1/18, No. 38; Minutes of the Council of Foreign Plantations, 14 May 1672, ibid. No. 56. The victualling of these ships was to be done by independent contractors, in England and in New England ports. It was already a practice in Barbados to send ships to New England for victualling; cf. Council of Barbados to the Commissioners of the Navy, 4 Mar. 1673, Adm 1/3545, 1152.

But the problem was not tackled systematically; there was no means of doing so. Evertsen's fleet cruised in the Caribbean in 1673, those of Binckes and d'Estrées from 1676.[1] English colonists were naturally restive while Dutchmen and French-men roamed at will. Atkins and Vaughan sent home some bitter comments,[2] for which the Lords of Trade had no real answer. And the story of neglect that came from the Leeward Islands, the group most vulnerable of all the English settlements in the West Indies, was exactly the same. An Administration that was unable to supply effective naval defence to two colonial Govern-ments was not likely to cope even in the feeblest fashion with a third. Governor Stapleton, aware of its difficulty, sensibly sug-gested that the Governors of Barbados and of the New England colonies should be instructed to send assistance to the Leeward Islands 'upon occasion of a rupture',[3] but this remained a sug-gestion only, for local jealousies were always apt to cut across broad strategic schemes of this type. The Council of St. Christopher, echoing Lynch in Jamaica, objected that Barbados in 1674 should be favoured with the protection of two frigates; had not Barbados 60 sloops of its own for coastal guard?[4] In contrast, the Leeward Islands 'station' (if its minute embryo may be so called) enjoyed only the intermittent services of a ketch, generally not even seaworthy. Stapleton asked repeatedly for a frigate to be sent, pointing out that the expense of maintaining it there might be offset against the losses the Customs sustained because of the uncurbed activities of the Dutch privateersmen.[5]

This plea was taken up seriously by the interim Committee of Trade in February 1675. Since the French by now had six men-of-war permanently stationed in the Antilles, the Commit-tee recommended that five or six frigates should 'constantly attend' the Leeward Islands, and that a Court of Admiralty should be established there for their better organization.[6] Arlington assured Stapleton in June that the security of his

[1] Binckes took Cayenne on 4 May 1676. d'Estrées recaptured it in December.
[2] Cf. Atkins to Lords Committee, 6/16 Dec. 1676, 8/18 Feb. 1677, CO 29/2, 148–50; Vaughan to Coventry, 26 June 1677, CO 138/3, 144.
[3] 'A particular accompt of the Leeward Islands', 17 July 1672, CO 153/2, 41–45.
[4] Minutes of the Council of St. Christopher, 26 Mar. 1674, CO 1/31, No. 29.
[5] Stapleton to the Council of Plantations, 7 Mar. 1674, ibid. No. 19.
[6] Cf. also their recommendations to the King in a letter of 13 Jan. 1676, CO 391/1, 61.

command was a matter of 'infinite concern' to the King.[1] Infinite concern or no, nothing happened to alleviate Stapleton's
position; and 'things not mended', as the Lords Committee
sensibly observed in an exhaustive report of April 1677,[2] 'grow
worse'. A war with France was expected that year, and all
colonial Governors were so notified. In March the Navy Commissioners were again debating how best to supply a sloop for
the Leeward Islands, a 5th-rate frigate for Barbados, and
another to convey the Earl of Carlisle to Jamaica and to stay
there for the service of the Island.[3] Everyone was now alive to
the importance of the defence of the Caribbean. Williamson
wrote Stapleton, who needed no telling, 'If we doe not look well
about us in time, I am afraid how dear it may one time or other
cost us.'[4] The Lords Committee's report remarked how the
Ministers of France had taken their colonies in the Antilles

under their wings, doing all things that might make them prosper,
as designing thereby to become masters of the sugar-trade. . . . They
are become not only of equal force either to Spain or to England in
those seas but stand suspected to be strong enough to conquer all. . . .
They are swelled, at home, into a vaster Fleet than what almost they
have harbours to contain.

Victory in the Leeward Islands, as the events of 1666 had
proved, depended on the timing of the first blow. Clearly the
French, already armed and prepared by land and sea, would
again win the day. 'If war comes', Southwell observed to
Ormond in Ireland, 'expect the loss of the plantations.'[5]

War did not come in 1677, but its arrival was as confidently
expected in 1678. Coventry had warned the West-India Governors of a possible breach with France;[6] and the King told Atkins
in April that he was expected to give every assistance to the

[1] Arlington to Stapleton, 23 June 1675, CO 153/2, 11.
[2] 'A Report from the Lords of the Committee of Trade & Plantations touching
the Leeward Islands', 25 Apr. 1677, signed by Anglesey, Bridgewater, Craven,
Essex, Fauconberg, G. Cartaret, J. Ernle, and R. Southwell; Bodl., MS. Rawl.
A. 295, ff. 45 et seq.
[3] The Admiralty was to consider 'how such may be provided for with best
husbandry to His Majesty'. Was it best to 'hyre convenient merchant vessells' for
this purpose? The answer was no; 29 Mar. 1677, Adm 2/1748, 28–29; 27 Oct. 1677,
ibid. 109. *Hunter* and *Jersey* were allotted to Carlisle, *Hunter* to carry 40 tons of
Purbeck stone for the fortifications.
[4] Williamson to Stapleton, 30 Oct. 1677, CO 389/4, 93.
[5] Southwell to Ormond, 19 June 1678, HMC Ormond, vi. 386.
[6] On 30 Dec. 1677; Add. MS. 25120, f. 123.

Leeward Islands if trouble came.[1] The Lords Committee knew that a force at sea 'was necessary above all things—inasmuch as between taking all and losing all, there seems no middle way left'.[2] In May, therefore, Pepys was instructed to estimate the cost of maintaining three 4th- or 5th-rate frigates in the Leewards.[3] But the *détente* begun by the wrecking of d'Estrées's fleet in April, continued by the arrangement of a pact between Stapleton and de Blénac on St. Christopher in July, and concluded by the European Treaty of Nijmegen in August, took the urgency out of this matter; and Pepys's estimate did not come up for consideration until the following May (1679).

Its figures must have startled the Lords Committee, for he calculated that the costs of such a naval maintenance in the Leewards would amount to £43,400 per annum.[4] The new Privy Councillors believed in retrenchment; far from expending more on Caribbean defence, they at once recalled the two frigates at Jamaica to save money.[5] An Order-in-Council of 6 June instructed that every means possible should be taken to reduce the American expenses,[6] but a week later the Lords Committee advised that there should be no reduction in the naval establishment for the Leeward Islands[7]—a somewhat grandiose reference to the ketch that was still all that Stapleton saw from one year's end to the other.

The following table illustrates the naval policy of the Administration at this time:

[1] The King to Atkins, 16 Apr. 1678, CO 389/6, 245. The King also hastened Carlisle's departure to Jamaica within the fortnight, 'lest after that his passage might not be safe'; Daniel Finch to Sir John Finch, 13 Feb. 1678, HMC Finch, ii. 40.

[2] Lords Committee to the King, 25 Apr. 1678, CO 153/2, 273–99.

[3] Order-in-Council, 15 May 1678, Adm 1/5138, 1179.

[4] 200 men per 4th-rate, 110 per 5th-; 30s. per man per 28-day month; 20s. per man per 28-day month for victuals; 30s. per man per 28-day month for wear and tear of ships. Total per month = £3,620; 12 May 1679, CO 153/2, 387.

[5] Orders, 25 May 1679, Adm 2/1749, 3.

[6] APCC, i. 1277. An estimate of 1676 reckons the American expenses thus: for the Leeward Islands, £3,200; for Jamaica, £4,500; for New York, £1,500; for Virginia, £9,000. Total = £17,200; HMC Lindsey, 110.

[7] 13 June 1679, APCC, i. 1281; cf. CO 1/43, No. 70; CO 324/4, 62. Their report of 22 May 1679 calls the Leewards 'a considerable parcell' of the King's plantations, and again stresses the necessity of opposing the French; CO 1/43, No. 61. It was on these grounds, too, that they objected to Carlisle's project to import people from the Leewards to Jamaica, 'since they are of great defence to the other plantations in opposition to the French'.

	No. of men	Time (months)
For the service of Jamaica, 1 ship of the 5th-rate, vizt. *Success*	90	13
For the service of Barbados, 1 ship of the 5th-rate, vizt. *Europa*	115	13
For the service of the Leeward Is., 1 ship of the 6th-rate, vizt. '*Deptford* ketch' . . .	30	13

This scheme was designed to fit into the major plan to reduce the entire naval expenditure of the country to a maxim of £300,000 per annum.[1]

Stapleton, advised of this, expressed a hope that some better vessel would be sent him, and suggested once more that the three ships sent to the West Indies would do the King more service if they patrolled together.[2] Again no comment was made on this notion. Although the Lords Committee did try to obtain an 'able frigate' for Stapleton,[3] they were unsuccessful, and he had to put up with the *Deptford* ketch once more. 'It is my duty', said this admirable officer, 'to be as silent as satisfied with what is sent.'[4]

The increase of piracy in the Caribbean in the 1680's, and Sir Thomas Lynch's consequent complaint that it was the great want of a frigate that had made those villains increase in numbers and impudence,[5] induced the Lords Committee to see to it that Jamaica at least was more regularly supplied. (They even managed at last to find a better frigate for the Leewards, the *Francis*, which was sent out in 1683 with 30 soldiers aboard and no less than three years' provisions[6]—indeed a quite phenomenal

[1] 'A Project of what force of shipping His Majesty may employ abroad when the whole charge of HM Navy shall not exceed £300,000 per annum'; June 1679. There were also two 4th-rate frigates stationed at Newfoundland, 400 men for 9 months; Adm 2/1740, 263. The establishment for colonial defence was set at £12,816; CO 1/43, No. 70.

[2] Stapleton to Lords Committee, 26 Oct. 1680, CO 1/46, No. 25.

[3] Cf. JLTP, 1 Oct. 1679, CO 391/3, 70–72; 3 Apr. 1679, Adm 2/1748.

[4] Stapleton to Lords Committee, 15 Nov. 1680, CO 1/46, No. 44. After a Carib raid on Montserrat he declared he would 'pursue the villans tho' in Shallops'; 20 Dec. 1682, CSPC 1681–5, 860.

[5] Lynch to Lords Committee, 6 Nov. 1682, CO 138/4, 114.

[6] The Lords recommended its dispatch on 28 Oct. 1682; CO 391/4, 68. (*Francis* was, however, lost at sea in May 1684.) When Stapleton sent home the *Deptford*

piece of planning). Moreover, Lynch in Jamaica did not share the view of Dutton in Barbados that a King's ship was the Governor's private property, and cheerfully dispatched the *Ruby* from Port Royal to Nevis to aid Stapleton's expedition against the Caribs of Dominica. Defensive solidarity among the colonies was still, however, far to seek; Lynch, a generous and intelligent man, was naturally apt to take generous and intelligent action, but a sense of personal responsibility was slow in developing among the planter class. (Indeed, there is a formidable case for the argument that it never developed at all.) However that may be, it can at least be said that the Restoration Administration became keenly alive to its responsibilities in regard to the naval defence of the West Indies; yet, despite this, it was unable to implement them adequately. Louis XIV, had he wished it, might very easily have encompassed the ruin of the English colonies in the Caribbean. But he was content to show his flag there while he preoccupied himself with the extension of his European frontiers. It was this preoccupation that granted to the English Administration—strengthened if not purified by the Revolution of 1689—the precious gift of time: the time it required to reap the benefit of the far-sighted commercial policy of the Restoration era, the time to make the naval defence of the Caribbean the natural corollary of the enumeration of its produce.[1]

Military defence in the West Indies in this period rested on an equally precarious basis. The planters relied on their own militia and horse. Barbados in 1661 could muster four regiments of foot and two of horse, the charge of this force being defrayed by a tax on imported liquors.[2] Francis Lord Willoughby worked hard to raise a double regiment of two or four thousand

in April 1680, he had remarked that he hoped that if any man-of-war was sent out, it would be provided for a West-India and not for a Channel voyage; CO 1/44, No. 48.

[1] A ketch was stationed as a permanency in Virginia from 1684; the *Dartmouth* (4) took up its station in the Leeward Islands from 1686. James II's zeal in naval affairs is illustrated by his dispatch of Sir Robert Holmes and four frigates (Commission, 21 Aug. 1687, in CSPC 1685–8, 1411), to the Caribbean to quell the pirates; (Cf. MS. Rawl. A. 189, f. 13, 'What Sir Robert Holmes desires for his present expedition to the West Indies'.) For the development of the Jamaica 'station' and Leeward Islands 'station', see Ruth Bourne, *Queen Anne's Navy in the West Indies* (New Haven, 1939), and Pares, *War and Trade in the West Indies* (Oxford, 1936).

[2] Minutes of the Council of Barbados, 9–10 May 1661, CO 29/1, 44–52.

men under the King's colours—though not, of course, in the King's pay. His own view was that the importance of the Island was such that it merited a standing army of 500 soldiers well paid and equipped, with another 1,000 more distributed among the Leeward Islands[1]—but even to make such an observation was pointless. Nevertheless, Barbados could muster a formidable force, sufficient to impress de Ruyter at a distance in 1665 and d'Estrées at closer quarters in 1678. Henry Willoughby was able to raise 1,500 men and 30 pressed merchantmen for his expedition to St. Christopher in 1666; Willoughby himself took a thousand men with him on his last voyage.[2] Next year his brother found over 4,000 fighting-men in Barbados, but the quality of these may be judged by his comment, 'God send us Peace or 2 good Regiments at least'.[3] But although the arrival of Sir Tobias Bridge's regiment may have served to answer this prayer, it seemed a dubious blessing to the inhabitants.[4] The planters wished to be protected, yes—but they disliked and distrusted the presence of soldiers, seeing in it at once an economic burden and a political danger to the Island's liberties. Even so, the Assembly, always contrary, was unwilling to allow Willoughby to send the regiment down to the Leewards, as he wished to do.[5] Was not Barbados a more important plantation than any in the Leewards—more deserving, therefore, of the protection of the King's troops?

While the sense of Barbadian grievance grew—a general grievance, to which particular issues attached themselves like burrs—the Administration sent orders to Willoughby in the spring of 1668 to disband Bridge's regiment, for the war was officially over. The French attitude concerning the restoration

[1] Willoughby to the King, 4 Nov. 1663, CO 1/17, No. 89; 12 May 1666, CO 1/20, No. 92.
[2] Of which the French captured 800, with a ransom value each of 3,000 lb. sugar—according to a letter to Harley, 11 Oct. 1666, in HMC Portland, iii. 301.
[3] W. Lord Willoughby to the King, 9 July 1667, CO 1/21, Nos. 71, 108. Cf. also 'Some Observations on the Island of Barbados', 1667: 'To compel men that have neither land, house, goods, wife or children or pay, to be sometimes 4 or 5 days together on duty without so much as victuals, save what they stole, was extremely severe—but this was their practice, and till the arrival of Sir Tobias Bridge's Regiment there were not 40 men in pay'; ibid., No. 170.
[4] Rumour served Barbados well. de Blénac, who was there in Jan. 1666, reckoned that the Island could muster eighteen to twenty thousand foot and 3,000 horse.
[5] Minutes of the Council of Barbados, 17–28 Oct. 1668, CO 29/1, 173–7.

and restitution of the English half of St. Christopher grew daily more surly, however, and the order was countermanded in July, to Willoughby's relief if not to that of the Barbadians.[1] Nor were Bridge's soldiers better pleased; Sir Tobias reminded the King in 1670 that the regiment had by then served three years in Barbados, and in the first two years had drawn only two months' pay.[2] Codrington and the Council, now compelled to pay for the soldiers' upkeep out of the 4½ per cent., petitioned for the disbandment of the regiment while the planters grew increasingly restive.[3] Fortunately Sir Charles Wheler, the first Governor of the Leeward Islands, had a use for 200 of the troops; better these, he remarked, than 500 tapsters and tailors.[4] Bridge's force was therefore reduced to two companies of 80 men each, including officers, and settled in St. Christopher. A Commission to Wheler as captain of one company and to Stapleton (then Governor of Montserrat) as captain of the other under Wheler's authority was issued in February 1671.[5] The remainder were disbanded. The 'old raised men' of the regiment were offered 38 acres of land in either Jamaica or the Leeward Islands.[6] A corporal should have 50 acres, a captain 400.[7] It is not unlikely that these offers were accepted, and doubtless, too, some martial spirits went to stiffen the backbone of the privateering fraternity in Jamaica.

Barbados anyway was relieved at this outcome; Sir Tobias Bridge was still able to raise eight companies of foot for his Tobago expedition of December 1672;[8] and Sir Peter Colleton was able to report to the Council of Trade and Foreign Plantations in May 1673 that the strength of the Island had been in no way impaired. The militia at that time consisted of two regi-

[1] Cf. Willoughby to the King, 21 July 1668, CO 1/23, No. 20.

[2] Bridge to the King, 10 Mar. 1670, CO 1/25, No. 14.

[3] It was the recommendation of the Council of Plantations that these troops should be in the royal pay 'for one year'; Report to the King, 14 Feb. 1671, CO 389/5, 86–87.

[4] 'Proposals of Sir Charles Wheler', 9 Feb. 1671, CO 1/26, No. 21; Wheler to Arlington, 8 June 1671, ibid. No. 72.

[5] Commissions, 24 Feb. 1671, CO 153/1, 19.

[6] Barbados was not included, for there was no land and less prospects for the small estate-owner in that Island. It seems that only six men actually went there; Lynch to Arlington, 7 June 1671, CO 1/26, No. 71.

[7] 14 Mar. 1671, CO 153/1, 28. Further instructions concerning settlement and disbandment are in CO 1/27, No. 36, and T 54/2, 135, 316.

[8] Bridge to Arlington, 15 Dec. 1672, CO 1/29, No. 63.

ments of horse and six of foot—or, in other words, 1,000 cavalry and 4,000 infantry.[1] The figures Atkins sent home in 1676 were more inflated. He reckoned that the whole defensive force might amount to 10,000 horse, foot, and dragoons.[2] Dutton's of 1681, however, confirms Colleton's rather than Atkins's report estimate.[3]

In the Leeward Islands the military situation was always uncertain. Nevis in 1671 possessed a regiment of trained bands, with a militia of 100 horse, under Russell's command; Antigua in the charge of Colonel Philip Warner could raise 900 foot; while Stapleton's Montserrat had 1,000 men in arms. There was no fortification worthy of the name in any of the Islands. Wheler reckoned that the French had a force of 1,200 professional soldiers distributed in French St. Christopher, Martinique, and Guadeloupe.[4] After de Ruyter's attack on Martinique in July 1674, France based there two regiments of Poitou and Navarre, and reinforced her force on St. Christopher. Stapleton complained how disgraceful it was that the English soldiers on St. Christopher—by 1676 reduced to 110, and 'but 2 files of men in pay'—should be 'naked and starving' under the eyes of the French.[5] Of the militia in the other islands, Stapleton never expected to find '$\frac{2}{3}$ in the field, much less on service'.[6] Accordingly, he sent an agent home to solicit these problems with the Lords Committee of Trade.

The Administration was well aware of Stapleton's difficulties and the dangers that might spring from them. Danby in 1675 managed to pay the two years' arrears of the companies' pay, together with those of Stapleton himself. The interim Committee had suggested in January that a fund should be established for the regular supply of the forces in the Leeward Islands, and a month later recommended that this should be found from the $4\frac{1}{2}$ per cent. revenue, and that the King should contribute £500 towards the building of a fort at Cleverley Point in

[1] 'The President and Council of Barbados to the Councell of Forrain Plantacons', 25 May 1673, CO 389/5, 154–6.
[2] Atkins to Lords Committee, 4/14 July 1676, CO 1/37, No. 22.
[3] CO 1/47, No. 7. A report of 1683, in Sloane MS. 2441, ff. 1–22, makes it: horse, 57 officers, 1,005 men; foot, 186 officers, 4,906 men.
[4] Wheler to the Council of Plantations, 9 Dec. 1671, CO 1/27, No. 52.
[5] Stapleton to the Council of Plantations, 17 Mar. 1675, CO 1/34, No. 24.
[6] 'Answers of Governor Sir William Stapleton to the 32 Heads of Inquiry', 22 Nov. 1676, CO 1/38, No. 65.

St. Christopher. Arms, ammunition, and field-carriages, at a total cost of £990, should be sent out. But apparently His Majesty did not think fit at that time 'to signify his pleasure on the said large report of particulars'.[1] There were military expenses enough to meet: 1,000 troops had to be sent to Virginia that summer to deal with Bacon's rebellion and its aftermath. Thus, although it was arranged in August 1676 that 57 soldiers should be transported to St. Christopher to make the complement there up to 200 once more, a warrant authorizing their dispatch was not issued until 11 months had passed; and when, in January 1678, these recruits did at last arrive in the Leewards, Stapleton reported wearily that they were without arms, ammunition, or money.[2]

The report presented by the Lords Committee in April 1677 was, however, the preface to some well-meaning administrative activity. On 1 June Danby was instructed to find the necessary £500 for the fort, and to make arrangements with the Master of the Ordnance about a supply of war stores for the Islands.[3] The creditors of Francis Lord Willoughby (still besieging the Lord Treasurer) must wait until the soldiers, again in arrears, had been paid.[4] It was one thing, however, to recommend the institution of a fund, but another to find the cash to put in it. What was not being claimed as 'defalcations' of the 4½ per cent. revenue by its Farmers was already anticipated. To the Lords Committee's recommendation in 1679 that the duty should be applied for one year to the building of a fort in *each* Island, Stapleton quite correctly retorted that the duty was incapable of bearing any such burden. Nevertheless, an Order-in-Council was issued accordingly, and the sum to be contributed by the King raised to £1,500. Stapleton (perhaps with relish) again pointed out that this sum would not even pay the masons.[5] Official suggestions as to the welfare of the Leewards began

[1] 'Report of the Lords Committee . . . touching the Leeward Islands', 25 Apr. 1677, MS. Rawl. A. 295, ff. 45 et seq.
[2] Order-in-Council, 13 July 1677, Adm 1/5132, 702; Stapleton to the Lords Committee, 19 Jan. 1678, CO 1/42, No. 13.
[3] CO 153/2, 219–22. In June 1677 there was less than a barrel of powder in St. Christopher and only two in Montserrat; APCC, i. 1141.
[4] Treasury Lords to Danby, 23 July 1677, Add. MS. 9764, f. 3.
[5] Cf. JLTP, 1 Oct. 1679, CO 391/3, 70–72; CO 153/2, 397; APCC, i. 1319; Stapleton later suggested that the £1,500 might be used in the building of one fort in one Island, and considered Nevis the best for the work; CO 1/42, No. 39.

to dry up at their source. For, while Pepys was presenting his dismaying estimate of a secure naval establishment in the Islands, Monmouth, as Captain-General, had given the Lords a similar shock in regard to the cost of the land forces. To keep 1,000 soldiers in arms and pay there would cost the country £6,053. 16s. 8d.[1] It was a figure to place on the file; it was not an expense an insolvent Administration could meet.

With the passing of the immediate danger of a war with France the immediate interest failed. By 1682 the two companies in St. Christopher were again four years in arrears, and the troops were once more watching the monthly French pay-parades just beyond the English lines.[2] When the agent for the Leewards, Christopher Jeaffreson, made a fresh appeal for arms for St. Christopher, the Lords Committee returned him a dusty answer, desiring 'my Lord Dartmouth to enquire whether any order be in the office of the Ordnance that the several plantations should furnish their Stores at their own Charge'.

Jeaffreson commented ruefully on his situation:

I proceeded to petition the King for cannon, shot, arms, and ammunition for the fort. The 1st petition was lost; the 2nd I preferred was read, & by order referred to the Lords of the Committee. This order cost me 2 & 50s. and sixpence, before I could get it to Sir Ph. Lloyd's clerk; and it produced nothing but another reference to the Earl of Dartmouth. I made my application twice or thrice to HLpp. [Sunderland], who told me, if we could find money he would find all we wanted. I was no stranger to such rubs.

His cynical view of the Administration and its servants can hardly be blamed.

Mr. Blathwayt further says that the Lords of the Council should be reminded by letters of the same authorities of the wants of the Island, at least twice every year. But without a gratification of 20 or 30 guineas to himself at the least, I doubt much the effect of the letters or anything else.[3]

[1] Order-in-Council, so instructing Monmouth, dated 15 May 1678, CO 153/2, 381; 20 Jan. 1679, CO 1/43, No. 4.
[2] Cf. Stapleton to Lords Committee, 26 July 1681, 25 Mar. 1682, CO 153/3, 16–20, 37–38. The French were paid ninepence a day; CO 1/54, No. 29. The Lords Committee indeed reported the matter to the King (7 Feb. 1682, CO 153/3, 27–30), and the Treasury Commissioners were asked to look into it (ibid. 31–32), but Blathwayt calculated in Aug. 1684 that the foot companies were still owed £8,333. 12s.; T 64/88, 137.
[3] JLTP, 25 Jan. 1683, CO 391/4, 140; 1 Feb. 1683, Jeaffreson, op. cit. ii. 29–30,

Small wonder, if this is true, that Jamaica always delayed appointing an agent in London because of the expenses involved!

Jamaica itself began as a garrison, and always retained something of this aspect. As already noted, Lord Windsor was given permission in 1662 to retain in arms 150 horse and 400 foot; and before he left the Island, he had set up a militia of 100 officers and 1,840 men. In 1663 the annual military establishment for Jamaica was set at £2,500, out of which £400 was allotted to the Major-General in command of the forces, and £500 to the soldiers' pay. This figure was too small, as the actual outlay in the previous year, 1662, had been some £5,500. The establishment was therefore raised to £5,000 in 1665.[1] Sir Thomas Modyford reported in October 1664 that five good regiments of militia had been raised,[2] but he claimed later that it was only his decision to grant letters of marque against the Spaniard that kept the guards up to strength. John Style in 1669 reckoned that the fighting strength of the Island amounted to some 1,580 men. He pointed out that in D'Oyley's day there had been a considerable army of 'young and lusty' men, but now the young and lusty were out a-privateering, about 800 all told.[3] Thus Modyford's subsequent request, to have leave to keep 1,000 privateers in pay because of the French and Spanish menace, was really more sensible than sinister. By 1671, however, Jamaica could muster six regiments of foot and one of horse.[4] The only fortifications were at Port Royal, and the fear of a coastal invasion was always acute in consequence. Lynch wrote in 1673 how great were his difficulties: a vast country to be kept by a few men, a port to be defended without ships, fortifications to be built without money. How strange it was that Jamaica 'should not be as much considered for the King's interest as Barbados had been for Lord Willoughby's'. When

59. (In CO 391/4 is an entry dated 24 Jan. 1685, that since Dec. 1676 only £4,780 worth of ordnance stores had been sent to St. Christopher, Barbados, New Hampshire, Jersey, Virginia, and New York.)

[1] MS. Rawl. A. 347; 25 Dec. 1663, CO 138/1, 110; £3,539. 8s. 7d. for the soldiers, £2,000 for the Governor; Egerton MS. 2395, f. 351. Compare the Bombay establishment: £7,000 in 1665; CSPD 1665–6, 92.

[2] 'A view of the condicon of Jamayca', 1 Oct. 1664, CO 1/18, No. 108.

[3] Style to Morice, 14 Jan. 1669, CO 1/24, No. 8.

[4] Livingstone, *Sketch Pedigrees*, says there were 2,720 officers and soldiers in Jamaica in 1670.

the war with the Dutch began, Lynch wrote gloomily that it was highly probable that very soon a letter from Jamaica would be 'a Novelty'.[1]

But, while Sir Henry Morgan had a say in the Island's destiny —and he was its Lieutenant-Governor, with minor vexatious interruptions, for 13 years—Jamaica regarded itself as a floating cruiser in a Spanish sea, whose best defence was attack, whose true land frontiers were the shores of Campeachy in the west and Havana to the north-west. Land forces were therefore looked on as a secondary consideration—though not so secondary that Morgan was pleased to find only three hours' supply of powder in store there in 1675,[2] and this despite the fact that an estimate of nearly £7,000 for supplying Jamaica with ordnance stores had been approved the previous year. Both Morgan and Colonel Thomas Modyford, junior, had a natural talent for military organization, and by 1678 there were some 4,000 men in arms. Carlisle, reporting this, warned the Lords Committee that this figure was 'security'—rumour had magnified it ten times, and rumour here was a useful servant.

Carlisle had brought with him two companies, 200 of the King's troops, the first to set foot in the Island. They had been hastily mustered in London in 1678,[3] but the inhabitants of Jamaica were never very certain whether these troops were designed for their protection against a foreign foe or for their own suppression by the King. The presence of so large a force in pay in Jamaica naturally made the English Administration the more eager to obtain a permanent revenue from the Island. Indeed, the dispatch of the troops, and the hope of gaining this fixed revenue, were closely connected from the outset. The estimate for the expenses of this force was presented to the Privy Council only two days before the order was sent to the Lords Committee to draft a law for the passage of a perpetual Revenue Act in Jamaica.[4] Had the constitutional struggle with the Assembly been won by the Crown, doubtless Jamaica would have been the base of our first imperial garrison, with a standing

[1] Lynch to Worsley, 6 Apr. 1673, CO 1/30, No. 21; 8 July 1673, CO 389/5, 174.
[2] Morgan to Williamson, 13 Apr. 1675, CO 1/34, No. 55.
[3] Royal warrant, 17 July 1677, CO 1/41, No. 18.
[4] Estimate, £3,762. 5s. 4d., 14 Nov. 1677, APCC, i. 1174; order to Committee, 16 Nov. 1677, ibid. 1176. The actual expenditure in Jamaica from 1 Mar. 1679 to 1 May 1680 was £3,635. 13s. 10d.; Sloane MS. 2724, f. 65.

army paid for by the planters. But the struggle was lost; and so, by an Order-in-Council of 3 November 1680 the two companies were disbanded. Not only this, it was ordered that the salaries of the Governor, the Deputy-Governor, and Lieutenant-General, 'at present paid out of the English Exchequer', were to be retrenched.[1] The allowance of £600 that had been made for the maintenance of the fortifications was also to cease. Retrenchment, it turned out, involved the abolition of the posts of Deputy-Governor and Major-General altogether. The original suggestion to do this came from the Treasury, as was now—in this new era of colonial audit—only proper. 'Its being a hard thing', commented Lawrence Hyde to Carlisle, in language typical of Treasurers in all ages, 'will be no argument to those that are hardened in doeing such kind of things every day.'[2] From interfering in every detail of the colonial government in the Island, Whitehall now turned to a policy of washing its hands. Its palm had not been crossed with colonial silver; and it had therefore no money with which to purchase a sword.

[1] CSPC 1677–80, 1569.
[2] L. Hyde to Carlisle, 27 Aug. 1681, Sloane MS. 2724, f. 106. Virginia's garrison was disbanded the following year.

VII

CONCLUSION

THE history of Charles II's reign illustrates the perplexed efforts of Crown and Parliament—sometimes in harmony, but oftener at odds—to maintain and improve a weak structure of government; but a further revolution in the status of the Crown (1689) was necessary before these efforts could meet success. In the meantime, the affairs of an already extensive colonial empire had to await their definitive settlement.

Although to seek in isolation a 'colonial policy' amid the confusions of politics is somewhat to distort the outlook of seventeenth-century statesmen, it is nevertheless the case that the Crown consistently regarded the American settlements as a single estate, its own particular patrimony. It therefore tried to centralize the control of that estate on the basis of the Prerogative. This policy is most plainly seen in action in the West-India colonies, where the effort was anyway most worth the making. Crown, Parliament, and the expanding mercantile interest all valued these island possessions at a high rate, and it was around their sub-tropical produce, so eagerly sought in European markets, that what Adam Smith later called the 'commercial system' was fashioned. This system was animated by accepted principles that defined the most favourable balance of trade. To promote the prosperity of the West-India colonies was to promote the wealth and welfare of the whole nation: on this there was no domestic controversy. Crown and Parliament therefore co-operated amicably to build this system on a statutory basis.

The decade from 1660 to 1670 was, however, too crowded with foreign and domestic complication to allow any priority to the handling of colonial business. The Acts of Trade defined the channels of colonial commerce in general, and those of the West-India trade in particular, by confining Caribbean produce to English ships and consigning it to English ports; but the various bureaux that were set up to regulate this traffic lacked executive authority, and thus drive. Jamaica, a legacy from

Cromwell, was given royalist civil government (1662), and an able planter-Governor (1664), and thereafter left to its own devices, which proved nefarious. Barbados and the Leeward Islands were removed from their former proprietary control (1663–4)—a form of governance ill-suited to the ideas of latter-day royalism—but then their affairs fell out of official sight. There was as yet no close supervision of local colonial government. It required the successes of France in the West Indies in the war of 1666–7 to awaken the English Administration to full realization of the weakness of the English plantations in the Caribbean.

Moreover, the fall of Clarendon in 1667 was a signal for a Parliamentary investigation into the mismanagement of the nation's affairs. The colonial account came in for scrutiny. The settlement of Crown authority in Barbados and the Leewards had assured—on paper—a secure revenue. William Lord Willoughby (Governor 1667–73) was expected to restore the *status quo ante bellum* in the Islands, pay a regimental garrison, and still provide that revenue. The discovery that this could not be done roused the Administration to activity. The revenue was farmed out among eager West-India merchants (1670), new Councils of Trade and Plantations were established (1670, 1672), Commissioners of the Customs were appointed under the control of the Treasury (1671), a new Charter was granted to and new stock raised for the African Company (1672), and the old proprietary province of 'Carliola' was finally split into two —a separate Government being set up in the Leeward Islands for their better security and control (1671). The reins of local colonial government were now drawn in; two Governors were summarily dismissed. From 1674 the members of a Governor's Council were nominated by the Crown in his official Instructions. The Governor had now to translate from paper to practice an order to transmit all colonial legislation to the Crown for its confirmation or disallowance; similarly, the tenets of the Acts of Trade had now to be properly enforced.

The duty of $4\frac{1}{2}$ per cent., imposed in 1663 on exports from Barbados and the Leewards, was now used as a lever to prise open these colonies for further infiltration by royal officials not responsible to the local government itself. Revenue farmers' agents, revenue collectors, 'naval' officers, African Company factors, office-holders appointed by the Crown by Letters

Patent under the Great Seal—all these now took up key positions in the West Indian world. Barbados under a Governor sympathetic to the planters' interests protested against this new dispensation, but could not make its protest good against the Crown's resolve to put the plantation house and its accounts in order.

Jamaica, a colony State-aided from the outset, had also quickly developed a sense of its own importance. This had been reinforced by seven years of successful freebooting against the Spanish power in America, connived at by the English Government, which hoped that these tactics would force in the door of the Spanish trade monopoly. This hope was soon seen to be vain, in London at least; and so the Treaty of Madrid (1670), by taking international law 'beyond the Line', was intended to put an end to Jamaica's period of independent action, and to begin an era of lawful trade with Spanish American colonies. This hope too was to prove empty. For Jamaica's privateering could not be ended by the stroke of an official pen, and its natural turbulence affected domestic politics. In the sight of the Crown, Jamaica was a conquest, whose form of government was therefore a matter solely in the royal discretion. Jamaica's cry that the King's subjects were all freeborn and had the right to the protection of the 'laws of England' was therefore not one that appealed to the home authorities, who heard in it only a charge against the rights of the Crown—in fact an echo of Parliamentary disaffection. The Lords Committee of Trade (1675) thus worked hard and long to assert the royal authority in the Island; to make, in the King's words, 'a plantation of Jamaica, and not a Christian Algiers'. Nevertheless, their attempt to impose a dictated form of government on the colonists, by tacking a *corpus* of law to a perpetual Revenue Act, was defeated after four years' effort (1677–81). It failed because the scheme controverted fundamental principles of law. (Consequently in its subsequent attack on the Charters of other American colonies, the Crown took care to make its stand on secure legal ground.) The immediate result was the shelving of the project to obtain a perpetual revenue from the West-India colonies. The system of fiscal supervision was, however, improved: a colonial Auditor-General, whose agents supplemented the local Receivers, was appointed (1680), and the $4\frac{1}{2}$ per cent. Farm was replaced by a direct collection of this duty by royal officials (1684)—with a marked improvement in the amount returned. The year 1685 saw heavy duties placed on Barbadian sugars precisely because the planters were so well able to pay.

West-India development requires to be read in the context of the political history of old England and New England alike. The effort to assert the authority of the Crown has its parallel in English politics (and James II's Dominion of New England surely embodied many of his ideas for the authoritarian government of old England); while New England's 'independency' proved to be contagious along the whole length of the American frontier. The traders from the Northern Colonies eventually came under the royal displeasure, but it was their West-India customers who first felt the curb. The Caribbean colonies, unlike those of New England, were unprotected by Charter, and thus the administrative grip could be tightened without legal difficulty.

Even so, this grip could never be entirely effective while no comprehensive scheme for the defence of the Caribbean frontier existed. The institution of a system of imperial defence was the *quid pro quo* expected by the West-India planters in return for their resignation of their old ways of open trading to all parts of the world. The English Government was aware of this commitment and did its best to meet it, but it lacked the necessary resources to do so. It had neither the ships, the men, nor the money, on call. Left ill-defended, the planters took issue with constitutional and economic interference from Whitehall with a genuine sense of grievance, which not all the efforts of loyal and able Governors like Lynch and Stapleton could ever remove. Jamaicans suspected that the troops brought there by Carlisle in 1678 were there less to defend them than to overawe them into accepting the Crown's 'new model' of government. Frigates came to the West Indies as frequently as an overtaxed Admiralty could arrange, but there were never more than two there at any one time, and Dutch and French fleets-of-war patrolled the Caribbean without hindrance throughout the 1670's. Moreover, this absence of the King's ships left the colonial coast clear for the 'interlopers', illicit traders from Salem, Guinea, Curaçao. Thus, any form of autocratic government, in America as in England, was bound to fail in no very long run while there were no effective armed forces in pay to give it power. The failure of the scheme to raise a perpetual revenue made impossible the establishment of West-India naval and military stations, and so left the Caribbean till the 1720's a prey of the smuggler and the pirate. It should be remembered, however, that the English Administration did its best to make the Indies secure.

The Restoration period indeed witnessed the heyday of the West-India economy. Under the aegis of Charles II's government Jamaica began her upward climb to fortune. 'Rich and famous' Barbados was already on her plateau of success. It was, indeed, England's possession of these islands while the sun was strong upon them that gave point and purpose to the construction of that close circle, 'sea-power, commerce, and colonies', whose interaction G. L. Beer defined 40 years ago as 'The Old Colonial System' of England. The chorus of 'Groans of the Plantations', symptoms of a genuine, and eventually a killing, *malaise*, only opened as the period closed. The Stewarts were, in their way, utilitarians: American resources were plainly there to be made the best use of. The growth and prosperity of the West-India colonies, the success of the plantations there, provide indeed the best yardstick for testing the efficiency and common sense that animated that much-abused 'commercial system', first set on its institutional basis by Charles II and his brother.

APPENDIX

RETURNS OF THE 4½ PER CENT. DUTY IN BARBADOS AND THE LEEWARD ISLANDS
1670–88

THE 4½ per cent. Duty on exported produce, payable in kind, was granted to the King by the Assemblies of Barbados and the Leeward Islands in 1663–4 in return for a free grant of land-titles and/or in consideration of the costs of defence.[1] Until 1670 half the Duty was granted to the two Governors Willoughby, and the other half directly to the costs of administration in the Islands, once the creditors of the first Earl of Carlisle had been satisfied—which of course they never were throughout this period. In 1670 the whole of

Date	Amount[2]			Reference[3]
Michaelmas–Michaelmas	£	s.	d.	
1670–1	673	6	8	E 405/402, 329.
1671–2	5,078	10	8	SP 46/157; E 401/1948–9.
1672–3	1,161	15	7	SP 46/152 (vi); E 401/1951.
1673–4	10,865	0	0	E 405/301; GD 32/8.
1674–5	8,478	4	10	E 405/403; GD 32/9.
1675–6	5,993	15	0	T 33/13; E 405/404.
1676–7	800	0	0	E 405/405; T 33/14.
1677–8	3,650	0	0	E 405/406–7.
1678–9	6,885	8	8	SP 46/152 (xii–xiii).
1679–80	1,550	0	0	SP 46/152 (xiv); E 405/409.
1680–1	650	0	0	SP 46/152 (xvii–xviii).
1681–2	8,407	1	4	SP 46/152 (xviii–xix).
1682–3	3,297	14	9½	SP 46/152 (xx–xxi).
1683–4	1,603	3	2½	SP 46/152 (xxii–xxiii).
1684–5	8,993	7	5	T 38/253.
1685–6	—	—	—	'There is not any perfect state of the yeare 1685, nor can it be made by reason the journals of that yeare are not to be found.' T 38/253.
1686–7	8,260	0	0	Add. MS. 10119, f. 215.
1687–8	5,000	0	0	

[1] Add. MS. 10119, f. 42.

[2] These figures represent the sums paid into the English Exchequer, not the yield to the Farmers.

[3] I am indebted to Dr. D. G. Chandaman of the University of Glasgow for the majority of these references.

the Duty was farmed for seven years at an annual rent of £7,000 payable into the English Exchequer.[1] The Farmers' rent-payments were very unsatisfactory,[2] but their lease was renewed in 1677 for a further seven years, at a reduced annual rent of £5,300.[3] In 1684-5 the revenue was brought under direct collection, and the goods received in respect of the Duty, principally sugar, were shipped to England for sale.[4]

[1] Cal. T.B. iii (i), 472, 627; iii (ii), 1217.
[2] Ibid. iv. 357; v (i), 60; vii (i), 514–15; Add. MS. 28089, f. 41.
[3] Cal. T.B. v (ii), 836, 961.
[4] Ibid. viii (ii), 600.

BIBLIOGRAPHY

I. MANUSCRIPTS

(a) PUBLIC RECORD OFFICE

Colonial Office

CO 1/14–54.   Colonial Papers, 1660–85. Correspondence between colonial Governments and the various Plantations Committees and Councils, together with Reports and other material.
CO 318/1–2.   West Indies. Trade and General, 1624–1808.
CO 323/4.   Ordnance and stores for the Plantations.
CO 324/1–4.   Plantations General, 1662–96. (Entry-books.)
CO 326/1.   Trade, 1635–96. Inventory of books and papers of the old Plantation Office.
CO 326/2.   Trade, 1660–1732. General Index by subjects. (P.R.O. Index, 8302.)
CO 326/6–7.   General Index. (P.R.O. Index, 8306–7.)
CO 388/2.   Original Papers of the Lords Committee of Trade, Books A and B, 1662–93.
CO 389/1–6, 8, 9. Plantations Entry-Books, 1660–85.
CO 389/10.   Council of Trade and Foreign Plantations, 1672–4. (34 pp.)
CO 389/11–12.   Entry-Books of the Lords Committee of Trade, 1673–96.
CO 389/35.   Plantations. Entry-Books of Occurrences, 1678–89.
CO 390/6.   Customs-House Accounts, 1677–1731.
CO 391/1–5.   Journals of the Lords Committee of Trade, 1675–85.

THE WEST INDIES
Barbados

CO 5/274.   MSS. Lists of Acts of Barbados, 1648–1758.
CO 29/1–3.   Commissions, Instructions, &c., 1627–88.
CO 30/1.   Printed Acts, 1643–1762.
CO 30/3.   MSS. Acts, 1649–1704.
CO 31/1.   Council and Sessional Papers, 1660–86.
CO 33/13.   Shipping Returns, 1678–89.

Jamaica

CO 138/1–4.   Entry-Books, 1661–87.
CO 139/1–2.   Acts, 1661–82.
CO 140/1, 3, 4.   Sessional Papers, 1661–85.
CO 140/2.   Journal of the Assembly from 1664.
CO 142/13.   Shipping Returns, 1680–1705.

Leeward Islands

CO 8/1.   Acts of Antigua, 1668–1708.
CO 10/3, 166. Antigua and defence, 1667.

CO 153/1–3.   Council and Sessional Papers, 1670–89.
CO 154/1, 2, 4–6. Acts, 1644–1758.
CO 155/1.   Sessional Papers, 1680–95.
CO 157/1.   Shipping Returns, 1683–1787.
CO 260/3, 46.   St. Vincent. Miscellany from 1668.

State Paper Office

SP 9/18, 25, 27, 28, 165, 214, 244. Miscellany of Plantations affairs.
SP 29/87, 231, 253, 271, 391a, 366. Joseph Williamson's Notebooks.
SP 29/359.   Admiralty Warrants and passes, 1673–85.
SP 94/44–70.   Spain, 1660–84.
SP 104/174b.   Entry-Book of Commissions, Instructions, &c., 1664–70.

Privy Council Office

PC 5/1.   Plantation Register, from 1678.

Gifts and Deposits

GD 24/30.   Plantation shipping, 1682.
GD 24/36, 3, 4, 8, 11, 26, 49. Shaftesbury Papers.
GD 26/92.   Letter from William Lord Willoughby, Oct. 1668.
GD 32/43–44.   King's Warrants, 1667–85.

Admiralty

Adm 1/3545.   West Indies, 1673–4.
Adm 1/3554.   Jamaica, 1684–5.
Adm 1/5138–9. Admiralty Orders-in-Council, 1673–89.
Adm 2/1, 1725, 1732–9. Outletters, 1660–89.
Adm 2/1726.   Orders and Instructions, 1679–84.
Adm 2/1740, 1745–54. Lords' letters, 1660–84.
Adm 2/1755.   Vice-Admiralty Courts, 1663–84.
Adm 7/168.   Estimates, 1673–89.
Adm 8/1.   Naval dispositions, 1673–88.
Adm 106/3117. List of Ships, 1660–7.
Adm 110/1.   Outletters, 1683–9.
Index 10667.   Register of the Navy, 1660–85.

Pipe Office

E 351/6.   African Company, June 1661.
E 351/1254–6. The 4½ per cent. duty in the Leeward Islands, 1670–7.
E 351/1560–2. Accounts of Lord Windsor, Governor of Jamaica. June 1661–November 1662.
E 351/1563.   Accounts of Sir Thomas Modyford, Governor of Jamaica. December 1664–December 1668.
E 351/1564.   Accounts of Sir Charles Lyttelton, Deputy-Governor of Jamaica. October 1662–4.
E 351/2966.   Accounts of Receivers, Act of Navigation, &c., 1660–2.
E 351/2967.   Accounts of John Locke, Secretary of the Council of Foreign Plantations, 1673.

Audit Office

(Note: AO 1/312/1236 = Bundle 312, Roll 1236.)

AO 1/3.   African Company, June 1661.
AO 1/312/1236.   Accounts of Sir William Stapleton, Governor of the
                          Leeward Islands, July 1672–July 1686.
AO 1/607/65.   Accounts of returns from Navigation Act, 1660–2.
AO 1/607/67–68.   Accounts of the farm of the logwood duties, 1662–9.
AO 1/756/792. ⎫
AO 1/757/801–2. ⎬   Plantations accounts, 1671–2.
AO 1/758/803–7. ⎭
AO 1/843/1132–3.   Accounts of Barbados and the Leeward Islands,
                          1684–5.
AO 1/1274/248a.   Drax, brandy. Feb. 1660–1.
AO 1/1274/248b.   Windsor, £21,200. June 1661–2.
AO 1/1274/248d.   Windsor, charges. Feb.–Nov. 1662.
AO 1/1274/250.   Lyttelton, fortifications. 1662–4.
AO 1/1274/251.   Windsor, charges. 1662.
AO 1/1274/252.   Modyford, salary. 1664–8.
AO 1/1274/253.   Lynch, salary as Lieutenant-Governor. 1671–5.
   The above are all warrants on the establishment of Jamaica.
AO 1/2303/2.   Locke's accounts for the Council of Foreign Planta-
                          tions, 1672.
AO 3/305/1–2.   Plantation accounts, 1667–8, 1681–2.

Treasury

T 11/1, 8, 9.   Letters relating to Customs, 1667–85.
T 38/253.   4½ per cent., Barbados and Leeward Islands.
T 54/1–2.   Warrants not relating to money, 1667–85.
T 64/88.   Blathwayt's Entry-Book, 1680–97.
T 70 (African Company Papers).[1]
T 70/1, 10.   Letters from West Africa and West Indies, 1678–82.
                         (P.R.O. Index 8731.)
T 70/12.   Letters from the West Indies, 1683–98.
T 70/15, 16.   Letters and accounts from Africa and the West Indies,
                         1678–84.
T 70/20.   Committee of Goods: Africa and the West Indies, 1678–81.
T 70/75.   Royal Company of Adventurers' Minutes, 1664–72.
T 70/76–80.   Royal African Company Minutes: Court of Assistants,
                         1673–87.
T 70/100.   General Court, 1671–1720.
T 70/169.   Petitions to the Crown, 1681–96.
T 70/185.   Journal of accounts, 1674–81.
T 70/186.   Transfer Book, 1677–87.
T 70/646.   Barbados, 1662–4.
T 70/869–71.   Jamaica, 1665–9, 1675–7.

   [1] I have not been able to include in this book any account of the slave trade
to the West Indies, but I allow this short list to stand as it may prove of service.

(b) BRITISH MUSEUM

Additional Manuscripts

8133c, f. 237. 1677–8.   Inter-plantation trade.

9764, f. 3. 23 July 1677.   Debts of Francis Lord Willoughby.

9787–8. 1674–8.   Entry Book of Council of Trade expenses.

10119, f. 166b. 1701.   A comment on the 'last farm' of the Leeward Islands.

11268, ff. 66, 68–72. 29 June, 22 July 1670.   Minutes of the Council of Jamaica, Modyford's Commission to Morgan, &c.

11268, ff. 73, 79. 31 Jan. 1672.   Panama, and Modyford's complicity.

11410, f. 10. 1663.   List of privateers in Jamaica.

11410, f. 16. 1663.   D'Oyley's Report to Clarendon.

11410, ff. 372, 377. 27 June ⎫
                    7 Sept. ⎬ 1671. Letters of Lynch to Arlington.
                    17 Dec. ⎭

11410, f. 490. 5, 9 Mar. 1672.   Lynch to Lyttelton, Arlington.

11410, f. 560. 5 July 1672.   Lynch to Arlington.

11410, f. 623. c. 1670.   Worsley and the privateers of Jamaica.

11602, f. 37. Nov. 1690.   The loss of the *Coventry* and St. Christopher—gentlemen and 'tarpaulins' on H.M. ships.

12408, ff. 1–10.   Edward Long's notes on the early history of Jamaica.

12410–14.   The same.

12422, f. 63.   Barham's Account of Jamaica.

12423, ff. 94–95.   Interloping in Barbados and Jamaica.

12429. 1680.   Blathwayt's Patent as Auditor-General, &c.

12430.   Beeston's *Journal.*

15898, f. 130. 1680?   Windward and leeward—winds in the Caribbean.

15898, ff. 127–49.   Commission and Instructions to Sir Richard Dutton, Barbados.

✓ 15948, ff. 121, 140.   Letters from Thomas Povey, c. 1670.

✓ 17018, ff. 61, 89. 1674–7.   Affairs of Jamaica.

✓ 17019, f. 37. July 1678–9.   Account of the revenue in Jamaica.

21134, f. 42. c. 1730.   Barbados and the Irish trade.

21947, f. 59. 15/25 May 1667.   On winds, &c.

22617, ff. 141, 149. 16 Feb. 1694.   The naval office in Barbados.

25115, f. 300. 5 Nov. 1661.   On sugar refining, aliens in the plantations, &c.

✓ 25120, ff. 43, 47, 51, 57, 69–72, 74, 84, 96, 118, 120, 123, 129, 132–8, 143. 1674–8. Letters from Secretary Sir Henry Coventry to Atkins, Vaughan, Carlisle, &c., on colonial affairs.

27382, f. 191. 1690?   Justice in Barbados.

28089, ff. 41–43. 1684.   The end of the Farm of the 4½ per cent.

28749, f. 170. 1700.   Patentees in Barbados.

✓ 30218, f. 190. 13 Feb. 1682.   On the dependence of plantations, Acts of Trade cases, &c.

✓ 33413, f. 39. Sept. 1666–8.   Parliament and Clarendon's fall.

33845, f. 13. 1741.   Memoirs of the Government of Barbados. (Cf. Duke, p. 268, *infra.*)

34729, f. 112. 1660.   Commission of the Council of Trade.

36785, f. 29. 1668–9. Plantations imports, exports.

36807, f. 1. 10/20 May 1672. Godolphin to Arlington on logwood.

38350, ff. 205–12. c. 1790. Various Proclamations and Commissions concerning Jamaica.

38714, ff. 67–73. 2–15 Sept. 1684. William Blathwayt's papers, new system of collection of 4½ per cent. Revenue.

38861, f. 9. 15 Nov. 1678. Blathwayt at Council debates.

38861, f. 16. 6 Mar. 1666. Rights of Lord High Admiral in war.

38861, ff. 18–20. 12–14 Feb. 1668. Privy Council Committees.

Egerton Manuscripts

2395, ff. 241, 243, 245, 251, 267, 270, 276–7, 301, 351, 463, 466, 479b, 483–4, 487, 490, 501, 531, 574, 598, 614, 617. Plantation affairs, 1660–78. Thomas Povey's collection.

2543, ff. 123, 205. Modyford's paper, 'Your Maties Interest in the West Indies.'
Committees of the Privy Council.

Sloane Manuscripts

856, f. 37. 1661. Jamaica.

2441, ff. 1–22. 1683. 'State' of Barbados.

2724, ff. 23, 33, 65, 106, 108, 211, 225, 236. 1678–81. Jamaica.

2902, f. 117. 1676–7. Plantations, imports, and exports.

2902, f. 151. 1700. Value of Jamaican exports.

2902, f. 173b. 23 Dec. 1697. Plantation trade review.

3662, ff. 52–60. John Scott's Description of Barbados.

3828, ff. 205 et seq. The sugar controversy, 1670–1.

3861, ff. 62–67. c. 1675. The King's territories in America.

3894, f. 194. 16 Dec. 1670. Royal Society's inquiries to Lynch.

4020, f. 22. Jan. 1671/2–June 1673. Corbett's 'Memoriall' of Jamaica.

Harleian Manuscripts

1510, ff. 787, 791. Jan.–Feb. 1668. Prize in Jamaica and Barbados.

1511, f. 38. Prize in Barbados, and Edwin Stede's case.

1511, f. 314. 28 Jan. 1676. Vaughan's accounts.

6806, f. 188. 1691. 4½ per cent. accounts.

7310, ff. 149, 226, 235. Feb. 1694. Stede and the negro trade, plantation debts, &c.

Stowe Manuscripts

201, f. 145. 1673. William Lord Willoughby on Tobago.

256, f. 305. May 1672. Godolphin on logwood.

324, f. 3. Account of the establishment of the 4½ per cent. at Barbados.

(c) WESTMINSTER ABBEY MUNIMENTS

There is a series of letters in this depository from Sir James Modyford in Jamaica to Sir Andrew King (merchant, and later sub-Governor of the Royal African Company) in London, 1667–72. They contain a considerable amount of illustrative matter on West-India conditions in general. The

Manuscript Numbers are W.A.M. 11348–9, 11351–2, 11417–18, 11683, 11686, 11689, 11691, 11693, 11697–702, 11704, 11906–40 inclusive. Cf. my article in *Jamaica Historical Review*, October 1952, pp. 36–60.

(*d*) BODLEIAN LIBRARY

Rawlinson Manuscripts

A. 171, f. 199. 1687.   Orders to the naval officer in Jamaica.

A. 175.   John Scott's projected history of the West Indies, and other matter on Scott.

A. 189, f. 13. n.d. (1687).   Holmes's projected expedition to the West Indies.

A. 197–9.   Register of the Navy.

A. 255. 27 Feb. 1666.   Commission and Instructions to Modyford, &c.

A. 295, ff. 45 et seq.   Lords Committee's Report on the Leeward Islands, April 1677.

A. 347. 1660–4.   Jamaica: D'Oyley's reports, &c.

A. 478, f. 48. *c.* 1668.   Worsley on the plantation trade.

A. 478, f. 53. Dec. 1668.   Worsley on Jamaican affairs.

A. 478, f. 88. *c.* 1668.   The Acts of Trade and the plantations.

B. 250, f. 59. 1680–4.   Jamaica's exports.

Clarendon Manuscripts and Papers

82, f. 152. 16 Oct. 1664.   Francis Lord Willoughby's report on Barbados.

88, ff. 40–43.   Gains of Dutton in Barbados.

104, f. 38. 25 Nov. 1663.   Dutch seizures in the West Indies.

State Papers, Appendix V (unprinted), 509. 1661.   Hyde's notes on the affairs of America.

State Papers, Appendix V (unprinted), 529.   Barbados, &c.

II. PRINTED DOCUMENTS

Calendar of State Papers, Colonial Series (America and West Indies), vol. i, 1574–1660; vol. ii, 1661–8; vol. iii, 1669–74; vol. iv, 1675–6; vol. v, 1677–80; vol. vi, 1681–5; vol. vii, 1685–8.

Acts of the Privy Council, Colonial Series, vol. i, 1613–80; vol. ii, 1680–1720.

Calendar of State Papers, Venetian, vols. xxii–xxxviii, 1660–75.

Parliament—*Journal of the House of Lords*, vols. v, vii, viii, ix, x; *Journal of the House of Commons*, vols. iii, iv, vii, viii; Anchitell Grey's *Debates of the House of Commons from . . . 1667 to 1694* (10 vols., London, 1769); Cobbett's *Parliamentary History*, vol. iv (London, 1808); L. F. Stock, *Proceedings and Debates of British Parliaments respecting North America*, vol. i (Washington, 1924).

DAVENPORT, F. G., *European Treaties bearing on the History of the United States*, vol. ii, Washington, 1929.

WATERS, W., *Check-list of American Laws, Charters, and Constitutions of the 17th and 18th centuries, in the Huntington Library*, San Marino, 1936.

Journals of the House of Assembly of Jamaica, 1664–1826, vol. i (f. 14), Kingston, 1811–29. (P.R.O. CO 140/2.)

MACDONALD, W., *Select Charters and other Documents illustrative of American History, 1606–1775*, 2 vols., New York, 1899, 1904.

Historical Manuscripts Commission

Report II (Lyttelton)	1664
Report IV (de la Ware)	1665
(Bath)	1665
Report VI (Ingilby)	1669
Report VII (F. Graham)	1682–4
(Finch)	1666–7
(Verney)	1679
(House of Lords)	1664
Report VIII (Portsmouth, I)	1663
(Trinity House, I)	1674
(Braybrooke, I)	1662
Hodgkin, I	1673
Montagu	1682
Kenyon	1680
Hastings, II	1663
Johnstone	1670
Downshire, I	1670
Dartmouth, I	1675
Beaufort	1678
Buccleuch, II	1683
Buccleuch–Whitehall, I	1669
Lindsey	1671–4, 1676
Heathcote	1661–5
Ormonde, IV–V–VI–VII	1677–82
Finch, I–II	1651–67, 1678–83
Portland, III	1660–70
Le Fleming	1667–79

III. SECONDARY SOURCES

Source Material

ANDREWS, C. M., 'Materials in British Archives for American Colonial History', *American Historical Review*, x (1908), 325–49.

—— 'Lists of Reports and Representations of the Plantation Councils 1660–74, the Lords of Trade 1675–96, and the Board of Trade 1696–1782, in the Public Record Office', Report, American Historical Association, 1913.

—— Guide to the Materials for American History to 1783 in the Public Record Office of Great Britain. 2 vols., Washington, 1912–14.

ANDREWS, C. M., DAVENPORT, F. G., Guide to the MSS. Materials for the History of the United States to 1783, in the British Museum, in minor London Archives, and in the Libraries of Oxford and Cambridge. Washington, 1908.

DAMPIERRE, J. DE, Essai sur les sources de l'histoire des Antilles françaises, 1492–1664. Société de l'École des Chartes, vi, Paris, 1904.

GEROULD, J. T., Sources of English History in the 17th Century, 1603–1689, in the University of Minnesota Library. Minneapolis, 1921.

GRIFFIN, G. G., A Guide to the Material for American History in British Depositories. Washington, 1946.

HIGHAM, C. S. S., The Colonial Entry-Books. (Helps for Students of History, No. 45.) London, 1921.

JAMESON, J. F., 'Guide to the Items relating to American History in the Reports of the English Historical Manuscripts Commission', Report, American Historical Association, 1898.

SAINSBURY, W. N., 'The British Public Record Office and the Materials in it for Early American History', *Journal of the American Antiquarian Society*, viii, 1893.

Trade and Administration

ANDERSON, A., *A Deduction of the Origins of Commerce*. 4 vols., London, 1801.

ANDREWS, C. M., *British Committees, Councils, and Commissions for Trade and Plantations, 1622–75*. Baltimore, 1908.

—— *The Colonial Period of American History*. 4 vols., New Haven, 1933–8.

ASHLEY, MAURICE, *Financial and Commercial Policy under the Cromwellian Protectorate*. Oxford, 1934.

BEER, G. L., *The Origins of the Old Colonial System, 1579–1660*. New York, 1908.

—— *The Old Colonial System*. 2 vols., New York, 1912.

BIEBER, R. P., *The Lords of Trade and Plantations, 1675–1696*. Allentown, Philadelphia, 1919.

—— 'British Plantation Councils of 1670–4', *English Historical Review*, xl (1925), 93–106.

BROWN, L. F., *The First Lord Shaftesbury*. New York, 1933.

CHALMERS, GEORGE, *Opinions of Eminent Lawyers on Various Points of English Jurisprudence, chiefly concerning the Colonies, Fisheries, and Commerce of Great Britain*. 2 vols., London, 1814.

CLARKE, M. P., 'The Board of Trade at Work', *American Historical Review*, xvii (1911), 17–43.

COLLINS, E. D., 'Studies in the Colonial Policy of England'. Report, American Historical Association, i, 1900.

CRUMP, H. J., *Colonial Admiralty Jurisdiction in the 17th Century*. London, 1931.

DICKERSON, O. M., *American Colonial Government, 1696–1765*. Cleveland, 1912.

EGERTON, H. E., 'The system of colonial administration of the Crown colonies in the 17th and 18th centuries compared with the system prevailing in the 19th century', *Transactions of the Royal Historical Society*, iv. i (1918), 190–218.

—— 'The 17th- and 18th-century Privy Council in its relations with the Colonies', *Journal of Comparative Legislation*, iii. vii (1925), 1–16.

EVANS, F. M. G., *The Principal Secretary of State*. Manchester, 1923.

HARPER, L. A., *The English Navigation Laws*. New York, 1939.

HOON, E. E., *The Origin of the English Customs System*. New York, 1938.

JACOBSEN, G. A., *William Blathwayt: a 17th-century Administrator*. New Haven, 1932.

JOHNSON, E. A. J., *American Economic Thought in the 17th Century*. London, 1932.

KAYE, P. L., *The Colonial Executive prior to the Restoration*. Baltimore, 1900.

KAYE, P. L., *English Colonial Administration under Lord Clarendon*. Baltimore, 1905.

LABAREE, L. W., *Royal Government in America*. New Haven, 1930.

—— *Commissions and Instructions to Royal Governors in America and the West Indies, 1670–1776*. 2 vols., New York, 1935.

MACKAY, D. C. (ed.), *Essays in the History of Modern Europe*: 'The Logwood Trade in the 17th and 18th Centuries', by A. M. Wilson. New York, 1936.

NETTELS, CURTIS, 'England and the Spanish-American Trade, 1680–1715', *Journal of Modern History*, iii (1931), 1–33.

OSGOOD, H. L., *The American Colonies in the 17th Century*. 3 vols., New York, 1905–7.

ROOT, W. T., 'The Lords of Trade and Plantations', *American Historical Review*, xxiii (1917), 20–41.

RUSSELL, E. B., *The Review of American Colonial Legislation by the King-in-Council*. New York, 1915.

West Indies

BARBOUR, VIOLET, 'Privateers and Pirates of the West Indies', *American Historical Review*, xvi (1911), 529–66.

CRUICKSHANK, E. A., *The Life of Sir Henry Morgan*. Toronto, 1935.

CUNDALL, F., *The Governors of Jamaica in the 17th Century*. London, 1936.

DUKE, W., *Some memoirs of the first settlement of Barbados and other of the Caribbee Islands, with the succession of Governors and Commanders-in-Chief of Barbados to the year 1741*. Barbados, 1741; reprint, Boston, 1939.

EDWARDS, BRYAN, *The History, Civil and Commercial, of the British Colonies in the West Indies*. 3 vols., London, 1801. (The fifth edition, 1819, is the best.)

HARING, C. H., *The Buccaneers in the West Indies in the 17th Century*. London, 1910.

HARLOW, VINCENT T., *Barbados, 1625–85*. Oxford, 1926.

HIGHAM, C. S. S., *The Development of the Leeward Islands under the Restoration, 1660–85*. Cambridge, 1921.

HUSSEY, R. D., 'Spanish Reaction to Foreign Aggression in the Caribbean to about 1680', *Hispanic American Historical Review*, ix (1929), 286–302.

Interesting Tracts relating to the Island of Jamaica. St. Jago de la Vega, Jamaica, 1800.

JEAFFRESON, J. C., *A Young Squire of the 17th Century (Christopher Jeaffreson)*. 2 vols., London, 1878.

List of Works in the New York Public Library relating to the West Indies. *Bulletin of the New York Public Library*, xvi (1912), 1–8.

LIVINGSTONE, N. B., *Sketch Pedigrees of some of the Early Settlers in Jamaica*. Kingston, Jamaica, 1909.

LONG, EDWARD, *The History of Jamaica*. 3 vols., London, 1774. (There is no adequate modern survey.)

NEWTON, A. P., *The European Nations in the West Indies, 1492–1688*. London, 1933.

PITMAN, F. W., *The Development of the British West Indies, 1700–63*. New Haven, 1917.

RAGATZ, L. J., *The West Indian Approach to the Study of American Colonial History*. London, 1934.

SAINT-YVES, G., *Les premières relations des Antilles françaises et des Antilles anglaises*. Paris, 1902.

WATTS, A. P., *Une Histoire des colonies anglaises aux Antilles de 1649 à 1660*. Paris, 1924.

WHITSON, A. M., *The Constitutional Development of Jamaica, 1664–1729*. Manchester, 1929.

WILLIAMSON, J. A., *The Caribbee Islands under the Proprietary Patents*. Oxford, 1923.

INDEX

Acadia, 96.
Acts of Trade, *see* Trade, Acts of.
Admiralty, Commissioners of, 41, 44.
Africa, 104.
African Companies, *see* Royal African
Company; Royal Company of Adventurers trading into Africa.
Aix-la-Chapelle, peace of, 105.
Albemarle, Duke of (General George
Monk), 15, 25; on Jamaica committee, 43; supports Modyford, 61;
allows Modyford to grant letters of
marque, 93–94, 100; death, 117; and
Willoughby, 126.
Allegiance and Supremacy, Oath of,
25; Assemblymen to take, 174.
Alliance, Triple, *see* Triple Alliance.
Allington, Lord, 148 n. 3.
Amsterdam, merchants of, 73.
Anglesey, Earl of (Arthur Annesley), 5,
8; on Jamaica committee, 43; diary
quoted, 173 n. 3.
Anguilla, 30.
Annesley, Arthur, *see* Anglesey, Earl of.
Antigua, 128 n. 6, 130–1, 138, 237, 247.
Antilles, Greater, 23.
— Lesser, 23, 98.
Arlington, Earl of (Henry Bennet), 15–
16; Modyford's recommendations to,
61; in Madrid, 66, 76; Secretary of
State, 83; connives at privateering,
85; answers Moledi, 87; supported
for once by Clarendon, 88; relations
with Modyford, 99–100; listens to
Worsley, 107; orders calling-in of
privateers, 109; approves Treaty of
Madrid (1670), 116; warns Modyford,
116; relations with Willoughby, 126;
fall of, 157–8; warns Jamaica of invasion threat, 218.
Aruba, 23.
Ashley, Viscount, *see* Shaftesbury, Earl of.
Assemblies, colonial, their pretensions
to parliamentary status, 19–20.
Atkins, Sir Jonathan, Governor of
Barbados, 19, 154; views on nomination of Council, 154–5; instructions,

155–6; Lords of Trade and, 162,
178 ff.; Coventry's advice to, 186–7;
recalled, 190; d'Estrées and, 225.
Avès, 226.

Bacon's rebellion in Virginia, 248.
Bahamas, 98, 180, 229, 232.
Barbados, plea of, for free trade, 3; bad
debts in, 12; laws of, 14; politics in,
22, 25–26, 27, 29–30; dislike of
Willoughby in, 32; Council of, 33;
complaints of, 34–35; Assembly in,
legality of, 36–37; rumours from, 42;
views of, on Jamaica, 50; regiment
for defence of, 129; not altruistic,
132; Council of, to be likeminded,
145–6; Council of, nominated by
Crown, 154–5; royal patentees in,
180–2; laws of, Gentlemen-Planters'
views on, 190; Council of, no longer
nominated, 200; suggests alternative
to 4½ per cent., 207 n. 2; dislike of
soldiery in, 245; militia forces of,
244 ff.
Barbuda, 180.
Barrillon, French ambassador in London, 231.
Barwicke, Sam, 129, 131 n. 2, 146.
Batteville, Spanish ambassador in London, 68, 70, 72, 75–76, 90.
Beckford, Peter, secretary of Jamaica,
222.
Beef Island, 217, 229 n. 2.
Beeston, William, his journal, 42, 197,
199.
Bell, Governor of Barbados, 39.
Bennet, (Sir) Henry, *see* Arlington, Earl
of.
Berkeley, Sir William, Governor of
Virginia, 138 n. 1.
Bermuda, 5, 74, 156.
Billop, Captain, case of, 166 n. 3.
Binckes, Admiral, fleet of, 240.
Blathwayt, William, 159 n. 1, 190, 196;
patent as Auditor-General, 204; consults North, C.J., 209; and piracy,
233–4.

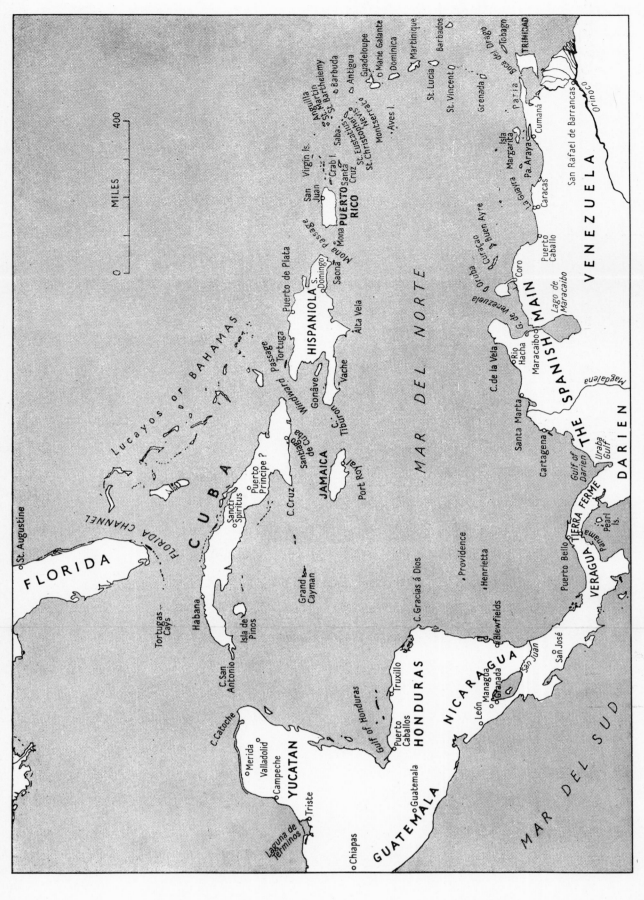

THE WEST INDIES IN THE MID-SEVENTEENTH CENTURY

MILES
0 — 400

FLORIDA

St. Augustine

FLORIDA CHANNEL

Tortugas Cays

Habana

C.San Antonio

C U B A

Isla de Pinos

Sancti Spiritus

Puerto Principe ?

C.Cruz

Santiago de Cuba

Grand Cayman

JAMAICA

Port Royal

Lucayos or BAHAMAS

Windward passage

Tortuga

Puerto de Plata

HISPANIOLA

Gonâve

C. Tiburon

Vache

Alta Vela

Saona

S.Domingo

Mona passage

Mona

PUERTO RICO

Santa Cruz

San Juan

Virgin Is.

Crab I.

Saba

St.Eustatius

St.Christopher

Nevis

Montserrat

Anguilla

St.Martin

St.Barthélemy

Barbuda

Antigua

Guadeloupe

Marie Galante

Dominica

Martinique

St. Lucia

St. Vincent

Barbados

Grenada

Aves I.

MAR DEL NORTE

Providence

Henrietta

C.Gracias á Dios

Truxillo

Puerto Caballos

HONDURAS

Gulf of Honduras

NICARAGUA

León

Managua

Granada

Bluefields

San Juan

San José

C.Catoche

Merida

Valladolid

Campeche

YUCATAN

Triste

Laguna de Terminos

Chiapas

GUATEMALA

Guatemala

MAR DEL SUD

VERAGUA

Panama

Pearl Is.

Puerto Bello

Gulf of Darien

Uraba Gulf

TIERRA FERME

DARIEN

THE SPANISH MAIN

Cartagena

Santa Marta

C.de la Vela

Rio Hacha

Maracaibo

Lago de Maracaibo

Coro

Curaçao

Buen Ayre

Oruba

G. de Venezuela

Puerto Caballo

Caracas

La Guayra

Pa. Araya

Cumaná

Isla Margarita

San Rafael de Barrancas

VENEZUELA

Paria

Pa. de Drago

Tobago

TRINIDAD

Orinoco

Magdalena